ABNORMAL PSYCHOLOGY: NEW RESEARCH

ABNORMAL PSYCHOLOGY: NEW RESEARCH

HELEN D. FRIEDMAN
AND
PAULINA K. REVERA
EDITORS

Nova Science Publishers, Inc.
New York

For permission to use material from this book please contact us:
Telephone 631-231-7269; Fax 631-231-8175
Web Site: http://www.novapublishers.com

Library of Congress Cataloging-in-Publication Data

Abnormal psychology : new research / editors, Helen D. Friedman and Paulina K. Revera.
p. ; cm.
Includes bibliographical references and index.
ISBN 978-1-60692-636-9 (hardcover)
1. Psychology, Pathological. I. Friedman, Helen D. II. Revera, Paulina K.
[DNLM: 1. Mental Disorders--therapy. 2. Adolescent Behavior--psychology. 3. Child Behavior Disorders--psychology. 4. Parent-Child Relations. 5. Psychopathology. WM 140 A1526 2009]
RC454.4.A22 2009
616.89--dc22

2008054297

Published by Nova Science Publishers, Inc. ✝ New York

CONTENTS

PREFACE

Abnormal psychology studies people who are consistently unable to adapt and function effectively in a variety of conditions. Biological, cognitive, emotional, and developmental psychology are all different types of the above-mentioned state. This new book specifically discusses depression, self-harm, perception without awareness, the psychological aspect of alcoholism, attachment-related memory in children, the psychology of fear, and dyslexia. In addition, intervention and treatment programs are examined.

Chapter 1 - Currently, there is a renewed interest for the concept of avoidance in the field of depression research (e.g., Moulds, Kandris, Starr, & Wong, 2007; Ottenbreit & Dobson, 2004). A recent hypothesis is that rumination, which refers to constant dwelling on negative mood and its causes, functions as an avoidance strategy in depression (see Moulds et al., 2007). Hitherto, this idea remained untested in a clinically depressed group. The present study examined the relationship between rumination and avoidance. A clinical sample of depressed inpatients (n = 37) completed self-report measures of avoidance, rumination, depression, and anxiety. Results showed that rumination is significantly associated with cognitive forms of avoidance, even when controlled for anxiety levels. These findings are consistent with the hypothesis that rumination functions as a (cognitive) avoidance strategy, and extend prior observations of such association to a clinical group. As a whole, the results further underscore the potential value of the construct of avoidance in the conceptualization of depression.

Chapter 2 - The "spectrum of self-harm" is commonly used to describe a wide range of behaviors of different levels of severity, all with overlapping risk factors, spanning health-risk behavior (such as reckless driving or sexual activity), deliberate non-suicidal self-injury (in the form of cutting, burning, or other superficial tissue damage without conscious suicidal intent), suicide attempts, and actual death by suicide. Extensive research in self-harm so far has focused on predisposing factors, including demographic (i.e., gender, age), biological (i.e., neurotransmitter abnormalities, hypersensitivity to emotional response, slow return-to-baseline), temperamental (i.e., shy/withdrawn, emotionally-reactive, or impulsive), environmental (i.e., childhood abuse, family conflict), and intrapersonal (i.e., psychopathology, low self-esteem) diatheses. However, although predisposing factors identify those at increased risk, not much is known about how these factors are connected with self-harm outcomes. Considering that the central goal of clinical intervention with those who self-harm is to replace maladaptive patterns of thinking and behavior with more adaptive ones, a more practical focus of research and theory would be potential pathogenic mechanisms that link risk factors to self-harm outcomes.

In this chapter, we proposed a theoretical model that linked Joiner's (2005) theory of suicide to our own model of affect regulation as a critical mechanism in the development, escalation, and maintenance of self-harm behaviors. This proposed model draws upon the existing research, existing theories, and unstated theories that appear to underlie self-harm research. By integrating models of self-harm into one comprehensive theory that considers predisposing, precipitating, and maintenance factors in light of the mechanisms of emotion dysregulation and maladaptive coping, researchers and clinicians alike can lay the groundwork for further study informed by the literature.

Chapter 3 - For many years, the study of dyslexia relied heavily on exclusionary definitions. In turn, dyslexics were defined simply in terms of a reading score that was far below a specific reading age when IQ, socio-educational, emotional, neurological, and psychiatric reasons had also been excluded. Two problems emerged from such an approach, one being conceptual and one being related to the assessment of dyslexia. This chapter advocates that dyslexia concept is better understood only if attention is drawn to the wide range of problems and the constitutional nature of the difficulties encountered by individuals with dyslexia. Therefore, four major stands in current dyslexia research are discussed: (a) the nature of the phonological impairment that is mainly associated with a pervasive problem at the level of underlying phonological representations, (b) the nature of naming speed and automaticity impairments that are seen either as a consequence of an impairment of a timing mechanism or are attributed to abnormal cerebellar functioning, providing a more neuropsychological explanation for dyslexia, (c) the nature of the cognitive deficits that are more general and modality unspecific, such as deficits at information processing level, and (d) the nature of language based problems attributed to impaired semantic, syntactic and/or orthographic awareness. The ultimate aim is to understand the biological basis of the disorder and how this brain-based disposition can lead to subtle impairments at the cognitive and behavioral levels. It is concluded that with the advent of cognitive neuroscience which revolutionizes the medical approach we can build unitary definitions and models of dyslexia, making it possible to study links between brain and behavior in this specific developmental disorder.

Chapter 4 - For many years, the study of dyslexia relied heavily on exclusionary definitions. In turn, dyslexics were defined simply in terms of a reading score that was far below a specific reading age when IQ, socio-educational, emotional, neurological, and psychiatric reasons had also been excluded. Two problems emerged from such an approach, one being conceptual and one being related to the assessment of dyslexia. This chapter advocates that dyslexia concept is better understood only if attention is drawn to the wide range of problems and the constitutional nature of the difficulties encountered by individuals with dyslexia. Therefore, four major stands in current dyslexia research are discussed: (a) the nature of the phonological impairment that is mainly associated with a pervasive problem at the level of underlying phonological representations, (b) the nature of naming speed and automaticity impairments that are seen either as a consequence of an impairment of a timing mechanism or are attributed to abnormal cerebellar functioning, providing a more neuropsychological explanation for dyslexia, (c) the nature of the cognitive deficits that are more general and modality unspecific, such as deficits at information processing level, and (d) the nature of language based problems attributed to impaired semantic, syntactic and/or orthographic awareness. The ultimate aim is to understand the biological basis of the disorder and how this brain-based disposition can lead to subtle impairments at the cognitive and behavioral levels. It is concluded that with the advent of cognitive neuroscience which revolutionizes the medical approach we can build unitary definitions and models of dyslexia, making it possible to study links between brain and behavior in this specific developmental disorder.

Chapter 5 - Depressed caregivers who present for parenting assistance often display excess difficulties with maintaining positive parent-child interactions and report that they cannot manage their children's problem behaviours. In addition to this, they often report other life stressors such as marital distress, lack of social support and/or socioeconomic disadvantage. This confluence of problems means that engaging depressed caregivers in parenting services can be challenging and depression is believed to impede successful intervention outcomes. For example, research has shown that depressed participants are at increased risk of intervention dropout and that they more often fail to maintain positive parenting behaviours (Assemany & McIntosh, 2002; Forehand, Furey & McMahon, 1984). However, others have suggested that engagement in parenting interventions in order to improve parent-child relationships may provide additional benefits such as reducing caregiver stress and depressive symptoms (Sameroff, 2004). In this randomised controlled trial of Parent-Child Interaction Therapy (PCIT), we assessed depression using three methods -- an interview, a self-report questionnaire and observation. We anticipated that nonattendance and attrition would be higher in depressed compared to nondepressed caregivers. In addition, those who attended 12 weeks of treatment (n = 68) were compared to those on a supported waitlist (n = 27); we expected that caregivers receiving PCIT would have greater declines in depressive symptoms than those on the waitlist. Participants were female caregivers (age M = 34, SD = 8.9) and their young children (ages 3 to 7). Caregivers were at risk of child maltreatment based on a child maltreatment inventory and reported that their children had clinical levels of externalising symptoms. Survival analysis showed that attrition was similar to previous studies of PCIT and there was no significant difference in attrition rate when depressed and nondepressed caregivers were compared. Measures of attendance such as the number of missed appointments also did not differ between groups. Regarding parenting outcomes, treatment participants showed greater improvements in observed interactions with their children than those on waitlist. Yet, the anticipated difference between depressed and nondepressed caregivers was not found; groups did not differ when we compared observed interactions with children prior to treatment and during treatment, with the exceptions of reflections/descriptions and negative talk. When depression was compared, it declined similarly and rapidly for caregivers regardless of whether they were receiving PCIT or were on the waitlist. Caregiver depression does not correlate with attendance and length of PCIT or observed parent-child interactions when participants are female caregivers with high risk of maltreatment and children with behaviour problems. In summary, study findings suggest that PCIT is an effective intervention for improving the observed parenting skills of both depressed and nondepressed caregivers with young children, but PCIT is not directly implicated in reducing caregivers' depressive symptoms.

Chapter 6 - Epidemiological research shows that about 30 percent of the general population will develop an anxiety disorder at some point in life (Kessler, Koretz, Merikangas, & Wang, 2004). Unsurprisingly, much research is invested in unveiling the processes that are responsible for the origin and maintenance of anxiety disorders, as well as in the principles that constitute the core of successful treatment. The general efficacy of exposure-based treatments for these disorders is irrefutable. Nevertheless, return of fear after successful exposure is a common finding and constitutes a challenge for clinical practice and fear research.

According to contemporary learning theories, fear can be acquired through an associative learning process. In a fear conditioning procedure a neutral stimulus (the Conditioned Stimulus or CS) comes to evoke fear after it was repeatedly paired with an aversive stimulus (the Unconditioned Stimulus or US). From this perspective extinction – a decrease in conditioned responding to the CS due to repeated presentations of the CS alone – can be viewed as an experimental model for exposure therapy. Return of conditioned responses after extinction then can be seen as a model for relapse after treatment. Experimental research suggests that during a fear acquisition procedure the reinforced CS (CS+) does not only become a valid predictor for the US but also acquires a negative connotation that is resistant to extinction. This is in line with the clinical observation that even after avoidance behavior has been drastically reduced through exposure, spider fearful individuals continue to consider spiders as negative animals (Baeyens, Eelen, Van den Berg, & Crombez, 1989). This remaining negative valence after extinction/exposure might function as an affective-motivational source for return of fear. Procedures that alter the valence of the fear eliciting stimulus after extinction/exposure (e.g., counterconditioning procedures) might then be effective in diminishing return of fear.

In this chapter, we will give an overview of the research literature on the role of affective valence in (return of) fear. In addition, we discuss results of an animal (mice) study that was designed to investigate the impact of a counterconditioning procedure after extinction on return of conditioned responding.

Chapter 7 - Studies on neuropsychological functions in alcoholism have reported a range of impairments including visuo-spatial abilities, attention, memory, executive functions and social cognition. On the basis of neuropsychological studies as well as imaging data different models have been proposed for the interpretation of these deficits. The present chapter aims to give an overview of findings concerning the neuropsychology of alcoholism by reviewing investigations on cognitive functions as well as imaging and electrophysiological data. In addition, the potential contribution of drinking variables, family history of alcoholism, gender and affective variables as well as the presumable relevance of cognitive deficits for the treatment of alcoholism will be discussed.

Chapter 8 - Is it possible to perceive stimulus information even when there is no awareness of perceiving? This question has been the focus of considerable research and discussion for more than 100 years (see Adams, 1957, for a review of earlier studies). However, despite the numerous experimental reports suggesting that our behavior and thoughts may be influenced by unconscious processes, research on perception without awareness has usually been plagued by continual controversy (Merikle, 1992). Much of this controversy stems directly from the logic underlying the task-*dissociation paradigm*, which has traditionally been the most widely followed approach to address that issue.

Although various versions of this paradigm have been used, the basic assumption underlying all versions is that unconscious perception can be demonstrated via a dissociation between two different indices or measures of perception. One *direct* measure (e. g., stimulus recognition) would reflect the effect of a perceived stimulus on the instructed responses to that stimulus (which is typically assessed by a measure of accuracy at the instructed task). Such a direct effect is assumed to indicate whether any relevant stimulus information is consciously perceived. A second *indirect* measure of stimulus perception would be an uninstructed effect of the task stimulus on behavior, which is assumed to be also sensitive to unconsciously perceived information. As an illustration, a well-known indirect effect is semantic priming (see also the Stroop's (1935) interference effect), which consists of a facilitation of responses (in terms of speed and/or accuracy) to a target stimulus (e.g., CAT) when it is preceded by a semantically related (prime) word (e.g., DOG), than when the preceding prime word is unrelated to the target (e.g., ARM). A dissociation is demonstrated whenever there is a reliable indirect effect by a stimulus that is unaccompanied by any direct effect of that stimulus. In other words, perception without awareness would be demonstrated whenever the indirect measure of perception (e.g., semantic priming) shows some sensitivity to stimuli under conditions on which the direct measure shows null sensitivity.

Chapter 9 - Depression during adolescence is both a normal phenomena and cause for concern, with the sequelae sometimes including poorer academic and occupational outcomes, social withdrawal, and suicide. The etiology of depression, especially during adolescence has been associated with a number of factors, including biological factors (Riddle and Cho, 1989), early physiological and psychological trauma (Toolan, 1981), psychological and psychosocial factors (National Institute of Mental Health, 1981). There have also been attempts to understand depression as a result of intrapsychic factors, such as a failure to individuate (Blos, 1968), insecure attachments (Armsden, McCauley, Greenberg, Burke and Mitchell, 1990) negative parental representations, and object relations that lack self-other differentiation (Blatt, Wein, Chevron, and Quinlan, 1979).

The separation-individuation process, where adolescents attempt to let go of their dependence on their parents, in a process similar to that which occurs in infancy, is central to adolescent development. The quality of attachment to the primary caregiver also impacts upon the ability of adolescents to re-negotiate the changes in these attachments. Parental representations both conscious and unconscious are also related to adjustment in adolescence. Self-report measures of perceptions of maternal care as being either over-protective or uncaring; have also been related to depression, suicidal thoughts and disrupted interpersonal relationships (Blatt, Wein, Chevron, and Quinlan, 1979).

During childhood the estimates of rates of depression do not tend to show gender differences, yet by adolescence females are diagnosed with depression at twice the rate that males are – and this gender difference in epidemiology remains throughout adulthood (Angold and Worthman, 1993). This would suggest that the causal and maintaining factors are in some way related to gender. The present study examines from a psychoanalytic perspective, the intrapsychic factors associated with symptoms of depression in adolescents, and in particular gender differences are examined.

A non-clinical sample of 81 adolescents was assessed on a number of theoretically related measures: separation-individuation; anaclitic depression; introjective depression; attachment style; parental representations, and symptoms of depression. The aim of this study was to analyse the factors that mediate the relationship between parenting variables and symptoms of depression in adolescent males and females.

Chapter 10 - Despite the growing awareness of culture within psychology, critics contend that understandings of culture remain largely superficial. Hermeneutics is a way of thinking interpretively about cultural meanings and discerning their specific manifestations that helps to remedy this situation. Hermeneutics offers a comprehensive theory of culture that (a) details how the self is embedded in culture, (b) highlights culture's inherently moral nature, and (c) provides conceptual tools for approaching culture in specific encounters. It can be utilized by psychotherapists not only to help understand clients from different cultural backgrounds but also to better recognize how the dominant Western cultural outlook, individualism, influences psychotherapy theory, research, and practice. These concepts are applied to cross-cultural cases.

In: Abnormal Psychology: New Research
Editor: Helen D. Friedman and Paulina K. Revera
ISBN: 978-1-60692-636-9

Short Communication

RUMINATION AND AVOIDANCE IN DEPRESSION: THE RELATIONSHIP BETWEEN RUMINATION, AVOIDANCE AND DEPRESSION IN DEPRESSED INPATIENTS

Filip Raes*, Heleen Vandromme and Dirk Hermans
Department of Psychology
University of Leuven, Belgium

ABSTRACT

Currently, there is a renewed interest for the concept of avoidance in the field of depression research (e.g., Moulds, Kandris, Starr, & Wong, 2007; Ottenbreit & Dobson, 2004). A recent hypothesis is that rumination, which refers to constant dwelling on negative mood and its causes, functions as an avoidance strategy in depression (see Moulds et al., 2007). Hitherto, this idea remained untested in a clinically depressed group. The present study examined the relationship between rumination and avoidance. A clinical sample of depressed inpatients (n = 37) completed self-report measures of avoidance, rumination, depression, and anxiety. Results showed that rumination is significantly associated with cognitive forms of avoidance, even when controlled for anxiety levels. These findings are consistent with the hypothesis that rumination functions as a (cognitive) avoidance strategy, and extend prior observations of such association to a clinical group. As a whole, the results further underscore the potential value of the construct of avoidance in the conceptualization of depression.

Keywords: rumination, avoidance,depression

* Department of Psychology, University of Leuven, Tiensestraat 102, 3000 Leuven, Belgium
Tel : ++ 32 - (0)16 - 32.58.92
Fax : ++ 32 - (0)16 - 32.60.99
E-mail: filip.raes@psy.kuleuven.be

INTRODUCTION

Although the concept of avoidance has been – and still is – mainly used in relation to the conceptualization and treatment of anxiety states (see e.g., Barlow, 2002), there is recently an increased interest in the study of avoidance in depression research (e.g., Cribb, Moulds, & Carter, 2006; Moulds, Kandris, Starr, & Wong, 2007; Ottenbreit & Dobson, 2004; Williams & Moulds, 2007). In fact, as rightly noted by some (e.g., Ottenbreit & Dobson, 2004), it is probably more correct to speak of a *renewed* interest for the concept of avoidance in the field of depression research. Indeed, in 1973 Ferster already posited in his behaviour analytic theory that a large part of the behavioural repertoire of depressed persons, on a functional level, can best be viewed as avoidance and escape behaviour: "*Escaping from an aversive environment (internal or external), or avoiding aversive conditions altogether, becomes the predominant mode of action*" (Martell, Addis, & Jacobson, 2001, p. 29).

Later (behaviour analytic) approaches towards depression, mainly placed emphasis on the lack of positive reinforcement in the learning history and current context of depressed persons. The idea that avoidance might play a – possibly even more important – role was largely neglected by both academics and clinicians (see Ottenbreit & Dobson, 2004). However, as mentioned, recently a change has been taking place, with an increasing interest for the topic of avoidance in relation to depression. This is not least to the credit of people like Neil Jacobson and colleagues with the advancement of their contextual model of depression (e.g., Jacobson, Martell, & Dimidjian, 2001; Martell et al., 2001). In these authors' thoroughly revised model of behavioural activation in depression, Ferster's idea of avoidance as a key maintaining factor of depression and depressed mood, again takes a central position.

Ottenbreit and Dobson (2004) noted the lack of a good instrument in the literature to assess different subtypes of avoidance. Therefore, they developed the multidimensional Cognitive-Behavioral Avoidance Scale (CBAS). The CBAS measures avoidance across four factors: behavioural-social, behavioural-nonsocial, cognitive-social, and cognitive-nonsocial.

The past two decades have also witnessed a steadily increased interest in the concept of rumination in relation to depression (see e.g., Papageorgiou & Siegle, 2003). Rumination refers to the tendency to constantly dwell on negative mood, and on the possible causes and implications of sad and depressed feelings (Nolen-Hoeksema, 1987, 1991). A vast body of literature indicates that rumination represents a cognitive vulnerability factor for depression onset and depressive relapse (e.g., Nolen-Hoeksema, 2004, for a review). Very recently, depression researchers have started to study the concept of avoidance and rumination jointly. This new line of research was instigated by the idea that rumination might be conceptualised as an avoidance strategy, both in a cognitive and overt-behavioural sense (see Moulds et al., 2004, for a review).

Borkovec (e.g., Borkovec, Alcaine, & Behar, 2004) proposed that anxious worry may be viewed as a cognitive avoidance response in anxiety states in general, and generalised anxiety disorder in particular. Given the many commonalities between worry and rumination (e.g., Fresco, Frankel, Mennin, Turk, & Heimberg, 2002) the idea has been put forward that rumination may function as a cognitive avoidance response in depression, similar to worry in the case of anxiety (Moulds et al., 2007; McLaughlin, Sibrava, Behar, & Borkovec, in press; Raes, 2005; Watkins & Moulds, 2005). The key idea here is that rumination functions as a cognitive avoidance mechanism in that it attenuates the activation of sharp emotional responses. It is further hypothesized that this dampening of intense affect is brought about by the fact that rumination represents an abstract, rather than concrete thinking style (cf. the reduced concreteness theory for worry; Stöber & Borkovec, 2002). But rumination is not only thought to function as an avoidance response on a *cognitive* level. From a functional-analytic perspective, rumination is also hypothesized to also promote *behavioural* avoidance, since a good deal of depressed persons' ruminative thinking can be conceptualised as avoidance of more active overt behaviour (e.g., more adaptive approach behaviours; see Addis & Martell, 2004; Jacobson et al., 2001; Martell et al., 2001).

So far, no more than two studies have explored the hypothesized relationship between rumination and several forms of avoidance (Cribb et al., 2006; Moulds et al., 2007). These preliminary investigations, both conducted in non-clinical student samples, indeed show that rumination is linked to different subtypes of avoidance. The question remains, however, to what extent those observations also apply to a clinical sample of depressed patients. In fact, replication in a clinically depressed sample was identified by Moulds et al. (2007) as an important next step in the study of the interrelation between rumination and avoidance. Furthermore, to the best of our knowledge, the newly developed innovative CBAS has not been employed in any studies in the literature using clinically depressed respondents. Moulds et al. (2007) further noted that future research should also study the relationship between rumination and experiential avoidance. To address these absences in the current literature, we explored the relationship between rumination and different forms of avoidance (i.e., cognitive, behavioural, and experiential) in clinically depressed patients. Based upon the hypothesis that rumination represents an avoidance response, we predicted significant and positive correlations between rumination and different types of avoidance.

METHOD

Participants

Thirty-seven patients (22 women) participated in the study. Their mean age was 41.14 years (*SD* = 13.25; range = 21–64). They were inpatients at the University Psychiatric Centre (University of Leuven) and started treatment for depression. Inclusion criterium was a DSM-IV diagnosis of Major Depressive Disorder without psychotic features (APA, 1994). Patients were interviewed using the mood modules of the Structured Clinical Interview for DSM-IV (SCID; First, Gibbon, Spitzer, & Williams, 1996; Dutch version: van Groenestijn, Akkerhuis, Kupka, Schneider, & Nolen, 1999). All patients participated on a voluntary basis. The study was approved by the Ethical Committee of the Faculty of Psychology and Educational Sciences, University of Leuven.

Instruments

Beck Depression Inventory (BDI-II). The BDI-II (Beck, Steer, & Brown, 1996) is a widely used self-rating measure for severity of depressive symptoms and consists of 21 four-choice statements. Participants are asked to mark the statements that best describe how they felt during the past two weeks. The Dutch version by van der Does (2002) is used, for which adequate reliability is reported with Cronbach's alpha of .92 and .93 in a psychiatric and student population, respectively (van der Does, 2002).

Symptom Checklist – Anxiety subscale (SCL-90 ANX). The SCL-90 (Arrindel & Etema, 2005) is a multidimensional self-report scale for psychopathology. The Anxiety subscale measures feelings of generalized anxiety and consists of 10 items, which are rated on a 5-point scale (*not at all* to *very much*). Good reliability and validity is reported (Arrindel & Etema, 2005).

Cognitive-Behavioral Avoidance Scale (CBAS). The CBAS (Ottenbreit & Dobson, 2004) is a 31-item self-report scale measuring avoidance across four factors: behavioral-social (BS; e.g., 'I find that I often want to leave social gatherings'), behavioral-nonsocial (BN; e.g., 'I quit acitivities that challenge me too much'), cognitive-social (CS; 'I fail to discuss/address tension that builds in a relationship'), and cognitive-nonsocial (CN; 'I avoid making decisions about my future'). Items are rated on a 5-point scale, range from 1 (*not true at all for me*) to 5 (*extremely true for me*). Good reliability and validity is reported (Ottenbreit & Dobson, 2004). The Dutch version by Vandromme, Raes, Defranc, and Hermans (in press) was used, for which adequate reliability and validity is reported as well (Vandromme et al., in press). Confirmatory Factor Analyses showed that the original 4-factor model provided the best fit for the Dutch CBAS as well (Vandromme et al., in press).

Rumination on Sadness Scale (RSS). The RSS (Conway, Csank, Holm, & Blake, 2000) is a 13-item questionnaire measuring rumination on sadness. Items are rated on a 5-point scale (*not at all* to *very much*) for the extent to which they reflect the participant's responses to sadness. All items are preceded by the frame sentence 'when I feel sad, down, or blue …'. Sample items are '… I repeatedly analyze and keep thinking about my sadness', '… I get absorbed in thinking about why I am sad and find it difficult to think about other things'. The RSS has demonstrated good internal consistency (α = .91), high concurrent validity with the Ruminative Response Scale (RRS; Nolen-Hoeksema & Morrow, 1991; r = 0.81), and good convergent and discriminant validity (for more details, see: Conway et al., 2000; Luminet, 2004). The Dutch translation by Raes, Hermans and Eelen (2003) was used (α = .84).

Acceptance and Actionhehr Questionnaire (AAQ). The AAQ (Hayes et al., 2004) is a 9-item self-report scale measuring experiential avoidance. Experiential avoidance refers to attempt to avoid, control or escape from particular (negative) private experiences, such as bodily sensations, emotions, thoughts, memories, and behavioural predispositions. Items are rated on a 7-point scale, ranging from 1 (*never true*) to 7 (*always true*). Internal consistency for the AAQ for the current sample was adequate (α = .62).

PROCEDURE

Participants were tested during the first week(s) after their admittance to the hospital. All participants gave informed consent and were tested individually. The test session started with the SCID, after which the BDI-II was completed. The SCL-90 Anxiety Subscale, C-BAS, RSS, and AAQ were given to the participants, who were allowed to complete these questionnaires in their room, after which they were returned to the experimenter.

RESULTS

Table 1 presents the mean scores on the questionnaire measures. The mean score on the BDI-II (28.05) indicates that the current sample suffers from moderately severe depression (Beck et al., 1996). In order to explore associations between questionnaire measures, we calculated correlations between all measures (see Table 2). Following Moulds et al. (2007) we also recalculated these correlations, controlling for anxiety (i.e., SCL-90 Anxiety subscale scores), given that avoidance is a known key feature of anxiety states. These partial correlations are presented in Table 3.

Table 1. Means, standard deviations, and range for all variables of interest

	M (*SD*)	range
BDI-II	8.05 (11.43)	6 - 49
SCL-A	30.30 (9.70)	10 - 50
CBAS-T	80.84 (23.99)	44 - 138
CBAS-BS	20.89 (8.74)	8 - 40
CBAS-BN	18.43 (5.87)	8 - 30
CBAS-CS	16.24 (5.91)	7 - 29
CBAS-CN	25.03 (7.68)	10 - 40
RSS	45.24 (8.05)	33 - 65
AAQ	44.68 (6.63)	62 - 58

Note. BDI = Beck Depression Inventory; SCL-ANX = Symptom Checlist Anxiety subscale; CBAS-T = Cognitive-Behavioral Avoidance Scale, Total score; CBAS-BS = Cognitive-Behavioral Avoidance Scale, Behavioral Social subscale; CBAS-BN = Cognitive-Behavioral Avoidance Scale, Behavioral Nonsocial subscale; CBAS-CS = Cognitive-Behavioral Avoidance Scale, Cognitive Social subscale; CBAS-CN = Cognitive-Behavioral Avoidance Scale, Cognitive Nonsocial subscale; RSS = Rumination on Sadness Scale; AAQ = Acceptance and Action Questionnaire.

Table 2 shows that the majority of the measures were positively correlated. RSS scores (rumination) correlated with all measures, besides with the Anxiety subscale of the SCL-90, and was only marginally associated with the Behavioral-Nonsocial subscale of the CBAS and the AAQ (both *ps* $< .10$). BDI-II scores correlated significantly with all measures, except with the Cognitive-Social subscale of the CBAS.

Table 2. Correlations between questionnaire measures

	BDI-II	SCL-A	CBAS-T	CBAS-BS	CBAS-BN	CBAS-CS	CBAS-CN	RSS
SCL-A	.42**							
CBAS-T	.43**	.10						
CBAS-BS	.49**	.19	.88***					
CBAS-BN	.34*	.26	.88***	.81***				
CBAS-CS	.19	-.13	.77***	.56***	.50**			
CBAS-CN	.35*	-.02	.84***	.57***	.77***	.60***		
RSS	.52**	.19	.44**	.34*	.29†	.41*	.38*	
AAQ	.36*	.52**	.34*	.19	.36*	.22	.36*	.31†

Note. BDI = Beck Depression Inventory; SCL-A = Symptom Checlist Anxiety subscale; CBAS-T = Cognitive-Behavioral Avoidance Scale, Total score; CBAS-BS = Cognitive-Behavioral Avoidance Scale, Behavioral Social subscale; CBAS-BN = Cognitive-Behavioral Avoidance Scale, Behavioral Nonsocial subscale; CBAS-CS = Cognitive-Behavioral Avoidance Scale, Cognitive Social subscale; CBAS-CN = Cognitive-Behavioral Avoidance Scale, Cognitive Nonsocial subscale; RSS = Rumination on Sadness Scale; AAQ = Acceptance and Action Questionnaire.
† $p < .10$. *$p < .05$. **$p < .01$. ***$p < .001$.

Although anxiety scores were not significantly related to CBAS scores, we nevertheless decided, in order to reduce any possible influence of anxiety on the findings, to repeat the above correlational analyses with anxiety scores partialled, as recommended by Moulds et al. (2007; see Table 3). When controlled for anxiety, rumination remained significantly related with CBAS Total scores and with both Cognitive subscales of the CBAS. The correlations between the RSS and the Behavioral-Social and Behavioral-Nonsocial CBAS-subscales were in the predicted direction, but not statistically significant (respective *p*s being <.10 and < .15). Table 3 further shows that the correlation between rumination and experiential avoidance (AAQ) was reduced to marginal significance ($p < .10$). We also note that depression scores remained significantly correlated with CBAS Total scores and scores on the Behavioral-Social and Cognitive-Nonsocial subscales of the CBAS. The correlations between the BDI-II and the Behavioral-Nonsocial and Cognitive-Social subscales were marginally significant ($p < .10$).

Table 3. Correlations between questionnaire measures controlling for anxiety

	BDI-II	CBAS-T	CBAS-BS	CBAS-BN	CBAS-CS	CBAS-CN	RSS
CBAS-T	.39**						

CBAS-BS	.45**	.88***					
CBAS-BN	.27	.89***	.80***				
CBAS-CS	.27	.79***	.60***	.56**			
CBAS-CN	.39*	.84***	.58***	.71***	.60***		
RSS	.49**	.42**	.32†	.25	.44**	.39*	
AAQ	.18	.34*	.11	.28†	.34*	.44**	.25

Note. BDI = Beck Depression Inventory; SCL-ANX = Symptom Checlist Anxiety subscale; CBAS-T = Cognitive-Behavioral Avoidance Scale, Total score; CBAS-BS = Cognitive-Behavioral Avoidance Scale, Behavioral Social subscale; CBAS-BN = Cognitive-Behavioral Avoidance Scale, Behavioral Nonsocial subscale; CBAS-CS = Cognitive-Behavioral Avoidance Scale, Cognitive Social subscale; CBAS-CN = Cognitive-Behavioral Avoidance Scale, Cognitive Nonsocial subscale; RSS = Rumination on Sadness Scale; AAQ = Acceptance and Action Questionnaire.

$^{\dagger}p < .10$. $^{*}p < .05$. $^{**}p < .01$. $^{***}p < .001$.

CONCLUSION

This study investigated the relationship between rumination, avoidance and depression in a clinical sample of depressed inpatients. As predicted, there were significant correlations between rumination, avoidance, and depression. Furthermore, rumination was positively correlated with all included subtypes of avoidance, although for behavioural-nonsocial avoidance and experiential avoidance, the correlation was only marginally significant. When controlled for anxiety, rumination remained significantly correlated with the cognitive subtypes of avoidance (Cognitive-Social and Cognitive-Nonsocial CBAS-subscales). This confirms that the association between cognitive avoidance and rumination is independent of anxiety in depressed patients. The relationships between rumination on the one hand and the behavioural subtypes of avoidance and experiential avoidance on the other hand, were in the predicted direction but not statistically significant.

As a whole, the results are partially consistent with the hypothesis that rumination functions as an avoidance mechanism. Whereas we did observe that rumination is indeed associated with cognitive forms of avoidance, the relationship between rumination and behavioural and experiential forms of avoidance was not supported. In previous studies, all conducted in non-clinical (student) groups, rumination was found to correlate with both cognitive and behavioural subtypes of avoidance (Cribb et al., 2006), or with behavioural forms only (Moulds et al., 2007). One possible explanation for the fact that in the present study rumination was only significantly correlated with cognitive avoidance is that our sample consisted of clinically depressed participants, whereas previous studies were conducted in non-clinical samples. A second explanation is that we used a different self-report measure for anxiety (SCL-90 Anxiety subscale vs. Beck Anxiety Inventory, BAI, in the studies of Cribb et al., 2006, and Moulds et al., 2007). However, the BAI and SCL-90 Anxiety subscale correlate very highly ($r > .80$; Steer, Ranieri, & Beck, 1993), making it less likely that this may have caused for our pattern of results to be somewhat different from those obtained in earlier studies with non-clinical participants.

A third and in our opinion most plausible explanation for the fact that in our study rumination was not significantly associated with behavioural forms of avoidance, is the self-report questionnaire used to measure rumination. Whereas we used the Rumination on Sadness Scale (RSS; Conway et al., 2000), previous studies employed the Ruminative Response Scale (RRS; Nolen-Hoeksema & Morrow, 1991). The RRS has been criticized for containing items that overlap with depression symptoms (Conway et al., 2000; Segerstrom, Tsao, Alden, & Craske, 2000). Several items of the RRS, like 'I think about my feelings of fatigue and achiness', 'I think about how passive and unmotivated I feel', and 'I think "Why can't I get going?"' clearly tap into the diagnostic cluster of energy loss in depression. People scoring high on such items can be expected to not engage relatively frequently in all kinds of activities, and thus, can be expected to score high on the behavioral subscales of the CBAS, not necessarily because there is a link between rumination and behavioural avoidance. Interestingly, when those items related to depression symptoms were deleted from the RRS in the Moulds et al. study (2007), rumination was no longer associated with CBAS-scores. In the present study, we used the RSS, which was specifically developed to overcome some of the problems with the RRS, e.g., overlap with depression symptom measures. As such, the RSS can be considered as a more pure measure of rumination, less confounded with depressive symptomatology.

When interpreting the results, several limitations should be taken into account (see also Moulds et al., 2007). First, only self-report measures were used. Second, the correlational nature of the present study prevents causal interpretations. Third and finally, our sample size was relatively small; replication in a larger sample could strengthen the present findings.

Notwithstanding these limitations, this study is the first to our knowledge to explore the relationship between rumination and avoidance in a clinically depressed group. We observed that rumination, even when controlled for anxiety levels, is significantly related with cognitive subtypes of avoidance. This supports the recent hypothesis that rumination may function as a cognitive avoidance strategy (e.g., Moulds et al., 2004; McLaughlin et al., in press, Watkins & Moulds, 2005): because of its abstract nature, rumination is thought to assist in the attenuation of sharp affect. Rumination can thus be considered to be under the control of negative reinforcement, that is, the (cognitive) avoidance of intense emotional responses linked to concrete thoughts, memories, or images. The fact that this relationship remained when anxiety was partialled, further supports the value of the construct of avoidance, notably cognitive avoidance, in the conceptualization of depression (see also Moulds et al., 2007; Ottenbreit & Dobson, 2004).

References

Arrindel, W. A., & Ettema, J. H. M. (2005). *Symptom checklist (SCL-90): Handleiding bij een multidimensionale psychopathologie-indicator.* [Symptom checklist (SCL-90): Manual of multidimensional psychopathology indicator]. Amsterdam: Harcourt Test Publishers.

Barlow, D. A. (2002). *Anxiety and its disorders: The nature and treatment of anxiety and panic* (2nd ed.). New York: Guilford Press.

Beck, A. T., Steer, R. A., & Brown, G. K. (1996). *Beck Depression Inventory – second edition*. San Antonio, TX: The Psychological Corporation.

Borkovec, T. D., Alcaine, O., & Behar, E. (2004). Avoidance theory of worry and generalized anxiety disorder. In R. G. Heimberg, C. L. Turk, & D. S. Mennin (Eds.), *Generalized anxiety disorder: Advances in research and practice* (pp. 77-108). New York: Guilford Press.

Conway, M., Csank, P. A. R., Holm, S. L., & Blake, C. K., 2000. On assessing individual differences in rumination on sadness. *Journal of Personality Assessment, 75,* 404-425.

Cribb, G., Moulds, M. L., & Carter, S. (2006). Rumination and experiential avoidance in depression. *Behaviour Change, 23,* 165-176.

Ferster, C.B. (1973). A functional analysis of depression. *American Psychologist*, 28, 857-870.

First, M. B., Spitzer, R. L., Gibbon, M., & Williams, J. B. W. (1996). *Structured Clinical Interview for DSM-IV Axis I Disorders: Patient Edition (SCID-I/P, Version 2.0).* Washington, DC: American Psychiatric Press.

Fresco, D. M., Frankel, A. N., Mennin, D. S., Turk, C. L., & Heimberg, R. G. (2002). Distinct and overlapping features of rumination and worry: The relationship of cognitive production to negative affective states. *Cognitive Therapy and Research, 26,* 179-188.

Hayes, S. C., Strosahl, K. D., Wilson, K. G., Bissett, R. T., Pistorello, J., Toarmino, D., Polusny, M., A., Dykstra, T. A., Batten, S. V., Bergan, J., Stewart, S. H., Zvolensky, M. J., Eifert, G. H., Bond, F. W., Forsyth J. P., Karekla, M., & McCurry, S. M. (2004). Measuring experiential avoidance: A preliminary test of a working model. *The Psychological Record*, 54, 553-578.

Jacobson, N. S., Martell, C. R., & Dimidjian, S. (2001). Behavioral activation treatment for depression: Returning to contextual roots. *Clinical Psychology: Science and Practice, 8,* 255-270.

Luminet, O. (2004). Assessment and measurement of rumination. In C. Papageorgiou & A. Wells (Eds.), *Rumination: Nature, theory, and treatment of negative thinking in depression* (pp. 187–215). Chichester, England: Wiley.

Martell, C. R., Addis, M. E., & Jacobson, N. S. (2001). *Depression in context: Strategies for guided action.* New York: Norton.

McLaughlin, K., Sibrava, N., Behar, E., & Borkovec, T. D. (in press). Recurrent negative thinking in emotional disorders: Worry, depressive rumination, and trauma recall. In S. Sassaroli, G. Ruggerio, & R. Lorenzini (Eds.), *Worry, need of control, and other core cognitive constructs in anxiety and eating disorders.* Milan, Italy: Raphael Cortina Publisher.

Moulds, M. L., Kandris, E., Starr, S., & Wong, A. C. M. (2007). The relationship between rumination, avoidance and depression in a non-clinical sample. *Behaviour Research and Therapy, 45,* 251-261.

Nolen-Hoeksema, S. (1987). Sex differences in unipolar depression: Evidence and theory. *Psychological Bulletin, 101,* 259-282.

Nolen-Hoeksema, S. (1991). Responses to depression and their effects on the duration of depressive episodes. *Journal of Abnormal Psychology, 100,* 569-582.

Nolen-Hoeksema, S. (2004). The response styles theory. In C. Papageorgiou & A. Wells (Eds.), *Depressive rumination: Nature, theory, and treatment* (pp. 107-124). Chichester, UK: John Wiley & Sons.

Nolen-Hoeksema, S., & Morrow, J. (1991). A prospective study of depression and posttraumatic stress symptoms after a natural disaster: The 1989 Loma Prieta Earthquake. *Journal of Personality and Social Psychology, 61,* 115-121.

Ottenbreit, N. D., & Dobson, K. S. (2004). Avoidance and depression: The construction of the Cognitive-Behavioral Avoidance Scale. *Behaviour Research and Therapy, 42,* 293-313.

Papageorgiou, C., & Siegle, G. J. (2003). Rumination and depression: Advances in theory and research. *Cognitive Therapy and Research, 27,* 243-245.

Raes, F. (2005). *Specificity of autobiographical memory: An experimental investigation of the functional aspects and a prospective investigation of the predictive value for depression.* Unpublished doctoral dissertation, University of Leuven, Leuven, Belgium.

Raes, F., Hermans, D., & Eelen P. (2003). De Nederlandstalige versie van de Ruminative Response Scale (RRS-NL) en de Rumination on Sadness Scale (RSS-NL) [The Dutch version of the Ruminative Response Scale (RRS-NL) and the Rumination on Sadness Scale (RSS-NL)]. *Gedragstherapie, 36,* 97-104.

Segerstrom, S. C., Tsao, J. C. I., Alden, L. E., & Craske, M. G. (2000). Worry and rumination: Repetitive thought as a concomitant and predictor of negative mood. *Cognitive Therapy and Research, 24,* 671-688.

Steer, R. A., Ranieri, W. F., & Beck, A. T. (1993). Further evidence for the validity of the Beck Anxiety Inventory with psychiatric outpatients. *Journal of Affective Disorders, 7,* 195-205.

Stöber, J., & Borkovec, T. D. (2002). Reduced concreteness of worry in generalized anxiety disorder. *Cognitive Therapy and Research, 26,* 89-96.

Van der Does, A. J. W. (2002). *Handleiding bij de Nederlandse bewerking van de BDI-II* [Manual of the Dutch version of the BDI-II]. San Antonio, TX / Lisse, the Netherlands: The Psychological Corporation / Swets Test Publishers.

Vandromme, H., Raes, F., Defranc, A., & Hermans, D. (in press). De Nederlandstalige versie van de Cognitive-Behavioral Avoidance Scale (CBAS-NL). [The Dutch version of the Cognitive-Behavioral Avoidance Scale]. *Gedragstherapie.*

Watkins, E. R., & Moulds, M. (2005). Distinct modes of ruminative self-focus: Impact of abstract versus concrete rumination on problem solving in depression. *Emotion, 5,* 319-328.

Williams, A. D., & Moulds, M. L. (2007). Cognitive avoidance of intrusive memories: Recall vantage perspective and associations with depression. *Behaviour Research and Therapy, 45,* 1141-1153.

Research and Review Studies

In: Abnormal Psychology: New Research
Editor: Helen D. Friedman and Paulina K. Revera
ISBN: 978-1-60692-636-9

Chapter 1

THE SPECTRUM OF SELF-HARM IN ADOLESCENCE AND YOUNG ADULTHOOD: MOVING TOWARD AN INTEGRATIVE MODEL OF PATHOGENIC MECHANISMS

Christa D. Labouliere, M.A. and Marc S. Karverh
University of South Florida, Tampa, Florida, USA

ABSTRACT

The "spectrum of self-harm" is commonly used to describe a wide range of behaviors of different levels of severity, all with overlapping risk factors, spanning health-risk behavior (such as reckless driving or sexual activity), deliberate non-suicidal self-injury (in the form of cutting, burning, or other superficial tissue damage without conscious suicidal intent), suicide attempts, and actual death by suicide. Extensive research in self-harm so far has focused on predisposing factors, including demographic (i.e., gender, age), biological (i.e., neurotransmitter abnormalities, hypersensitivity to emotional response, slow return-to-baseline), temperamental (i.e., shy/withdrawn, emotionally-reactive, or impulsive), environmental (i.e., childhood abuse, family conflict), and intrapersonal (i.e., psychopathology, low self-esteem) diatheses. However, although predisposing factors identify those at increased risk, not much is known about how these factors are connected with self-harm outcomes. Considering that the central goal of clinical intervention with those who self-harm is to replace maladaptive patterns of thinking and behavior with more adaptive ones, a more practical focus of research and theory would be potential pathogenic mechanisms that link risk factors to self-harm outcomes.

In this chapter, we proposed a theoretical model that linked Joiner's (2005) theory of suicide to our own model of affect regulation as a critical mechanism in the development, escalation, and maintenance of self-harm behaviors. This proposed model draws upon the existing research, existing theories, and unstated theories that appear to underlie self-harm research. By integrating models of self-harm into one comprehensive theory that considers predisposing, precipitating, and maintenance factors in light of the mechanisms of emotion dysregulation and maladaptive coping, researchers and clinicians alike can lay the groundwork for further study informed by the literature.

INTRODUCTION

The "spectrum of self-harm" is commonly used to describe a wide range of behaviors of different levels of severity, all with overlapping risk factors, spanning health-risk behavior (such as reckless driving or sexual activity), deliberate non-suicidal self-injury (in the form of cutting, burning, or other superficial tissue damage without conscious suicidal intent), suicide attempts, and actual death by suicide (King, Ruchkin, & Schwab-Stone, 2003). It seems contrary to all human survival instincts when people intentionally attempt to end their own lives or deliberately hurt themselves (Joiner, 2005). Nevertheless, self-harming behaviors are relatively common in the general population, with between 5-23% of adolescents (Grunbaum, Kann, & Kinchen, 2004; Jacobson & Gould, 2007; Lewinsohn, Rohde, & Seeley, 1996) and as many as one third of college students (Gratz, 2001) engaging in self-harmful behaviors at some point in their lives. The most deadly variety of self-harm, suicide, occurs once every 18 minutes in the United States – approximately 30,000 deaths per year (CDC WISQARS, 2008).

Extensive research in self-harm so far has focused on predisposing factors, including demographic (i.e., gender, age), biological (i.e., neurotransmitter abnormalities, hypersensitivity to emotional response, slow return-to-baseline), temperamental (i.e., shy/withdrawn, emotionally-reactive, or impulsive), environmental (i.e., childhood abuse, family conflict), and intrapersonal (i.e., psychopathology, low self-esteem) diatheses (e.g., Evans, Hawton, & Rodham, 2004; Jacobson & Gould, 2007; Joiner, Brown, & Wingate, 2005). However, although predisposing factors identify those at increased risk, not much is known about how these factors are connected with self-harm outcomes. In addition, predisposing factors typically are static and therefore not as amenable to treatment. Considering that the central goal of clinical intervention with those who self-harm is to replace maladaptive patterns of thinking and behavior with more adaptive ones, a more practical focus of research and theory would be precipitating and maintenance factors relative to self-harm behavior. This is consistent with the perspective from Dialectical Behavior Therapy that adequate therapeutic intervention with those who self-harm requires an understanding of the connection between predisposing antecedents, precipitating antecedent links, and maintaining consequences (Linehan, 1993). Thus, the aim of self-harm research and theory needs to shift toward gaining a better understanding of why and how predisposing factors lead to self-harm behavior. Self-harm research and theory would then more directly contribute toward informing researchers and practitioners on how to intervene with at-risk individuals.

It seems that the burning question in self-harm research needs to shift from "Which risk factors predict self-harm?" to "What are the interacting mechanisms that act upon predisposing and precipitating risk factors that result in maintained self-harm behavior?" Implicit in this question are numerous interrelated assumptions. The first critical assumption is that there is a clear definition of self-harm behavior. Other assumptions are that there is clear understanding of predisposing factors, precipitating factors, and maintenance factors. Finally, there is the assumption that there are potential mechanisms acting upon risk factors that account for the development, maintenance, and escalation in self-harm behaviors. This chapter will focus on examining the assumptions, that is, describing and exploring what is known and what needs to be resolved in order to have a better understanding of the pathogenic mechanisms that contribute to self-harm behavior. The aim is to move the field toward the development and dissemination of interventions for youths and young adults that are specifically responsive to the pathogenic mechanisms that drive self-harm behavior. Considering that Tarrier, Taylor, and Gooding (2008) recently concluded that "when the treated sample is principally adolescent, then suicide behavior is difficult to treat" (p. 100), it is imperative that theory and research help identify the critical mechanisms that need to be altered in order to prevent self-harm behavior in adolescents and young adults. Identification of these mechanisms will allow us to refine our existing treatments or develop new ones that focus on ameliorating the critical mechanisms involved in self-harm behavior. Theory and research on mechanisms of self-harm behavior are needed in order to alter Tarrier et al.'s discouraging conclusion and provide real world practitioners with interventions that are correctly focused and effective.

The Problem of Self-Harm

Despite extensive research on self-harm behaviors, estimates of the prevalence of self-harm vary hugely. Estimates have varied from as low as 5% to as high as 17% in samples of high school students (Gould, Greenberg, Velting, & Shaffer, 2003; Hawton, Rodham, Evans, & Weatherall, 2002; Lloyd-Richarson, Perrin, Dierker, & Kelley, 2007; Muehlenkamp & Gutierrez, 2004; Ross & Heath, 2002). Among college students, rates of self-harm have been found between 8-38% (Brener, Hassan, & Barrios, 1999; Favazza, DeRosear, & Conterio, 1989; Gratz, 2001; Gratz et al., 2002; Whitlock, Eckenrode, & Silverman, 2006). Part of the difficulty in determining the prevalence of and studying self-harm is the inability of the research and clinical community to come to a consensus on the nomenclature associated with self-harmful behaviors (O' Carroll, Berman, Maris, Moscicki, Tanney, & Silverman, 1996; Silverman, Berman, Sanddal, O'Carroll, & Joiner, 2007). The term *self-harm* has multiple meanings: in the United Kingdom, where much of the research is conducted, the term is synonymous with *deliberate self-harm* and refers to all instances of deliberate injury, regardless of suicidal intent, a construct similar to the European term "parasuicide." *Parasuicide* is not commonly used in North American literature, but refers to two discrete concepts: 1) either all episodes of bodily harm survived with or without intent to die (Karver & Caporino, 2005), or 2) episodes without intent, typically excluding repetitive acts (Skegg, 2005). This construct of parasuicide does not differentiate between *suicide attempts*, episodes of self-harm (i.e., overdose, hanging, cutting, jumping from high places, etc.) in which there was at least some intent to die, and also more repetitive acts of self-harm motivated by inter- or intrapersonal factors in which there may be no conscious attempt to die. From this perspective, all acts of self-harm, regardless of intent, are considered on a spectrum of life-threatening behavior (Brezo, Paris, Barker, Tremblay, Vitaro, Zoccolillo, et al., 2007). Research on the high likelihood of persons who self-harm without suicidal intent later progressing into suicidal acts supports this position (Cooper et al., 2005; Owens et al., 2002; Sansone, Songer, & Sellbom, 2006).

However, characterizing all self-harm acts irrespective of motive may be overly simplistic, as research has shown differences between the two behaviors. Most recently, in an investigation of differences between adolescents engaging in non-suicidal self-injurious behavior and adolescents attempting suicide, Muehlenkamp & Gutierrez (2004) found that while depression and suicidal ideation differentiate self-harming adolescents from controls, only attitudes toward life differentiated between non-suicidal self-injurious and suicide-attempting groups. Those adolescents with many negative life events and strongly negative global attitudes towards life were far more likely to attempt suicide and have a wish to die. This suggests that persons with more positive attitudes toward life may engage in non-suicidal self-injurious behavior for motives very different from those who attempt suicide with a desire to die (Muehlenkamp & Gutierrez, 2004). Even amongst those classified as suicide attempters, those who express an intent to die make more lethal attempts and are typically more depressed and hopeless than those who make suicide attempts for other reasons (Groholt et al., 2000). This research supports the position that, while suicide and non-suicidal self-injury may exist on a spectrum of self-harm with many common precursors, there are likely phenomenological and potentially mechanistic differences between the two acts (Favazza, 1987; 1992; 1998; Muehlenkamp & Gutierrez, 2004; Pattison & Kahan, 1983; Tuisku, Pelkonen, Karlsson, Kiviruusu, Holi, Ruuttu, et al., 2006; Winchel & Stanley, 1991).

More consistent with a categorization versus continuum perspective, in North America, suicide attempts are considered separately from non-suicidal self-harm, and the term *self-harm* is used more specifically to refer to repetitive episodes of bodily harm without suicidal intent and typically excludes methods of high lethality (Skegg, 2005). From this perspective, suicide attempts and non-suicidal self-harm are qualitatively different, motivated and maintained by different mechanisms (e.g., wish to die vs. problematic coping mechanism in order to live). The North American definition of self-harm usually overlaps with the construct of *self-injurious behavior*, which is typically defined as self-inflicted superficial tissue damage, such as self-cutting or self-burning, without a conscious intent to die (Claes & Vandereycken, 2007; Claes, Vandereycken, & Vertommen, 2005; Herpertz, 1995). Unfortunately, confusion in terminology is increased because the terms self-injurious behavior and *self-mutilation* are often used interchangeably, although the former typically refers to repetitive or superficial injuries and the latter more often refers to serious bodily injury, such as castration, amputation, or enucleation of the eye, which occur often without suicidal intent in the context of psychosis (Claes, Vandereycken, & Vertommen, 2005; Herpertz, 1995). The terms self-mutilation and self-injurious behavior are also sometimes used to describe stereotypical self-harm, such as head-banging, often present in pervasive developmental disorders (Fulcher, 1984; Kress, 2003). These forms of self-injury are considered to be driven by quite different mechanisms relative to youths and young adults who make suicide attempts or engage in nonsuicidal self-injury in response to unbearable distress (Favazza, 1987; 1992; 1998). The picture becomes further muddied when *risky behavior*, defined as "risk taking and health-compromising behaviors that most profoundly affect mortality, morbidity, disability, and social problems," is considered within the realm of self-harm (Perez, 2005, p. 38). Although these risky acts, including substance abuse, fighting, eating disorders, delinquency, aggression, and reckless sexuality or driving, are rarely consciously suicidal and often are not directly completed in order to harm oneself, these youths often report not caring if they experience harm and their risky behaviors are commonly risk factors for progressing to more serious self-injury or suicidality (Afifi, Cox, & Katz, 2007; Bae, Ye, Chen, Rivers, & Singh, 2005; Karver & Tarquini, under review; King et al., 2003). Given this panoply of terms and behaviors around self-harm, how are we to understand the development of self-harm if it cannot even be clearly defined?

The two major positions – viewing all self-harmful behaviors on a spectrum (i.e., parasuicide) as opposed to viewing self-harmful behaviors categorically (i.e., non-suicidal self-injurious behavior versus suicide attempt) – have competed in the research of suicidology for years, and most researchers have touted one viewpoint or the other rather than making efforts to reconcile the two. For example, Favazza (1998) states that "a basic understanding is that a person who truly attempts suicide seeks to end all feelings whereas a person who self-mutiliates seeks to feel better" (p. 261). On the other hand, Stanley, Winchel, Molcho, Simeon, & Stanley (1992) state that "individuals who engage in the various forms of self-harm ... may share common biochemical and behavioral features. All forms of self-harm have in common the inability to resist a self-injurious impulse. In terms of their shared differences, these patients can be represented on a continuum with regard to seriousness and aggresivity of self-injury" (p. 154).

However, a recent theory has grown in prominence, the Joiner interpersonal-psychological theory of suicidality (Joiner, 2005; Stellrecht, Gordon, Van Orden, Witte, Wingate, Cukrowicz, et al., 2006), which incorporates both viewpoints. According to Joiner's model, although risky behavior, self-injurious behavior, and suicide attempts may all have qualitatively different motivations and (sometimes ambiguous) suicidal intent in the mind of the executor, all self-harmful behaviors exist on the same continuum. The actions with lower-suicidal intent (i.e., risky behaviors or non-suicidal self-injurious behavior) have different initial motivators, but still increase a person's capability to later engage in true suicidal actions. According to this theory, the acquired capability to enact lethal self-harm, coupled with a perception of burdensomeness and thwarted belonging, paves the way for subsequent actions with higher suicidal-intent (Joiner, 2005; Stellrecht et al., 2006). Although this theory partially reconciles the dimensional and categorical viewpoints of suicidality and contributes toward an increased understanding of risk of future self-harm and death by suicide, it does not address the mechanisms that differentiate the various types of self-harm. It may be that certain mechanisms are common to all forms of self-harm, whereas others are specific to certain types of self-harm. This also implies that some mechanisms may be critical contributors to some forms of self-harm but are completely irrelevant to other forms of self-harm. In order to get to this level of understanding, one needs to be able to differentiate between different types of self-harm. This of course returns one to the issue of addressing the confusing lack of standardization of nomenclature in the literature.

Silverman et al. (2007) recently suggested a standard nomenclature for the field of suicidology. This nomenclature represents an update of O'Carroll's (1996) classic suicide nomenclature article. Parallel to our perspective, they suggest that clear definitions are needed to advance the science in this field. Thus, Silverman et al. (2007) have proposed that the following definitions be adopted by clinicians, researchers, and other key stakeholders:

- *Suicide* refers to "self-inflicted death with evidence (either explicit or implicit) of intent to die" (Silverman, et al., 2007, p. 273).
- *Suicide attempt* refers to "a self-inflicted, potentially injurious behavior with a nonfatal outcome for which there is evidence (either explicit or implicit) of intent to die" (Silverman et al., 2007, p. 273). A suicide attempt would include behaviors of low lethality where there is evidence of conscious suicidal intent (i.e., the ingestion of five aspirin when the person believed this to be a lethal dose, etc.) as well as behaviors of high lethality where there is no directly expressed intent but obvious

implicit intent (i.e., the ingestion of three bottles of pills combined with liquor because the person "had a headache and wanted the pain to go away," etc.), regardless of whether injury results.

Silverman et al. (2007) have also proposed definitions for self-harm behavior in which there is no or ambiguous intent to die. Whereas the proposed nomenclature is helpful for focusing research relative to gaining understanding of the causes of suicide and suicide attempts, it may be less helpful relative to self-harm behavior in which there is not an intent to die. Silverman et al. (2007) state that "persons engage in self-harm behaviors when they wish to use the appearance of intending to kill themselves in order to attain some other end" (pg. 272). Although this definition of the self-harm term is meant to encompass all self-harming behaviors where there is no intent to die, it is problematic because it assumes a mechanism behind the behavior which may not be consistent with the mechanisms actually driving youths' non-suicidal self-injury. The key point here is that this definition assumes an external function of self-harm behavior; that is, it assumes that self-harming individuals want to appear to others "as if" they are trying to die by suicide. Quite to the contrary, recent research suggests that most nonsuicidal intent self-injury is driven by internal functions such as affect regulation (i.e. releasing emotional pressure, getting rid of intolerable emotions) or self-punishment (to express anger just to one self; Klonsky, 2007). Many other researchers have also expressed a similar viewpoint (Favazza, 1998; Haas & Popp, 2006; Herpertz, 1995; Kumar, Pepe, & Steer, 2004; Laye-Gindhu & Schonert-Reichl, 2005; Linehan, 1993; Nixon, Cloutier, & Aggarwal, 2002; Rodham, Hawton, & Evans, 2004; Skegg, 2005; Suyemoto, 1998; Zlotnick, Donaldson, Spirito, & Pearlstein, 1997). Given these data, this leads to the suggestion that the O'Carroll et al. (1996) and Silverman et al. (2007) definitions need further refinement in order to allow research to more thoroughly investigate the mechanisms behind all self-harm behavior.

From the perspective of understanding mechanisms of self-harm, it is necessary to use a definition of non-suicidal self-injury that does not include a mechanism in the definition. Thus, the following terms and definitions are suggested:

- *Self-injurious behavior* would refer to the commission of any socially unacceptable behavior involving deliberate and direct injury to one's own body severe enough for tissue damage to result without conscious suicidal intent (Claes & Vandereycken, 2007; Winchel & Stanley, 1991).
- *Self-harm* will refer to the wider spectrum of episodes of self-directed bodily damage, regardless of intent and lethality. Self-harm will function as an umbrella-term for both suicidality and self-injurious behavior that is not consciously suicidal. This self-harm term is suggested to replace the term suicide-related behavior recommended by Silverman et al. (2007) because it removes the assumption that all self-injurious behavior is related to suicide [although we do agree, consistent with Joiner (2005), that any self-harm behavior likely increases the risk of future self-harm and risk of suicide].

Given potentially increased understanding of the term self-harm behavior, the next logical step in understanding mechanisms of self-harm is to examine the assumption that there exists clear understanding of the risk factors for self-harm behavior. Three areas, predisposing factors, precipitating factors, and maintenance factors, can be examined when looking at the overlapping risk factors for risky behavior, self-injurious behavior, and suicidal acts (behaviors that vary in severity on the spectrum of self-harm).

RESEARCH ON RISK FACTORS FOR SELF-HARM

Risk factor research utilizes correlational designs to identify variables that are associated with an increased risk of the occurrence of some problematic condition (such as self-harm behaviors). For a variable to be a risk factor, those who have the risk factor should have a greater prevalence of the problematic condition than those who do not have the risk factor. Risk factors for self-harm can be separated into three distinct categories: predisposing factors, precipitating factors, and maintenance factors. Separating risk factors into these categories, as opposed to viewing them all simultaneously as just risk factors, moves one closer to a view of risk factors being part of a model of the mechanisms that lead to self-harm behavior. The first category of risk factors consists of *predisposing factors*. These are fairly early or long-standing risk factors that often create an initial level of risk or vulnerability for other risk factors. These often include biological and genetic features, past behaviors, or past historical events in the environment experienced by an individual (Bryan & Rudd, 2006). These have been the most common type of risk factor examined in the self-harm risk literature.

The second category of risk factors consists of *precipitating factors*. These are environmental and life events (stressors) that are thought to serve as immediate triggers for problematic behaviors and conditions. These often include interpersonal stressors (i.e. recent conflict, recent loss, recent humiliation) but can also include intrapersonal events (i.e. emotional crisis, intense self-criticism, intoxication; e.g. Beautrais, Joyce, & Mulder, 1997; Schnyder, Valach, Bichsel, & Michel, 1999). The third category of risk factors consists of *maintenance factors*. These are the internal and external events that follow a behavior and contribute toward the continuation/repetition of the behavior in the future. These include social and automatic positive and negative reinforcement of self-harm behavior (Nock & Prinstein, 2004). Examining these risk factors within the aforementioned categories allows researchers and theorists to start to differentiate the potential mechanisms that effect self-harm behaviors.

PREDISPOSING FACTORS

Numerous biological, environmental, and personality variables have been suggested to predispose youths and young adults to engaging in self-harm behavior (e.g. Bridge et al., 2006; Spirito & Esposito-Smythers, 2006). However, these risk factors, many extensively researched, do not necessarily reveal the mechanisms by which a vulnerable individual engages in self-harm behavior. However, given that not all predisposing risk factors are equally present in all individuals who later engage in self-harm behavior, these predisposing factors may suggest that there are multiple mechanisms by which individuals later engage in self-harm behavior.

Ethnicity. Self-harm is a problem that exists across genders, ages, ethnicities, and socioeconomic status. Although self-injurious behavior has typically been considered a problem most prevalent in young Caucasian females (Muehlenkamp & Gutierrez, 2004), current research suggests that this may present a skewed picture, since most research is conducted with females in countries of predominantly Caucasian populations (Shaw, 2002). Statistically, in the United States, persons of Caucasian or Latino descent are more likely to engage in self-harming behaviors (Borrill, Burnett, Atkins, Miller, Briggs, Weaver, et al., 2003; Muehlenkamp & Gutierrez, 2004; 2007; Zayas, Lester, Cabassa, & Fortuna, 2005), with African-American females (Garlow, Purselle, Heninger, 2005) and Asian-American college students (Whitlock, Eckenrode, & Silverman, 2006) at reduced risk for self-injury. Most notably, Hispanic teens, especially Hispanic female teens, have been found to be the highest demographic risk group for suicide attempts (Hallfors, Waller, Ford, Halpern, Brodish, & Iritani, 2004; Zayas, Lester, Cabassa, & Fortuna, 2005) and Native American high school students have also been identified as an ethnic group with a very high rate of suicidality (Range, Leach, McIntyre, Posey-Deters, Marion, Kovac, et al., 1999). However, more studies assessing ethnic and cultural differences in self-harm and potential differences in mechanisms of self-harm (e.g. acculturative difficulties, attitudes toward death) are needed, particularly studies that utilize large-scale epidemiological samples.

Gender. Despite extensive research, it is still inconclusive whether gender differences exist in self-injurious behavior; several studies have found more women than men self-injure (Briere & Gill, 1998; Laye-Gindhu & Shonert-Reichl, 2005; Muehlenkamp & Gutierrez, 2007; Ross & Heath, 2002; Stanley et al., 2001), while others suggest that self-injurious behavior may occur at equal rates in both genders (Garrison, Cheryl, McKeown, et al., 1993; Gratz, 2001; Hawton, Hall, Simkin, Bale, Bond, Codd, et al., 2003; Klonsky, Otlmanns, & Turkheimer, 2003; Muehlenkamp & Gutierrez, 2004; Zoroglu, Tuzun, Sar, et al., 2003), although females may be more likely to receive treatment for their injuries (Olfson, Gameroff, Marcus, Greenberg, & Shaffer, 2005). However, there is no debate regarding the gender differences present in suicidality: while females are three times as likely as males to attempt suicide (Krug, Dahlberg, Mercy, Zwi, & Lozano, 2004), males are four times more likely than females to die by suicide, perhaps reflecting their increased likelihood of having certain critical precipitating factors (e.g. access to more lethal means, intoxication, aggression; Anderson & Smith, 2003; Bridge, Goldstein, & Brent, 2006; Center for Disease Control, 2007). Additional research is needed to examine potential gender differences in mechanisms of self-harm.

Age. Self-injurious behavior typically has its age of onset earlier in adolescence than suicide attempts, suggesting that self-injurious behavior may be a precursor to suicidality for some teens (Izutsu, Shimotsu, Matsumoto, Okada, Kikuchi, Kojimoto, et al., 2006; Muehlenkamp & Gutierrez, 2004; Tuisku et al., 2006). Although many studies are retrospective in nature and therefore subject to various distortions, findings are relatively consistent across clinical and community samples that self-injury typically begins between the ages of 12 and 14 (Kumar, Pepe, & Steer, 2004; Meuhlenkamp & Gutierrez, 2004; 2007; Nixon, Cloutier, & Aggarwal, 2002; Nock & Prinstein, 2004; Ross & Heath, 2003). Suicide attempt rates have been found to be highest early in high school (ninth and tenth grade) rather than later (National Center for Health Statistics, 2007). On the other hand, rates of death by suicide are typically low prior to age 15, rapidly increase in late adolescence and are even higher for young adults (CDC, 2007). Connor and Goldston (2007) suggest that increasing rates of death by suicide by age may be related to increased suicidal capability and greater exposure to dangerous precipitating factors such as substance use. Nonetheless, research is lacking on developmental differences in the mechanisms that lead to varying types of self-harm behavior.

Temperament factors. As opposed to demographic predisposing risk factors, temperament factors are more revealing as to potential mechanism behind self-harm behavior. In the classic definition, Rothbart, Ahardi, and Evans (2000) define *temperament* as the "individual differences in reactivity and self-regulation assumed to have a constitutional basis" (pg. 123). Although a tremendous number of constructs have been labeled as being dimensions of temperament, Rothbart et al. (2000) suggest that most identified constructs fall within the domains of Desire to Approach/Positive Affect, Fearfulness/Behavioral Inhibition, Irritability/Anger, Orienting (which is sensitivity to noticing internal and external stimuli), and Effortful Control (which is the ability to inhibit a dominant response for a less dominant response). Interestingly, several of these temperaments are seen as predisposing risk factors for self-harm. Persons with approach-oriented temperaments (impulsivity or sensation seeking) have been found to be at higher risk of engaging in self-harm behaviors (Fergusson, Woodward, & Horwood, 2000; Simeon, Cohen, Stein, Schmeidler, & Spadaccini, 1997; Stanley, Winchel, Molcho, Simeon, & Stanley, 1992). On the other hand, adolescents and adults with behaviorally inhibited temperaments (e.g. shy, withdrawn, avoiding) have also been found to be at-risk for all varieties of self-harm (Callahan, 1993; Goldston, Reboussin, & Daniel, 2006). Individuals high in the temperament domain of irritability/anger also appear to be at elevated risk. Specifically, several researchers have found an association between individuals with high levels of internalized anger and engagement in self-harm behaviors (Claes, Vandereycken, & Vertommen, 2007; Nixon, Cloutier, & Aggarwal, 2002). Additionally, it appears that being high on the Orienting domain of temperament increases vulnerability for self-harm. Research has shown that those who are very highly sensitive to emotional stimuli (i.e., highly responsive to emotional stimuli and experience emotions particularly intensely), may be more likely to be overwhelmed by their emotions and to engage in self-injury and suicide attempts (Haines, Williams, Brain, & Wilson, 1995; Henry, M'Baïlara, Desage, Gard, Misdrahi, & Vieta, 2007; Linehan, 1993; Nock & Mendes, 2008). Finally, being low in effortful control may also increase vulnerability. Linehan (1993) proposed that some individuals appear to have difficulty inhibiting initial emotional responses, that is, they are slow to return to their emotional baseline after becoming emotionally aroused. She suggested that these person are then at heightened risk for self-harm behavior. As of yet, evidence of this association has not been established.

As with the aforementioned predisposing risk factors, the presence of temperamental risk factors may indicate some level of vulnerability; however, their presence alone does not mean self-harm behavior will occur. Instead it is hypothesized that there could be a mechanism by which temperamental risk factors interact bidirectionally with the social environment in that those persons with certain temperament types may expose themselves to greater stressors and precipitating risk factors (Caspi, Sugden, & Moffitt, 2003). For example, teens who are impulsive may be more likely to get themselves into stressful situations that challenge their ability to cope, placing them at greater risk for self-harmful behavior.

Genetic and neurobiological factors. Given that temperamental factors are most likely associated with biological or genetic underpinnings and that they may be associated with self-harm behavior, it makes sense to directly examine genetic and neurobiological predisposing risk factors for self-harm behavior. Consistent with this perspective, twin and family studies suggest that suicidality has a clear genetic component (Brent et al., 2002; Brent et al., 2003; Glowinski et al., 2001; Qin et al., 2003; Roy and Segal, 2001; Runeson & Asberg, 2003), and that the contribution of genetics may be between 30-50% (Fu et al., 2002; Statham et al., 1998). This genetic risk appears independent of risk for other psychopathology such as mood disorders (Egeland & Sussex, 1985; Qin et al., 2003; Runeson & Asberg, 2003). More specifically, there is some research evidence linking the serotonin transporter gene (Belliver et al, 2000; Bondy et al., 2000; Courtet et al., 2001; Fusar-Poli, Allen, & Cortesi, 2007; Gorwood et al., 2000; Joiner, Brown, & Wingate, 2005; Purselle & Nemeroff, 2003), TPH gene (Fusar-Poli, Allen, & Cortesi, 2007; Joiner, Brown, & Wingate, 2005; Rujescu et al., 2003a), and COMT gene (Joiner, Brown, & Wingate, 2005; Nolan et al., 2000; Rujescu et al., 2003b) to suicidality. Hyperactivity of the HPA axis (Nemeroff, Owens, Bissette, Andorn, & Stanley, 1988; Arato, Banki, Bissette, & Nemeroff, 1989), white matter hyperintensities (Ahearn, Jamison, Steffens, et al., 2001; Ehrlich, Noam, Lyoo, Kwon, Clark, & Renshaw, 2003; 2004), and abnormalities of the orbitofrontal and prefrontal cortex (Monkul, Hatch, Nicoletti, Spence, Brambilla, Lacerda, et al., 2007) have also all been consistently found in those who attempt and die by suicide.

Lower serotonergic and heightened adrenergic activity have also been somewhat consistently associated with suicidality (Cremniter et al., 1999; Joiner, Brown, & Wingate, 2005; Mann & Malone, 1997; Placidi et al., 2001; Spreux-Varoquax et al., 2001; van Heeringen, 2003; Westrin & Nimeus, 2003), whereas abnormalities in the dopamine system and lowered levels of fatty acids have been less consistently associated with suicidality (Huan, Hamazaki, & Sun, 2004; Mann, 2003; Lalovic, Levy, Canetti, Sequeira, Montoudis, & Turecki, 2007; Sublette, Hibbeln, Galfalvy, Oquendo, & Mann, 2006). However, as associations between the dopamine system and fatty acid levels and impulsivity and violent behaviors have consistently been found (Sublette, Oquendo, & Mann, 2006), the role of these neurochemical systems should be further studied in the context of self-harm, considering the overlap in vulnerabilities of impulsivity and anger. Despite some interesting genetic and neurobiological findings that suggest biological predisposing risk factors, extremely little is known about how these factors may lead to self-harm behavior. More studies are needed to elucidate exactly how the mechanisms of genetic and neurobiological factors interact with environmental factors to lead a person to self-harming behavior.

Environmental factors. Environmental factors serve as predisposing risk factors when the at-risk individual has been exposed to the harmful environment early in development and/or chronically in the present. For example, self-injurious behavior has been traditionally associated in adolescence with cold, perfectionistic, overbearing mothers in conjunction with uninvolved, overpowered fathers (Wanstall & Oei, 1989); however, similar explanations (i.e., the refrigerator mother) were proposed as etiological factors for schizophrenia and eating disorders but were not supported empirically. Although this connection has not been established in the self-harm literature, it is worth noting recent research that has found an association between cold, unemotional, uninvolved family environments and habituation to emotional pain (Vangelisti, Maguire, Alexander, & Clark, 2007). This overlaps with Joiner's (2005) theory that people become more capable of harming themselves when they habituate to physical or emotional pain. Relatedly, self-harm has been empirically associated with poor parent-youth relationships (Fotti et al., 2006), parental criticism (Wedig & Nock, 2007), experiencing high levels of family conflict (Lowenstein, 2005), and a chaotic or unsafe home life (Dube, Anda, Felitti, Chapman, Williamson, & Giles, 2001). In addition, a history of abuse, particularly physical or sexual abuse, has been found to be more likely in self-harming populations (Gratz, 2003; Whitlock, Eckenrode, & Silverman, 2006). Prior sexual abuse, in particular, appears to be a specific predisposing risk factor for self-injury (Kisiel & Lyons, 2001; Lipschitz, Winegar, Nicolaou et al., 1999; Zoroglu, Tuzun, Sar et al., 2003). It has been hypothesized that disruptive family environments (with abuse serving as an extreme example) increase vulnerability to self-harm in that persons are exposed to emotionally invalidating environments.

In her work on borderline personality disorder, a core feature of which is self-harmful behavior, Marsha Linehan described the etiological significance of an *invalidating environment*. The invalidating environment can manifest itself in many forms, but a defining characteristic is the tendency of others in the environment "to respond erratically and inappropriately to private experience (e.g., beliefs, thoughts, feelings, sensations, etc.) and in particular to be insensitive to private experience… [often responding] in an extreme fashion" (Linehan, 1993, p. 3). Over time, a youth may not learn appropriate emotional regulation if their emotional internal experiences are often met with nonattuned responses by parents, siblings, and teachers (i.e., instances of anger or sadness are met with either nonresponsiveness or an overly extreme punitive response). Often, youth in an invalidating environment will not learn to appropriately label and modulate their emotions, tolerate stress, or to trust their own personal emotional responses as valid (Linehan, 1993); as a result, they remain emotionally immature, unable to adequately cope with and often trying to inhibit their emotional expression, and may feel intolerable distress when confronted with strong affect states. Developmentally, over time, this type of environment, in interaction with a predisposition toward impulsivity, shyness, or high emotional reactivity, can raise vulnerability to precipitants of self-harming behaviors.

The invalidating environment can take many forms. Although much emphasis has been placed on nonresponsive or inappropriately responsive parenting (Linehan, 1993), there are several other chronic social environments associated with increased risk for self-harm. Experiencing chronic discrimination or oppression because of one's race, sexual orientation, or gender identity (Grossman & D'Augelli, 2007; Skegg, 2005), being chronically victimized or bullied at school (Lowenstein, 2005), experiencing social isolation (Skegg, 2005), or experiencing school failure (Orpinas, Basen-Engquist, Grunbaum, & Parcel, 1995) are types of invalidating environments that have been associated with increased risk of self-harm. Likewise, persons from disadvantaged backgrounds, such as being of low socioeconomic status, are often targets of invalidation and are overrepresented in self-harming groups (Ayton, Rasool, Cattrell, 2003). These environmental factors are believed to interact with biological and temperamental risk factors in individuals who are vulnerable to self-harm; in turn, these factors are believed to produce and to be affected by a constellation of personality or intrapersonal factors that are commonly found in self-harming populations.

Personality or intrapersonal factors. Finally, a number of personality/intrapersonal factors have been found to be related to increased vulnerability to self-harm behavior. Many persons who engage in self-harming behaviors have been found to demonstrate a variety of social skills deficits, especially deficits in problem solving (Nock & Mendes, 2008; Speckens & Hawton, 2005) and coping skills (Linehan, 1993; McAuliffe et al., 2006). Often, self-harming individuals have difficulty expressing their emotions (Kisiel & Lyons, 1999) and often try to suppress their thoughts and emotions (Najmi, Wegner, & Nock, 2007), common byproducts of exposure to an invalidating environment (Linehan, 1993). In self-harming females, body image disturbance, self-criticism, and perfectionism have commonly been found to indicate vulnerability to self-harm (Donaldson, Spirito, & Farnett, 2000); in self-harming individuals of both genders, self-esteem tends to be lower and negative rumination may be higher than for those who do not self-harm (Laye-Gindhu & Schonert-Reichl, 2005). Neuroticism and general psychopathology tend to be higher in self-harming populations (Haw, Hawton, Houston, & Townsend, 2001), including depression (Haw, Hawton, Houston, & Townsend, 2001; Haw, Houston, Townsend, & Hawton, 2002; Ross & Heath, 2002), social phobia (Haw, Hawton, Houston, & Townsend, 2001), post-traumatic stress disorder (Harned, Najavits, & Weiss, 2006), substance abuse, anxiety disorders, schizophrenia (Haw, Hawton, Houston, & Townsend, 2001), antisocial behavior (Laye-Gindhu & Schonert-Reichl, 2005; Verona, Sachs-Ericsson, & Joiner, 2004), obsessive-compulsive disorder (Apter, Horesh, Gothelf, Zalsman, Erlich, Soreni, et al., 2003), eating disorders, psychotic disorders, and personality disorders (Haw, Hawton, Houston, & Townsend, 2001). Although these comorbid disorders and other intrapersonal factors often precede the onset of self-harm and indicate increased vulnerability to self-harm, these risk factors are not sufficient to indicate a causal mechanism for self-harm in that many persons with these vulnerabilities do not engage in self-harm behaviors. Thus, a mechanism of self-harm behavior likely includes more than just predisposing risk factors.

PRECIPITATING FACTORS

Although individuals who evince biological, environmental, and personality predisposing factors are at-risk to engage in self-harm behavior, most never actually progress to self-harm. It is in the presence of precipitating factors such as stressful events that individuals become more likely to engage in self-harm behavior (Muehlenkamp & Gutierrez, 2004). Essentially, these precipitating factors trigger existing vulnerabilities within an individual, leading to self-harm behavior. Although this diathesis-stress model (e.g. Schotte & Clum, 1982) is more revealing about the process of self-harm behavior, a weakness of this model is that the precipitating event can be viewed as the critical mechanism, when in fact, the critical mechanisms that lead to self-harm behavior may actually be related to how the person internally and the environment externally respond to the precipitating event and its consequences. Nonetheless, given the variety of events that have been found to precipitate self-harm behavior, examination of these precipitating factors may help to reveal the mechanisms by which individuals later engage in self-harm behavior.

Interpersonal difficulties. Interpersonal difficulties have been clearly noted as the most common precipitating events for self-harm behavior (Beautrais, Joyce, & Mulder, 1997). Beautrais, Joyce, & Mulder (1997) found that 24% of youth making a serious suicide attempt reported a recent relationship breakdown as the most common precipitating factor, and 26.4% reported other interpersonal difficulties, such as arguments with family or friends, as the primary precipitant. This finding was corroborated by Lowenstein (2005), who found that adolescents often engaged in suicidal behavior and non-suicidal self-injury after conflicts with family or in other important relationships. Abandonment or the threat of abandonment (Wanstall & Oei, 1989), peer or parental rejection (Hilt, Cha, & Nolen-Hoeksema, 2008;

Yates, Tracy, & Luthar, 2008), separation from a loved one, and refusal of demands (Wanstall & Oei, 1989) are other commonly reported interpersonal triggers for acts of self-harm. Although these interpersonal events have commonly been found to immediately proceed self-harm behavior, these precipitating factors are also not sufficient to indicate a causal mechanism for self-harm in that most individuals, even vulnerable individuals, do not engage in self-harm behaviors at the occurrence of these interpersonal events. Thus, further exploration of possible precipitants seems warranted.

Legal/disciplinary difficulties. Legal difficulties, problems with the police, and disciplinary issues have been found to be the second leading precipitating event for self-harm behavior in adolescents and young adults (Beautrais, 2003; Beautrais, Joyce, & Mulder, 1997). Recently, in a prospective longitudinal study, it was found that, even after controlling for other risk factors, being a recent victim of a physical attack–assault, being accused of a crime, being arrested, being sent to jail, and being involved in a court case were all legal/crime related predictors of self-harm behavior (Yen, Pagano, Shea, et al, 2005). Bridge, Goldstein, and Brent (2006) also concluded that legal and disciplinary problems are often the immediate triggers for self-harm behavior and suicide, especially in vulnerable youths (e.g. impulsive, aggressive). Again, as with interpersonal precipitating events, it is suspected that there are more proximal mechanisms that occur following precipitating events that may be the most immediate precursors of self-harm behavior. Furthermore, suicide autopsy studies have revealed that often there is no clear *external* precipitating event for self-harm behavior (Maltsberger, Hendin, Haas, & Lipschitz, 2003).

Intrapersonal difficulties. Surprisingly, the literature on precipitants of self-harm behavior has focused on external events and has ignored internal events as potential triggers for self-harm behavior. On the other hand, considering that much of this literature is based on what has been learned from psychological autopsies (which relies on interviewing persons who knew the person who died by suicide), it is perhaps to be expected that internal triggers would be missed. Recently, a number of studies have found that it is often the internal affective states that result from external events with which the individual cannot successfully cope that are the reasons persons engage in self-harm behavior (Gratz, 2003; Jacobson & Gould, 2007; Klonsky, 2007; Laye-Gindhu & Schonert-Reichl, 2005; Messer & Fremouw, 2008; Polk & Liss, 2007). Persons who self-harm often report an intolerable affective state to which they are unable to appropriately respond as the impetus for their self-harmful acts (Gratz, 2003; Jacobson & Gould, 2007; Klonsky, 2007; Laye-Gindhu & Schonert-Reichl, 2005; Linehan, 1993; Messer & Fremouw, 2008; Polk & Liss, 2007). When persons with deficient coping skills and problems with emotion regulation face strong affective states, tension escalates severely, emotional resources are exhausted and/or paralyzed, and ultimately self-harm behaviors are utilized to reduce the tension and escape from overwhelming affect or a painful situation (Tamas, Kovacs, Gentzler, Tepper, Gadoros, et al., 2007). This internal escalation often occurs when vulnerable people try to inhibit their experiences of guilt, depression, frustration, anxiety, or feelings of failure (which often follow external precipitating events; Laye-Gindhu & Schonert-Reichl, 2005; Namji, Wegner, & Nock, 2007) rather than dealing with their problems directly. Given the recent empirical work in the areas of coping and emotion regulation, it is suspected that intrapersonal processes are critical antecedent components in the mechanisms by which persons engage in self-harm behavior.

Maintenance Factors (Consequences)

Although antecedent intrapersonal processes appear to be critical mechanisms behind engagement in self-harmful behavior, extensive behavioral research has long indicated that consequences often are required for the maintenance of any problematic behavior (Miltenberger, 2008). Thus, it is likely that consequences (besides death by suicide which is a fairly uncommon self-harm behavior) also serve a maintenance function in self-harming behavior. Consequences of self-harm can be post behavior stimuli that serve as *negative reinforcers*, wherein a noxious stimulus is removed as the result of an action making the action more likely to occur in the future, or *positive reinforcers*, wherein a positive stimulus is added as the result of an action making the action more likely to occur in the future (Fahmy & Jones, 1990). Negative reinforcers, such as escape from overwhelming affect, demands, or an unpleasant situation, often result from self-harm, making self-harm behavior more likely to be repeated. Survivors of self-harm often cite the desire to escape their emotional pain and tension or alleviate guilt as primary reasons for self-harm (Kumar, Pepe, & Steer, 2004; Skegg, 2005). Not surprisingly, many individuals who engage in self-harmful behaviors have a history of multiple hospitalizations for self-harmful behavior; often hospitalization serves to release an individual from overwhelming demands - negative reinforcement (Carr & Diamond, 1985). Positive reinforcers, such as relief, pleasure, relaxation, calm, regained control, or a return to the sense of self from a dissociative state, are also common in the aftermath of self-harm and are often cited as reasons for engaging in self-harming behavior (Kumar, Pepe, & Steer, 2004; Skegg, 2005; Wanstall & Oei, 1989). Nonetheless, negative reinforcement, in the form of removal of a noxious stimulus such as overwhelming painful affect, may be the most powerful motivator for self-injurers (Machoian, 2001).

While negative reinforcement in the form of removal of high levels of negative emotion may motivate the initial episode of self-harm, it is also likely to maintain this maladaptive emotion regulation strategy over more adaptive strategies (Machoian, 2001). Consistent with the principles of reinforcement, on the next occasion that their level of negative emotion rises, individuals who self-harmed in the past will be less likely to engage in problem-focused coping or adaptive emotion regulation strategies and increasingly likely to turn to the maladaptive strategy that brought them emotional relief in the past, self-harm. Self-harm behavior increases while other coping strategies decrease due to differential reinforcement; the maladaptive emotion regulation strategy of self-harm that brought symptom relief in the past is more likely to be chosen because it was reinforced. Other strategies are not used, are thus not reinforced, and then are pushed out of the coping repertoire. Over time, as other adaptive strategies drop off, the maladaptive self-harm strategy may become less effective, and engaging in self-harm itself may cause additional problems and emotional stress (i.e., other people's reactions, feelings of shame, etc.). When the previously reinforcing behavior of self-harm no longer brings the same level of relief from emotional pain, self-harm may increase in frequency or severity, an "extinction burst" that occurs when a previously reinforced behavior is no longer reinforced at the same level. The danger, of course, is that this can cause an escalating cycle of increasing self-harm behavior in order to achieve the same level of relief as was previously received by lower level self-harmful behavior.

Borrowing from the behavioral literature, Nock & Prinstein (2004; 2005) added that the consequences of self-harmful behavior can be either *automatically-* or *socially-reinforcing*.

Automatic negative reinforcement refers to an individual's use of self-harm for affect regulation purposes, such as reducing tension or other intolerable emotions. *Automatic positive reinforcement* refers to an individual's use of self-harm to create a desirable physiological or psychological state, such as generating feelings of relief or desiring to feel anything after a state of depersonalization or numbness, even if the feeling was pain. Automatic reinforcement, usually automatic negative reinforcement, is consistently the most commonly endorsed reason for engaging in self-harm (Gratz, 2003; Jacobson & Gould, 2007; Klonsky, 2007; Laye-Gindhu & Schonert-Reichl, 2005; Linehan, 1993; Messer & Fremouw, 2008; Polk & Liss, 2007). However, the socially reinforcing elements of self-harm also play a role in the behavior's maintenance.

Nock and Prinstein (2004; 2005) define *social negative reinforcement* as an individual's use of self-harm to escape from interpersonal or environmental demands, such as avoiding punishment or work. *Social positive reinforcement* is defined as an individual's use of self-harm to communicate with or gain a reaction or access to services from others, such as receiving attention from parents or peers, eliciting help from others, expressing how sad or angry a person feels, or gaining admittance to treatment. Social reinforcement is less commonly endorsed as a motive for self-harm (Herpertz, 1995; Lloyd-Richardson, Perrine, Dierker, & Kelley, 2007; Nock & Prinstein, 2004; 2005). Although self-harming behaviors may not consciously be committed in order to manipulate others and receive reinforcement, even those who engage in self-harm for a variety of reasons may still be likely to continue the behavior because of these factors (Hilt, Cha, & Nolen-Hoeksema, 2008; Jacobson & Gould, 2007; Levenkron, 1998; Linehan, 1993; Lloyd-Richardson, Perrine, Dierker, & Kelley, 2007; Nock & Prinstein, 2004; 2005). As self-harm often has positive consequences, the use of self-harm in response to negative emotional states and situations may become habitual and cyclical over time (Nixon, Cloutier, & Aggarwal, 2002). Although maladaptive, self-harm provides a means of social and more importantly emotional control to those who otherwise have difficulties with emotional expression and adaptive coping. In summary, emerging risk factor research, reviewed in this section of this chapter, indicates that risk factors may not exist as isolated contributors to risk but may interact within the context of certain theorized mechanisms to heighten risk of self-harm behavior.

THEORIES OF SELF-HARM

As we have demonstrated, the literature contains an abundance of studies on risk factors for self-harm behavior, but most of the research has been conducted separate from any guiding theory of self-harm. As mentioned initially in this chapter, risk factor research needs to move from examining relationships with self-harm behavior to identifying the pathogenic mechanisms that lead to self-harm behavior. A limited number of theories about mechanisms of self-harm behavior can be inferred from the research literature; closer examination appears warranted as an important first step.

Affect regulation theory of self-harm. The many studies that have explored the functions of self-harm, emotion regulation and self-harm, and coping and self-harm appear to support an affect regulation model of self-harm. An affect regulation model would need to focus on regulation of negative emotion, as negative emotion and not positive emotion has been repeatedly linked to self-harm (Herpertz, 1995; Klonsky, 2007; Laye-Gindhu & Schonert-Reichl, 2005; Nixon, Cloutier, & Aggarwal, 2002). Before one can fully understand and test the relationships between constructs in any proposed model, it is important that clear definitions be used to avoid confusion that can impede progress. Thus, we begin with the following definitions as a starting point in understanding the role of affect regulation in self-harm theory.

The term *affect* refers to a superordinate category that includes all valenced emotional states, whether positive or negative (Scherer, 1984). *Affect regulation*, therefore, refers to a number of processes individuals utilize in order to consciously or unconsciously influence these affective states (Rottenberg & Gross, 2007). When a conscious effort, this affect regulation process is often referred to as "coping" in the common parlance. However, traditionally in the emotion, stress, and coping literatures, *coping* refers to responses that address both the emotions associated with the stressful situation and the problem of the stressful situation itself, whereas *emotion regulation* refers to the specific subset of coping behaviors that addresses the emotions associated with the stressful situation but not the external source of the stressful situation itself. Although emotion regulation can be considered a subset of coping, the two types of affect regulation can be differentiated based on whether the response is meant to address internal or external demands. One can refer to affect regulation strategies as coping when considering cognitive or behavioral responses designed to alter the stressful stimulus itself, whereas the term emotion regulation can be used when referring to cognitive or behavioral responses designed to maintain or alter the emotional state resulting from the experience or processing of the stressful stimulus. Although these two terms can differentiate between variants of affect regulation, in practice, the two processes of coping and emotion regulation often occur together, either simultaneously or sequentially. For example, negative emotions that are stressful even independent of the stressful situation must often be down-regulated before the stressful situation itself can be addressed; without such emotion regulation, more instrumental forms of coping cannot occur effectively (Folkman & Moskowitz, 2004).

Growing interest in affect regulation in the self-harm literature has focused on pathogenic processes such as deficits in emotion regulation or coping. However, despite the importance of this area of research and many researchers suggesting that affect regulation plays a primary role in self-harm (Favazza, 1988; Favazza, 1992; Favazza, 1998; Gratz, 2001; Gratz, 2003; Linehan, 1993; Suyemoto, 1998), there has been no affect regulation theory to guide researchers. Thus, in this section, we propose an *affect regulation theory of self-harm.* It is proposed that when precipitating factors in the environment tax an individual's ability to respond (i.e., life stressors), they will often elicit negative emotions (i.e., anger, anxiety, or depression) that must be appropriately regulated. However, lacking adequate emotion regulation or coping skills, at-risk individuals become overwhelmed by their environment and their emotional experiences and experience unrelenting distress. They then turn to self-harm behaviors as what they believe to be their only means to regulate their overwhelming negative affect. Although these maladaptive avoidant emotion regulation and coping strategies may be effective at reducing negative emotions in the short-term (i.e. through denial or suppression, etc.), these tactics actually cause negative emotions to increase in the long-term (Kashdan, Barrios, Forsyth, Steger, 2006). Unfortunately, if a person is uncomfortable using adaptive coping strategies such as expressing or trusting their emotions and maladaptive tactics work even slightly in the short-term, the maladaptive self-harm strategies become reinforced, and the person comes to rely on these maladaptive strategies without realizing that their affect regulation strategies are ineffective in the long term, as difficult emotions and problems are never addressed. With problems being inadequately addressed or avoided altogether, negative emotions associated with the problem actually increase. Ironically, the presence of high levels of unrelenting negative emotion makes it increasingly difficult for persons to perform appropriate coping and emotion regulation strategies (Linehan, 1993). Problems and the emotions they elicit become continually avoided, levels of negative emotions rise higher and higher, and become overwhelming. With their coping repertoire composed of ineffective strategies and their ability to regulate their emotions overtaxed, the negative mood state may become intolerable, precipitating further self-harm as a desperate emotion regulation strategy. Over time, the maladaptive self-harm strategy becomes less effective, and if this heightened frequency or severity of self-harm is reinforced (in the form of providing additional relief from negative emotion or concern and attention from others in the environment), a cycle of escalating maladaptive emotion regulation can ensue. As the ability to regulate emotions and cope adaptively deteriorates over time, self-harm continues to escalate, potentially to a lethal degree.

Consistent with the proposed theory, there appears to be empirical support for the notion that those who self-harm have deficient emotion regulation and coping strategies (e.g. Cantanzaro, 2000). Suicidal individuals are more likely to utilize avoidant (Spirito et al., 1996) and maladaptive emotion regulation strategies (Curry, et al., 1992), such as thought and emotion suppression, nonacceptance of emotional responses, or use of drugs or alcohol as distraction, and they have fewer adaptive coping strategies in their repertoire in general (Rotherham-Borus, Trautman, Dopkins, & Shrout, 1990). Numerous researchers have found that the the most commonly attributed motive for self-injurious behavior is emotion regulation (Favazza & Conterio, 1989; Herpertz, 1995; Laye-Gindhu & Schonert-Reichl, 2005; Muehlenkamp & Gutierrez, 2004; Nixon, Cloutier, & Aggarwal, 2002). Studies of both adolescents and adults with self-injury often cite that self-injurious behavior provides temporary relief from anxiety and depersonalization (Favazza & Conterio, 1989), and amongst populations of adolescent self-injurers, the top two reasons for engaging in this behavior were to reduce depression and tension (Nixon, Cloutier, & Aggarwal, 2002). Despite being such a maladaptive method of coping, over 60% of adolescent self-injurers report experiencing emotional relief after they injure themselves (Kumar, Pepe, & Steer, 2004); similarly, "escape from a negative or overwhelming mood state" is also a commonly endorsed motive for suicide attempts, showing continuity in negative automatic reinforcement processes between the two self-harm behaviors (Groholt, Ekeberg, & Haldorsen, 2000; Hjelmeland & Groholt, 2005). Additionally, continuity and progression of emotion dysregulation and self-harm severity is shown by hospitalized adolescents who have attempted suicide at least once; they have been found to show higher levels of emotion dysregulation and a greater number of self-injurious behaviors than hospitalized self-harm ideators who have never engaged in any self-harm behavior (Zlotnick, et al., 1997). Similarly, persons who have attempted suicide multiple times demonstrate greater use of maladaptive emotion regulation strategies than single attempters and engage in more severe forms of non-suicidal self-injury (Esposito, Spirito, Boergers, & Donaldson, 2003).

Considering that persons who engage in self-harm often do so for the purpose of regulating overwhelming emotion, self-harm behaviors can therefore be viewed as an emotion-focused coping mechanism, albeit a maladaptive one (Alderman, 1997; McAllister,

2003). Reports from those who self-injure often express that emotional pain and both physiological and psychological tension escalate until it is absolutely intolerable and dissociation sometimes occurs; at this point, the person engages in self-harm in order to deal with the overwhelming mood state (Favazza, 1998; Simeon & Favazza, 2001; Nock & Prinstein, 2004; 2005). Self-harm has been recognized as a response to overwhelming emotional states, but has rarely been researched in light of the vast body of the stress and coping literature. Nevertheless, self-harm research supports the union of these literatures via the hypothesized affect regulation model of self-harm, with special emphasis on the interplay between emotion regulation, coping, and self-harm behavior.

Joiner model of suicidality. Identifying and measuring pathogenic affect regulation processes is critical in understanding how self-harm behavior comes about; however, this only addresses part of the mechanism behind self-harm behavior. Missing from affect regulation theories of self-harm is the process by which individuals actually become capable of hurting themselves. One of the most influential theories of suicidal behavior to emerge in recent years is that by Thomas Joiner (2005), who proposes that few people are capable of self-harm behavior. The central idea of Joiner's theory is that serious suicidal behavior requires the acquired *suicidal capability*, through habituation to pain and fear, to enact lethal self-injury. In other words, suicide attempts do not readily occur unless the ability to enact lethal self-injury is already in place. By this theory, persons who engage in self-harm behavior must previously overcome strong innate self-preservation instincts that are present in all human beings. Joiner suggests that the repeated experience of or witnessing of physical and emotional pain may make it easier for individuals to break this self-preservation threshold. His theory explains why past self-harm behavior (experience of pain) or suicidality in close family or friends (witnessing pain) increases the risk of future self-harm. It also follows that aggression toward others (giving and witnessing pain), is expected to lower the self-preservation threshold. Other behaviors also make sense in how they potentially increase suicidal capability – careless, reckless, risky behavior like drunk driving, eating disorders, or drug abuse, by definition has the individual engaging in behavior that reduces fear of pain and fear of being harmed; thus the person habituates to increasing levels of pain. All of these circumstances make the natural aversion toward harming one self less fear inducing.

However, it is suggested that this acquired ability to enact lethal self-harm is necessary but not sufficient (Stellrecht, Gordon, Van Orden, Witte, Wingate, et al., 2006; Van Orden, Witte, Gordon, Bender, & Joiner, 2008). This acquired capability is only activated in situations of stress and psychological pain in which the individual feels hopeless to change two important factors: *perceived burdensomeness*, the perception of being a burden to loved ones and being helpless to ever change this situation; and *thwarted belonging*, the perception that one does not belong, has no social support network, or is not valued by family, friends, or community (Stellrecht, Gordon, Van Orden, Witte, Wingate, et al., 2006). When perceived burdensomeness and thwarted belonging are high, the person is said to have high *suicidal desire.* Despite this high desire, risk of self-harm is only elevated if the individual also has suicidal capability (Joiner et al., 2007).

Much like the Affect Regulation model, there is also a great deal of empirical support for the Joiner model of self-harm behavior. A history of self-harm, whether risky behavior, self-injurious behavior, or suicide attempts, has been found to drastically raise the risk for completed suicide or increasingly lethal suicide attempts (Cooper et al., 2005; Owens, Horrocks, & House, 2002), even after controlling for other important moderators such as psychopathology or negative life events. Much research has also linked perceived burdensomeness to suicide: for example, suicide notes written by those who completed suicide demonstrated more perceived burdensomeness than those who survived, and perceived burdensomeness correlates highly with both past number of suicide attempts and indices of current suicidal symptoms (Joiner, 2005). Similarly, suicidal ideation correlates highly, both in the community and in high-risk populations, with both perceived burdensomeness and low levels of belonging (DeCatanzaro, 1995; Van Orden, Witte, Gordon, Bender, & Joiner, 2008). This theory coincides well with the observation that those who commit or attempt suicide often are socially isolated (Skegg, 2005), recently divorced or widowed (Joiner, 2005), or have perceptions of low social support (Evans, Hawton, & Rodham, 2005). While there are many more persons who have these risk factors than ever engage in self-harm, the critical combination with suicidal capability addresses both the low base rate of self-harm as well as proposes a reason why certain people may be more vulnerable (e.g. doctors witness a great deal of pain which increases their suicidal capability; Joiner, 2005).

Need for Integrative Theory

The Joiner model, although impressively explaining who is most at-risk for engaging in self-harm behavior and explaining how persons actually go about being able to harm themselves, does not get to the specific mechanisms that explain why certain precipitating events are responded to with self-harm behavior or not. The presence of perceived burdensomeness and thwarted belonging may be important risk factors but they do not reveal the mechanisms that lead to self-harm behavior. In a complementary fashion, the affect regulation model addresses how vulnerability through predisposing risk factors and interaction with precipitating factors leads to maladaptive responses, but does not address how individuals actually become capable of hurting themselves. In addition, neither model fully integrates the tremendous literature that includes predisposing and precipitating antecedent risk factors and the recent literature on maintenance factors. Therefore, this chapter presents an integrative model of how a person progresses along the spectrum of self-harming behavior that includes predisposing, precipitating, and maintenance factors and incorporates the Affect Regulation model of self-harm and the Joiner model of suicidality.

An Integrative Model of Self-Harming Behavior in Adolescence and Young Adulthood

Hypothesized relationships among the core constructs in our model are presented in Figure 1. Biological and/or temperamental characteristics are hypothesized to interact with early and/or long-standing environmental factors to contribute to the development of individuals with varying intrapersonal/personality characteristics. Varying combinations of these predisposing risk factors create individuals who are particularly vulnerable to self-harm. These individuals often have a constellation of intrapersonal traits that both develop from and

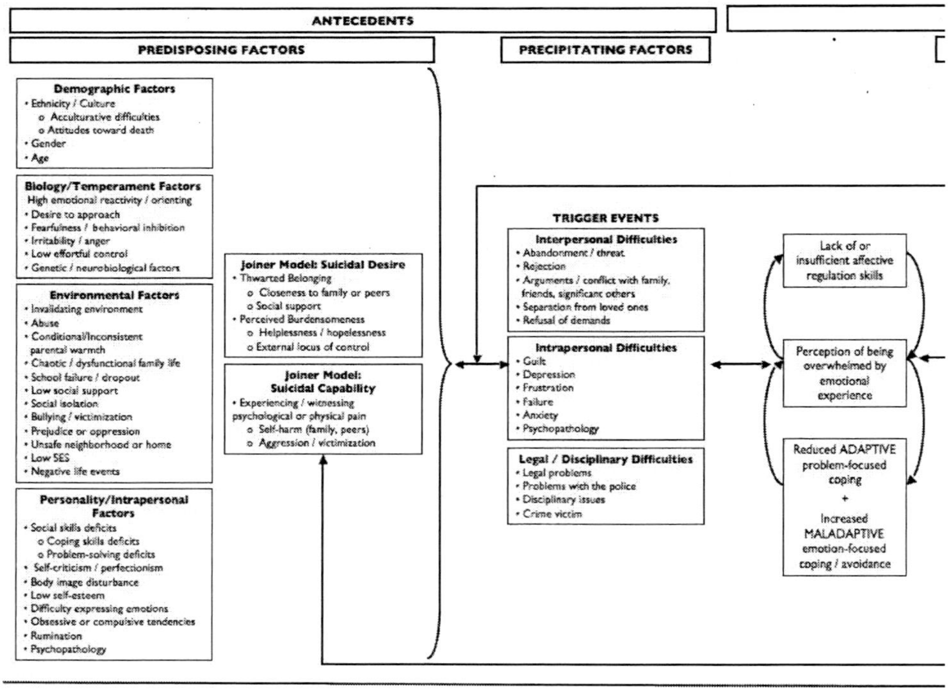

interact with biological, temperamental, and environmental factors to form a predisposing diathesis for self-harm. We see Joiner's model fitting within a conceptualization of predisposing intrapersonal vulnerabilities. Certain individuals develop negative feelings/suicidal desire as a result of a sense of thwarted belonging and/or thwarted efficacy (they experience a great deal of psychological pain, feel helpless to do anything about it, and worry about being a burden upon others). In addition, Joiner's model also makes an important contribution to predisposing environmental factors – some individuals witness and/or experience physical and/or psychological pain (self-harm by peers or family, victim or purveyor of aggression, etc.) which leaves them more vulnerable to being capable of engaging in self-harm behavior.

These predisposing factors can be viewed as a vulnerability that is activated in the face of triggering events, the precipitating factors. These precipitating factors may be interpersonal, legal/disciplinary, or intrapersonal in nature. In fact, sometimes the interpersonal and legal/disciplinary factors trigger the intrapersonal factors, which then serve as additional precipitating triggers for self-harm behavior. Furthermore, not only are predisposing factors activated by precipitating factors, they also sometimes help create the precipitating events in the first place. For example, an impulsive individual may be at heightened risk of self-harm following interpersonal conflict; the nature of their impulsivity may also increase the likelihood of there being a precipitating interpersonal conflict.

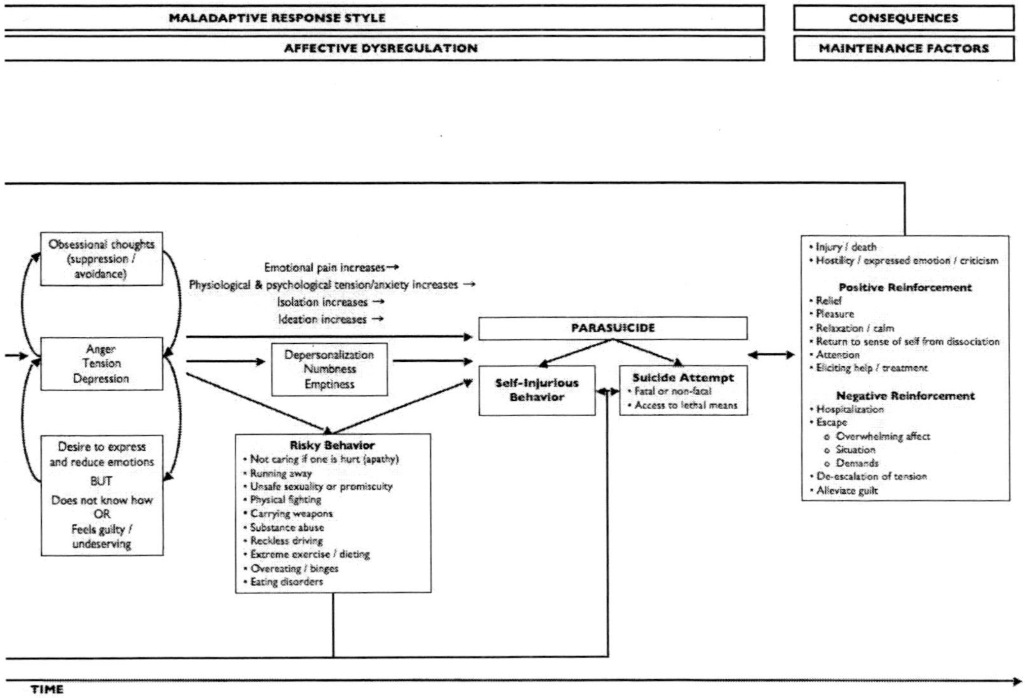

Figure 1. An integrative model of self-harm that includes predisposing, precipitating, and maintenance factors in light of the interacting mechanisms of emotion dysregulation and maladaptive coping.

When a vulnerable individual (e.g. emotionally sensitive, high suicidal desire) encounters any number of precipitating factors, we believe that the individual's response style (maladaptive or adaptive) plays a critical role in the mechanism by which self-harm behavior develops or does not occur. Those individuals who, in the face of precipitating events, have inadequate affect regulation skills or are unable to utilize proper skills when under duress, are more likely to respond with increased emotion-focused coping, increased emotional avoidance skills, and decreased problem-focused coping. It is hypothesized that these maladaptive responses (avoidance of dealing with problems, suppression of emotions) often lead to an inability to adequately address the precipitating problem, the arousing of and an inability to cope with strong affective states, and the individual's perception of being overwhelmed by the emotional experience. Over time, the continual avoidance of the problem and associated feelings may actually increase the feelings of being overwhelmed and also increase the frequency of triggering events (i.e., not addressing the problem may lead to additional fights with family or increased depression, leading to increased perceptions of being overwhelmed and increased usage of avoidant coping in a cyclical manner). This cycle of maladaptive coping is likely to lead to emotion dysregulation in the form of increased anger, tension, or depression, mood states commonly associated with self-harm. The individual may wish to express their painful emotions, but unable to cope adaptively, this does not happen because the individual does not know how to appropriately express him/herself or feels guilty and undeserving. This inability to cope only increases the negative mood state (i.e., anger, tension, or depression) and perception of emotional pain. Over time, these cycles of maladaptive coping and emotion dysregulation interact and escalate, often resulting in an increase in both social isolation and self-harm ideation. Individuals, when faced with ineffective coping strategies, will often attempt new maladaptive coping mechanisms in an attempt to find an effective response to their emotional pain. Thus, one will often see individuals engage in any number of risky (substance use, eating disorders, sexuality, etc.) behaviors in attempts to escape their negative mood state.

However, this rarely solves the problem and may even lead to an increase in trigger events and negative affect (i.e., destructive consequences of sexual risk-taking, delinquency, or substance abuse can lead to increased conflict with families or partners, etc.). Physiological and psychological tension increases to an intolerable level, and depersonalization, emotional numbness, or emptiness (factors commonly reported as directly preceding acts of self-harm) often occur. At the height of emotion dysregulation, this mood state is so intolerable that nearly anything will be done to escape it; unfortunately, the vulnerable individual has nowhere to turn, with the ability to cope overtaxed and the ability to appropriately express his or her pain underdeveloped. Interestingly, at this time, most individuals will not engage in self-harm behavior, due to our natural self-preservation instincts and fears of experiencing pain. However, according to Joiner's model, those individuals who have experienced or witnessed much emotional and physical pain will gradually increase their self-harm capability. Desperate to feel better and escape the agony of their mood state, those individuals able to cross the self-preservation threshold will turn to self-harm as a release, a method of coping and regulating their affect. Once someone has become capable of enacting self-harm, they are now at-risk for attempting suicide even if they only initially enacted self-injurious behavior. As the onset of self-injurious behavior is usually earlier than the onset of suicide attempts, it is possible that the cycles of emotion dysregulation and maladaptive coping increase in severity with time, moving a person further along the trajectory of self-harm towards progressively more lethal acts. The consequences of these acts (e.g. escape from overwhelming affect or difficult situations, elicitation of help from others) may further reinforce the self-harm behavior and extinguish adaptive responses, resulting in repetitive self-harm that increases in severity over time.

Other possible relationships may exist amongst these constructs; however, we feel the proposed model is an excellent starting point for taking a more comprehensive look at how self-harm behavior develops, escalates, and is maintained over time.

CONCLUSION

There has been substantial progress in the self-harm literature relative to understanding risk factors for self-harm behavior. A growing number of studies have moved beyond just examining predisposing risk factors. New research is emerging that examines potential pathogenic mechanisms that link predisposing risk factors to self-harm outcomes. This research is starting to move in the direction of answering the question "what are the interacting mechanisms that act upon predisposing and precipitating risk factors that result in maintained self-harm behavior?" In this chapter, we proposed a theoretical model that linked Joiner's (2005) theory of suicide to our own model of affect regulation as a critical mechanism in the development, escalation, and maintenance of self-harm behaviors. Our intention in presenting this integrated model was to present a means for organizing the vast number of risk factor variables that have been identified in the self-harm literature. In addition, it is hoped that this model will provide a framework to guide future research. This proposed model draws upon the existing research, existing theories, and unstated theories that appear to underlie some of the self-harm research.

It is our hope that the next wave of self-harm research will explore hypothesized relationships presented in our model of self-harm. This research will require bridging risk factor research that has previously been separate. These risk factors will need to be examined in mediational models that connect predisposing, precipitating, and maintaining risk factors to self-harm outcomes through mediating pathogenic mechanisms. As our chapter has shown, researchers are beginning to study variables that are more informative relative to self-harm mechanisms. However, this research has been handicapped due to issues of unclear nomenclature and a lack of a comprehensive and integrated guiding theory. By integrating the models of self-harm into one comprehensive theory that considers predisposing, precipitating, and maintenance factors in light of the mechanisms of emotion dysregulation and maladaptive coping, researchers and clinicians alike can lay the groundwork for further study informed by the literature. In addition, researchers will be able to examine how Joiner's (2005) model of perceived burdensomeness, thwarted belonging, and suicidal capability fits relative to prior research on predisposing and precipitating risk factors, mechanisms of affect regulation, and mechanisms of reinforcement of self-harm behavior. To the degree that our proposed model is used to guide future research, suicidologists and practitioners can potentially gain better understanding of how self-harm functions as a coping mechanism in the face of emotion dysregulation, how emotion dysregulation interacts with an individual's coping repertoire to promote maladaptive coping, whether certain types of affect regulation tactics are more strongly associated with self-harm, how maladaptive affect regulation is maintained and escalated by short term reinforcement processes, and how alternative coping strategies can be embraced and endorsed to counteract this negative tendency. In addition, research should explore whether there are different subtypes of persons who self-harm and if these different subtypes have different mediational trajectories and maintenance factors. With this research, effective interventions can be developed that specifically target pathogenic mechanisms of self-harm. Such research appears especially critical given that effective interventions have yet to be clearly identified for vulnerable adolescents and young adults (Tarrier, Taylor, & Gooding, 2008).

References

Afifi, T. O., Cox, B. J., & Katz, L. Y. (2007). The associations between health risk behaviours and suicidal ideation and attempts in a national representative sample of young adolescents. *The Canadian Journal of Psychiatry, 52*, 666-674.

Ahearn, E. P., Jamison, K. R., Steffens, D. C. et al. (2001). MRI correlates of suicide attempt history in unipolar depression. *Biological Psychiatry, 50*, 266-270.

Alderman, T. (1997). *The scarred soul: Understanding and ending self-inflicted violence.* Oakland, CA: New Harbinger.

Anderson, R. N., & Smith, B. L. (2003). Death: Leading causes for 2001. *National Vital*

Statistics Report, 52, 1-86.

Apter, A., Horesh, N., Gothelf, D., Zalsman, G., Erlich, Z., Soreni, N., & Weizman, A. (2003). Depression and suicidal behavior in adolescent inpatients with obsessive compulsive disorder. *Journal of Affective Disorders, 75*, 181-189.

Arato, M., Banki, C. M., Bissette, G., & Nemeroff, C. B. (1989). Elevated CSF CRF in suicide victims. *Biological Psychiatry, 25*, 355-359.

Ayton, A., Rasool, H., & Cottrell, D. (2003). Deliberate self-harm in children and adolescents: Association with social deprivation. *European Child & Adolescent Psychiatry, 12*, 303-307.

Bae, S., Ye, R., Chen, S., Rivers, P., & Singh, K. (2005). Risky behaviors and factors associated with suicide attempt in adolescents. *Archives of Suicide Research, 9,* 193-202.

Baker, R., Thomas, S., Thomas, P. W., & Owens, M. (2007). Development of an emotional processing scale. *Journal of Psychosomatic Research, 62*, 167-178.

Beautrais, A. L. (2003). Life course factors associated with suicidal behaviors in young people. *American Behavioral Scientist, 46*, 1137-1156.

Beautrais, A. L. ,Joyce, P. R., & Mulder, R. T. (1997). Precipitating factors and life events in serious suicide attempts among youths aged 13 through 24 years. *Journal of the American Academy of Child and Adolescent Psychiatry, 36*, 1543-1551.

Belliver, F., Szoke, A., Henry, C., Lacoste, J., Bottos, C., Nosten-Bertrand, M., et al. (2000). Possible association between serotonin transporter gene polymorphism and violent suicide behavior in mood disorders. *Biological Psychiatry, 48*, 319-322.

Bondy, B., Erfurth, A., de Jonge, S., Kruger, M., & Meyer, H. (2000). Possible association of the short allele of the serotonin transporter promoter gene polymorphism (5-HTTLPR) with violent suicide. *Molecular Psychiatry, 5,* 193-195.

Borrill, J., Burnett, R., Atkins, R., Miller, S., Briggs, D., Weaver, T., et al. (2003). Patterns of self-harm and attempted suicide among white and black mixed-race female prisoners. *Criminal Behavior and Mental Health, 13*, 229-240.

Brener, N. D., Hassan, S. S., & Barrios, L. C. (1999). Suicidal ideation among college students in the United States. *Journal of Consulting and Clinical Psychology, 67*, 1004-1008.

Brent, D. A., Oquendo, M., Birmaher, B., Greenhill, L., Kolko, D., et al. (2002). Familial pathways to early-onset suicide attempt: Risk for suicidal behavior in offspring of mood-disordered suicide attempters. *Archives of General Psychiatry, 59*, 801-807.

Brent, D. A., Oquendo, M., Birmaher, B., Greenhill, L., Kolko, D., et al. (2003). Peripubertal suicide attempts in offspring of suicide attempters with siblings concordant for suicidal behavior. *American Journal of Psychiatry, 160*, 1486-1493.

Brezo, J., Paris, J., & Turecki, G. (2006). Personality traits as correlates of suicidal ideation, suicide attempts, and suicide completions: a systematic review. *Acta Psychiatrica Scandinavica, 113,* 180-206.

Bridge, J. A., Goldstein, T. R., & Brent, D. A. (2006). Adolescent suicide and suicidal behavior. *Journal of Child Psychology and Psychiatry, 47*, 372–394.

Briere, G., & Gil, E. (1998). Self-mutilation in clinical and general population samples: Prevalence, correlated, and functions. *American Journal of Orthopsychiatry, 68*, 609-620.

Bryan, C. J., & Rudd, M. D. (2006). Advances in the assessment of suicide risk. *Journal of Clinical Psychology, 62*, 185-200.

Callahan, J. (1993). Blueprint for an adolescent suicidal crisis. *Psychiatric Annals, 23*, 263-270.

Cantanzaro, S. J. (2000). Mood regulation and suicidal behavior. In Joiner, T. E., & Rudd, M. D. (Eds.), *Suicide Science: Expanding the Boundaries* (pp. 81-103). New York: Kluwer Academic / Plenum Publishers.

Carr, E. G., & Diamond, V. M. (1985). Reducing behavior problems through functional communication training. *Journal of Applied Behavior Analysis, 18*, 111-126.

Caspi, A., Sugden, K., & Moffitt, T. E. (2003). Influence of life stress on depression: moderation by a polymorphism in the 5-HTT gene. *Science, 301*, 386-389.

Center for Disease Control, (2007). Suicide Trends Among Youths and Young Adults Aged 10--24 Years --- United States, 1990—2004. *Morbidity and Mortality Weekly Report, 56*(35), 905-908.

Center for Disease Control, National Center for Injury Prevention and Control. (2008). Web-based Injury Statistics Query and Reporting System (WISQARS). Retrieved on April 27, 2008 from http://webapp.cdc.gov/sasweb/ncipc/mortrate.html.

Claes, L., & Vandereycken, W. (2007). Self-injurious behavior: Differential diagnosis and functional differentiation. *Comprehensive Psychiatry, 48*, 137-144.

Claes, L., Vandereycken, W., & Vertommen, H. (2005). Self-care versus self-harm: Piercing, tattooing, and self-injuring in eating disorders. *European Eating Disorders Review, 13*, 11-18.

Claes, L., Vandereycken, W., & Vertommen, H. (2007). Self-injury in female versus male psychiatric patients: A comparison of characteristics, psychopathology, and aggression regulation. *Personality and Individual Differences, 42*, 611-621.

Conner, K. R., & Goldston, D. B. (2007). Rates of suicide among males increase steadily from age 11 to 21: Developmental framework and outline for prevention. *Aggression and Violent Behavior, 12*, 193-207.

Cooper, J., Kapur, N., Webb, R., Lawlor, M., Guthrie, E., Mackway-Jones, K., & Appleby, L. (2005). Suicide after deliberate self-harm: A 4-year cohort study. *American Journal of Psychiatry, 162,* 297-303.

Courtet, P., Baud, P., Abbar, M., Boulenger, J. P., Castelnau, D., Mouthon, D., et al. (2001). Association between violent suicidal behavior and the low activity allele of the serotonin transporter gene. *Molecular Psychiatry, 6*, 338-341.

Cremniter, D., Jamain, S., Kollenbach, K., Alvarez, J.-C., Lecrubier, Y. et al. (1999). CSF 5-HIAA levels are lower in impulsive as opposed to nonimpulsive violent suicide attempters and control subjects. *Biological Psychiatry, 45*, 1572-1579.

Curry, J. F., Miller, Y., Waugh, S., & Anderson, W. (1992). Coping responses in depressed, social maladjusted, and suicidal adolescents. *Psychological Reports, 71*, 80-82.

DeCatanzaro, D. (1995). Reproductive status, family interaction, and suicidal ideation: Surveys of the general public and high-risk group. *Ethology and Sociobiology, 16*, 385-394.

Donaldson, D., Spirito, A., & Farnett, E. (2000). The role of perfectionism and depressive cognitions in understanding the hopelessness experienced by adolescent suicide attempters. *Child Psychiatry and Human Development, 31*, 99-111.

Dube, S. R., Anda, R. F., Felitti, V. J., Chapman, D. P., Williamson, D. F., & Giles, W. H. (2001). Childhood abuse, household dysfunction, and the risk of attempted suicide throughout the lifespan: Findings from the Adverse Childhood Experiences Study. *Journal of the American Medical Association, 286*, 3089-3096.

Egeland, J., & Sussex, J. (1985). Suicide and family loading for affective disorders. *Journal of the American Medical Association, 254*, 915-918.

Ehrlich, S., Noam, G. G., Lyoo, J. K., Kwon, B. J., Clark, M. A., Renshaw, P. F. (2003). Subanalysis of the location of white matter hyperintensities and their association with suicidality in children and youth. *Annals of the NY Academy of Science, 1008,* 265-268.

Ehrlich, S., Noam, G. G., Lyoo, J. K., Kwon, B. J., Clark, M. A., Renshaw, P. F. (2004). White matter hyperintensities and their associations with suicidality in psychiatrically hospitalized children and adolescents. *Journal of the American Academy of Child and Adolescent Psychiatry, 43*, 770-776.

Esposito, C., Spirito, A., Boergers, J., & Donaldson, D. (2003). Affective, behavioral, and cognitive functioning in adolescents with multiple suicide attempts. *Suicide and Life-Threatening Behavior, 33*, 389-399.

Evans, E., Hawton, K., & Rodham, K. (2005). In what ways are adolescents who engage in self-harm or experience thoughts of self-harm different in terms of help-seeking, communication, and coping strategies? *Journal of Adolescence, 28*, 573-587.

Fahmy, V., & Jones, R. S. P. (1990). Theories of the aetiology of self-injurious behavior: A review. *The Irish Journal of Psychology, 11*, 261-276.

Favazza, A. (1987). *Bodies under siege: Self-mutilation in culture and psychiatry.* Baltimore, MD: Johns Hopkins University Press.

Favazza, A. R. (1992). Repetitive self-mutilation. *Psychiatric Annals, 22,* 60-63.

Favazza, A. R. (1998). The coming of age of self-mutilation. *Journal of Nervous and Mental Disorders, 186*, 259-268.

Favazza, A. R., & Conterio, K. (1989). Female habitual self-mutilators. *Acta Psychiatrica Scandinavia, 79*, 283-289.

Favazza, A. R., DeRosear, L., & Conterio, K. (1989). Self-mutilation and eating disorders. *Suicide and Life Threatening Behavior, 19*, 352–361.

Fergusson, D. M., Woodward, L. J., & Horwood, L. J. (2000). Risk factors and life processes associated with the onset of suicidal behavior during adolescence and young adulthood. *Psychological Medicine, 30*, 23-39.

Folkman, S., & Moskowitz, J. T. (2004). Coping: Pitfalls and promise. *Annual Review of Psychology, 55*, 745-774.

Fotti, S. A., Katz, L. Y., Afifi, T. O., & Cox, B. J. (2006). The associations between peer and parental relationships and suicidal behaviours in early adolescents. The Canadian Journal of Psychiatry, 51, 698-703.

Fu, Q., Heath, A. C., Bucholz, K. K., Nelson, E. C., Glowinski, A. L., Goldberg, J., et al. (2002). A twin study of genetic and environmental influences on suicidality in men. *Psychological medicine, 32*, 11-24.

Fulcher, G. (1984). A review of self-injurious behavior (SIB). *Australia and New Zealand Journal of Developmental Disabilities, 10,* 51-67.

Fusar-Poli, P., Allen, P., & Cortesi, M. (2007). Acute tryptophan depletion and suicidality. *Journal of Psychophysiology, 21*, 72-73.

Garlow, S. J., Purselle, D., & Heninger, M. (2005). Ethnic differences in patterns of suicide across the life cycle. *American Journal of Psychiatry, 162,* 319-323.

Garrison, C. Z., Addy, C. L., McKeown, R. E., Cuffe, S. P., et al. (1993). Nonsuicidal physically self-damaging acts in adolescents. *Journal of Child and Family Studies, 2*, 339-352.

Glowinski, A. L., Bucholz, K. K., Nelson, E. C., Fu, Q., Madden, P. A. F., et al. (2001). Suicide attempts in an adolescent female twin sample. *Journal of the American Academy of Child and Adolescent Psychiatry, 40*, 1300-1307.

Gould, M. S., Greenberg, T., Velting, D. M., & Shaffer, D. (2003). Youth suicide risk and preventive interventions: A review of the past 10 years. *Journal of the American Academy of Child & Adolescent Psychiatry. 42*, 386-405.

Goldston, D. B.m Reboussin, B. A., Daniel, S. S. (2006). Predictors of suicide attempts: State and trait components. *Journal of Abnormal Psychology. 115*, 842-849.

Gorwood, P., Batel, P., Ades, J., Hamon, M.,& Boni, C. (2000). Serotonin transporter gene polymorphisms, alcoholism, and suicidal behavior. *Biological Psychiatry, 48*, 259-264.

Gratz, K. (2001). Measurement of deliberate self-harm: Preliminary data on the deliberate self-harm inventory. *Journal of Psychopathology and Behavioral Assessment, 23*, 253-263.

Gratz, K. L., Conrad, S. D., & Roemer, L. (2002). Risk factors for deliberate self-harm among college students. *American Journal of Orthopsychiatry. 72*, 128-140.

Gratz, K. L. (2003). Risk factors for and functions of deliberate self-harm: An empirical and conceptual review. *Clinical Psychology Science and Practice, 10*, 192-205.

Groholt, B., Ekeberg, O., & Haldorsen, T. (2000). Adolescents hospitalized with deliberate self-harm: The significance of an intention to die. *European Child and Adolescent Psychiatry, 9*, 244-254.

Grossman, A. H., & D'Augelli, A. R. (2007). Transgender youth and life-threatening behaviors. *Suicide and Life-Threatening Behavior, 37*, 527-537.

Grunbaum, J. A., Kann, L., Kinchen, S., et al. (2004). Youth risk behavior surveillance – United States, 2003. In Services DoHaH (Ed.), *Surveillance Summaries* (pp. 1-96). Atlanta: Centers for Disease Control and Prevention.

Haines, J., Williams, C. L., Brain, K. L., & Wilson, G. V. (1995). The psychophysiology of self-mutilation. *Journal of Abnormal Psychology, 104*, 471-489.

Hallfors, D. D., Waller, M. W., Ford, C. A., Halpern, C. T., Brodish, P. H., & Iritani, B. (2004). Adolescent depression and suicide risk: Association with sex and drug behavior. *American Journal of Preventive Medicine, 27*, 224-230.

Harned, M. S., Najavits, L. M., & Weiss, R. D. (2006). Self-harm and suicidal behavior in women with comorbid PTSD and substance dependence. *The American Journal on Addictions, 15*, 392-395.

Hass, B. & Popp, F. (2006). Why do people injure themselves? *Psychopathology, 39,* 10-18.

Haw, C., Hawton, K., Houston, K., & Townsend, E. (2001). Psychiatric and personality disorders in deliberate self-harm patients. *The British Journal of Psychiatry: The Journal of Mental Science, 178*, 48-54.

Haw, C., Houston, K., Townsend, E., & Hawton, K. (2002). Deliberate self-harm patients with depressive disorders: Treatment and outcome. *Journal of Affective Disorders, 70*, 57-65.

Hawton, K., Hall, S., Simkin, S., Bale, L., Bond, A., Codd, S., et al. (2003). Deliberate self-harm in adolescents: a study of characteristics and trends in Oxford, 1990-2000. *Journal of Child Psychology and Psychiatry, 44*, 1191-1198.

Hawton, K., Rodham, K., Evans, E., & Weatherall, R. (2002). Deliberate self harm in adolescents: Self report survey in schools in England. *British Medical Journal, 325*, 1207-1211.

Henry, C., M'Baïlara, K., Desage, A., Gard, S., Misdrahi, D., & Vieta, E. (2007). Towards a reconceptualization of mixed states, based on an emotional-reactivity dimensional model. *Journal of Affective Disorders, 101*, 35-41.

Herpertz, S. (1995). Self-injurious behavior. Psychopathological and nosological characteristics in subtypes of self-injurers. *Acta Psychiatrica Scandinavia, 91*, 57-68.

Hilt, L. M., Cha, C. B., & Nolen-Hoeksema, S. (2008). Nonsuicidal self-injury in young adolescent girls: moderators of the distress-function relationship. *Journal of Consulting and Clinical Psychology, 76*, 63-71.

Hjelmeland, H., & Groholt, B. (2005). A comparative study of young and adult deliberate self-harm patients. *Crisis, 26*, 64-72.

Huan, M., Hamazaki, K, Sun, Y., et al. (2004). Suicide attempt and n-3 fatty acid levels in red blood cells: a case-control study in China. *Biological Psychiatry, 56*, 490-496.

Izutsu, T., Shimotsu, S., Matsumoto, T., Okada, T., Kikuchi, A., Kojimoto, M., et al. (2006). Deliberate self-harm and childhood hyperactivity in junior high school students. *European Child and Adoelscent Psychiatry, 15*, 172-176.

Jacobson, C. M., & Gould, M. (2007). The epidemiology and phenomenology of non-suicidal self-injurious behavior among adolescents: A critical review of the literature. *Archives of Suicide Research, 11*, 129-147.

Joiner, T. E. (2005). *Why People Die By Suicide.* Cambridge, MA: Harvard University Press.

Joiner, T. E., Brown, J. S., & Wingate, L. R. (2005). The psychology and neurobiology of suicidal behavior. *Annual Reviews in Psychology, 56*, 287-314.

Joiner, T., Kalafat, J., Draper, J., Stokes, H., Knudson, M., Berman, A. L., & McKeon, R. (2007). Establishing standards for the assessment of suicide risk among callers to the National Suicide Prevention Lifeline. *Suicide and Life-Threatening Behavior, 37*, 353-365.

Karver, M. S. and Caporino, N. (2005). Parasuicide. In N. J. Salkind (Ed). *The Encyclopedia of Human Development: Vol. 3* (pp. 957-959). Thousand Oaks, CA: Sage Publications.

Karver, M. S. & Tarquini, S. (manuscript under review). Prediction of Suicide Related Behaviors in Youths Receiving Treatment.

Kashdan, T. B., Barrios, V., Forsyth, J. P., Steger, M. F. (2006). Experiential avoidance as a generalized psychological vulnerability: Camparisons with coping and emotion regulation strategies. *Behaviour Research and Therapy, 44,* 1301-1320.

King, R. A., Ruchkin, V. V., & Schwab-Stone, M. E. (2003). Suicide and the 'continuum of adolescent self-destructiveness': Is there a connection? In R. A. King & A. Apter (Eds.), *Suicide in children and adolescents* (pp. 41-62). Cambridge: Cambridge University Press

Kisiel, C. L., & Lyons, J. S. (2001). Dissociation as a mediator of psychopathology among sexually abused children and adolescents. *American Journal of Psychiatry, 158,* 1034-1039.

.Klonsky, E. D. (2007). The functions of deliberate self-injury: A review of the evidence. *Clinical Psychology Review, 27*, 226-239.

Klonsky, E. D., Oltmanns, T. F., & Turkheimer, E. (2003). Deliberate self-harm in a nonclinical sample: prevalence and psychological correlates. *American Journal of Psychiatry, 160*, 1501-1508.

Krug, E. G., Dahlberg, L. L., Mercy, J.A., Zwi, A. B., Lozano, R. (Eds.; 2004). World report on violence and health. 2004 May. Retrieved December 8, 2006, from http://www.who.int/violence_injury_prevention/violence/world_report/wrvh1/en.

Kumar, G., Pepe, D., & Steer, R. A. Adolescent psychiatric inpatients' self-reported reasons for cutting themselves. *Journal of Nervous and mental Discease, 192,* 830-836.

Lalovic, A., Levy, E., Canetti, L., Sequeira, A., Montoudis, A., & Turecki, G. (2007). Fatty acid composition in postmortem brains of people who completed suicide. *Journal of Psychiatry and Nueroscience, 32*, 363-370.

Laye-Gindhu, A., & Schonert-Reichl, K. A. (2005). Nonsuicidal self-harm among community adolescents: Understanding the "whats" and "whys" of self-harm. *Journal of Youth and Adolescence, 34*, 447-457.

Levenkron, S. (1998). *Cutting: Understanding and overcoming self-mutilation.* New York: Norton.

Lewinsohn, P. M., Rohde, P., & Seeley, J. R. (1996). Adolescent suicidal ideation and attempts: Prevalence, risk factors, and clinical implications. *Clinical Psychology Science and Practice, 3,* 25-46.

Linehan, M. M. (1993). *Skills training manual for treating borderline personality disorder.* New York: Guilford Press.

Lipschitz, D. S., Winegar, R. K., Nicolaou, A. L., Hartnick, E., Wolfson, M., & Southwick, S. M. (1999). Perceived abuse and neglect as risk factors for suicidal behavior in adolescent inpatients. *Journal of Nervous and Mental Disease, 187*, 32-39.

Lloyd-Richardson, E. E., Perrin, N., Dierker, L., & Kelley, M. L. (2007). Characteristics and functions of non-suicidal self-injury in a community sample of adolescents. *Psychological Medicine, 37*, 1183-1192.

Lowenstein, L. F. (2005). Youths who intentionally practise self-harm. In J. Merrick & G. Zalsman (Eds.), *Suicidal behavior in adolescence: An international perspective* (pp. 95-104). London, England: Freund Publishing House.

Machoian, L. (2001). Cutting voices: Self-injury in three adolescent girls. *Journal of Psychosocial and Nursing Mental Health Services, 39*, 22-29.

Maltsberger, J. T., Hendin, H., Haas, P., & Lipschitz, A. (2003). Determination of precipitating events in the suicide of psychiatric patients. *Suicide and Life-Threatening Behavior, 33*, 111-119.

Mann, J. J. (2003). Neurobiology of suicidal behavior. *National Review of Neuroscience, 4*, 819-828.

Mann, J. J., & Malone, K. M. (1997). Cerebrospinal fluid amines and higher-lethality suicide attempts in depressed inpatients. *Biological Psychiatry, 41*, 162-171.

McAllister, M. (2003). Multiple meanings of self harm: A critical review. *International Journal of Mental Health Nursing, 12*, 177-185.

McAuliffe, C., Corcoran, P., Keeley, H. S., Arensman, E., Bille-Brahe, U., de Leo, D., et al. (2006). Problem-solving ability and repetition of deliberate self-harm: A multicentre study. *Psychological Medicine, 36*, 45-55.

Messer, J. M., & Fremouw, W. J. (2008). A critical review of explanatory models for self-mutilating behaviors in adolescents. *Clinical Psychology Review, 28*, 162-178.

Miltenberger, R. G. (2008). Behavior modification. In M. Hersen & A. L. Gross (Eds.), *Handbook of clinical psychology, vol 2: Children and adolescents* (pp. 626-652). Hoboken, NJ, US: John Wiley & Sons Inc.

Monkul, E. S., Hatch, J. P., Nicoletti, M. A., Spence, S., Brambilla, P., Lacerda, A. L. T., et al. (2007). Fronto-limbic brain structures in suicidal and non-suicidal female patients with major depressive disorder. *Molecular Psychiatry, 12*, 360-366.

Muehlenkamp, J. J., & Gutierrez, P. M. (2004). An investigation of differences between self-injurious behavior and suicide attempts in a sample of adolescents. *Suicide and Life-Threatening Behavior, 34*, 12-23.

Muehlenkamp, J. J., & Gutierrez, P. M. (2007). Risk for suicide attempts among adolescents who engage in non-suicidal self-injury. *Archives of Suicide Research, 11*, 69-82.

Najmi, S., Wegner, D. M., & Nock, M. K. (2007). Thought suppression and self-injurious thoughts and behaviors. *Behaviour Research and Therapy, 45*, 1957-1965.

National Center for Health Statistics. (2007). *Health, United States, 2007*. Washington, DC: Department of Health and Human Services. Retrieved on May 20, 2008 from http://www.cdc.gov/nchs/data/hus/hus07.pdf.

Nemeroff, C. B., Owens, M. J., Bissette, G., Andorn, A. C., & Stanley, M. (1988). Reduced corticotropin releasing factor binding sites in the frontal cortex of suicide victims. *Archives of General Psychiatry, 45*, 577-579.

Nixon, M. K., Cloutier, M. A., & Aggarwal, S. (2002). Affect regulation and addictive aspects of repetitive self-injury in hospitalized adolescents. *Journal of the American Academy of Child and Adolescent Psychiatry, 40*, 1062-1069.

Nock, M. K., & Mendes, W. B. (2008). Physiological arousal, distress tolerance, and social problem-solving deficits among adolescent self-injurers. *Journal of Consulting and Clinical Psycholgoy, 76*, 28-38.

Nock, M. K., & Prinstein, M. J. (2004). A functional approach to the assessment of self-mutilative behavior. *Journal of Counseling and Clinical Psychology, 72*, 885-890.

Nock, M. K., & Prinstein, M. J. (2005). Contextual features and behavioral functions of self-mutilation among adolescents. *Journal of Abnormal Psychology, 114,* 140-146.

Nolan, K. A., Volvavka, J., Czobor, P., Cseh, A., Lachman, H., et al. (2000). Suicidal behavior in patients with schizophrenia is related to the COMT polymorphism. *Psychiatric Genetics, 10*, 117-124.

O' Carroll, P. W., Berman, A. L., Maris, R. W., Mascicki, E. K., Tanney, B. L., & Silverman, M. M. (1996). Beyond the tower of Babel: A nomenclature of suicidology. *Suicide and Life Threatening Behavior, 23*, 237-252.

Olfson, M., Gameroff, M. J., Marcus, S. C., Greenberg, T., & Shaffer, D. (2005). National trends in hospitalization of youth with intentional self-inflicted injuries. *American Journal of Psychiatry, 162*, 1328-1335.

Orpinas, P. K., Basen-Engquist, K., Grunbaum, J. A., & Parcel, G. S. (1995). The co-morbidity of violence-related behaviors with health-risk behaviors in a population of high school students. *Journal of Adolescent Health, 16*, 216-225.

Owens, D., Horrocks, J., & House, A. (2002). Fatal and non-fatal repetition of self-harm. Systematic review. *British Journal of Psychiatry, 323,* 135-138.

Pattison, E. M., & Kahan, J. (1983). The deliberate self-harm syndrome. *American Journal of Psychiatry, 140*, 867-872.

Perez, V. W. (2005). The relationship between seriously considering, planning, and attempting suicide in the Youth Risk Behavior Survey. *Suicide and Life Threatening Behavior, 35*, 35-49.

Placidi, G. P. A., Oquendo, M. A., Malone, K. M., Huang, Y.-Y., Ellis, S. P., & Mann, J. J. (2001). Aggressivity, suicide attempts, and depression: Relationship to cerebrospinal fluid monoamine metabolite levels. *Biological Psychiatry, 50*, 783-791.

Polk, E., & Liss, M. (2007). Psychological characteristics of self-injurious behavior. *Personality and Individual Differences, 43*, 567-577.

Purselle, D. C., & Nemeroff, C. B. (2003). Serotonin transporter: A potential substrate in the biology of suicide. *Neuropsychopharmacology, 28*, 613-619.

Qin, P., Agerbo, E., & Mortensen, P. B. (2003). Suicide risk in relation to socioeconomic, demographic, psychiatric, and familial factors: a national register-based study of all suicides in Denmark 1981-1987. *American Journal of Psychiatry, 160*, 765-772.

Range, L. M., Leach, M. M., McIntyre, D., Posey-Deters, P. B., Marion, M. S., Kovac, S. H., et al. (1999). Multicultural perspectives on suicide. Aggression and Violent Behavior, 4, 413-430.

Rodham, K., Hawton, K., & Evans, E. (2004). Reasons for deliberate self-harm: Comparison of self-poisoners and self-cutters in a community sample of adolescents. *Journal of the American Academy of Child and Adolescent Psychiatry, 43*, 80-87.

Ross, S., & Heath, N. (2002). A study of the frequency of self-mutilation in a community sample of adolescents. *Journal of Youth and Adolescence, 31*, 67-77.

Ross, S., & Heath, N. L. (2003). Two models of adolescent self-mutilation. *Suicide and Life-Threatening Behavior, 33*, 277-287.

Rothbart, M. K., Ahadi, S. A., & Evans, D. E. (2000). Temperament and personality: Origins and outcomes. *Journal of Personality and Social Psychology, 78*, 122-135.

Rotherham-Borus, M. J., Trautman, P. D., Dopkins, S. C., & Shrout, P. E. (1990). Cognitive style and pleasant activities among female adolescent suicide attempters. *Journal of Consulting and Clinical Psychology, 58*, 554-561.

Rottenberg, J., & Gross, J. J. (2007). Emotion and emotion regulation: A map for psychotherapy researchers. *Clinical Psychology: Science and Practice*, 323-328.

Roy, A., & Segal, N. L. (2001). Suicidal behavior in twins: a replication. *Journal of Affective Disorders, 66*, 71-74.

Rujescu, D., Giegling, I., Gietl, A., Hartman, A. M., & Moller, H.-J. (2003b). A functional single nucleotide polymorphism (V158M) in the COMT gene is associated with aggressive personality traits. *Biological Psychiatry, 54*, 34-39.

Rujescu, D., Giegling, I., Sato, T., Hartman, A. M., & Moller, H.-J. (2003a). Genetic variations in tryptophan hydroxylase in suicidal behavior: analysis and meta-analysis. *Biological Psychiatry, 54*, 465-473.

Runeson, B., & Asberg, M. (2003). Family history of suicide among suicide victims. *American Journal of Psychiatry, 160*, 1525-1526.

Sansone, R. A., Songer, D. A., & Sellbom, M. (2006). The relationship between suicide attempts and low-lethal self-harm behavior among psychiatric inpatients. *Journal of Psychiatric Practice, 12*, 148-152.

Scherer, K. (1984). On the nature and function of emotion: A component process approach. In K. R. Scherer & P. E. Ekman (Eds.), *Approaches to emotion* (pp. 293-317). Hillsdale, N J: Erlbaum.

Schnyder, U., Valach, L., Bichsel, K., & Michel, K. (1999). Attempted suicide: Do we understand the patients' reasons? *General Hospital Psychiatry, 21*, 62-69.

Schotte, D. E., & Clum, G. A. (1982). Suicide ideation in a college population: A test of a model. *Journal of Consulting and Clinical Psychology, 50*, 690-696.

Shaw, S. (2002). Shifting conversations on girls' and women's self injury. *Feminism and Psychology, 12*, 191-219.

Silverman, M. M., Berman, A. L., Sanddal, N. D., O'Carroll, P. W., & Joiner, T. E. (2007). Rebuilding the Tower of Babel: A revised nomenclature for the study of suicide and suicidal behaviors Part 2: Suicide-related ideations, communications, and behaviors. *Suicide and Life-Threatening Behavior, 37*, 264-277.

Simeon, D., Cohen, L. J., Stein, D. J., Schmeidler, J., & Spadaccini, E. (1997). Comorbid self-injurious behaviors in 71 female hair-pullers: A survey study. *Journal of Nervous and Mental Disease, 185*, 117-119.

Simeon, D., & Favazza, A. R. (2001). Self-injurious behaviors: Phenomenology and assessment. In D. Simeon & E. Hollander (Eds.), *Self-injurious behaviors: Assessment and treatment* (pp. 1-28). Washington, DC: American Psychiatric Press.

Skegg, K. (2005). Self-harm. *The Lancet, 366*, 1471-1483.

Speckens, A. E. M., & Hawton, K. (2005). Social problem solving in adolescents with suicidal behavior: A systematic review. *Suicide and Life Threatening Behavior, 35*, 365-387.

Spirito, A., & Esposito-Smythers, C. (2006). Attempted and completed suicide in adolescence. *Annual Review of Clinical Psychology, 2*, 237-266.

Spirito, A., Francis, G., Overholser, J., & Frank, N. (1996). Coping, depression, and adolescent suicide attempts. *Journal of Clinical Child Psychology, 25*, 147-155.

Spreux-Varoquaux, O., Alvarez, J. C., Berlin, I., Batista, G., Despierre, P. G. et al. (2001). Differential abnormalities in plasma 5-HIAA and platelet serotonin concentrations in violent suicide attempters: Relationships with impulsivity and depression. *Life Science, 69*, 647-657.

Stanley, B., Winchel, R., Molcho, A., Simeon, D., & Stanley, M. (1992). Suicide and the self-harm continuum: Phenomenological and biochemical evidence. *International Review of Psychiatry, 4,* 149-155.

Stanley, B., Gameroff, M. J., Michalsen, V., & Mann, J. J. (2001). Are suicide attempters who self-mutilate a unique population? *American Journal of Psychiatry, 158*, 427-432.

Statham, D. J., Heath, A. C., Madden, P. A. F., Bucholz, K. K., Bierut, L., et al. (1998). Suicidal behavior: An epidemiological and genetic study. *Psychological Medicine, 28*, 839-855.

Stellrecht, N. E., Gordon, K. H., Van Orden, K., Witte, T. K., Wingate, L. R., Cukrowicz, K. C., et al. (2006). Clinical applications of the In terpersonal-Psychological Theory of attempted and completed suicide. *Journal of Clinical Psychology: In Session, 62*, 211-222.

Sublette, M. E., Hibbeln, J. R., Galfalvy, H., Oquendo, M. A., & Mann, J. J. (2006). Omega-3 Polyunsaturated Essential Fatty Acid Status as a Predictor of Future Suicide Risk. *American Journal of Psychiatry, 163*, 1100-1102.

Sublette, M. E., Oquendo, M. A., & Mann, J. J. (2006). Rational approaches to the neurobiologic study of youth at risk for bipolar disorder and suicide. *Bipolar Disorders, 8*, 526-542.

Suyemoto, K. L. (1998). The functions of self-mutilation. *Clinical Psychology Review, 18*, 531-554.

Tamas, Z., Kovacs, M., Gentzler, A. L., Tepper, P., Gadoros, J. et al., (2007). The relations of temperament and emotion self-regulation with suicidal behaviors in a clinical sample of depressed children in Hungary. *Journal of Abnormal Child Psychology, 35*, 640-652.

Tarrier, N., Taylor, K., & Gooding, P. (2008). Cognitive-behavioral interventions to reduce suicide behavior: A systematic review and meta-analysis. *Behavior Modification, 32*, 77-108.

Tuisku, V., Pelkonen, M., Karlsson, L., Kiviruusu, O., Holi, M., Ruutu, T., Punamaki, R. L., & Marttunen, M. (2006). Suicidal ideation, deliberate self-harm behavior and suicide attempts among adolescent outpatients with depressive mood disorders and comorbid axis I disorders. *European Child and Adolescent Psychiatry, 15*, 199-206.

van Heeringen, K. (2003). The neurobiology of suicide and suicidality. *Canada Journal of Psychiatry, 48*, 292-300.

Van Orden, K. A., Witte, T. K., Gordon, K. H., Bender, T. W., & Joiner, T. E. (2008). Suicidal desire and the capability for suicide: Tests of the Interpersonal-Psychological Theory of suicidal behavior among adults. *Journal of Consulting and Clinical Psychology, 76*, 72-83.

Vangelisti, A. L., Maguire, K. C., Alexander, A. L., & Clark, G. (2007). Hurtful family environments: Links with individual, relationship, and perceptual variables. Communication Monographs, 74, 357-385.

Verona, E., Sachs-Ericsson, N., & Joiner, T. E., Jr. (2004). Suicide attempts associated with externalizing psychopathology in an epidemiological sample. *American Journal of Psychiatry, 161*, 444-451.

Wanstall, K., & Oei, T. P. S. (1989). Delicate wrist cutting behavior in adult psychiatric patients: A review. *Austalian Psychologist, 24*, 13-25.

Wedig, M. M., & Nock, M. K. (2007). Parental expressed emotion and adolescent self-injury. *Journal of the American Academy of Child and Adolescent Psychiatry, 46,* 1171-1178.

Westrin, A., & Nimeus, A. (2003). The dexamethasone suppression test and CSF-5-HIAA in relation to suicidality and depression in suicide attempters. *European Psychiatry, 18*, 166-171.

Whitlock, J., Eckenrode, J., & Silverman, D. (2006). Self-injurious behaviors in a college population. *Pediatrics, 117*, 1939-1948.

Winchel, R. M., & Stanley, M. (1991). Self-injurious behavior: A review of the behavior and biology of self-mutilation. *American Journal of Psychiatry, 148,* 306-317.

Yates, T. M., Tracy, A. J., & Luthar, S. S. (2008). Nonsuicidal self injury among "privileged" youths" longitudinal and cross-sectional approaches to developmental process. *Journal of Consulting and Clinical Psychology, 76*, 52-62.

Yen, S., Pagano, M. E., Shea, M. T., Grilo, C. M., Gunderson, J. G., Skodol, A. E., et al. (2005). Recent life events preceding suicide attempts in a personality disorder sample: Findings from the Collaborative Longitudinal Personality Disorders Study. *Journal of Consulting and Clinical Psychology, 73*, 99-105.

Zayas, L. H., Lester, R. J., Cabassa, L. J., & Fortuna, L. R. (2005). Why do so many Latina teens attempt suicide? A conceptual model for research. *American Journal of Orthopsychiatry, 75*, 275-287.

Zlotnick, C., Donaldson, D., Spirito, A., & Pearlstein, T. (1997). Affect regulation and suicide attempts in adolescent inpatients. *Journal of the American Academy of Child and Adolescent Psychiatry, 36*, 793-798.

Zoroglu, S. S., Tuzun, U., Sar, V., Tutkun, H., Savas, H. A., Ozturk, M., et al. (2003). Suicide attempt and self-mutilation among Turkish high school students in relation with abuse, neglect and dissociation. *Psychiatry and Clinical Neurosciences, 57*, 119-126.

In: Abnormal Psychology: New Research
Editor: Helen D. Friedman and Paulina K. Revera
ISBN: 978-1-60692-636-9

Chapter 2

MODELING OF DYSLEXIA: IS A UNITARY MODEL OF DYSLEXIA POSSIBLE?

Timothy C. Papadopoulos1[a], George K. Georgiou[b] and Sotirios Douklias[c]

[a]Department of Psychology, University of Cyprus
[b]Department of Educational Psychology, University of Alberta
[c]Department of Psychology, University of Cyprus

ABSTRACT

For many years, the study of dyslexia relied heavily on exclusionary definitions. In turn, dyslexics were defined simply in terms of a reading score that was far below a specific reading age when IQ, socio-educational, emotional, neurological, and psychiatric reasons had also been excluded. Two problems emerged from such an approach, one being conceptual and one being related to the assessment of dyslexia. This chapter advocates that dyslexia concept is better understood only if attention is drawn to the wide range of problems and the constitutional nature of the difficulties encountered by individuals with dyslexia. Therefore, four major stands in current dyslexia research are discussed: (a) the nature of the phonological impairment that is mainly associated with a pervasive problem at the level of underlying phonological representations, (b) the nature of naming speed and automaticity impairments that are seen either as a consequence of an impairment of a timing mechanism or are attributed to abnormal cerebellar functioning, providing a more neuropsychological explanation for dyslexia, (c) the nature of the cognitive deficits that are more general and modality unspecific, such as deficits at information processing level, and (d) the nature of language based problems attributed to impaired semantic, syntactic and/or orthographic awareness. The ultimate aim is to understand the biological basis of the disorder and how this brain-based disposition can lead to subtle impairments at the cognitive and behavioral levels. It is concluded that with the advent of cognitive neuroscience which revolutionizes the medical approach we can

---

[1]Timothy C. Papadopoulos, PhD Department of Psychology, University of Cyprus, P.O. Box 20537, 1678, Nicosia, Cyprus, TEL: +357 22 892079; FAX: +357 22 892071; E-mail: tpapadop@ucy.ac.cy. This work was supported by EU-UCY Grants for Applied Research Projects for Cyprus to the first author (Grant No. 8037-16013).

build unitary definitions and models of dyslexia, making it possible to study links between brain and behavior in this specific developmental disorder.

Keywords: dyslexia, cognitive, phonological, and morphological deficits, theories' convergence

Is a Unitary Model of Dyslexia Possible?

There is no unanimity concerning the definition of dyslexia. Some employ it broadly as the equivalent of reading disability (Aaron, Kuchta, & Grapenthin, 1988; Apthorp, 1995). Yet others offer diverse definitions which include indications of genetic or inherited cause (Olson, 1999, 2002), presence of structural brain abnormalities (Cohen & Dehaene, 2004; Paulesu et al., 2001), observation of behaviour manifestations of cognitive deficits (for a review, see Scarborough, 1998a, 1998b), comorbidity with a general language disability along with a reading problem (Peterson, McGrath, Smith, & Pennington, 2007) or attention deficits (Chadwick, Taylor, Taylor, Heptinstall, & Danckaerts, 1999; Jakobson & Kikas, 2007; Papadopoulos, Constantinidou, & Douklias, 2008b). Regardless of the definition under investigation, dyslexia is considered by many as a specific learning disability which initially shows itself by difficulty in manipulating the sounds of speech and the rapid (serial) naming of stimuli and later by problems in learning to read and erratic spelling (for a review, see Grigorenko, 2001). Noticeably, a thorough assessment of dyslexia requires the use of multiple criteria and necessitates the development of definitions that are both psychologically and educationally useful. The aim of the present review is to get around the problem of the dyslexia by examining the convergence of different theories and approaches.

In a recent review of dyslexia research, Vellutino, Fletcher, Snowling, and Scanlon (2004) summarized some of the most important findings evaluating the hypothesized causes of specific reading disability (or dyslexia) over the past four decades. In relation to typical reading, authors support that it is considered a linguistic skill, contrary to the popular belief, for many decades, that it is primarily a visual skill. Phonological abilities, phonological decoding, alphabetic knowledge, and naming speed along with basic cognitive skills, such as verbal working memory and information processing skills, play a significant role in early reading development. In contrast, orthographic, semantic, and syntactic skills carry greater weight than phonological and cognitive skills in later years. By analogy then, the former set of skills accounts for the reliable and robust differences observed between poor and normal readers and tends to be the primary cause for reading disability in early years. Similarly, orthographic, semantic and syntactic deficits, in most cases, are a likely consequence of longstanding reading disorder or a comorbid oral language disorder. The question is whether and how these skills can be seen together in a way that can permit integration of the cognitive and linguistic frames of reference in a comprehensive study of sub-processes or subtypes of reading disability. The present chapter, therefore, addresses this issue of a possible integrative account of phonological, cognitive, and linguistic deficits of dyslexia in three main parts, with the least possible overlap between them: (a) the first part is devoted largely to the phonological and naming deficits, (b) the second focuses on the cognitive, namely, verbal working memory, information processing, the cerebellum and motor deficits in dyslexia, and the auditory and temporal aspects of speech, and (c) the last section on the morphological and syntactic deficits of dyslexia.

PHONOLOGICAL AWARENESS AND DYSLEXIA

To date, an accumulated body of evidence has established the causal role of phonological awareness in reading (e.g., Blachman, 1984; de Jong & van der Leij, 1999; McBride-Chang & Kail, 2002; Parrila, Kirby, & McQuarrie, 2004; Schatschneider, Fletcher, Francis, Carlson, & Foorman, 2004; Torgesen, Wagner, & Rashotte, 1994). Phonological awareness has been defined as the awareness of and access to the sound structure of one's oral language (Wagner & Torgesen, 1987). It involves the awareness of the most basic speech units of a language – phonemes – as well as of larger units, such as rimes and syllables.

Several tasks have been used to measure phonological awareness. These tasks vary in complexity and the level of phonological awareness assessed. The simplest tasks involve rhyme, alliteration detection, and sound categorization. More complex tasks involve manipulation of phonemes. The first of these tasks is phoneme deletion. A subject is presented with a spoken word (e.g., *cat*) and is required to mentally delete a particular sound (e.g., /k/) and say what remains (*/at/*). Other tasks measuring awareness at the phoneme level include phoneme counting (e.g., "Tap out each sound in */cake/*), phoneme blending (e.g., What does */c/*, */a/*, */t/* say?), phoneme reversal (e.g., Say the sounds of */pen/* backwards), spoonerisms, where the initial sounds of two words are switched (e.g., David Beckham becomes Bavid Deckham), and Pig Latin (e.g., stripe becomes tripe-say).

Beginning readers have only rudimentary phonological awareness skills and fine-grained awareness of the sound structure of words typically develops hand in hand with reading instruction (e.g., Ziegler & Goswami, 2005). Prior to reading instruction, children often develop awareness of rhyme and alliteration but have more difficulty segmenting and counting the individual sounds in words. In comparison to their normally developing peers, dyslexic children demonstrate pronounced deficits in phonological awareness (e.g., Bruck, 1992; Ramus et al., 2003). However, because fine-grained phonological awareness does not typically develop in the absence of reading instruction, some researchers have suggested that deficits in phonological awareness are a consequence rather than a cause of reading failure (e.g., Morais, 2003).

Several lines of research have supported the view that deficits in phonological awareness are causally related to reading difficulties and do not represent either a developmental delay or are not simply consequences of poor reading ability. First, a plethora of studies have demonstrated that phonological awareness measured prior to or at the onset of reading instruction successfully predicts reading performance in later years even after controlling for possible confounding variables (Kirby, Parrila, & Pfeiffer, 2003; Manis, Doi, & Bhadha, 2000; Muter & Snowling, 1998; Wagner et al., 1997). For example, Parrila and his colleagues (2004) examined the concurrent and future predictive influence of phonological processing measures on reading development in a 4-year-longitudinal study. The results demonstrated that phonological awareness, measured in grade 1, was the strongest predictor of grade 3 reading after controlling for the effect of prior reading skills (word identification measured in grade 1). Furthermore, phonological awareness measured in kindergarten and grade 1 accounted for unique variance in all reading measures, even after measures of other non-phonological processing variables (articulation rate, verbal short-term memory, and rapid naming speed) were taken into account. Similarly, Kirby et al. (2003) reported that phonological awareness measured in kindergarten was a strong predictor of reading performance in the first two years of schooling, after controlling for general intelligence and prior reading achievement (measured with letter recognition).

Juel (1988) traced the reading development of 54 children from Grade 1 to Grade 4. One of the most important findings was that children who were poor readers at the end of grade 4 entered grade 1 with little phonological awareness, and by the end of grade 4, still had not achieved the level of decoding skill that the good readers had achieved at the beginning of grade 2. The probability of a child remaining a poor reader throughout the period studied was extremely high (.88), as was the probability of a good first-year reader maintaining a good reading performance in later grades (.87).

The majority of the studies with dyslexic children measure reading and processing skills after there has been a considerable interaction between them. This raises problems in terms of the direction of causality. The question that many researchers were called to answer was whether phonological awareness was a cause of reading difficulties or a consequence itself of reading. The approach that a number of researchers have used to provide an answer to this question is to compare the profiles of reading and processing skills in younger normal and older dyslexic groups that have been carefully matched on a measure of reading skill (i.e., word identification or reading speed). A causal role in dyslexia is suggested for those component skills that are significantly worse in the dyslexic group compared to younger normal children at the same reading level (Bryant & Coswami, 1986). The basic rationale for this conclusion is that if reading development is responsible for the development of a processing skill, older dyslexic subjects should be at least as strong in that processing skill when compared to younger normal subjects at the same reading level. In one of these studies, Swan and Goswami (1997) examined the performance of 15 dyslexic children, 15 reading age-matched controls and 15 chronologically age-matched controls on several literacy skills. Chronologically age-matched controls were significantly better than any of the other two groups in all the measures used in the study. Importantly, dyslexics were significantly poorer than reading age-matched controls on phoneme tapping and initial/final phoneme judgment tasks.

In addition, experimental studies have demonstrated that training in phonological awareness effectively facilitates learning to read (e.g., Ball & Blachman, 1991; Blachman et al., 2004; Lovett, Steinbach, & Frijters, 2000). For example, Nicolson, Fawcett, Moss, Nicolson, and Reason (1999) conducted an intervention study with 32 reading-disabled children (mean age = 7.6 years) and reported that the intervention group which received phonics based treatment improved significantly in mean reading standard score (from 89.0 to 92.8), whereas a control group of reading-disabled children who received no intervention made no significant improvement.

Phonological awareness deficits appear also to be a persistent feature of dyslexia (Birch & Chase, 2004; Pennington, Van Orden, Smith, Green, & Haith, 1990; Wilson & Lesaux, 2001). Adults with childhood diagnosis of dyslexia have more difficulty with phoneme segmentation, deletion, and manipulation tasks than reading-level matched controls. Adult dyslexics' performance on tasks measuring phonological awareness of larger sub-lexical features such as rhyme or onset and rime is comparable to reading-level matched controls.

However, more recent findings suggest that the deficit may be located at the speed of accessing the phonological representations rather than at the quality of the phonological representations (e.g., Georgiou, Parrila, & McQuarrie, 2005; Parrila, Georgiou, & Corkett, 2007).

Deficits in phonological awareness have also been found in studies with more transparent orthographies, such as Arabic (e.g., Abu-Rabia, Share, & Mansour, 2003), Czech (Caravolas, Vólin, & Hulme, 2005), Dutch (e.g., de Jong, 2003), Hebrew (e.g., Share, 2003), Greek (e.g., Papadopoulos, Charalambous, Kanari, & Loizou, 2004; Porpodas, 1999), Finnish (e.g., Puolakanaho, Poikkeus, Ahonen, Tolvaven, & Lyytinen, 2004), and Italian (e.g., Brizzolara et al., 2006). However, there are studies that have challenged the existence of phonological awareness deficits in dyslexics learning to read in an orthographically transparent language (*German*: Wimmer, 1993; *Greek*: Georgiou, Parrila, Papadopoulos, & Zarouna, 2008). These researchers have argued that the effect of consistent spelling-sound correspondences in orthographically transparent languages is sufficiently powerful to secure children's phonological awareness skills.

Ziegler and Goswami (2005) suggested that phonological awareness tasks may be easier for dyslexic readers in orthographically transparent languages. Readers in these languages receive consistent feedback because there is little pronunciation ambiguity. The consistency of feedback along with systematic phonics instruction facilitates the development of phonological awareness (e.g., Seymour, Aro, & Erskine, 2003). In contrast, in English, the development of phonological awareness is more complex because English exhibits both forward (from graphemes to phonemes) and backward (from phonemes to graphemes) irregularity. In fact, phonological awareness develops much more rapidly in normally developing readers in transparent orthographies compared to children learning to read in English (e.g., Durgunoglu & Öney, 1999) and may explain why deficits in phonological awareness have not always been detected in children and adults learning to read in orthographically transparent languages (e.g., Goswami, 2002; Seymour et al., 2003).

By itself the phonological-core deficit does not account for all that is known about the development of reading problems. Other verbal abilities are equally strong predictors of reading outcomes, not only from kindergarten but also from younger ages (e.g., de Jong & Olson, 2004). Furthermore, phonology-based training programs have not been able to prevent or remediate reading difficulties completely (e.g., Torgesen et al., 2001), and some children who are successfully helped in learning to decode nevertheless fall behind at later stages in reading ability (e.g., Slavin et al., 1996). Thus, while the existence of a phonological core deficit and its potency in disrupting reading acquisition is generally undisputed, subsequent hypotheses have sought to expand on this idea in various ways.

In sum, phonological awareness has been considered as the number one cause of individual differences in reading development. Three lines of evidence support this conclusion. First, remediation studies with at-risk children showed that by improving phonological awareness there is a substantial improvement in reading ability. Second, phonological awareness has been shown to be a good predictor of reading ability even after the influence of possible confounding variables, such as general intelligence and letter knowledge, has been ruled out. Third, studies with younger children and older dyslexics that have been carefully matched on a measure of reading skill indicated that dyslexics perform poorer on measures of phonological awareness. Despite the consensus on the importance of phonological awareness, researchers have begun to look into alternative explanations regarding other possible causes of individual differences in reading. The most prominent alternative explanation maintains that individual differences in reading are caused by a deficit in rapid naming speed (Wolf & Bowers, 1999).

RAPID NAMING SPEED AND DYSLEXIA

Rapid naming speed has been defined as the ability to name as fast as possible visually presented and highly familiar symbols, such as objects, colors, digits, and letters (e.g., Wagner & Torgesen, 1987). The faster the children are in naming visually presented stimuli the better their reading ability is expected to be. Rapid naming performance has been shown to distinguish average from poor readers during childhood (e.g., Badian, Duffy, Als, & McAnulty, 1991; Cornwall, 1992; Wolf, Bally, & Morris, 1986) and into adulthood (Felton, Naylor, & Wood, 1990; Korhonen, 1995). In addition, even after statistically controlling for IQ (Cornwall, 1992), reading experience (Badian, 1993; Parrila et al., 2004), articulation rate (Parrila et al., 2004), speed of processing (e.g., Bowey, McGuigan, & Ruschena, 2005), letter knowledge (e.g., Kirby et al., 2003), and, most importantly, phonological awareness (e.g., Bowers, 1995; Kirby et al., 2003; Manis et al., 2000), rapid naming has survived as a predictor of reading.

The rapid naming test was first developed by Denckla and Rudel (1974) and was called the Rapid Automatized Naming (RAN) test. The test has been used frequently during the last three decades in studies investigating the association between rapid naming and reading (e.g., Bowers & Swanson, 1991; Compton, 2003; Kirby et al., 2003; Manis et al., 2000; Schatschneider et al., 2004; Wagner et al., 1997). During the RAN test, participants are presented with a series of visual stimuli, typically between 30 and 50 items in length, which they are asked to name as quickly as possible. Timing starts at the beginning of articulation of the first stimulus and ends when articulation of the last stimulus is completed. Despite the fact that it is relatively easy to measure, it is extremely hard to improve (de Jong & Vrielink, 2004).

Although the cause of variability in children's naming speed is not fully understood, converging evidence suggests that a deficit in rapid naming speed is a characteristic of reading difficulty from the early stages of reading (Wolf et al., 1986) to adulthood (Birch & Chase, 2004; Korhonen, 1995). For example, Korhonen (1995) carried out a longitudinal study with 9 dyslexic children followed from age 9 until age 18. A control group of 10 normally developing readers was matched on gender, age, general intelligence, and socioeconomic status. Results showed that the group of dyslexic children was significantly slower in rapid naming in comparison to the matched control group throughout this developmental period of interest. Similarly, Badian et al. (1991) examined the linguistic profiles of 60 boys in kindergarten, grade 2 and grade 4. The subjects were 7 dyslexics, 7 mildly dyslexics, 30 average, and 16 good readers. Across the three ages, the greatest differences between the four groups were found in rapid naming, syntactic awareness, and verbal memory. Group strengths and weaknesses were apparent already in kindergarten and maintained until grade 4. The kindergarten tasks which most effectively predicted reading group membership at grade 4 were letter sounds and rapid naming. These two measures predicted 4th grade reading group membership with close to 100 percent accuracy.

The importance of rapid naming in predicting reading ability and differentiating between poor and good readers has also been repeatedly shown in orthographically transparent languages. For example, de Jong and van der Leij (1999) demonstrated that when phonological awareness, verbal short-term memory, and naming speed were measured in kindergarten, only naming speed was a significant predictor of grade 1 and grade 2 reading outcomes. Likewise, Wimmer, Mayringer, and Landerl (2000) found that German-speaking Austrian children classified as having a naming speed deficit upon school entry continued to be impaired in naming speed at the end of grade 3. These children also showed deficits in reading speed compared to children with no naming speed deficit.

An important methodological issue with rapid naming tasks is the question of appropriate control groups. Many studies that have examined the relationship between rapid naming and dyslexia have not tested whether dyslexic readers are impaired on rapid naming tasks relative to reading-level matched controls (e.g., McBride-Chang & Manis, 1996; Manis et al., 2000; Meyer, Wood, Hart, & Felton, 1998). Additionally, those studies that have compared dyslexics with both age-matched and reading-level matched controls have reported conflicting findings. Some studies have found that dyslexics were impaired on rapid naming compared to age-matched controls but not relative to reading-level matched controls (Griffith & Snowling, 2001; Muneaux, Ziegler, Truc, Thomson, & Goswami, 2004), whereas other studies have reported that dyslexic readers demonstrate deficits relative to both age- and reading level-matched controls (e.g., Wolf, 1991). In addition, one study reported changing patterns over development in a cross-sectional study: younger dyslexic children did not demonstrate deficits on rapid naming tasks relative to reading level-matched controls, but dyslexic adolescents' rapid naming was impaired relative to both age- and reading level-matched controls (Pennington, Cardoso-Martins, Green, & Lefly, 2001).

To summarize, several researchers motivated by the observation that some children with adequate phonological awareness were still becoming poor readers started to seek alternative explanations. Unassailable evidence led them to consider rapid naming speed as the second core deficit in reading disabilities. First, rapid naming was found to account for variance in reading over and above the one accounted for by phonological awareness. Second, dyslexic children were found to be significantly slower than reading age-matched controls on rapid naming speed measures. Finally, in languages with transparent orthographies, children experience difficulties with rapid naming speed rather than with phonological awareness.

The Double-Deficit Hypothesis

On the basis of the cumulative data supporting the independent role of phonological awareness and rapid naming speed on reading, Wolf and Bowers (1999) developed an alternative conceptualization of reading disabilities, the double-deficit hypothesis. According to this hypothesis, four groups of children are expected to be identified: a group with normal reading, a group with deficits only in rapid naming speed, a group with deficits only in phonological awareness, and a double-deficit group with difficulties in both rapid naming speed and phonological awareness.

Children in the double-deficit group tend to have the most severe difficulties in learning to read. For example, Wolf, O'Rourke, Gidney, Lovett, Cirino, and Morris (2002) found that children in the double-deficit group had the lowest scores on word identification, word attack and reading comprehension. The double-deficit hypothesis has also been replicated in adults (Miller et al., 2006) and with children in other languages (i.e., *German*: Wimmer et al., 2000; *Greek*: Papadopoulos, Georgiou, & Kendeou, in press; and *Spanish*: Escribano, 2007). Wolf and Bowers (1999) interpreted this pattern of findings as an indication that when both rapid naming and phonological awareness deficits co-occur, there are only few compensatory mechanisms available that the child can rely on to overcome his or her difficulties.

However, Schatschneider, Carlson, Francis, Foorman, and Fletcher (2002) raised concerns with respect to the use of arbitrary cutoff scores on identifying the different deficit groups. They demonstrated that, because phonological awareness and RAN were correlated with each other, children in the double-deficit group could have a lower level of phonological awareness than children in the single-phonological deficit group and have slower RAN than children in the single-naming deficit group. In this case, it would be difficult to determine whether the poorer performance of the double-deficit group was due to having two deficits or rather to having more severe deficits. Compton, Defries, and Olson (2001) nicely demonstrated that categorizing children into subtypes based on arbitrary cutoffs of continuous variables that are correlated resulted in groups that differed in their level of phonological awareness. Importantly, when the groups were matched on phonological awareness and RAN (i.e., the double-deficit group and the RAN deficit group were matched on RAN, and the double-deficit and the phonological-deficit group were matched on phonological awareness), many of the differences in reading disappeared.

In conclusion, it would suffice to say here that the need for further research on the double-deficit hypothesis is deemed necessary before the suggested subtypes of children with reading difficulties can be fully conceptualized. Probably differential remedial work targeting the diverse needs experienced by these groups would be enough to provide some extra validation of this sub-grouping.

Cognitive Deficits and Dyslexia

Although there is a consensus that phonological and naming speed skills are related to typical and atypical reading development, the role that other cognitive processes play in reading acquisition is an issue considerably less agreed upon. More than a decade ago, Share and Stanovich (1995) suggested that phonological deficits have not been found to be attributable to nonphonological factors such as IQ, semantic processing, and visual processing. This has at least two implications: (a) that phonological processing is either an independent *module* of the mind, something that functions independently and is not even developmentally affected by more basic cognitive processes, or (b) if the alternative is true, the negative results can be explained by the fact that the researchers have not found the correct underlying cognitive processes to explain phonological processing and reading difficulties. Similarly, controversial is the evidence from the naming speed deficit hypothesis. Although it is suggested that dysfluency in name retrieval is caused by a hypothesized timing deficit that impairs temporal integration of a word's component letters, the evidence to support this hypothesis is tenuous and the issue has become controversial (Torgesen, Wagner, Rashotte, Burgess, & Hecht, 1997) particularly, in relation to the double deficit hypothesis (e.g., Compton et al., 2001; Schatschneider et al., 2002), as shown in the previous section. Thus, the question remains: Is naming retrieval or rapid naming also an independent module of the mind?

Even if the phonological processes and/or rapid naming are independent and *modularized* and reading difficulties do not generalize into tasks unrelated to reading, we still have the problem of unexplained variance in reading ability. Although correlations between phonological processing and word recognition ability are high (for useful reviews see Beaton, 2004; Snowling, 2000) and, similarly, between rapid naming and speed of word identification and speed of letter-sound decoding (Manis et al., 2000; Wolf, Bowers, & Biddle, 2000) they still leave reading variance unaccounted for. In this case, our question turns as follows: Do other cognitive processes add to the explanatory power of a model predicting reading acquisition?

The answer is affirmative and certainly important when considering the possible phenotypic variability exhibited by children with dyslexia. The possibility, for instance, that there may be a substantial number of children with dyslexia whose phonological decoding, phoneme awareness, or raping naming skills are at the average compared to same age peers but who still perform significantly lower in word reading tasks (Morris et al., 1998) may have significant implications for individual differences at the level of neurobiology or treatment. Thus, a multivariate approach is essential for addressing phenotypic variability. For this reason, four different hypotheses are examined next: (a) the auditory temporal processing, (b) the short-term/working memory, (c) the information-processing, and (d) the cerebellar deficit hypothesis.

Auditory Temporal Processing Deficit Hypothesis

One of the earliest hypotheses that have been tested examining the cognitive deficits of children with dyslexia is the relationship between speech perception and production or the temporal processing hypothesis of dyslexia (Tallal, 1980). More recently, Goswami (2003) has advanced this hypothesis to an auditory magnocellular deficit that seems to affect the discrimination of phonemes via deficits in auditory rapid (transient) processing, analogous to the visual deficit, a proposal that is similarly challenging. Generally, it has hypothesized that children who have a better mastery of phonology – as exhibited by their ability to hear spoken words accurately and articulate speech sounds clearly – can more readily gain a metalinguistic appreciation of the phonological structure of the words. In contrast, children with subtle deficits in speech perception or auditory rapid processing may also exhibit serious phonological problems (Mody, Studdert-Kennedy, & Brady, 1997; Richardson, Thomson, Scott, & Goswami, 2004). Tallal and Stark (1982) have early on hypothesized that more fundamental weaknesses in auditory temporal processing may underlie speech perception deficits, resulting eventually in reading disabilities. The examination of this hypothesis has led to the so-called 'rapid processing deficit' theory suggesting that children with dyslexia have difficulties in making rapid temporal judgments when stimuli are presented closely spaced in time. In spite of that, the demonstration of a relationship between speech perception and phonological awareness does not necessarily establish that problems in speech perception are causally related to reading difficulties. To answer this question, Reed (1989) examined the effects of stimulus modality on the retention of temporal order, by testing the most impaired readers in her sample on an auditory and a visual temporal judgment task. Although she found significant increase in errors in the auditory version, as the presentation interval between the two given tones was decreased, the same was not observed in the case of the visual temporal judgment task. This led Reed to suggest that the worse performance on the auditory task 'may reflect a basic perceptual deficit rather than a deficit in the retention of temporal order' (p. 287). Similarly, Snowling (2001) has also found that not all children with dyslexia have problems with auditory tests. Furthermore, Georgiou, Protopapas, Papadopoulos, Skaloumpakas, & Parrila (in press) examining the correlations between auditory temporal processing, phonological sensitivity measures, and word reading performance, have also found that they are only weakly correlated. However, Richardson et al. (2004) have found that individual differences in auditory tasks requiring amplitude envelope rise time processing explain significant variance in phonological processing, and that, developmentally, amplitude envelope cues may be fundamental in establishing well-specified phonological representations. Overall, the evidence from this area of research is not yet conclusive and, for this reason, it is has received great criticism. It may suffice to say that further research that would replicate the positive findings to date is deemed necessary in order to reach a conclusion about how poor readers deficits in speech related tasks or to a general auditory deficit in temporal processing are related to their characteristically impaired phonological ability, and so to reading.

Short-Term or Working Memory Deficit Hypothesis

Memory processes have been among the most researched cognitive processes in children with reading disabilities for the last 30 years (Swanson, Cooney, & McNamara, 2004). Verbal and visual-spatial working memory (WM) deficits, in particular, have frequently been identified, as markers of dyslexia, with individuals with the disorder exhibiting significantly weaker verbal WM than visualspatial WM skills (Papadopoulos et al., 2004; Siegel & Ryan, 1989; Vellutino, Scanlon, & Spearing, 1995). For some, these difficulties are considered as manifestations of the underlying cognitive deficits in phonology and language skills as opposed to specific problems with working memory (WM) and short-term memory (STM) (Schatschneider et al., 2004; Snowling, 2000; Wagner et al., 1997). For others, they are mostly attributed to deficits at the level of information processing, considering particularly the significance of memory span to reading and comprehension as a function of cognitive processing speed (Bisanz, Das, Varnhagen, & Henderson, 1992; Das, Mensink, & Mishra, 1990; Das, Mok, & Mishra, 1993; Papadopoulos, 2001). In sum, the question is whether the working memory deficits are independent of phonological processing and, subsequently, a significantly related factor to word recognition and to dyslexia.

In a comprehensive review of the literature on the relationship between working memory and reading difficulties, Savage, Lavers, and Pillay (2007) suggested that the nature of the tasks used to assess working memory may be particularly important to answer this question. With regard to the relationship between phonological processing and WM, the authors virtually argue that because any assessment of phonological ability involves some working memory component, it is important to assess working memory using different type of tasks, namely, STM and WM. The former assess storage capacity and the latter have both storage and processing components. By including both of them in the assessment of phonological skills, one may more accurately test whether STM or WM tasks contribute independent variability on phonological processing. For instance, Snowling, Hulme, Smith, and Thomas (1994) failed to show a relation between children's STM and performance on the phonological sound categorization task, wherein a child has to choose the 'odd-word out' from a set of words such as *cat, mat, sat, car*. In contrast, Oakhill and Kyle (2000) found that WM predicted independent variability on the phonological sound categorization task, probably because performing correctly on this task requires simultaneous processing and storage. On the basis of such findings, Savage et al. (2007) concluded that in making sense of the relationship between phonological processing and WM, it is deemed necessary to consider the type and demand of the task involved as well as the developmental level of children and the element of WM involved (see Anthony & Francis, 2005; Papadopoulos, Kendeou, & Spanoudis, 2008a; and Papadopoulos, Spanoudis, & Kendeou, in press, for further discussion on the conceptualization of phonological processing).

With regard to the relationship between working memory and reading difficulties, a rather influential model has been the multi-component proposal by Baddeley (for a review see, Baddeley, 1999). Baddeley describes working memory as a complex and flexible system, relying primarily on a central executive system that interacts with a set of two '*slave*' storage systems used for temporary storage of different clusters of information. One of these systems is the *phonological loop* that is responsible for the temporary storage of verbal information. The second storage system, the *visual sketchpad*, is responsible for the storage of visual/spatial information and plays an important role in the generation and manipulation of mental images. Both storage systems are in direct contact with the central executive system, allowing it to offload some of its short-storage functions, thereby freeing a portion of its own capacity for performing more demanding information processing tasks.

Investigations from this perspective, when applied to reading deficits, focus primarily on the use or operation of the phonological loop (Siegel, 1993; for a comprehensive review). For example, individuals with reading difficulties perform lower than controls on the production of pronunciations for nonsense words (Gathercole & Baddeley, 1993) and on word reading accuracy measures, suggesting a deficit in the phonological system (e.g., Hansen & Bowey, 1994). The question, however, is whether the deficits observed in the use or operation of the phonological loop system may be partially attributed to deficiencies in the controlling functions of the central executive itself, given that the phonological loop is partially controlled by the central executive. Relevant studies provide inconclusive evidence to this question. Swanson, Ashbaker, and Lee (1996) have supported that when children with reading difficulties perform tasks with high processing demands, they tend to be poorer in recalling both verbal and visual-spatial information compared to typically developing peers. However, other studies (e.g., de Jong, 1998; Swanson & Ashbaker, 2000) suggest that difficulties in executive processing may also contribute to the poor WM performance of poor readers above and beyond their deficits in phonological processing, which implies impairment in executive functioning. Thus, either both central executive and the phonological loop are important to typical or atypical reading development (Baddeley, 1992) or the ability group differences are due to a domain general system. Jerman and Swanson (2005) are more in favor of a domain general system synthesis, as they have found no differences in effect sizes when they divided tasks in terms of those that have visual/spatial WM and those that have verbal WM. In other words, their results have showed that the WM problems of children with reading difficulties were not merely due to the failure of the phonological coding. Even more, when they entered reading as a variable in which to assess the interaction of domain specificity, no interaction was observed. Consequently, they argued that WM deficits are not domain-specific and that the influence of WM on cognitive measures is probably independent of various academic domains. This rather overarching effect of WM on dyslexia, in turn, has probably led researchers to look for answers about the reasons behind the disorder into information processing theories.

Information-Processing Deficit Hypothesis

The impact of cognitive revolution in the 60s has been substantial on both applied and theoretical psychologists and educators studying dyslexia and other types of learning disabilities. The movement toward redefining intelligence as cognitive processes and, thereby question the makeup of traditional IQ tests, could be considered as the most important impact of this revolution. Within this cognitive frame, alternative – to traditional IQ measures – psychometric approaches were developed, eliminating achievement from the measure of ability. One of the most influential information processing theories[2] in reading development and dyslexia is the Planning, Attention, Simultaneous, and Successive (PASS) processing theory, suggested by Das and his colleagues. Because thorough reviews of PASS model and related research are presented elsewhere (e.g., Das, Naglieri, & Kirby, 1994; Naglieri & Rojahn, 2004; Papadopoulos et al., 2004; Papadopoulos, Das, Parrila, & Kirby, 2003) only a brief summary is provided here, with specific emphasis on PASS theory's application to the study of reading difficulties.

The PASS theory of cognitive processes is based largely on the psychological work of Luria (e.g., 1980). The maintenance of attention, the processing and storing of information, and the management and direction of mental activity comprise the activities of the operational units that work together to produce cognitive functioning (Das et al., 1994). *Arousal-Attention*, the first unit, comprises of basic behaviors such as the orienting reflex, as well as instances of complex attentional behavior involved in discrimination learning and selective attention, which in turn, allows the allocation of resources and effort. While attentional skills such as ability for shifting and resistance to distraction are certainly important for reading, children with reading difficulties usually do not exhibit problems with these tasks. The second functional unit includes *Simultaneous and Successive coding* of information. Simultaneous processing involves the arrangement of incoming information into a holistic pattern, or a gestalt, that can be "surveyed" in its entirety. For example, recognition of whole words by sight involves this kind of processing, as does comprehension of the meaning of a sentence or a paragraph (Papadopoulos, 2001). Successive processing refers to coding information in discrete, serial order where the detection of one portion of the information is dependent on its temporal position relative to other material. It is used in skills such as word decoding and spelling where the maintaining of the exact sequence or succession of letters in the word is crucial for completion (Naglieri, 2001; Papadopoulos, 2001, 2002). Successive

[2] with over 800 citations in the ISI Web of Knowledge and Scopus, April 2008

processing, therefore, is relatively broader than the specific tests for phonemic awareness, syntax awareness, or even short-term memory, which have been identified as the core 'processes' that separate dyslexics and normal readers (Siegel, 1993). Finally, *Planning* consists of programming, regulation, and verification of behavior. All of these are required in writing a composition and to a lesser extent in reading comprehension and word reading. Among the three operational units, successive and simultaneous processing is mainly important in the early stages of reading (Das, Parrila, & Papadopoulos, 2000; Papadopoulos, 2001). Dual-route theories of word recognition, for example, suggest that a word is recognized either through direct visual access or through phonological coding of its sounds. The first should relate more to simultaneous and the second more to successive processing. No task, however, solely requires simultaneous or successive processing; it is a matter of emphasis. Due to the importance of phonological coding and letter-by-letter processing in the early stages of word reading, successive processes are naturally expected to be more important at this level of processing. Simultaneous processing, in turn, is more strongly related to the development of letter recognition and later orthographic processing of the words, as child uses simultaneous processing when s/he has to identify each letter as an orthographic unit (Kirby, Booth, & Das, 1996; Papadopoulos, 2001; Papadopoulos & Kendeou, 2008).

Research to date, utilizing the PASS theory, has much to offer to the definition of dyslexia with findings that coincide mostly with those from the relevant to STM and WM research. Poor readers seem to have difficulty in the successive processing tasks such as random word sequences or word series, sentence repetition and speech rate (Das et al., 1993, 1994; Kirby et al., 1996; Papadopoulos et al., 2003; Snart, Das, & Mensink, 1988). They have been also found to have weak morphology-dependent skills and inferior performance compared to their chronologically matched peers on measures of planning (Kirby et al., 1996; Parrila, 1995; Snart et al. 1988) and, to a less extent, to measures of attention (Das et al., 1990; Snart et al., 1988, Papadopoulos et al., 2008b). Finally, group differences between poor and typically developing readers have also been observed in the case of the simultaneous processing tasks, accounting for significant independent variance on reading performance and, particularly, reading comprehension (Kendeou, Papadopoulos, & Christou, 2007; Kirby et al., 1996; Papadopoulos, 2001; Shankweiler et al., 1995).

A closer examination of these deficits with regard to reading and comprehension, does affirm the pattern that successive and attention tasks are more strongly related to word decoding, whereas planning and simultaneous tasks are more strongly linked to comprehension. If that is the case, then by linking phonological coding and articulation to successive processing, we can account for the association between short-term memory span and reading, a factor that is also found to be very weak in the reading performance of unskilled readers (Papadopoulos, Kendeou, Demetriou, & Demetriou, 2007). In contrast, by associating comprehension to simultaneous processing, we can support the idea that simultaneous processing may contribute early on to what has become known as *outside-in* skills of emergent literacy (Whitehurst & Lonigan, 1998). Indeed, Kendeou & Papadopoulos (2009) have found that performance on the Woodcock Reading Mastery Test-Revised (WRMT-R) depends primarily on cognitive skills and particularly, simultaneous processing. Thus, in a sense, the information processing deficit hypothesis offers a broader theoretical approach to the explanation of dyslexia than the WM deficit hypothesis. In contrast, the so-called cerebellar deficit hypothesis seems to provide a more specific approach about the functional architecture of children who are not able to read.

Cerebellar Deficit Hypothesis

Two recent empirically innovative hypotheses that have been proposed for the nature of dyslexia are the Dyslexia Automatization Deficit (Nicolson & Fawcett, 1990) and the Cerebellar Deficit (Nicolson, Fawcett, & Dean, 1995) hypotheses. The former hypothesis proposes that dyslexia leads to difficulties in becoming fluent in any skill (including non-literacy skills), whereas the latter attributes the literacy and automaticity problems to abnormal cerebellar function, providing a more neuropsychological explanation for dyslexia. Dysfunction at the level of articulatory skills, underlying human speech, is also immediately linked to cerebellar dysfunction. These skills are considered relatively complex motor skills taking years to develop and be mastered at a level of automaticity. Inability, consequently, to coordinate the thousands of neuromuscular events/second involved in translating abstract phonological representations into a code for the motor system is explained then by a cerebellar deficit. This is what, essentially, the recent research addresses as a problem in Rapid Automatized Naming (RAN; Wolf & Bowers, 1999). The cerebellar deficit hypothesis provides further explanations for the phonological based difficulties in dyslexic populations, by identifying the problem in producing the sounds in words and, thus, to a less rich representation of the phonological space. A further manifestation of the cerebellar difficulties, which is, however, evenly correlated to successful deployment of reading skills, is the impairment witnessed in balance and coordination of moves, and more specifically in the development of fine motor skills, among children with dyslexia. The cerebellar hypothesis provides, thus, a natural (neurophysiologic) explanation for the poor manual control of individuals exhibiting poor writing and spelling, symptoms that are intertwined with dyslexia. Nicolson and his colleagues (see for e.g., Reynolds, Nicolson, & Hambly, 2003) argue, indeed, that training on adaptive balance tasks can lead to all round improvements in coordination, self-belief and academic performance, enhancing, in a far transfer, reading performance as well.

In a recent meta-analysis of 17 studies that compared balance function between dyslexia and control samples, Rochelle and Talcott (2006) concluded that the association between balance deficits and dyslexia results primarily from the influence of third variables, other than reading skill. Among those are the substantial effects of Attention Deficit Hyperactivity Disorder (ADHD) and the relevant lowered IQ of the participating samples. Nicolson and Fawcett (1990; 1994) has, however, pointed out early on that it is difficult to account for motor or balance deficits on any hypothesis that is restricted specifically to reading. A number of tasks that work as good markers for reading failure, such as some phonological and rapid automatized naming tasks are characterized by demands on attentional resource allocation and this is the reason why children with dyslexia may be at a disadvantage to fare successfully these tasks. Thus, they support that if we see children with dyslexia suffering from 'a *general* learning deficit (for *any* skill) which is confined to the final stage of skill mastery – the stage where the skill normally becomes so fluent that it occurs *automatically*, without the need for conscious control (Fawcett & Nicolson, 1992; p. 508), then we can understand why some hypothesis, such as the phonological deficit hypothesis, do not account for the full range of findings related to dyslexia.

Even when memory or balance deficits are found, they do not always appear in the ways predicted by the cerebellar deficit hypothesis. For instance, Wimmer, Mayringer, and Raberger (1999) did not find that German children with dyslexia differed from controls on a balancing task, after controlling for attention deficits. In fact, ADHD was a better predictor of performance on the cerebellar task in their study than reading status. Similarly, Ramus, Pidgeon, and Frith (2003) in comparison of three hypotheses about dyslexia addressing (1) phonological processing deficits, (2) low-level auditory and visual deficits, and (3) cerebellar dysfunctions found the strongest support for phonological deficits, which occurred in the absence of the other types of deficits. However, about 59% of dyslexics were more than one standard deviation below controls in motor skills. The comorbidity with ADHD was considered as a possible explanation of at least part of this discrepancy.

Brain imaging studies provide some insight into the cerebellum hypothesis in dyslexia. Anatomical studies have found metabolic abnormalities (Rae et al., 1998), decreased grey matter density (Brown et al., 2001), and neural morphology asymmetry (Rae et al., 2002). In addition, functional imaging has showed reduced activation in motor and cerebellar regions while performing motor sequencing tasks (Nicolson et al., 1999; Price, 2008). Taken altogether, it appears that cerebellum is operationally engaged in a range of cognitive processes, including sequential stimulus processing, skill automatization and receptive language (for a review see Rochelle & Talcott, 2006). However, how and in what incidence difficulties in these abilities are seen in people with dyslexia is not yet very clear. It may suffice to say that their role in explaining reading problems and dyslexia is limited (Papadopoulos et al., 2007; Ramus, 2003).

Syntactic Awareness and Dyslexia

Recent research evidence points to a significant relationship between children's early phonological skills and their development in learning to read, as has been discussed. However, the potential significant effect of other language skills to the development of reading has been less well documented. According to Nation and Snowling (2004), early literacy skills are acquired from a foundation of spoken language, making it reasonable to expect that the nature of the reading system children develop will depend not only on phonological processing skills, but also on their relative proficiency of syntactic and semantic skills. Fluent reading requires that the meanings of single words be integrated at the sentence and text levels and that ongoing comprehension be monitored. Thus, sensitivity to the syntactic and semantic constraints of the language can be considered as a resource that 'assists' literacy development (Bohannon, Warren-Leubecker, & Helper, 1984; Willows & Ryan, 1986).

Syntactic (or grammatical) awareness refers to the ability of manipulating and reflecting on the grammatical structure of language. In order to assess this ability, several tasks have been used, such as word-order correction tasks, in which the words of a sentence are presented in a jumbled order and have to be rearranged and grammatical correction tasks, where a grammatical or morphological violation in a sentence has to be corrected. Syntactic awareness is a metalinguistic skill, distinct from the comprehension or production of a sentence. The reason for this lies in the fact that it concerns the ability to consider the structure rather than the meaning of a sentence. Several studies have shown that performance on measures of syntactic awareness in children improves with age and is related to reading ability (Bowey, 1986a, 1986b; Siegel & Ryan, 1989).

Due to its contribution to reading comprehension, the ability to manipulate the syntactic structure of spoken language is thought to be closely related to reading development (e.g., Bowey, 1986a; Demont & Gombert, 1996; Paris & Landauer, 1982). In addition, evidence also suggests that syntactic awareness may also facilitate reading development via contributing directly to word recognition. Tunmer et al. (Tunmer & Hoover, 1992; Tunmer, Nesdale, & Wright, 1987) argued that knowledge of the constraints of sentential context can provide enough information for unfamiliar words to be decoded successfully, especially for beginning readers, whose decoding skills are not yet fully automatic. Thus, children with well-developed syntactic awareness skills may benefit more from contextual information (Rego & Bryant, 1993; Tunmer & Hoover, 1992; Tunmer et al., 1987).

In line with this, Tunmer (1989) showed that second grade word recognition skills were predicted by first grade syntactic awareness skills, even after phonological awareness and general ability had been accounted for. Comparative studies of children with diverse reading ability skills also point to the relatively close relationship between syntactic awareness and word recognition. In a Tunmer et al. (1987) study, poor readers performed on two syntactic awareness tests lower than younger, reading-age matched controls, thus providing evidence that supports the notion that syntactic awareness deficits may be causally related to reading difficulties. Poor readers also face difficulties in comprehending syntactically complex sentences (Byrne, 1981; Mann, Shankweiler, & Smith, 1984), they form syntactically less complex sentences and tend to make more grammatical errors in spontaneous speech than good readers (Vogel, 1975). Furthermore, kindergarten children being at risk of developing reading problems tend to show a more limited use of syntax, when speaking, than typically developing children (Scarborough, 1990).

To date, several studies examining the role of syntactic awareness in reading development are characterized by various limitations. For example, they show difficulties to disentangle causal relations, as poor decoding skill has been confounded with poor reading comprehension. Poor syntactic awareness may well be a secondary consequence of this kind of limitations rather than a direct result of difficulties dealing with syntax (Smith, Macaruso, Shankweiler, & Crain, 1989) as poor phonological processing and deficient verbal memory with decoding deficits (Brady, 1986; Mann, Liberman, & Shankweiler, 1980; Snowling, 1991; Stanovich & Siegel, 1994) typically tend to co-occur. Also, Smith et al. (1989) provided evidence that syntactic comprehension and syntactic awareness are constrained by limitations of verbal working memory, by showing that poor readers perform equivalently to skilled readers on syntactic comprehension tests, when processing load is reduced. In order to measure syntactic awareness, word order correction tasks have been typically used, in which children have to put the words into a syntactically correct order, after hearing a scrambled sentence (e.g., Tunmer et al., 1987). Despite the fact that such tasks are sensitive to individual differences in language skills, the fact that sentences contain a variety of different syntactic structures makes it difficult to distinguish what linguistic factors account for task difficulty.

The central focus in studying syntactic awareness skills has been its relation to reading ability. Both word reading and reading comprehension have been considered to relate directly to syntactic awareness. It is thought that syntactic awareness skills aid not only word recognition skills by enabling a reader to use the syntactic constraints of a sentence to decode unfamiliar words (Rego & Bryant, 1993; Tunmer, 1989), but also reading comprehension by facilitating sentence- and text-level integration and monitoring skills (Tunmer & Bowey, 1984). Rego and Bryant (1993) showed that syntactic awareness predicted 5-year-olds' ability to use context to read words that they are unable to read in isolation. Similarly, Muter and Snowling (1998) found that 9-year-old's accuracy at reading words in context was also predicted by syntactic skills. Other studies pointed to a specific relation between word reading and syntactic awareness even after receptive vocabulary (Bowey, 1986a) or even variables such as short-term memory (Willows & Ryan, 1986) was accounted for, although this was not the case in studies that controlled for additional measures, such as sentence repetition (Bowey & Patel, 1988).

On the other hand, several studies have examined the relationship between syntactic awareness and reading comprehension. Tunmer (1989) found that syntactic awareness in Grade 1 predicts reading comprehension a year later by influencing decoding and listening comprehension, while the two skills were found to be highly correlated in 6- to 10-year-olds (Bowey, 1986b; Bowey & Patel, 1988). Weaknesses on measures of syntactic awareness skills in children with poor reading comprehension relative to chronologically-age matched good comprehenders have also been found using cross-sectional designs (Gaux & Gombert, 1999; Nation & Snowling, 2000; Siegel & Ryan, 1988). Syntactic awareness has also been shown to explain unique amounts of variance in reading comprehension skills, even after language and memory have been controlled for (Willows & Ryan, 1986).

In spite of these findings, the relation between syntactic awareness and reading ability is not yet clear: although a specific relation between syntactic awareness and either word reading ability or reading comprehension has been shown in some cases, it also seems that the relation is mediated by language skills. Late-acquired grammatical structures are among those skills that influence young readers' performance on syntactic awareness tasks.

Investigation of the possible contribution of grammatical sensitivity to early reading achievement is based on the investigation of alternative causal hypotheses concerning the key determinants of performance on grammatical sensitivity tasks. Two accounts that generate conflicting predictions in relation to the possible role of grammatical sensitivity in early reading have been distinguished by Gottardo, Stanovich, and Siegel (1996). According to a 'phonological processing limitation hypothesis' (Shankweiler, Crain, Brady, & Macaruso, 1992), underlying phonological processing deficits are the main cause of all language-related symptoms of poor word reading, including difficulties with grammatical error correction. This is consistent with a large body of evidence suggesting that children word-level reading difficulties have their origins in phonological processing difficulties, as has been already discussed in previous sections (Share, 1995; Stanovich, 1991; Wagner, Torgesen, & Rashotte, 1994; Wagner et al., 1997). Alternatively, Tunmer, Herriman, and Nesdale (1988) has proposed the 'cognitive capacity' account, according to which grammatical error correction assesses metalinguistic ability, which itself reflects underlying cognitive ability. Cognitive capacity is the underlying determinant, although phonological and grammatical sensitivity seem to make independent contributions to word reading skill.

According to this view of metalinguistic development, preliterate children with low levels of metalinguistic skills but high levels of cognitive skills are expected to show much greater improvement in metalinguistic skills during the school year than similar children with low levels of cognitive skills at school entry. These children should do reasonably well in learning to read even though their preliterate metalinguistic abilities may suggest otherwise. If so, metalinguistic ability is suggested to directly influence early reading development by mediating the effects of general cognitive ability.

In summary, the studies reported above support the view that children's syntactic awareness skills are related to their reading ability. Low syntactic awareness skills seem to impact upon reading development in at least two ways. Apart from facilitating text integration and comprehension monitoring, syntactic awareness may as well constrain the development of skilled word recognition by influencing the ease with which children learn to read words they could not read via simple decoding mechanisms (Nation & Snowling, 1998; Rego & Bryant, 1993). The findings of the above studies leave several questions unanswered, not least of which is the extent to which the relationship between syntactic awareness and reading is causal. In order for future research to address the precise nature of the relationships between syntactic awareness, other aspects of language processing, word recognition, and reading comprehension, longitudinal designs, and intervention studies are needed.

Morphological Awareness and Dyslexia

There are several reasons why morphological awareness should strongly relate to learning to read. Morphemes not only have phonological and syntactic properties, but also semantic (Mahony, Singson, & Mann, 2000). Morphological awareness is, thus, integrally related to other aspects of language knowledge and may provide a 'more general index of metalinguistic capability' than phonological or syntactic awareness considered alone (Carlisle, 1995, p. 192).

Moreover, the way the mature mental lexicons are organized provide an additional relation. Adult psycholinguistic studies have consistently shown that when processing complex words the use of morphological information is crucial (Clahsen, Sonnenstuhl, & Blevins, 2003; Nagy, Anderson, Schommer, Scott, & Stallman, 1989; Napps, 1989).

In line with this, Burani and Caramazza (1987) showed that root frequency affects the processing of morphologically complex words in alphabetical languages. Similar results in support of a morpheme-based mental lexicon have also been obtained for logographic languages such as Chinese (Zhou & Marslen-Wilson, 1995). Sandra (1994) argued that morphological knowledge may serve as a framework to efficiently store words, based on the fact that the mental lexicon of adult readers is morphologically organised. Thus, children with better developed morphological awareness skills may have an advantage in acquiring and retaining morphologically complex vocabulary.

This becomes crucial for expedited learning of morphologically complex vocabulary, if we take into account that such vocabulary may make up 60% to 80% of the new words acquired by school-aged children (Anglin, 1993). Vocabulary being a strong indicator of reading performance (Anderson & Freebody, 1981) points to the fact that morphological awareness should substantially influence reading development.

Morphological awareness may also provide readers with additional insight into the writing system (Nagy, Berninger, Abbott, Vaughan, & Vermeulen, 2003). Many writing systems incorporate both phonological and morphological information. Verhoeven,

Schreuder, and Baayen (2003) argued that that morphemes tend to receive a constant orthographic representation regardless of phonological shift due to affixation, as heal-health; and produce-production, based on the isomorphism principle. On the other hand, morphemes that are pronounced the same often differ in spelling, for example to-two-too.

Recent studies on the investigation of how morphological awareness is related to reading development measured the ability to decode both real words and nonwords (Carlisle, 1995; Casalis & Louis-Alexandre, 2000; Mahony et al., 2000). Their results pointed to a limited contribution of morphological awareness to decoding skills in early elementary grades after other decoding-related factors were considered. The weak relationship between awareness of derivational morphology and word reading can be attributed to the somewhat problematic inclusion of nonwords or single-morpheme words in the decoding test used. Although length itself can make test items more difficult for beginning readers, their morphological complexity may not indeed matter, when examining how phonological awareness and decoding relate. The inclusion of nonword items can even help to control for extraneous factors such as vocabulary size. However, because decoding such items does not require insights into morphological structure, the rationale of a possible strong relationship between morphological awareness and decoding of nonwords or even single-morpheme words is yet to be established. Evidence in support of this comes from intervention studies where morphological awareness training did not produce any significant effect on reading nonwords (Arnbak & Elbro, 2000). Thus, phonological awareness accounts for most of the variance in nonword and single-morpheme decoding tests, while morphological awareness only makes a very limited contribution, comes as no surprise. Recent research has shifted attention to the decoding of morphologically complex words in order to explain the relationship between morphological awareness and word reading (Mann & Singson, 2003; Nagy, Berninger, & Abbott, 2006).

Decoding of morphologically complex words may represent a type of morphological awareness, due to the requirement of coordination of orthographic and morphological cues to achieve the correct phonological representation. Morphological awareness seems to significantly influence the decoding of morphologically complex words, by enabling beginning readers to parse strings of letters at the right syllable boundary (e.g., mis-handle vs. mi-shandle). Verhoeven et al. (2003) and Nunes, Bryant, and Olsson (2003) have also shown that many of the seemingly inconsistent grapheme-phoneme conversion rules in English and Dutch are in fact morphologically governed. This can be the case for other alphabetic languages as well.

The importance of morphological awareness to word decoding skills has been found to increase with age. Morphological awareness has been found to account for significant decoding skill variance among French-speaking second-graders but not among first graders (Casalis & Louis-Alexandre, 2000). It has also been found that for third-graders, syllable length, but not frequency, contributed significantly to decoding speed and accuracy of morphologically complex words; for fifth graders, both syllable length and base frequency accounted for a significant variance (Carlisle & Stone, 2003). This suggests that older children are better able to capitalize on morphological cues to decode morphologically complex words. Mann and Singson (2003) showed that by fifth grade, the best predictor of decoding morphologically complex words is morphological awareness, not phonological awareness, after controlling for vocabulary. Nagy et al. (2003) found that for fourth and fifth graders, morphological awareness contributed more saliently to decoding of morphologically complex words when the words involved phonological shift. According to their model, while word decoding ability alone was the best predictor of decoding of morphologically complex words that did not involve phonological shift, word decoding ability and morphological awareness jointly contributed to the decoding of morphologically complex words that involved phonological shift.

The assumption underlying most studies is that morphological awareness is a contributing cause of reading development. However, neither comparative studies of good and poor readers nor studies using a within-group design and regression analysis license a causal conclusion. Several relations may exist between morphological awareness and reading development. In addition to morphological awareness being a contributing cause, the relationship could be reversed. Better morphological awareness may be attributed to extensive exposure to print. Another possibility is that the relationship between morphological awareness and learning to read is reciprocal. And finally, there might not be a direct relationship between morphological awareness and reading development, but more a co-variation with other factors. Longitudinal studies have suggested that among English-speaking children (Carlisle, 1995) and French-speaking children (Casalis & Louis-Alexandre, 2000) morphological awareness in kindergarten and first grade is a strong predictor of second-grade and even third grade reading comprehension (Carlisle, 1995; Carlisle & Fleming, 2003).

On the other hand, intervention studies can shed light on the question of causation. Morphological awareness skills training may benefit beginning readers. In a longitudinal study with Norwegian-speaking kindergarteners, Lyster (2002) found that morphological training not only had an immediate effect, but also a long-term effect on reading achievement. In addition, a recent intervention study by Nunes et al. (2003) with 7- and 8-year-old English-speaking children stands out in its theoretical approach and methodology. Nunes et al. (2003) found that the group that received morphological training outperformed the control group on the nonword items. The study provides evidence in favour of the view that morphological awareness may be the cause of better reading performance, but also suggests that morphological training may have a positive long-term effect on reading achievement.

Effects on reading comprehension have also been found among Mandarin-speaking children in intervention studies that emphasized the contribution of characters to the meanings of multi-character words (Anderson, Li, & Wu, 2004) but also in intervention studies that focused on the structures of compounds (Zhang, 2004), pointing to the fact that these positive effects of morphological instruction are not limited to alphabetic languages. Thus, recent cross-language evidence indicates that morphological training can significantly improve reading comprehension, but also that morphological awareness may be a cause of better reading.

Research evidence also suggests a reciprocal rather than a unidirectional relationship between morphological awareness and reading development. Carlisle (1988) and Templeton and Scarborough-Franks (1985) found that orthographic representations provided valuable clues to morphological structure. Thus, exposure to print may facilitate the development of morphological awareness.

Fowler and Liberman (1995) compared the performance of younger average readers and older poor readers matched on reading skill on morphological tasks. The results showed that younger average readers did not outperform older poor readers on the morphological tasks. This provides a more direct piece of evidence challenging the view that morphological awareness leads to better reading achievement. This finding is in contrast with studies on phonological awareness using a similar paradigm in which younger average readers consistently showed an advantage over older poor readers on phonological tasks (Bradley & Bryant, 1978; Fowler, 1990). Fowler and Liberman (1995) argued that this finding "leaves open the question of whether morphological weaknesses hamper reading acquisition or whether experience with the orthography promotes morphological sensitivity" (p.157). These findings along with the longitudinal and intervention studies discussed above suggest that the relationship between morphological awareness and reading may be reciprocal.

To summarise, studies using different designs and types of analysis have suggested that morphological awareness is a contributing cause of reading growth. However, the relationship between morphological awareness and reading development cannot be completely captured in any single simple theoretical relation. In order to further understand this relationship, it is important, first, to disentangle the relative roles of the various literacy-related factors, such as phonological awareness, syntactic awareness, vocabulary, decoding skills, working memory, and morphological awareness and, second, to expand the relevant hypotheses to populations with reading difficulties, as the nature of morphological processing in dyslexia is yet to be determined. Indeed, only a limited number of studies have investigated morphological awareness in dyslexia (e.g., Laxon, Rickard, & Coltheart, 1992). To recapitulate, although morphological awareness may not have a pronounced effect on the reading skills of beginning readers, its importance seems to increase over the elementary school years. Thus, the different aspects in morphological awareness should be considered in the field of reading acquisition, but also dyslexia research, especially when determining the implementation of possible compensatory strategies for disabled readers.

THE INTEGRATION OF THE DIFFERENT APPROACHES AND CORRELATES

Among the four major stands navigating the current review, the phonological deficit, the naming speed and automaticity impairments, the cognitive deficits, and the language-based problems, critical, as well, as sympathetic scholars may find creditable accounts of the contributions of these stands into the study of dyslexia to at least three fields: (a) to the field of assessment of dyslexia, delving into the potential cognitive or neuropsychological explanations of the disorder, (b) to the field of assessment of reading potential through instructional devices that can facilitate the development of relevant skills across theories, and (c) to techniques of remedial treatment that take individuals through their zones of proximal development, with the least possible guidance from the trainer's part, relying extensively on a aptitude-treatment interaction approach. As a result, the integration of these four stands provides a potential structure to bridge among the models/theories.

Starting from these premises, the aim of the current psychological research in dyslexia ought to be focused on how the different component skills relevant to reading and spelling, and the neuropsychological and/or biological factors underpinning them can be studied together to substantially increase the understanding of the disorder being manifest, apart from the presence of environmental risks. It is very legitimate to think that undue difficulty in learning to read is experienced when an individual is at the tail end of many distributions among the areas studied here. By implication, this means that in order to provide a fine-grained approach for exploring reading difficulties one must know what there is to be explained or modelled in the first place. In our view, the description of how different components operate is a useful step in conceptualizing the different skills that underlie normal reading and that are impaired in cases of dyslexia.

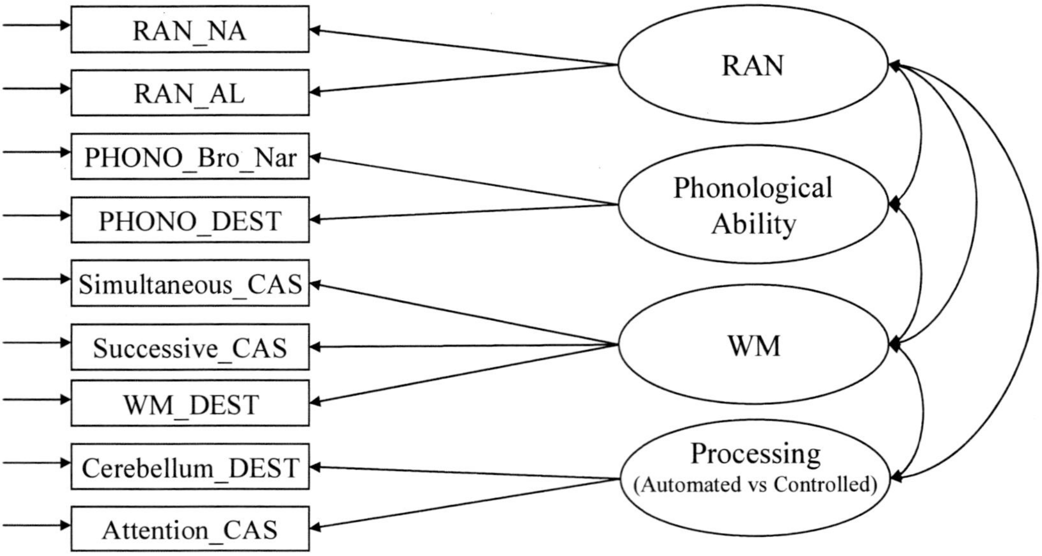

Note: RAN = Rapid Automatized Naming; RAN_NA = RAN Nonalphanumeric (Colors and Pictures); RAN_AL = RAN Alphanumeric; PHONO-Bro_Nar = Phonological tasks of Broad (Syllabic) and Narrow (Phoneme) Sensitivity; PHONO_DEST = Phonological tasks from the DEST-R battery; Simultaneous_CAS = Simultaneous processing tasks from the Cognitive Assessment System (CAS); Sucessive_CAS = Successive processing tasks from the CAS; WM_DEST = Working Memory tasks from the DEST-R; Cerebellum_DEST = Cerebellum tasks from the DEST-R; Attention_CAS = Attention tasks from the CAS

Figure 1. The baseline model of different cognitive and neuropsychological factors tested as a new possible frame for a unified theory for dyslexia

A possible frame for unifying research and theory is to relate cognitive models that specify the different components of dyslexia, their mode of operation and the relationships between them, with neuropsychological models and relevant brain-imaging data. Cognitive neuropsychology, with its origin in human experimental cognition, can provide data of considerable interest for testing theories of normal cognition with children exhibiting dyslexia or other disorders (for a review see Temple, 1997). These data, in turn, can allow the examination of the limitations of functional plasticity in development and the study of possible causal links between brain abnormality and reading difficulties (Cohen & Dehaene, 2004; Paulesu et al., 2001), leading probably to universal or unified theories about dyslexia. Indeed, Paulesu and his colleagues (2001) have recently concluded that dyslexia has a universal basis in the brain and can be characterized by the same neurocognitive deficit. The shallowness of orthography can only lead to less severe manifestation in reading behavior. Similarly, Papadopoulos, Kendeou, Nicolson, Fawcett, and Das (2008c) investigated the possibility for a unified theory for dyslexia exploring longitudinally the convergence among four theories that have been implicated in reading disability, which has been extensively discussed in the present paper: (1) an information processing theory, the Planning, Attention, Simultaneous, and Successive (PASS) theory (assessed with the Cognitive Assessment System, CAS; Naglieri & Das, 1997), (2) the Cerebellar Deficit theory (assessed with the Dyslexia Early Screening Test, DEST-R; Nicolson & Fawcett, 2004) (3) the phonological deficit hypothesis and (4) rapid automatized naming deficit hypothesis. Using Structural Equation Modelling and a large cohort of children, their results showed that four latent variables, namely, rapid automatized naming, phonological sensitivity, working memory, and processing capacity (as expressed by controlled versus automated processing), can explain longitudinally individual differences in reading. The authors concluded that the convergence of cognitive and neuropsychological approaches to understanding dyslexia is possible and that we are now closer than the past, to the formulation of unified theories (Figure 1 shows the baseline model that was tested as the most parsimonious model across ages). Current research (e.g., Simos et al., 2002) and monographs (Beaton, 2004) provide examples and argue in favour of this possible convergence between cognitive, neuropsychological or biological approaches.

A Final Word

In conclusion, nowadays dyslexia can be seen as the conversation between cognitive psychology and the neurosciences. Cognitive neuropsychology has emerged as an accepted tradition in this domain and has shed light on the modular architecture of cognitive processes involved in reading. However, on the principle that is important *not to miss what you are not looking for* we have argued that the future of research on dyslexia lies in its ability to break the boundaries of the various paradigms and build new theories that would integrate the various models and traditions into overarching explanations of the disorder. To attain this objective we need to depart from the correlational group studies approach and the solitary use of different approaches and adopt more widely model-driven approaches that will use large, preferably cross-cultural samples, multiple measures, and advanced statistics.

References

Aaron, P. G., Kuchta, S., & Grapenthin, C. T. (1988). Is there a thing called dyslexia? *Annals of Dyslexia, 38*, 33–49.

Abu-Rabia, S., Share, D., & Mansour, M. (2003). Word recognition and basic cognitive processes among reading disabled and normal readers in the Arabic language. *Reading and Writing: An Interdisciplinary Journal, 16*, 423-440.

Anderson, R. C., & Freebody, P. (1981). Vocabulary knowledge. In J. Guthrie (Ed.), *Comprehension and teaching: Research reviews* (pp.77–117). Newark, DE: International Reading Association.

Anderson, R. C., Li, W., & Wu, X. (2004, July). *Morphological instruction accelerates Chinese children's literacy development.* Paper presented at the annual meeting of the Society for the Scientific Study of Reading, Amsterdam, The Netherlands.

Anglin, J. M. (1993). Vocabulary development: A morphological analysis. Monographs of the Society of Research in Child Development, *58 (10, Serial No. 238)*, 1-165.

Anthony, J. L., & Francis, D. J. (2005). Development of phonological awareness. *Current Directions in Psychological Science, 14*, 255-259.

Apthorp, H. S. (1995). Phonetic coding and reading in college students with and without learning disabilities. *Journal of Learning Disabilities, 28*, 342–352.

Arnbak, E., & Elbro, C. (2000). The effects of phonological awareness training on the reading and spelling skills of young dyslexics. *Scandinavian Journal of Educational Research, 44,* 229–251.

Baddeley, A. D. (1992). Working memory. *Science, 255*, 556-559.

Baddeley, A. D. (1999). *Essentials of Human Memory*. Sussex, UK: Psychology Press.

Badian, N. A. (1993). Predicting reading progress in children receiving special help. *Annals of Dyslexia, 43*, 90-109.

Badian, N. A., Duffy, F. H., Als, H., & McAnulty, G. B. (1991). Linguistic profiles of dyslexics and good readers. *Annals of Dyslexia, 41*, 221-245.

Ball, E. W., & Blachman, B. A. (1991). Does phoneme segmentation training in kindergarten make a difference in early word recognition and developmental spelling? *Reading Research Quarterly, 24*, 49-66.

Beaton, A. (2004). *Dyslexia, reading, and the brain.* East Essex, UK: Psychology Press.

Birch, S., & Chase, C. (2004). Visual and language processing deficits in compensated and uncompensated college students with dyslexia. *Journal of Learning Disabilities, 37*, 389-410.

Bisanz, G. L., Das, J. P., Varnhagen, C. K., & Henderson, H. R. (1992). Structural components of reading time and recall for sentences in narratives: Exploring changes with age and reading ability. *Journal of Educational Psychology, 84*, 103-114.

Blachman, B. A. (1984). Relationship of rapid naming ability and language analysis skills to kindergarten and first-grade reading achievement. *Journal of Educational Psychology, 76*, 610-622.

Blachman, B. A., Schatschneider, C., Fletcher, J. M., Francis, D. J., Clonan, S. M., Shaywitz, B. A., et al. (2004). Effects of intensive reading remediation for second and third graders and a 1-year follow-up. *Journal of Educational Psychology, 96*, 444-461.

Bohannon, J. N., Warren-Leubecker, A., & Helper, N. (1984). Word order awareness and early reading. *Child Development, 55*, 1541–1548.

Bowers, P. G. (1995). Tracing symbol naming speed's unique contributions to reading disability over time. *Reading and Writing: An Interdisciplinary Journal, 7*, 189-216.

Bowers, P. G., & Swanson, L. B. (1991). Naming speed deficits in reading disability. *Journal of Experimental Child Psychology, 51*, 195-219.

Bowey, J. A. (1986a). Syntactic awareness in relation to reading skill and ongoing reading comprehension monitoring. *Journal of Experimental Child Psychology, 41*, 282–299.

Bowey, J. A. (1986b). Syntactic awareness in verbal performance from preschool in fifth grade *Journal of Psycholinguistic Research, 15*, 285–308.

Bowey, J. A., McGuigan, M., & Ruschena, A. (2005). On the association between serial naming speed for letters and digits and word-reading skill: Towards a developmental account. *Journal of Research in Reading, 28*, 400-422.

Bowey, J. A., & Patel, R. K. (1988). Metalinguistic ability and early reading achievement. *Applied Psycholinguistics, 9*, 367–383.

Bradley, L., & Bryant, P.E. (1978). Deficits in auditory organization as a possible cause of reading backwardness. *Nature, 271*, 746–747.

Brady, S. (1986). Short-term memory, phonological processing and reading ability. *Annals of Dyslexia, 36*, 138–153.

Brizzolara, D., Chilosi, A., Cipriani, P., Di Filippo, G., & Gasperini, F., et al. (2006). Do phonologic and rapid automatized naming deficits differentially affect dyslexic children with and without a history of language delay? A study of Italian dyslexic children. *Cognitive and Behavioral Neurology, 19*, 141-149.

Brown, W. E., Eliez, S., Menon, V., Rumsey, J. M., White, C. D., & Reiss, A. L. (2001). Preliminary evidence of widespread morphological variations of the brain in dyslexia. *Neurology, 56*, 781–783.

Bruck, M. (1992). Persistence of dyslexics' phonological deficits. *Developmental Psychology, 28,* 874-886.

Bryant, P. E., & Goswami, U. (1986). Strengths and weaknesses of the reading level design: A comment on Backman, Mamen, and Ferguson. *Psychological Bulletin, 100*, 101-103.

Burani, C., & Caramazza, A. (1987). Representation and processing of derived words. *Language and Cognitive Processes, 2*, 217–227.

Byrne, B. (1981). Deficient syntactic control in poor readers: Is a weak phonetic memory code responsible? *Applied Psycholinguistics, 2*, 210–212.

Caravolas, M., Vólin, J., & Hulme, C. (2005). Phoneme awareness is a key component of alphabetic literacy skills in consistent and inconsistent orthographies: Evidence from Czech and English children. *Journal of Experimental Child Psychology, 92*, 107-139.

Carlisle, J. F. (1988). Knowledge of derivational morphology and spelling ability in fourth, sixth, and eighth graders. *Applied Psycholinguistics, 9,* 247–266.

Carlisle, J. F. (1995). Morphological awareness and early reading achievement. In L. Feldman (Ed.), *Morphological aspects of language processing* (pp. 189–209). Mahwah, NJ: Lawrence Erlbaum Associates.

Carlisle, J. F., & Fleming, J. (2003). Lexical processing of morphologically complex words in the elementary years. *Scientific Studies of Reading, 7*, 239–253.

Carlisle, J. F., & Stone, C. (2003). The effects of morphological structure on children's reading of derived words. In E. Assink & D. Santa (Eds.), *Reading complex words: Cross-language studies* (pp. 27–52). Dordrecht, The Netherlands: Kluwer.

Casalis, S., & Louis-Alexandre, M. (2000). Morphological analysis, phonological analysis and learning to read French. *Reading and Writing: An Interdisciplinary Journal, 12*, 303–335.

Chadwick, O., Taylor, E., Taylor, A., Heptinstall, E., & Danckaerts, M. (1999). Hyperactivity and reading disability: A longitudinal study of the nature of the association. *Journal of Child Psychology and Psychiatry, 40*, 1039-1050.

Clahsen, H., Sonnenstuhl, I., & Blevins, J. (2003). Derivational morphology in the German mental lexicon: A dual mechanism account. In H. Baayen & R. Schreuder (Eds.), *Morphological structure in language processing* (pp. 125–155). Berlin: Mouton de Gruyter.

Cohen, L., & Dehaene, S. (2004). Specialization within the ventral stream: The case for the visual word form area. *Neuroimage, 22*, 466-476.

Compton, D. L. (2003). Modeling the relationship between growth in rapid naming speed and growth in decoding skill in first-grade children. *Journal of Educational Psychology, 95*, 225-239.

Compton, D. L., DeFries, J. C., & Olson, R. K. (2001). Are RAN and phonological deficits additive in children with reading disabilities? *Dyslexia, 7*, 125-149.

Cornwall, A. (1992). The relationship of phonological awareness, rapid naming, and verbal memory to severe reading and spelling disability. *Journal of Learning Disabilities, 25*, 532-538.

Das, J. P., Mensink, D., & Mishra, R. K. (1990). Cognitive processes separating good and poor readers when IQ is covaried. *Learning and Individual Differences, 2*, 423-436.

Das, J. P., Mok, M., & Mishra, R. K. (1993). The role of speech processes and memory in reading disability. *The Journal of General Psychology, 12*, 131-146.

Das, J. P., Naglieri, J. A., & Kirby, J. R. (1994). *Assessment of cognitive processes: The PASS theory of intelligence.* Boston, MA: Allyn & Bacon.

Das, J. P., Parrila, R. K., & Papadopoulos, T. C. (2000). Cognitive education and reading disability. In A. Kozulin & Y. Rand (Eds.), *Experience of mediated learning: An impact of Feuerstein's theory in education and psychology* (pp. 274-291). Oxford: Pergamon Press.

de Jong, P. F. (1998). Working memory deficits of reading disabled children. *Journal of Experimental Child Psychology, 70*, 75–96.

de Jong, P. F. (2003). Problems in the acquisition of fluent word decoding in Dutch children. In N. Goulandris (Ed.), *Dyslexia in different languages: Cross-linguistic comparisons* (pp. 33-52). London: Whurr Publishers.

de Jong, P. F., & Olson, R. K. (2004). Early predictors of letter knowledge. *Journal of Experimental Child Psychology, 88*, 254-273.

de Jong, P. F., & van der Leij, A. (1999). Specific contributions of phonological abilities to early reading acquisition: Results from a Dutch latent variable longitudinal study. *Journal of Educational Psychology, 91*, 450-476.

de Jong, P. F., & Vielink, L. O. (2004). Rapid Automatic Naming: Easy to measure, hard to improve (quickly). *Annals of Dyslexia, 54*, 65-88.

Demont, E., & Gombert, J. E. (1996). Phonological awareness as a predictor of recoding skills and syntactic awareness as a predictor of comprehension skills. *British Journal of Educational Psychology, 66,* 315–332.

Denckla, M. B., & Rudel, R. (1974). Rapid "automatized" naming of pictured objects, colors, letters, and numbers by normal children. *Cortex, 10*, 186-202.

Durgunoglu, A. Y., & Öney, B. (1999). A cross-linguistic comparison of phonological awareness and word recognition. *Reading and Writing: An Interdisciplinary Journal, 11*, 281-299.

Escribano, C. L. (2007). Evaluation of the double-deficit hypothesis subtype classification of readers in Spanish. *Journal of Learning Disabilities, 40*, 319-330.

Fawcett, A. J., & Nicolson, R. I. (1992). Automatization deficits in balance for dyslexic children. *Perceptual and Motor Skills,* 75, 507-529.

Felton, R. H., Naylor, C. E., & Wood, F. B. (1990). Neuropsychological profile of adult dyslexics. *Brain and Language, 39*, 485-497.

Fowler, A. (1990). Factors contributing to performance on phoneme awareness tasks in school-aged children. *Haskins Laboratories Status Report on Speech Research*, 103/104, 137–152.

Fowler, A., & Liberman, I. Y. (1995). The role of phonology and orthography in morphological awareness. In L. Feldman (Ed.), *Morphological aspects of language processing* (pp. 189–209). Mahwah, NJ: Lawrence Erlbaum Associates.

Gathercole, S. E., & Baddeley, A. D. (1993). *Working memory and language: Essays in cognitive psychology*. East Sussex, UK: Psychology Press.

Gaux, C., & Gombert, J. E. (1999). Implicit and explicit syntactic knowledge and reading in pre- adolescents. *British Journal of Developmental Psychology, 17*, 169–188.

Georgiou, G., & Parrila, R., & McQuarrie, L. (2005, July). *Phonological processing skills of adult compensated dyslexics.* A poster presented at the 3rd International Multilingualism and Dyslexia conference in Limassol, Cyprus.

Georgiou, G., Parrila, R., Papadopoulos, T. C., & Zarouna, E. (2008, March). *Cognitive underpinnings of dyslexia in an orthographically consistent language*. Poster presented at the 7th British Dyslexia Association (BDA) conference at Harrogate, York, England.

Georgiou, G., K., Protopapas, A., Papadopoulos, T. C., Skaloumpakas, C., & Parrila, R. K. (in press). Auditory temporal processing and dyslexia in an orthographically consistent language. *Cortex*.

Goswami, U. (2000). Phonological and lexical processes. In M. L. Kamil, P. D. Pearson, & R. Barr (Eds.), *Handbook of reading research* (Vol. 3, pp. 251-267). Hillsdale, NJ: Lawrence Erlbaum Associates.

Goswami, U. (2002). Phonology, reading development, and dyslexia: A cross-linguistic perspective. *Annals of Dyslexia, 52*, 141-163.

Goswami, U. (2003). Why theories about developmental dyslexia require developmental designs *Trends in Cognitive Sciences, 7*, 534-540.

Gottardo, A., Stanovich, K. E., & Siegel, L. S. (1996). The relationship between phonological sensitivity, syntactic processing, and verbal working memory in the reading performance of third-grade children. *Journal of Experimental Child Psychology, 63*, 563–582.

Griffith, Y. M., & Snowling, M. (2001). Auditory word identification and phonological skills in dyslexics and average readers. *Applied Psycholinguistics, 22*, 419-439.

Grigorenko, E. L. (2001). Developmental Dyslexia: An update on genes, brains, and environments. *Journal of Child Psychology and Psychiatry, 42*, 91-125.

Hansen, J., & Bowey, J. A. (1994). Phonological analysis skills, verbal working memory, and reading ability in second grade children. *Child Development, 65*, 938-950.

Jakobson, A., & Kikas, E. (2007). Cognitive functioning in children with and without Attention-Deficit/Hyperactivity Disorder with and without comorbid learning disabilities. *Journal of Learning Disabilities, 40*, 194-202.

Jerman, O., & Swanson, H. L. (2005). Working memory and reading disabilities: A selective meta-analysis of the literature. *Advances in Learning and Behavioral Disabilities, 18*, 1–31.

Juel, C. (1988). Learning to read and write: A longitudinal study of 54 children from first through fourth grades. *Journal of Educational Psychology, 80*, 437-447.

Kendeou, P., & Papadopoulos T. C. (2009). *Reading comprehension tests: What skills do they assess?* Manuscript submitted for publication.

Kendeou, P., Papadopoulos T. C., & Christou, E. (2007, July). *Bridging theories to better understand early reading difficulties*. Symposium paper presented at the 14th Annual Meeting of the Society for the Scientific Study of Reading (SSSR), Prague, Czech Republic.

Kirby, J. R., Booth, C. A., & Das, J. P. (1996). Cognitive processes and IQ in reading disability. *The Journal of Special Education, 29*, 442-456.

Kirby, J., Parrila, R., & Pfeiffer, S. (2003). Naming speed and phonological awareness as predictors of reading development. *Journal of Educational Psychology, 95*, 453-464.

Korhonen, T. T. (1995). The persistence of rapid naming problems in children with reading disabilities: A nine-year follow-up. *Journal of Learning Disabilities, 28*, 232-239.

Laxon, V., Rickard, M., & Coltheart, V. (1992). Children read affixed words and nonwords. *British Journal of Psychology*, 83, 407-423.

Lovett, M. W., Steinbach, K. A., & Frijters, J. C. (2000). Remediating the core deficits of developmental reading disability: A double-deficit perspective. *Journal of Learning Disabilities, 33*, 334-358.

Luria, A. R. (1980). *Higher cortical functions in man.* (2nd ed.). New York: Basic Books.

Lyster, S. H. (2002). The effects of morphological versus phonological awareness training in kindergarten on reading development. *Reading and Writing: An Interdisciplinary Journal, 15*, 261–294.

Mahony, D., Singson, M., & Mann, V. (2000). Reading ability and sensitivity to morphological relations. *Reading and Writing: An Interdisciplinary Journal*, *12,* 191–218.

Manis, F. R., Doi, L. M., & Bhadha, B. (2000). Naming speed, phonological awareness, and orthographic knowledge in second graders. *Journal of Learning Disabilities, 33*, 325-333.

Mann, V. A., Liberman, I. Y., & Shankweiler, D. (1980). Children's memory for sentences and word strings in relation to reading ability. *Memory and Cognition, 8*, 329–335.

Mann, V. A., Shankweiler, D., & Smith, S. T. (1984). The association between comprehension of spoken sentences and early reading ability: The role of phonetic representation. *Journal of Child Language, 11*, 627–643.

Mann, V., & Singson, M. (2003). Linking morphological knowledge to English decoding ability: Large effects of little suffixes. In E. Assink & D.Santa (Eds.), *Reading complex words: Cross-language studies* (pp. 1–25). Dordrecht, The Netherlands: Kluwer.

McBride-Chang, C., & Kail, R. (2002). Cross-cultural similarities in the predictors of reading acquisition. *Child Development, 73*, 1392-1407.

McBride-Chang, C., & Manis, F. R. (1996). Structural invariance in the associations of naming speed, phonological awareness, and verbal reasoning in good and poor readers: A test of the double-deficit hypothesis. *Reading and Writing: An Interdisciplinary Journal, 8*, 323-339.

Meyer, M. S., Wood, F. B., Hart, L. A., & Felton, R. H. (1998). Selective predictive value of rapid automatized naming in poor readers. *Journal of Learning Disabilities, 31*, 106-117.

Miller, C., Miller, S., Bloom, J., Jones, L., Lindstrom, W., Craggs, J., et al. (2006). Testing the doubled-deficit hypothesis in an adult sample. *Annals of Dyslexia, 56*, 83-102.

Mody, M., Studdert-Kennedy, M., & Brady, S. (1997). Speech perception deficits in poor readers: Auditory processing or phonological coding? *Journal of Experimental Child Psychology, 64*, 199-231.

Morais, J. (2003). Levels of phonological representation in skilled reading and in learning to read. *Reading and Writing: An Interdisciplinary Journal, 16*, 123-151.

Morris, R. D., Steubing, K. K., Fletcher, J. M., Shaywitz, S. E., Lyon, G. R., et al. (1998). Subtypes of reading disability: Variability around a phonological core. *Journal of Educational Psychology, 90*, 347–373.

Muneaux, M., Ziegler, J., Truc, C., Thomson, J., & Goswami, U. (2004). Deficits in beat perception and dyslexia: Evidence from French. *Neuroreport, 15*, 1255-1259.

Muter, V., & Snowling, M. (1998). Concurrent and longitudinal predictors of reading: The role of metalinguistic and short-term memory skills. *Reading Research Quarterly, 33*, 320–337.

Naglieri, J. A. (2001). Using the Cognitive Assessment System (CAS) with learning-disabled children. In A. S. Kaufman & N. L. Kaufman (Eds.), *Specific learning disabilities and difficulties in children and adolescents* (pp. 141-177). Cambridge, UK: Cambridge University Press.

Naglieri, J. A. & Das, J. P. (1997). *Das-Naglieri Cognitive Assessment System*. Itasca, IL: Riverside Publishing.

Naglieri, J. A., & Rojahn, J. (2004). Construct validity of the PASS theory and CAS: Correlations with achievement. *Journal of Educational Psychology, 96*, 174–181.

Nagy, W. E., Anderson, R. C., Schommer, M., Scott, J. A., & Stallman, A. C. (1989). Morphological families in the internal lexicon. *Reading Research Quarterly, 24,* 263–282.

Nagy, W. E., Berninger, V. W., & Abbott, R. C. (2006). Contributions of morphology beyond phonology to literacy outcomes of upper elementary and middle-school students. *Journal of Educational Psychology, 98*, 134–147.

Nagy, W. E., Berninger, V. W., Abbott, R. C., Vaughan, K., & Vermeulen, K. (2003). Relationship of morphology and other language skills to literacy skills in at-risk second-grade readers and at-risk fourth-grade writers. *Journal of Educational Psychology, 95*, 730–742.

Napps, S. E. (1989). Morphemic relationships in the lexicon: Are they distinct from semantic and formal relationships? *Memory and Cognition, 17*, 729–739.

Nation, K., & Snowling, M. J. (1998). Individual differences in contextual facilitation: Evidence from dyslexia and poor reading comprehension. *Child Development, 69*, 996–1011.

Nation, K., & Snowling, M. J. (2000). Factors influencing syntactic awareness skills in normal readers and poor comprehenders. *Applied Psycholinguistics, 21*, 229–241.

Nation, K., & Snowling, M. (2004). Beyond phonological skills: Broader language skills contribute to the development of reading. *Journal of Research in Reading, 27*, 342-356.

Nicolson, R. I., & Fawcett, A. J. (1990). Automaticity: A new framework for dyslexia research? *Cognition, 35*, 159-182.

Nicolson, R. I., & Fawcett, A. J. (1994). Comparison of deficits in cognitive and motor skills among children with dyslexia. *Annals of Dyslexia, 44*, 147-164.

Nicolson, R. I. & Fawcett, A. J. (2004). *The Dyslexia Early Screening Test-R.* London: The Psychological Corporation.

Nicolson, R. I., Fawcett, A. J., Berry, E. L., Jenkins, I. H., Dean, P., & Brooks, D. J. (1999). Association of abnormal cerebellar activation with motor learning difficulties in dyslexic adults. *Lancet, 353*, 1662–1667.

Nicolson, R. I., Fawcett, A. J., & Dean, P. (1995). Time-estimation deficits in developmental dyslexia: Evidence of cerebellar involvement. *Proceedings of the Royal Society of London Series B-Biological Sciences, 259*, 43-47.

Nicolson, R. I., Fawcett, A. J., Moss, H., Nicolson, M. K., & Reason, R. (1999). Early reading intervention can be effective and cost-effective. *British Journal of Educational Psychology, 69*, 47-62.

Nunes, T., Bryant, P., & Olsson, J. (2003). Learning morphological and phonological spelling rules: An intervention study. *Scientific Studies of Reading, 7*, 289–307.

Oakhill, J., & Kyle, F. (2000). The relation between phonological awareness and working memory. *Journal of Experimental Child Psychology, 75*, 152–164.

Olson, R. K. (1999). Genes, environment, and reading disabilities. In R. J. Sternberg & L. Spear-Swerling (Eds.), *Perspective on learning disabilities* (pp. 3-21). Boulder, CO: Westview Press.

Olson, R. K. (2002). Dyslexia: Nature and Nurture. *Dyslexia, 8*, 143-159.

Papadopoulos, T. C. (2001). Phonological and cognitive correlates of word-reading acquisition under two different instructional approaches. *European Journal of Psychology of Education, 16*, 549-567.

Papadopoulos, T. C. (2002). Predictors of reading development in at-risk kindergarten children. *Developmental Disabilities Bulletin, 30*, 173-198.

Papadopoulos, T. C., Charalambous, A., Kanari, A., & Loizou, M. (2004). Kindergarten intervention for dyslexia: The PREP remediation in Greek. *European Journal of Psychology of Education, 19*, 79-105.

Papadopoulos, T. C., Constantinidou, M., & Douklias, S. (2008b). *A longitudinal appraisal of cognitive deficits in children with attention deficits with and without comorbid reading difficulties*. Manuscript in preparation.

Papadopoulos, T. C., Das, J. P., Parrila, R. K., & Kirby, J. R. (2003). Children at-risk for developing reading difficulties: A remediation study. *School Psychology International, 24*, 340-366.

Papadopoulos T. C., Georgiou, G. K., & Kendeou, P. (in press). Investigating the double-deficit hypothesis in Greek: Findings from a longitudinal study. *Journal of Learning Disabilities*.

Papadopoulos, T. C., & Kendeou, P. (2008, July). *A longitudinal appraisal of the development of passage comprehension in Greek*. Symposium paper presented at the XXIX International Congress of Psychology (ICP), Berlin, Germany.

Papadopoulos T. C., Kendeou, P., Demetriou, S., & Demetriou, A. (2007, July). *Diagnosis of reading difficulties in Kindergarten and Grade 1 in Greek: The role of CAS and DEST-R*. Symposium paper presented at the 14th Annual Meeting of the Society for the Scientific Study of Reading (SSSR), Prague, Czech Republic.

Papadopoulos, T. C., Kendeou, P., Nicolson, R. I., Fawcett, A. J., & Das, J. P. (2008c, March). *Toward an integrative account of cognitive-neuropsychological model in dyslexia: Convergence of four theories*. Symposium paper presented at the 1st Pan-Hellenic Conference on Developmental Psychology, Athens, Greece.

Papadopoulos, T. C., Kendeou, P., & Spanoudis, G. (2008a). *Development and factor structure of phonological abilities in* Greek. Manuscript submitted for publication.

Papadopoulos, T. C., Spanoudis, G., & Kendeou, P. (in press). The dimensionality of phonological abilities in Greek. *Reading Research Quarterly*.

Paris, S., & Landauer, B. (1982). The development of cognitive skills in childhood. In B. Wolman (Ed.), *Handbook of developmental psychology* (pp. 333–349). Englewood Cliffs, NJ: Prentice-Hall.

Parrila, R. K. (1995). Vygotskian views on language and planning in children. *School Psychology International, 16*, 167-183.

Parrila, R., Georgiou, G., & Corkett, J. (2007). University students with a significant history of reading difficulties: What is and is not compensated? *Exceptionality Education Canada, 17*, 195-220.

Parrila, R., Kirby, J. R., & McQuarrie, L. (2004). Articulation rate, naming speed, verbal short-term memory, and phonological awareness: Longitudinal predictors of early reading development. *Scientific Studies of Reading, 8*, 3-26.

Paulesu, E., Demonet, J. F., Fazio, F., McCrory, E., Chanoine, V., Brunswick, N., et al. (2001). Dyslexia: Cultural diversity and biological unity. *Science, 291*, 2165-2167.

Pennington, B. F., Cardoso-Martins, C., Green, P. A., & Lefly, D. L. (2001). Comparing the phonological and the double deficit hypotheses for developmental dyslexia. *Reading and Writing: An Interdisciplinary Journal, 14*, 707-755.

Pennington, B. F., & Lefly, D. L. (2001). Early reading development in children at family risk for dyslexia. *Child Development, 72*, 816-833.

Pennington, B. F., Van Orden, G. C., Smith, S. D., Green, P. A., & Haith, M. (1990). Phonological processing skills and deficits in adult dyslexics. *Child Development, 61*, 1753-1778.

Peterson, R. L., McGrath, L. M., Smith, S. D., & Pennington, B. F. (2007). Neuropsychology and Genetics of Speech, Language, and Literacy Disorders. *Pediatric Clinics of North America, 54*, 543–561.

Porpodas, C. (1999). Patterns of phonological and memory processing in beginning readers and spellers of Greek. *Journal of Learning Disabilities, 32*, 404-416.

Price, C. (2008, March). *Neuro-imaging studies of developmental dyslexia.* Keynote address given at the British Dyslexia Association, Yorkshire, UK.

Puolakanaho, A., Poikkeus, A.-M., Ahonen, T., Tolvaven, A., & Lyytinen, H. (2004). Emerging phonological awareness differentiates children with and without familiar risk for dyslexia after controlling for general language skills. *Annals of Dyslexia, 54*, 221-243.

Rae, C., Harasty, J. A., Dzendrowskjy, T. E., Talcott, J. B., Simpson, J. M., Blamire, A. M., et al. (2002). Cerebellar morphology in developmental dyslexia. *Neuropsychologia, 40*, 1285–1292.

Rae, C., Lee, M. A., Dixon, R. M., Blamire, A. M., Thompson, C. H., Styles, P., et al. (1998). Metabolic abnormalities in developmental dyslexia detected by 1H magnetic resonance spectroscopy. *Lancet, 351*, 1849–1852.

Ramus, F. (2003). Developmental dyslexia: Specific phonological deficit or general sensorimotor dysfunction? *Current Opinion in Neurobiology, 13*, 212–218.

Ramus, F., Pidgeon, E., & Frith, U. (2003). The relationship between motor control and phonology in dyslexic children. *Journal of Child Psychology and Psychiatry, 44*, 712–722.

Ramus, F., Rosen, S., Dakin, S. C., Day, B. L., Castellote, J. M., White, S., et al. (2003). Theories of developmental dyslexia: Insights from a multiple case study of dyslexic adults. *Brain, 126*, 841-865.

Reed, M. (1989). Speech perception and discrimination of brief auditory cues in reading disabled readers. *Journal of Experimental Child Psychology, 48,* 270-292.

Rego, L. L., & Bryant, P. E. (1993). The connection between phonological, syntactic and semantic skills and children's reading and spelling. *European Journal of Psychology of Education, 8*, 235–246.

Reynolds, D., Nicolson, R. I., & Hambly, H. (2003). Evaluation of an exercise-based treatment for children with reading difficulties. *Dyslexia, 9*, 48-71.

Richardson, U., Thomson, J., Scott, S. K., & Goswami, U. (2004). Auditory processing skills and phonological representation in dyslexic children. *Dyslexia, 10*, 215-233.

Rochelle, K. S., & Talcott, J. B. (2006). Impaired balance in developmental dyslexia? A meta-analysis of the contending evidence. *Journal of Child Psychology and Psychiatry, 47*, 1159-1166.

Sandra, D. (1994). The morphology of the mental lexicon: Internal word structure viewed from psycholinguistic perspective. *Language and Cognitive Processes, 9*, 227–269.

Savage, R., Lavers, N., & Pillay, V. (2007). Working memory and reading difficulties: What we know and what we don't know about the relationship. *Educational Psychology Review, 19*, 185-221.

Scarborough, H. S. (1990). Very early language deficits in dyslexic children. *Child Development, 61*, 1728–1743.

Scarborough, H. S. (1998a). Early identification of children at risk for reading disabilities. In B. K. Shapiro, P. J. Accardo, & A. J. Capute (Eds.), *Specific reading disability: A view of the spectrum* (pp. 75-119). Timonium, MD: York Press.

Scarborough, H. S. (1998b). Predicting the future achievement of second graders with reading disabilities: Contributions of phonemic awareness, verbal memory, rapid naming, and IQ. *Annals of Dyslexia, 48*, 115-136.

Schatschneider, C., Carlson, C. D., Francis, D. J., Foorman, B. R., & Fletcher, J. M. (2002). Relationship of rapid automatized naming and phonological awareness in early reading development: Implications for the double-deficit hypothesis. *Journal of Learning Disabilities, 35*, 245-256.

Schatschneider, C., Fletcher, J. M., Francis, D. J., Carlson, C. D., & Foorman, B. R. (2004). Kindergarten prediction of reading skills: A longitudinal comparative analysis. *Journal of Educational Psychology, 96*, 265-282.

Seymour, P. H., Aro, M., Erskine, J. M. (2003). Foundation literacy acquisition in European orthographies. *British Journal of Psychology, 94,* 143-174.

Shankweiler, D., Crain, S., Brady, S., & Macaruso, P. (1992). Identifying the causes of reading disability. In P. Gough, L. Ehri, & R. Treiman (Eds.), *Reading acquisition* (pp. 275–305). Hillsdale, NJ: Lawrence Erlbaum.

Shankweiler, D., Crain, S., Katz, L., Fowler, A. E., Liberman, A. M., et al. (1995). Cognitive profiles of reading-disabled children: Comparison of language skills in phonology, morphology, and syntax. *Psychological Science, 6*, 149-156.

Share, D. L. (2003). Dyslexia in Hebrew. In N. Goulandris (Ed.), *Dyslexia in different languages: Cross-linguistic comparisons* (pp. 208-234). London: Whurr.

Share, D. L. (1995). Phonological recoding and self-teaching: Sine qua non of reading acquisition. *Cognition, 55*, 151–218.

Share, D. L. & Stanovich, K. E. (1995). Cognitive processes in early reading development: Accommodating individual differences into a model of acquisition. *Issues in Education, 1*, 1-57.

Siegel, L. S. (1993). Phonological processing deficits as the basis of a reading disability. *Developmental Review, 13*, 246-257.

Siegel, L. S., & Ryan, E. B. (1989). Development of working memory in normally achieving and subtypes of learning disabled children. *Child Development, 60,* 973–980.

Simos, G. P., Breier, J. I., Fletcher, J. M., Foorman, B. R., Castillo, E. M., & Papanicolaou, A. C. (2002). Brain mechanisms for reading words and pseudowords: An integrated approach. *Journal of Cognitive Neuroscience, 12*, 297-305.

Slavin, R. E., Madden, N. A., Dolan, L., Wasik, B. A., Ross, S., Smith, L., et al. (1996). Success for all: A summary of research. *Journal of Education for Students Placed at Risk, 1*, 41-76.

Smith, S. T., Macaruso, P., Shankweiler, D., & Crain, S. (1989). Syntactic comprehension in young poor readers. *Applied Psycholinguistics, 10*, 429–454.

Snart, F., Das, J. P., & Mensink, D. (1988). Reading disabled children with above-average IQ: A comparative examination of cognitive processing. *Journal of Special Education, 22*, 344-357.

Snowling, M. J. (1991). Developmental reading disorders. *Journal of Child Psychology and Psychiatry, 32*, 49–78.

Snowling, M. J. (2001). From language to reading and dyslexia. *Dyslexia,* 7, 37-46.

Snowling, M. J. (2000). *Dyslexia* (2nd ed). Oxford, UK: Blackwell Publishing.

Snowling, M. J., Hulme, C., Smith, A., & Thomas, J. (1994). The effects of phonetic similarity and list length on children's sound categorization performance. *Journal of Experimental Child Psychology, 58*, 160-180.

Stanovich, K. E. (1991). Discrepancy definitions of reading disability: Has intelligence led us astray? *Reading Research Quarterly, 26*, 7–29.

Stanovich, K. E., & Siegel, L. S. (1994). The phenotypic performance profile of reading-disabled children: A regression-based test of the phonological-core variable-difference model. *Journal of Educational Psychology, 86*, 24–53.

Swan, D., & Goswami, U. (1997). Phonological awareness deficits in developmental dyslexia and the phonological representations hypothesis. *Journal of Experimental Child Psychology, 66*, 18-41.

Swanson, H. L., & Ashbaker, M. (2000). Working memory, short-term memory, articulation speed, word recognition, and reading comprehension in learning disabled readers: Executive and/or articulatory system? *Intelligence, 28*, 1–30.

Swanson, H. L., Ashbaker, M. H., & Lee, C. (1996). Learning-disabled readers' working memory as a function of processing demands. *Journal of Experimental Child Psychology, 61*, 242-275.

Swanson, H. L., Cooney, J. B., & McNamara, J. K. (2004). Memory and learning disabilities. In: B.Y. Wong, (Ed.), *Learning about learning disabilities* (3rd ed.) (pp. 41-80). San Diego, CA: Academic Press.

Tallal, P. (1980). Auditory temporal perception, phonics and reading disabilities in children. *Brain and Language, 9*, 182–198.

Tallal, P., & Stark, R. E. (1982). Perceptual/motor profiles of reading impaired chidren with or without concomitant oral language deficits. *Annals of Dyslexia, 32*, 163-176.

Temple, C. M. (1997). Cognitive neuropsychology and its application to children. *Journal of Child Psychology and Psychiatry, 38*, 27-52.

Templeton, S., & Scarborough-Franks, L. (1985). The spelling's the thing: Knowledge of derivational morphology in orthography and phonology among older students. *Applied Psycholinguistics, 6,* 371–390.

Torgesen, J. K., Alexander, A. W., Wagner, R. K., Rashotte, C. A., Voeller, K., & Conway, T. (2001). Intensive remedial instruction for children with severe reading disabilities: Immediate and long-term outcomes from two instructional approaches. *Learning Disabilities, 34*, 33-58.

Torgesen, J. K., Wagner, R. K., & Rashotte, C. A. (1994). Longitudinal studies of phonological processing and reading. *Journal of Learning Disabilities, 27*, 276-286.

Torgesen, J. K., Wagner, R. K., Rashotte, C. A., Burgess, S., & Hecht, S. (1997). Contributions of phonological awareness and rapid automatic naming ability to the growth of word-reading skills in second to fifth grade children. *Scientific Studies of Reading, 1*, 161–185.

Tunmer, W. E. (1989). The role of language-related factors in reading disability. In D. Shankweiler & I. Y. Liberman (Eds.), *Phonology and reading disability: Solving the reading puzzle* (pp. 91–131). Ann Arbor: University of Michigan Press.

Tunmer, W. E., & Bowey, J. A. (1984). Metalinguistic awareness and reading acquisition. In W. E. Tunmer, C. Pratt, & M. L. Herriman (Eds.), *Metalinguistic awareness in children: Theory, research, and implications* (pp. 144–168). New York: Springer-Verlag.

Tunmer, W. E., Herriman, M. L., & Nesdale, A. R. (1988). Metalinguistic abilities and beginning reading. *Reading Research Quarterly, 23*, 134–158.

Tunmer, W. E., & Hoover, W. A. (1992). Cognitive and linguistic factors in learning to read. In P.Gough, L. Ehri, & R. Treiman (Eds.), *Reading acquisition* (pp. 175–214). Hillsdale, NJ: Erlbaum.

Tunmer, W. E., Nesdale, A. R., & Wright, A. D. (1987). Syntactic awareness and reading acquisition. *British Journal of Developmental Psychology, 5*, 25–34

Vellutino, F. R., Fletcher, J. M., Snowling, M. J., & Scanlon, D. M. (2004). Specific reading disability (dyslexia): What have we learned in the past four decades? *Journal of Child Psychology and Psychiatry, 45*, 2-40.

Vellutino, F., Scanlon, D. M., & Spearing, D. (1995). Semantic and phonological coding in poor and normal readers. *Journal of Experimental Child Psychology, 59*, 76-123.

Verhoeven, L., Schreuder, R., & Baayen, H. (2003). Units of analysis in reading Dutch bisyllabic pseudowords. *Scientific Studies of Reading, 7*, 255–271.

Vogel, S. A. (1975). *Syntactic abilities in normal and dyslexic children*. Baltimore: University Park Press.

Wagner, R. K., & Torgesen, J. K. (1987). The nature of phonological processing and its causal role in the acquisition of reading skills. *Psychological Bulletin, 101*, 192-212.

Wagner, R. K., Torgesen, J. K., & Rashotte, C. A. (1994). Development of reading-related phonological processing abilities: New evidence of bidirectional causality from a latent variable longitudinal study. *Developmental Psychology, 30*, 73–87.

Wagner, R. K., Torgesen, J. K., Rashotte, C. A., Hecht, S. A., Barker, T. A., Burgess, S. R., et al. (1997). Changing relations between phonological processing abilities and word-level reading as children develop from beginning to skilled readers: A 5-year longitudinal study. *Developmental Psychology, 33*, 468–479.

Whitehurst, G. J., & Lonigan, C. J. (1998). Child development and emergent literacy. *Child Development, 69*, 848-872.

Willows, D. M., & Ryan, E. B. (1986). The development of grammatical sensitivity and its relationship to early reading achievement. *Reading Research Quarterly, 21*, 253–266.

Wilson, A. M., & Lesaux, N. K. (2001). Persistence of phonological processing deficits in college students with dyslexia who have age-appropriate reading skills. *Journal of Learning Disabilities, 34*, 394-400.

Wimmer, H. (1993). Characteristics of developmental dyslexia in a regular writing system. *Applied Psycholinguistics, 14*, 1-33.

Wimmer, H., Mayringer, H., & Landerl, K. (2000). The double-deficit hypothesis and difficulties learning to read a regular orthography. *Journal of Educational Psychology, 92*, 668-680.

Wimmer, H., Mayringer, H., & Raberger, T. (1999). Reading and dual-task balancing: Evidence against the automatization deficit explanation of developmental dyslexia. *Journal of Learning Disabilities, 32*, 473–478.

Wolf, M. (1991). The word retrieval deficit hypothesis and developmental dyslexia. *Learning and Individual Differences, 3*, 205-223.

Wolf, M., Bally, H., & Morris, R. (1986). Automaticity, retrieval processes, and reading: A longitudinal study of average and impaired readers. *Child Development, 57*, 988-1000.

Wolf, M., & Bowers, P. G. (1999). The double-deficit hypothesis for the developmental dyslexias. *Journal of Educational Psychology, 91*, 415-438.

Wolf, M., Bowers, P. G., & Biddle, K. (2000). Naming speed processes, timing, and reading: A conceptual review. *Journal of Learning Disabilities, 33*, 387–407.

Wolf, M., O'Rourke, A. C., Gidney, C., Lovett, M., Cirino, P., & Morris, R. (2002). The second deficit: An investigation of the independence of phonological and naming-speed deficits in developmental dyslexia. *Reading and Writing: An Interdisciplinary Journal, 15*, 43-72.

Zhang, J. (2004). *Development and intervention of morphological awareness in Chinese*. Unpublished MA thesis, Beijing Normal University, Beijing.

Zhou, X., & Marslen-Wilson, W. (1995). Morphological structure in the Chinese mental lexicon. *Language and Cognitive Processes, 10*, 545–600.

Ziegler, J. C., & Goswami, U. (2005). Reading acquisition, developmental dyslexia, and skilled reading across languages: A psycholinguistic grain size theory. *Psychological Bulletin, 131*, 3-29.

In: Abnormal Psychology: New Research
Editor: Helen D. Friedman and Paulina K. Revera

ISBN: 978-1-60692-636-9

Chapter 3

OVERGENERAL ATTACHMENT MEMORY: OVERGENERAL ATTACHMENT-RELATED AUTOBIOGRAPHICAL MEMORY IN CHILDREN

***Jessica L. Borelli*[1,] *Daryn H. David,*[1] *Michael J. Crowley*[2] *and Linda C. Mayes*[2]**

[1]Yale University [2]Yale University Child Study Center.
New Haven, Connecticut, USA

This research was supported by grants from National Science Foundation and the Center for Mental Health Promotion awarded to the first author. Special thanks are due to Nicki Hunter, Eric Langlois, Donald F. Nathanson, and Erika McCarty for their assistance with data processing, to Susan Nolen-Hoeksema, Kelly Brownell, Doug Mennin, and Nancy Suchman for their comments on an earlier draft, and to all of the children and families who participated in this project

ABSTRACT

Overgeneral memory, or the tendency to report general rather than specific autobiographical memories, has been explored from different theoretical perspectives and has been linked to depressive and anxiety symptoms. Another perspective, attachment theory, suggests that individuals with a history of difficult parenting may show a bias toward remembering more general rather than specific autobiographical memories. At present, however, empirical work that may disentangle the important role of early relationships on autobiographical memory function is lacking. This study examined the associations among depressive symptoms, dismissing attachment, and the specificity of attachment-related memory in a sample of school-aged children. A total of 97 children between the ages of 8 and 12 completed the Child Attachment Interview and the Children's Depression Inventory. Results indicated that children with a dismissing

---

[1] jessica.borelli@yale.edu; Yale University, Department of Psychology, Box 208205, New Haven, CT, 06520; phone: (203) 432-1557; Fax: (203)-432-7172

attachment organization are not more likely to report clinically-significant levels of depressive symptoms as compared to other children. In addition, dismissing attachment moderates the association between depressive symptoms and memory specificity, such that for dismissing children, there are no group differences in memory specificity across clinical and non-clinical depression groups, whereas non-dismissing children with clinically-significant symptoms have lower specificity as compared to non-dismissing children with non-clinical levels of symptoms. Results are discussed in terms of their contribution to the literature on overgeneral memory.

Keywords: overgeneral autobiographical memory, attachment, depressive symptoms

Overgeneral Attachment-Related Autobiographical Memory In Children

The tendency to report general rather than specific episodic memories about specific experiences has been discussed from various theoretical perspectives and has been linked to a variety of factors, including depression (e.g., van Vreeswijk & de Wilde, 2004), childhood trauma (e.g, Kuyken & Brewin, 1995), post-traumatic stress disorder (PTSD; e.g, McNally, 1998), and dismissing attachment (e.g., Hesse, 1999). However, despite the phenotypic similarities between these various conceptualizations of overgeneral autobiographical memory (OGM), the integration of research findings and theory has been minimal. Empirical and theoretical synthesis of the phenomenon of OGM can inform our understanding of the links between OGM, depressive mood states, and dismissing attachment, as well as begin to elucidate the mechanisms underlying OGM.

The largest body of research examining this construct has focused on OGM in the context of autobiographical memory and its links with mood disorders. Findings of the association between depression and impoverished or overgeneral autobiographical memory in children (e.g., Vrielynck, Deplus, Philippot, 2007), adolescents (e.g., Kuyken & Howell, 2006), and adults (e.g., van Vreeswijk & de Wilde, 2004) saturate the literature. The majority of this line of research has been conducted using a cue-word paradigm called the Autobiographical Memory Test (AMT: Williams & Broadbent, 1986), in which participants are given cue words (e.g., happy) and are told to generate a specific autobiographical memory within a fixed amount of time.

According to Williams (1996), OGM serves the primary function of affect regulation: Williams' *affect regulation hypothesis* states that retrieving OGM protects the individual from experiencing the intense, primary negative emotion associated with specific incidents (e.g., Hermans, Raes, Iberico, & Williams, 2006). In support of this assertion, OGM is associated with higher scores on measures of avoidant coping (Hermans, Raes, Iberico, & Williams, 2006). Williams (1996) hypothesized that OGM develops in the context of difficult childhood experiences –indeed, research indicates that individuals who have experienced a traumatic event report fewer specific autobiographical memories (e.g., Dalgleish et al., 2003). This tendency towards OGM, though perhaps adaptive during initial times in which the individual experienced adversity (Williams, 1996), becomes maladaptive over time, placing the individual at increased risk for the development of depression or anxiety. In other words, individuals with OGM experience less negative affect in response to stressful events in the short term, but the avoidance of negative affect is related to deleterious outcomes in the long-term. In support of this, research indicates that individuals who demonstrate low-specific memory on the AMT experience less distress following a stressful cognitive task (e.g., Raes, Hermans, Williams, & Eelen, 2006), but are less likely to recover from a Major Depressive Disorder (MDD) episode (Brittlebank, Scott, Williams, & Ferrier, 1993), and have poorer problem solving strategies (Goddard, Dritschel, & Burton, 1996) and more difficulty imagining the future (Williams et al., 1996). Additionally, prospective research in adults indicates that OGM may be a risk factor for the development of increased depressive and anxiety symptoms following a stressor (van Minnen, Wessel, Verhaak, & Smeenk, 2005, but see Spinhoven et al., 2006).

However, in recent years investigators have proposed an alternate hypothesis regarding generative autobiographical memory retrieval (e.g. Rubin, 1996), called the *strategic inhibition process*, which postulates that in contrast to the folk belief that retrieving specific details regarding an event increases one's emotional arousal (Philippot, Baeyens, & Douilliez, 2006), in reality it inhibits it (Conway & Pleydell-Pearce, 2003). This has been supported by the results of recent studies (e.g, Philippot et al., 2006), and instead inspires the hypothesis that OGM may be caused by the fear of emotional arousal accompanying increased specificity rather than the experience of the arousal itself.

A separate theoretical perspective drawing from developmental and clinical psychology traditions suggests that a lack of autobiographical attachment memory specificity may be linked to the quality of one's early relationships with significant caregivers. Specifically, attachment theory postulates that OGM for attachment memories is a cornerstone of dismissing attachment. Attachment typically is assessed in adults using the Adult Attachment Interview (AAI; George, Kaplan, & Main, 1984, 1985, 1996), and in children using the recently-developed Child Attachment Interview (CAI; Target, Fonagy, & Shmueli-Goetz, 2003; Shmueli-Goetz, Target, Datta, & Fonagy, 2004). Both are semi-structured interviews where individuals are classified into one of three traditional attachment categories (autonomous, dismissing, preoccupied), and may also receive a classification of disorganized. The interview first prompts individuals to characterize their childhood relationships with their parents at a broad level by generating adjectival descriptors of the relationship (e.g., loving, strict) and then directs them to support these broad characterizations with specific memories of interactions with parents. These episodic memories are then coded for their relevance and detail (Shmueli-Goetz et al., 2004).

Theory predicts that individuals classified as dismissing are thought to be more likely to state an inability to recall specific childhood memories and to report generalities rather than specific episodes with parents despite extensive interviewer probing (Hesse, 1999; Main, 2000). Similar to individuals with OGM, adults and children classified as dismissing "use strategies that minimize, dismiss, devalue, or deny the impact of negative attachment experiences" (Crowell, Fraley, & Shaver, 1999, p. 442). Dismissing individuals are thought to be avoidant of the memory and emotional experience of negative experiences with attachment figures, and the strategies that they use on the AAI are thought to reflect this experiential avoidance, including denying the impact of negative childhood events while idealizing the positive aspects of their caregivers. According to theory, the dismissing individual "avoid(s) discussion or consideration of a range of strong affects, such as fear, anger, disappointment, hurt, and loneliness" (Allen & Land, 1999, p. 330), and a lack of memory specificity is thought to serve this underlying goal of experiential avoidance.

Theorists propose that this lack of memory specificity has its roots in early interactions with parents who reject or minimize the child's distress and do not encourage mental processing of the distress (e.g., Allen & Land, 1999; Main, 2000), thereby imparting the implicit message that times of distress are not worthy of reflection or deeper processing.

The tendency to focus on general attachment memories is thought to be a relatively stable phenomenon in dismissing individuals and one that is unrelated to depression. In fact, extant research does not support a link between dismissing attachment and depressive symptomatology (e.g., Tyrrell, Dozier, Teague, & Fallot, 1999). Importantly, attachment classification on the AAI is unrelated to other assessments of general autobiographical memory, verbal or performance intelligence (Bakermans-Kranenburg & van IJzendoorn, 1993), and performance on similar semi-structured interviews examining work experiences (Crowell et al., 1996). In other words, according to theory, OGM in dismissing individuals is specific to their discussion of attachment-related memories. To date, however, the link between attachment-related OGM, dismissing attachment, and depressive symptoms has not been examined.

Important distinctions regarding OGM exist between the autobiographical memory research literature and attachment theory. The first important distinction concerns the domain in which OGM is observed. Within the autobiographical memory literature, OGM is thought to be linked to all self-related autobiographical memories, or specifically to those that focus attention on the self in a threatening or evaluative way (Davis, 1987), whereas within the attachment framework, OGM is thought to be specific to memories relevant to experiences with primary caregivers. Second is the association of OGM with mood disorders. In the autobiographical memory literature, OGM is associated with MDD but is conceptualized not as an epiphenomenon of a mood state, but rather as a stable cognitive style that places individuals at risk for depression, which has been supported by research (e.g., van Minnen et al., 2005). In the attachment literature, OGM is thought to be related to dismissing attachment irrespective of the presence of mood disorder, and in fact research suggests that individuals with dismissing attachment do not have elevated rates of MDD relative to other types of insecure attachment (e.g., Tyrell et al., 1999). Therefore, whether a dismissing individual is depressed or not, one would expect him to show OGM for attachment topics.

The goal of this study was to begin to disentangle the interrelations between children's spontaneously-generated attachment memories, their attachment representations of primary caregivers, and their self-reported depressive symptoms. The association between depression and OGM on attachment measures has not been examined. Examining this association may afford an understanding of the developmental and relational roots of OGM, and may also inform our knowledge of the link between OGM and depression. Our hypotheses were twofold. First, we sought to evaluate the relationship between depressive symptoms and dismissing attachment. Based on previous findings with adults, we anticipated that dismissing children would not be more likely to report clinically-elevated levels depressive symptoms than children in other attachment categories. Second, in keeping with attachment theory, we predicted that dismissing children would show greater OGM independent of their levels of depressive symptoms, but that among non-dismissing children, a clinical level of depressive symptoms would be related to lower memory specificity. Given evidence that children's memory specificity is a function of age, with younger children reporting more general memories (Drummond et al., 2006), we controlled for age in all analyses.

METHOD

Participants

Ninety-seven children (56.6% boys) between the ages of 8 and 12 participated in the study. Participants were recruited from the community through a variety of means, including a mass mailing, flyers, and internet postings. Parents consented and children assented to participate in the study. The sample included 56.6% boys and of 43.3% girls with a mean age of 10.01 years old (35.1% 8, 18.5% 9, 16.5% 10, 15.5% 11 year-olds, and 14.4% 12 year-olds), with 86.6% Caucasian, 3.1% Hispanic, 3.1% African American, and 7.2% biracial children. Two children (2%) failed to complete the second study session due to schedule conflicts. Experimenters informed children that they could refuse to participate in any part of the study if they wished. Accordingly, data were missing due to failure to attend the second session (n = 2), refusal to answer questionnaires (n =4), and insufficient data due to skipped questions (n = 1). The cross-sectional design involved two sessions approximately one week apart which lasted 1.5 hours.

Measures

Attachment Interview. The Child Attachment Interview (CAI; Shmueli-Goetz et al.., 2004; Target et al., 1999) is a semi-structured interview designed for 8 to 13 year olds that previously has been used with clinical and non-clinical samples (Target, Fonagy, & Shmueli-Goetz, 2003), and consists of 19 questions concerning the child's current and past experiences with primary caregivers. Each interview is coded on 8 nine-point scales (e.g., Use of Examples) and is classified into one of four categories: secure, dismissing, preoccupied, and disorganized. The Use of Examples scale measures the "child's ability to provide specific episodes that are both relevant and detailed" (Shmueli-Goetz et al., 2004, p. 14), with higher scores indicating lower OGM.

Two different female doctoral students with extensive clinical training administered the interviews, which were then videotaped and transcribed, with both mediums utilized in the coding process. The interviews were then coded by researchers who had achieved coding reliability on the CAI with the authors of the measure and each other. Each interview was coded by one person and difficult cases were discussed and resolved between the two coders.

Test-retest reliability of scales and attachment classifications, internal consistency (ά = .94) and validity of the measure have been determined with both clinical and normative samples (Target et al., 2003). Attachment on the CAI is not predicted by age, gender, socioeconomic status, ethnicity, verbal IQ, or expressive language ability (Target et al., 2003).

Children's Depression Inventory. The Children's Depression Inventory (CDI; Kovacs, 1992) consists of 27-items designed to assess the behavioral, cognitive, emotional, and physiological features of depression. Participants choose one of three statements which best describes their symptoms over the past two weeks (e.g., "I am sad once in a while, ""I am sad many times," "I am sad all the time"). Responses are coded on a scale of 0 to 2, with higher scores indicating more severe depressive symptoms. For the purposes of these analyses, we grouped children based on whether their CDI score fell above or below the mild clinical cut-off of 13 (Kovacs, 1992). The psychometric properties of the CDI have been well-established (Kovacs, 1992).

Procedure

Participants and their parents arrived at the laboratory and immediately completed informed consent (parent), assent (child), and a brief demographic form. Child participants completed the CAI during the first session and the CDI during the second session. Questionnaires were administered via computer using a program called Computerized Assessment and Presentation Engine (Fisher & Mayes, 2001). Each question was presented individually in both visual and auditory domains, the latter consisting of a pre-recorded voice recording of each question and the response choices. Child participants used a computer touchscreen to input their responses to questionnaires. This procedure was designed to minimize the impact of reading ability on participants' responses as well as human error introduced by data entry procedures.

RESULTS

Descriptives

T-Tests revealed significant gender differences in the CAI Use of Examples scale scores. With respect to this score, findings indicate that boys have lower scores on Use of Examples. The results of a bivariate correlation revealed that Use of Examples was negatively associated with CDI depressive symptom total scores, $r = -.29$, $p < .01$. A Chi-Square examining attachment classification with respect to mother as a dismissing/not dismissing dichotomy revealed a significant gender difference in distribution, with boys having a greater dismissing-not dismissing ratio than girls ($p < .05$), but no other attachment category-specific differences were apparent. The results of an ANOVA indicated significant attachment group differences in age, $F\ (3, 93) = 3.64$, $p < .05$, indicating that preoccupied children were older than secure, dismissing, and disorganized children. Due to the presence of statistically significant age and gender differences in variables, age and gender were utilized as covariates in all further analyses.

Dismissing Attachment and Clinically-Significant Depressive Symptoms

In order to evaluate whether dismissing children are more likely to report clinically-significant levels of depressive symptoms as compared to other children, we conducted two Chi-square analyses, the first one examining differences across all four attachment classifications (secure, dismissing, preoccupied, disorganized) and the second evaluating dismissing children compared to all non-dismissing children (see Table 1). The result of the first Chi-square was statistically-significant, indicating that disorganized children have a greater clinically-depressed/non-clinically-depressed ratio than other attachment groups ($p < .05$). The result of the Chi-square comparing dismissing children to non-dismissing children was not statistically-significant, indicating that the ratio of clinically-depressed to non-clinically-depressed of dismissing children was not significantly different than that of non-dismissing children.

Table 1. Dismissing Attachment and Depressive Symptoms

Depressive Symptoms	linical Symptoms	Non-Clinical Symptoms	Group Differences
CDI Total Score			*Pearson Chi-Square*
CAI Attachment Classification with respect to mother			
dismissing	5.69 (3.57)	3	26
secure	4.00 (3.78)	2	36
preoccupied	5.83 (5.12)	0	6
disorganized	10.00 (7.91)	7	10
			14.69**
CAI Attachment Classification for mother			
dismissing	5.69 (3.97)	3	26
non-dismissing	5.82 (5.87)	9	52
			.33

Note. *$p < .05$; **$p < .01$; ***$p < .001$.

Dismissing Attachment, Depression Group, and Attachment-Related Memory

The second primary goal of this investigation was to evaluate the contributions of dismissing attachment and depression group in the prediction of memory specificity. Based on the theorizing that overgeneral memory is only found in dismissing children (e.g., Allen & Land, 1999), a categorical attachment variable was created comparing dismissing children ($n = 30$) to children in all other attachment categories ($n = 67$). Based on evidence suggesting that a child's attachment to his mother is more predictive of social developmental outcomes (e.g., Steele, Steele, Croft, & Fonagy, 1999), we report data using CAI classification with respect to mother. Importantly, all analyses were also conducted with respect to father and the pattern of findings was identical.

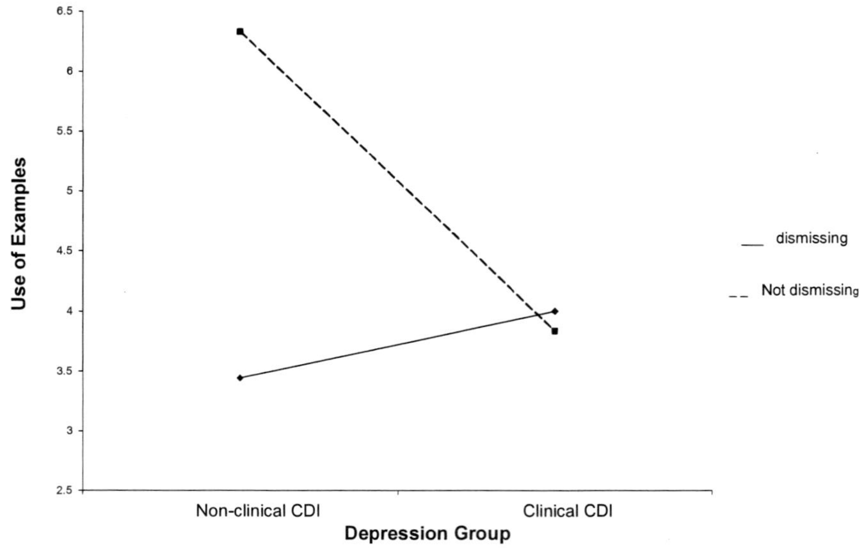

*Lower scores on Use of Examples Scale indicate reduced specificity of memories or higher OGM.

Figure 1. Interaction effect between dismissing Attachment and Depression Group in scores on Use of Examples Scale.

We evaluated these hypotheses using an ANCOVA: after controlling for age and gender, we entered the main effects of depression group and dismissing attachment and then entered an interaction term last (dismissing attachment x depression group), with Use of Examples as the dependent variable. Results revealed that age, F (1, 90) = 1.33, MSE = 2.73, p = ns, gender, F (1, 90) = 1.82, MSE = 2.73 , p = ns, and depression group, F(1, 90)= 2.28, MSE = 2.73, p = ns, were not significant contributors to the model, but that the main effect of dismissing attachment, F (1, 90)= 4.52, MSE = 2.73, $p < .05$, and the interaction between dismissing attachment and depression group, F (1, 90)= 6.12, MSE = 2.73, $p < .05$, were statistically significant. These findings indicated that dismissing children had lower memory specificity overall, and that among dismissing children, there are no group differences in memory specificity as a function of depression group. However, among children classified as secure, preoccupied, and disorganized, the previously documented relationship between clinically-significant symptoms of depression and low autobiographical memory specificity applies (see Figure 1).

Discussion

The tendency to provide overgeneral or non-specific memories of autobiographical experiences has been empirically linked to depression (e.g., van Vreeswijk & de Wilde, 2004) and theorized for its connection with dismissing attachment (e.g., Hesse, 1999). The autobiographical memory literature and attachment theory converge on the idea that OGM develops in reaction to adverse childhood experiences that prevent the individual from being cognitively aware of painful emotions in the short-term, but that ultimately result in deleterious outcomes later in development. To date, the links between depressive symptoms, dismissing attachment, and OGM have not been examined empirically. In an attempt to explore how children's cognitive models of their relationships with their caregivers may be related to the development of autobiographical memory processes, the current study evaluated associations among child-reported depressive symptoms, dismissing attachment classification, and attachment-related OGM in a sample of school-aged children.

Results revealed a nuanced relationship between these variables. Consistent with prior research, descriptive statistics revealed a negative association between depressive symptoms and memory specificity after controlling for age and gender: the greater the child's self-reported depressive symptoms, the lower his attachment-related memory specificity. Examining the link between OGM and depressive symptoms without taking dismissing attachment into account replicates previous findings of the link between depressive symptoms and OGM.

A central goal of this study was to evaluate whether dismissing children are more likely to report clinically-significant depressive symptoms. Given that both depressive symptoms and dismissing attachment have been implicated as correlates of OGM, evaluating whether high levels of depressive symptoms in dismissing children accounts for this relationship was essential. However, the results failed to support a link between clinically-elevated depressive symptoms and dismissing attachment classification in children, reducing the likelihood that depression is a common factor underlying the hypothesized association between dismissing attachment and OGM.

We also found that dismissing attachment moderated the link between depression group and attachment-related memory, such that for dismissing children, there were no differences in scores of OGM based on depression group, but for children not classified as dismissing (i.e., secure, preoccupied, or disorganized children), there was a group difference in memory specificity across depression group. This finding lends preliminary support to the assumption that OGM is unrelated to the presence of clinically-significant depressive symptoms in dismissing children (Hesse, 1999; Shmueli-Goetz et al., 2004). In contrast, children classified in other attachment categories only showed OGM if they also reported clinically-significant depressive symptoms. Therefore, at the broadest level, in this sample depressive symptoms are positively related to OGM if dismissing attachment is not taken into account, but when statistical models include dismissing attachment, the link between depressive symptoms and OGM drops out of the model. Furthermore, the association between dismissing attachment and OGM cannot be explained by higher rates of clinically-significant depressive symptoms in the dismissing group.

These findings can be interpreted in multiple ways. First, it appears that the previously documented association between depression and OGM does not hold for children classified as dismissing. This finding may be interpreted as reflecting the following: an absence of relation between depression and OGM in dismissing children, an underlying cognitive vulnerability to depression in the non-depressed dismissing children, or an underreporting of depressive symptoms among some dismissing children. There is evidence to support the notion that OGM may reflect an underlying vulnerability to depression: OGM is higher in individuals who were previously depressed (e.g., Mackinger et al., 2004) and predicts the onset of depression following a stressor in non-depressed adults (van Minnen et al., 2005, but see

Spinhoven et al., 2006). Alternatively, perhaps OGM is a stable trait in some (e.g., dismissing individuals) and an epiphenomenon of a depressed mood state in others (e.g., non-dismissing individuals). Additionally, perhaps there is a relation between depressive symptoms and OGM in dismissing children but reporting biases of dismissing individuals confound the effect. Research suggests that dismissing adults underreport psychological symptoms (Dozier & Lee, 1995; Kobak & Sceery, 1988), and this also may apply to dismissing children. The current study does not eliminate any of the competing interpretations but future research may be able to address these limitations through the use of multi-method and multiple informant designs.

Several additional caveats of the current study warrant mention. The first is that the study design was cross-sectional and correlational, precluding causal inferences. Attachment theory posits a link between rejecting or unresponsive parenting behavior and dismissing attachment (Ainsworth, 1967; Allen & Land, 1999; Main, 2000), but the link between specific types of caregiving behaviors and specific types of insecure attachment in middle childhood has not been established in this or other investigations. Nonetheless, our results do suggest that children's cognitive representations of relationships with their parents are concurrently related to autobiographical memory specificity.

Another important limitation of this study is the exclusive reliance on attachment-related autobiographical memories. Without a more general assessment of autobiographical memories, this study leaves open the possibility that findings can only be generalized to attachment-related topics. In other words, it is possible that the previously-observed depression-OGM relationship would be preserved in tasks tapping general autobiographical memory even while accounting for dismissing attachment. In fact, there is evidence that performance on an attachment interview is distinct from performance on non-attachment-related interviews involving autobiographical memory (Crowell et al., 1996). Future research addressing this topic would benefit from employing the AMT in conjunction with attachment interviews, in an attempt to further elucidate the links between depression, dismissing attachment, and the autobiographical memories for which OGM processes may be relevant.

In addition, future research ought to evaluate the influence of the affective memory valence on OGM in dismissing children. Some findings suggest that depression in adults is more strongly associated with OGM for positive, as opposed to negative, cues (e.g., Williams & Broadbent, 1986). Attachment theory predicts OGM in dismissing children both for positively and negatively valenced childhood events (Hesse, 1999; Main, 2000), but this has not been examined through empirical research. This study did not directly examine the links between memory valence and memory specificity, largely because on the CAI children generate their own adjectives, thereby constraining the researcher's ability to measure memory specificity for positive and negative cues. It is noteworthy, however, that in this sample low memory specificity was positively correlated with the tendency to describe relationships with parents with positive descriptors ($r = .74, p < .01$), indicating that the OGM observed in this sample is best accounted for by OGM for positively valenced descriptors.

Finally, this study employed a typically developing sample of children. For the purposes of the current investigation, which was preliminary in its investigation of attachment-related OGM, a low-risk, normative sample was desired. However, future research ought to incorporate longitudinal design, clinic samples of depressed children, multi-method assessment of psychopathology, multiple domains of autobiographical memory assessment, and the examination of high-risk populations.

This study offered a preliminary attempt to integrate different literatures' perspectives on lack of autobiographical memory specificity. Findings indicate that the previously-supported association between depression and OGM does not apply to children classified as dismissing –these children evidence similarly non-specific memories at high and low levels of depression. Future research should strive to continue to integrate the autobiographical memory and attachment literatures and to examine the potentially competing roles of dismissing attachment and depression in OGM.

REFERENCES

Ainsworth, M. D. (1967). *Infancy in Uganda: Infant care and the growth of love.* Oxford: Johns Hopkins Press.

Allen, J.P., & Land, D. (1999). Attachment in adolescence. In Cassidy, J., & Shaver, P.R., (Eds.), *Handbook of attachment: Theory, research, and clinicalapplications*. (pp. 319-335). New York: Guilford Press.

Bakermans-Kranenburg, M. J., & van IJzendoorn, M.H. (1993). A psychometric study of the Adult Attachment Interview: Reliability and discriminant validity. *Developmental Psychology, 29,* 870-879.

Brittlebank, A. D., Scott, J., Williams, J. M. G., & Ferrier, I. N. (1993). Autobiographical memory in depression: State or trait marker? *British Journal of Psychiatry, 162,* 118–121.

Conway, M. A., & Pleydell-Pearce, C. W. (2000). The construction of autobiographical memories in the self-memory system. *Psychological Review*, *107*, 261–288.

Crowell, J., Fraley, R.C., & Shaver, P. (1999). Measurement of individual differences in adolescent and adult attachment. In Cassidy, J. & Shaver, P.R., (Eds.),*Handbook of attachment: Theory, research, and clinical applications* (pp. 434-465). New York: Guilford Press.

Crowell, J.A., Waters, E., Treboux, D., O'Connor, E., Colon-Downs, C., Feider, O., Golby, B., & Posada, G. (1996). Discriminant validity of the Adult Attachment Interview. *Child Development, 67,* 2584-2599.

Dalgleish, T., Tchanturia, K., Serpell, L., Hems, S., Yiend, J., de Silva, P., & Treasure, J. (2003). Self-reported parental abuse relates to autobiographical memory style in patients with eating disorders. *Emotion, 3,* 211-222.

Davis, P. J. (1987). Repression and the inaccessibility of affective memories. *Journal of Personality and Social Psychology, 53,* 585-593.

Dozier, M., & Lee, Spring W. (1995). Discrepancies between self- and other-report of psychiatric symptomatology: Effects of dismissing attachment strategies.*Development and Psychopathology, 7,* 217-226.

Drummond, L.E. Dritschel, B., Astell, A., O'Carroll, R.E. & Dalgleish, Tim. (2006). Effects of age, dysphoria, and emotion-focusing on autobiographical memory specificity in children. *Cognition & Emotion, 20, 488-505.*

Fisher, S., & Mayes, L.C. (2001). Computerized assessment and presentation engine. (Version 3.0) [Computer software]. New Haven, CT: Yale University.

George, C., Kaplan, N., & Main, M. (1984, 1985, 1996.) *Adult Attachment Interview Protocol.* Unpublished manuscript, University of California at Berkeley.

Goddard, L., Dritschel, B., & Burton, A. (1996). Role of autobiographical memory in social problem solving and depression. *Journal of Abnormal Psychology, 105,* 609–616.

Hermans, D., Raes, F., Iberico, C., Williams, J.M.G. (2006) Reduced autobiographical memory specificity, avoidance, and repression. *Behavioral and Brain Sciences, 29,* 522.

Hesse, E. (1999). The Adult Attachment Interview: Historical and Current Perspectives.In Cassidy, J., & Shaver, P. (Eds.), *Handbook of Attachment: Theory, Research, and Clinical Applications* (pp. 395-433). New York: Guilford Press.

Holtgraves, T., & Hall, R. (1995) Repressors: What do they repress and how do they repress it? *Journal of Research in Personality, 29,* 306-317.

Kobak, R. R., & Sceery, A. (1988). Attachment in late adolescence: Working models, affect regulation, and representations of self and others. *Child Development, 59,* 135-146.

Kovacs, M. (1992). *Children's Depression Inventory Manual.* Los Angeles: Western Psychological Services.

Kuyken, W., & Brewin, C.R. (1995). Autobiographical memory functioning indepression and reports of early abuse. *Journal of Abnormal Psychology, 104,* 585-591.

Kuyken, W., & Howell, R. (2006). Facets of autobiographical memory in adolescents with major depressive disorder and never-depressed controls. *Cognition &Emotion, 20,* 466-487.

Mackinger, H. F., Leibetseder, M. F., Kunz-Dorfer, A. A., Fartacek, R. R., Whitworth, A. B., & Feldinger, F. F. (2004). Autobiographical memory predicts the course of depression during detoxification therapy in alcohol dependent men. *Journal of Affective Disorders, 78,* 61–65.

McNally, R. J. (1998). Experimental approaches to cognitive abnormality in posttraumatic stress disorder. *Clinical Psychology Review, 18,* 971–982.

Main, M. (2000). The Organized Categories of Infant, Child, and Adult Attachment: Flexible vs. inflexible attention under attachment-related stress. *Journal of theAmerican Psychoanalytic Association, 48,* 1055-1095.

Philippot, P., Baeyens, C., & Douilliez, C. (2006). Specifying emotional information: Regulation of emotional intensity via executive processes. *Emotion, 6,* 560- 571.

Raes, F., Hermans, D., Williams, J.M.G., & Eelen, P. (2006). Reduced autobiographical memory specificity and affect regulation. *Cognition and emotion, 20,* 402-429.

Rubin, D. C. (1996). *Remembering our past: Studies in autobiographical memories.* Cambridge, England: Cambridge University Press.

Shmueli-Goetz, Y., Target, M., Datta, A., & Fonagy, P. (2004). Child Attachment Interview (CAI) Coding and Classification Manual, Version V. Unpublished Manuscript, The Sub-Department of Clinical Health Psychology, University College London.

Spinhoven, P., Bockting, C.L.H., Schene, A.H., Koeter, M.W.J., Wekking, E.M., & Williams, J.MG. (2006). Autobiographical memory in the euthymic phase of recurrent depression. *Journal of Abnormal Psychology, 115,* 590-600.

Steele, H., Steele, M., Croft, C., & Fonagy, Peter. (1999). Infant-mother attachment at one year predicts children's understanding of mixed emotions at six years. *Social Development, 8,* 161-178.

Target, M., Fonagy, F., & Shmueli-Goetz, Y. (2003). Attachment representation in school-age children: the development of the child attachment interview (CAI). *Journal of Child Psychotherapy, 29,* 171-186.

Target, M., Fonagy, F., Shmueli-Goetz, Y., Datta, A., & Schneider, T. (1999). *The Child Attachment Interview (CAI) Protocol.* Unpublished manuscript, University College London.

Tyrrell, C., Dozier, M., Teague, G.B., & Fallot, R.B. (1999). Effective treatment relationships for persons with serious psychiatric disorders: The importance of attachment states of mind. *Journal of Consulting and Clinical Psychology, 67,*725-733.

van Minnen, A., Wessel, I., Verhaak, C., & Smeenk, J. (2005). The relationship between autobiographical memory specificity and depressed mood following a stressful life event: A prospective study. *British Journal of Clinical Psychology, 44,* 405 415.

van Vreeswijk, M. F., & de Wilde, E. J. (2004). Autobiographical memory specificity, psychopathology, depressed mood and the use of the Autobiographical Memory Test: a meta-analysis. *Behaviour Research and Therapy, 42,* 731-743.

Vrielynck, N., Deplus, S., Philippot, P. (2007). Overgeneral Autobiographical Memory and Depressive Disorder in Children. *Journal of Clinical Child and Adolescent Psychology, 36, 95-105*

Williams, J. M. G. (1996). Depression and the specificity of autobiographical memory. In D. C. Rubin (Ed.), *Remembering our past. Studies in autobiographical memory* (pp. 244-267). Cambridge, NY: Cambridge University Press.

Williams, J. M., & Broadbent, K. (1986). Autobiographical memory in suicide attempters. *Journal of Abnormal Psychology, 95,* 144-149.

Williams, J. M. G., Ellis, N. C., Tyers, C., Healy, H., Rose, G., & MacLeod, A. K. (1996). The specificity of autobiographical memory and imageability of the future. *Memory & Cognition, 24,* 116–125.

In: Abnormal Psychology: New Research
Editor: Helen D. Friedman and Paulina K. Revera
ISBN: 978-1-60692-636-9

Chapter 4

DEPRESSION AND A PARENTING INTERVENTION: CAN CAREGIVER DEPRESSION BRING A GOOD PARENTING INTERVENTION DOWN? THE CASE OF PARENT-CHILD INTERACTION THERAPY

Mark Scholes, Melanie J. Zimmer-Gembeck and Rae Thomas
School of Psychology, Griffith University, Queensland, Australia

ABSTRACT

Depressed caregivers who present for parenting assistance often display excess difficulties with maintaining positive parent-child interactions and report that they cannot manage their children's problem behaviours. In addition to this, they often report other life stressors such as marital distress, lack of social support and/or socioeconomic disadvantage. This confluence of problems means that engaging depressed caregivers in parenting services can be challenging and depression is believed to impede successful intervention outcomes. For example, research has shown that depressed participants are at increased risk of intervention dropout and that they more often fail to maintain positive parenting behaviours (Assemany & McIntosh, 2002; Forehand, Furey & McMahon, 1984). However, others have suggested that engagement in parenting interventions in order to improve parent-child relationships may provide additional benefits such as reducing caregiver stress and depressive symptoms (Sameroff, 2004). In this randomised controlled trial of Parent-Child Interaction Therapy (PCIT), we assessed depression using three methods -- an interview, a self-report questionnaire and observation. We anticipated that nonattendance and attrition would be higher in depressed compared to nondepressed caregivers. In addition, those who attended 12 weeks of treatment (n = 68) were compared to those on a supported waitlist (n = 27); we expected that caregivers receiving PCIT would have greater declines in depressive symptoms than those on the waitlist. Participants were female caregivers (age M = 34, SD = 8.9) and their young children (ages 3 to 7). Caregivers were at risk of child maltreatment based on a child maltreatment inventory and reported that their children had clinical levels of externalising symptoms. Survival analysis showed that attrition was similar to previous studies of PCIT and there was no significant difference in attrition rate when depressed and nondepressed caregivers were compared. Measures of attendance such as the number of missed appointments also did not differ between groups. Regarding parenting outcomes, treatment participants showed greater improvements in observed interactions with their children than those on waitlist. Yet, the anticipated difference between depressed and nondepressed caregivers was not found; groups did not differ when we compared observed interactions with children prior to treatment and during treatment, with the exceptions of reflections/descriptions and negative talk. When depression was compared, it declined similarly and rapidly for caregivers regardless of whether they were receiving PCIT or were on the waitlist. Caregiver depression does not correlate with attendance and length of PCIT or observed parent-child interactions when participants are female caregivers with high risk of maltreatment and children with behaviour problems. In summary, study findings suggest that PCIT is an effective intervention for improving the observed parenting skills of both depressed and nondepressed caregivers with young children, but PCIT is not directly implicated in reducing caregivers' depressive symptoms.

INTRODUCTION

Comprehensive literature reviews have documented that depressed mothers have difficulties maintaining positive parenting behaviours and have children with more mental health and behavioural problems (Downey & Coyne, 1990; Goodwin & Gotlib, 2002; Lovejoy, O'Hare, & Neuman, 2000). For example, compared to nondepressed caregivers, depressed caregivers have been found to be more negative when interacting with their children (Lovejoy et al.), and to have children who are more likely to develop internalising and externalising problems (Goodwin & Gotlib).

Caregivers with depression are likely to present to parenting interventions needing assistance with multiple problems, including child behavioural problems, marital distress, and/or other life stressors. Multiproblem families can create challenges for service providers who are attempting to work with caregivers to educate them in parenting skills and remediate parent-child relationships. The issue of how best to address each concern becomes important. It could be argued that the focus on one area may inadvertently impact positively on other areas. For example, it is possible that focusing on the parent-child relationship may promote functional improvements in both the child and the caregiver (Sameroff, 2004). This possibility has been of particular interest among those who provide interventions to improve parenting skills and child behaviour (see Webster-Stratton & Taylor, 2001).

The very general aims of most parenting interventions are to help parents have more positive relationships with their children, and to assist parents with skills to more competently and appropriately manage any child behaviour problems (Serketich & Dumas, 1996). Ultimately, better parenting and reduced child behavioural problems are expected to improve family and child life trajectories. Many reviews describe the various types of parenting interventions that have evidence of short-term effectiveness (see Webster-Stratton & Taylor, 2001; Thomas & Zimmer-Gembeck, 2007). However, parenting interventions do not help every family. Some families will dropout, fail to engage fully in the treatment, or fail to maintain positive changes beyond the time in treatment (Assemany & McIntosh, 2002). Due to these negative treatment outcomes, attempts have been made to identify the parent, child and family characteristics that increase or decrease the likelihood of success in parenting interventions. Maternal depression, socioeconomic disadvantage, and severity of the child's conduct problems are some characteristics that have been identified as potential moderators of treatment outcomes, which result in less positive outcomes for individuals and families (Assemany & McIntosh).

The focus in the study reported here was on maternal depression as a potential moderator of treatment outcome. There have been reports that maternal depression is predictive of treatment outcome, such as lower retention rates, and maternal depression has been found to be associated with reduced responsiveness to treatment in parenting interventions, such as less improvement in parent-child relationships when compared to nondepressed participants (e.g., Griest, Forehand, & Wells, 1981). However, in other studies such associations between depression and treatment outcomes have not been found (e.g., Kazdin, Mazurick, & Siegel, 1994). Consequently, it remains unclear whether maternal depression partially accounts for less positive caregiver and child outcomes in a parenting intervention.

Our first specific study aim was to compare patterns of intervention dropout and attendance between depressed and nondepressed caregivers. In addition, a randomised controlled study design was used to meet a second aim of comparing treatment participants to those in a supported waitlist comparison group. In each of the treatment and waitlist groups, nondepressed and depressed caregivers were identified and compared. In addition to assessing intervention attendance, parent-child interactions were observed and compared between groups to determine whether depression status was associated with differential responsiveness to the parenting intervention.

A third study aim was to examine whether completion of 12 weeks of a parenting intervention was associated with declines in caregivers' depressive symptoms. Improvements in depressive symptoms have been expected to be a correlate or outcome of participating in a parenting intervention, because of the provision of general support to caregivers, as well as the impact on maternal well-being that comes with improvements in parent-child relationships and associated reductions in family stress. Yet, there is limited evidence for such a side effect, and those researchers that have examined this question have found contradictory evidence; in some previous research it has been reported that maternal depressive symptoms improve as a by-product of participation in a parenting intervention (e.g., Hutchings, Appleton, Smith, Lane, & Nash, 2002), whereas in other studies this association has not been found (e.g., Irvine, Biglan, Smolkowski, Metzler, & Ary, 1999).

Measurement of Depression and Observations of Depressed Caregivers

To identify parents with depression, we used clinical interview, self-report, and observational methods. This system of measurement was more comprehensive than the techniques relied upon in most previous research in this area. Even though depression is recognised and accepted as a health priority area affecting large numbers of people for significant periods of time (Lovejoy et al., 2000; Nolen-Hoeksema, 2001), like many psychological constructs, the definition and measurement of depression continues to be debated (Tennen, Hall, & Affleck, 1995). The Diagnostic and Statistical Manual of Mental Disorders – Fourth Edition (DSM-IV, American Psychiatric Association [APA], 2001) has enabled researchers and clinicians to use a global definition of clinical depression based on specific criteria. Nevertheless, a variety of definitions of depression continue to appear in the research literature. This meant that it was best to use multiple methods and measures to better identify caregivers who met criteria for depression on different types of indicators.

In addition to using typical methods of assessing depression (i.e., a clinical interview and a depressive symptom inventory), an observational measure of depressive symptoms was developed for use in the current study. There has been limited use of observational methods for measuring depression. When observations have been used, it appears that the information gathered is somewhat divergent from self-report questionnaires and clinical interviews, and may have some advantages and disadvantages (Querido, Eyberg, & Boggs, 2001). The main advantage comes from the ability to include nonverbal behaviours (e.g., facial expressions, verbal quality, posture) as they relate to depressive symptomatology. Conversely, limitations include the inability to assess for exclusionary criteria, the lack of information about the stability of the presentation, and there are other characteristics of depression undetectable through observation.

No studies were located that have used observational methods as part of a set of measure that could be used to identify caregivers as depressed or nondepressed, but it seemed that observations should be used as a supplement to clinical interviews and self-report measures. For example, observed behaviours of parents have been found to differ when depressed and nondepressed caregivers are compared (Hops et al., 1987; Querido et al., 2001). In these studies, findings indicated that depressed caregivers show more negative affect (e.g., sad, anxious, dysphoric, self-focussed, despondency) rather than aggressive or irritable behaviour compared to nondepressed caregivers (Hops et al.; Radke-Yarrow, Nottelmann, Belmont, & Welsh, 1993). In contrast, in a separate study (Querido et al.), maternal depressive symptomatology (measured by the Beck Depression Inventory [BDI]; Beck, Steer & Brown, 1996) was assessed among 97 families with young children with oppositional defiant disorder. In this study, mothers who reported relatively more depressive symptomatology on the BDI had significantly more observed maternal physical negative behaviours (e.g., pushing, restraining, and hitting) as measured by the Dyadic Parent-Child Interaction Coding System – Second Edition (DPICS-II). However, no association was found between mothers' depressive symptomatology and maternal critical statements. Caregivers were all attending an intervention that provided assistance with parenting a young child (age 3-7) with behavioural problems. It was expected, therefore, that negative parenting behaviours may be prominent in participants, and would be more common and more resistant to change among depressed caregivers compared to nondepressed caregivers.

Parent-Child Interaction Therapy

The parenting intervention provided was Parent-Child Interaction Therapy (PCIT). PCIT is designed to improve the parent-child relationship and decrease behaviour problems via play and parental coaching. PCIT was specifically designed for children with significant behavioural problems and their caregivers (Eyberg, Boggs, & Algina, 1995; Thomas & Zimmer-Gembeck, 2007). In PCIT, the parent and child play together with a set of toys, while a therapist observes and coaches the parent from behind a one-way mirror with a microphone and earpiece device. PCIT has theoretical foundations in attachment theory and social learning theory (Foote, Eyberg, & Schuhmann, 1998). An aim in PCIT is to establish a nurturing relationship between the parent and child, while also learning to use appropriate disciplinary measures (i.e., selective attending and ignoring). Overall, the goal is to assist parents to create and attend to positive experiences with their children. Once the relationship between the parent and child has improved, additional disciplinary strategies (e.g., time out, removal of privileges) are coached. PCIT has been recognised as an empirically supported treatment for child behavioural problems (Chambless & Ollendick, 2000; Thomas & Zimmer-Gembeck, 2007; Webster-Stratton & Taylor, 2001).

PCIT has two phases – Relationship Enhancement (sometimes referred to as child-directed interaction or CDI) and Additional Skills (sometimes referred to as parent-direction interaction or PDI). The Relationship Enhancement phase is first and includes a didactic presentation on the PRIDE skills. These skills including teaching parents the importance of Praising, Reflecting, Imitating, Describing, and using Enthusiasm when interacting with their young children. Parents also are taught AVOID skills, which include limiting instructions, questions, and negative talk. This teaching session is followed by a series of coaching sessions targeted at meeting mastery criteria in these skills. Once these criteria are met over a course of sessions, caregivers enter the Additional Skills phase of PCIT. In this second phase, caregivers participate in a didactic session on effective instructions and consequences that can be used to manage significant child misbehaviours (i.e., removal of privileges and a time-out chair), followed by a series of coaching sessions designed to help caregivers gain competence and confidence in these skill. For more information about PCIT, see Hembree-Kigin and McNeil (1995).

We compared the outcomes of depressed caregivers with those of nondepressed caregivers. We also compared depressed and nondepressed caregivers who had been randomly assigned to PCIT treatment or a supported waitlist condition. A number of hypotheses were tested. First, depressed caregivers were expected to have higher rates of dropout than nondepressed caregivers. Depressed caregivers who completed 12 weeks of PCIT also were expected to 1) receive more personal support sessions (individual sessions that departed from the PCIT protocol), 2) to have a greater history of nonattendance and/or cancellations (DNA/CC) of scheduled appointments when compared to nondepressed caregivers, and 3) to have required more intensive treatment prior to completion of PCIT, including more sessions in the Relationship Enhancement Phase of PCIT compared to nondepressed caregivers.

Second, depressed caregivers, compared to nondepressed caregivers, were expected to have a lower percentage of positive behaviours (praises and reflections/descriptions) and a higher percentage of negative behaviours (questioning, giving instructions, and negative talk) when interacting with their children prior to participation in PCIT. Further, the percentage of praises and reflections/descriptions of depressed caregivers in treatment were expected to increase less than nondepressed caregivers in treatment from the pre- to the 12-week assessment, whereas the percentage of negative behaviours (questions, instructions, and negative talk) of depressed caregivers in treatment were expected to decrease less than nondepressed caregivers in treatment. We expected no changes in observed interactions between depressed or nondepressed caregivers and their children among those on the supported waitlist. Finally, we also investigated whether maternal depressive symptoms improved during involvement in treatment. We hypothesised that observed depressive symptoms would show greater improvements in the treatment group than in the supported waitlist.

METHOD

Participants

Participants were 95 female caregiver-child dyads who attended a university clinic for parenting assistance with a child between the ages of 3 and 7. Dyads were randomly allocated using a ratio of 2 to 1. Families were randomised to immediate PCIT or a supported waitlist. In total, there were 68 dyads who received PCIT and 27 who were allocated to a 12-week supported waitlist. Overall, 43% of families were referred from Department of Child Safety after a notification for maltreatment, whereas 17% were from government health agencies, 13% were self-referrals (often encouraged by Child Safety or similar agencies), and 27% were from other sources (e.g., paediatricians, schools). The mean age of female caregivers was 34 (SD = 8.9, range 20 to 58), and 87% were biological mothers. Other caregivers were stepmothers, grandmothers or foster carers. In regards to relationship status, 28% were married, 24% were in de facto relationships, 13% were separated/divorced, and 32% were single. The majority of caregivers were of low socioeconomic status, and most were Caucasian (96.8%) with other participants of Aboriginal or Torres Strait Islander descent. Children were aged 3 to 7 (age M = 60 months, SD = 20 months, range 27-98 months) with just a few children slightly younger than 3 and 1 child slightly older than 7 at pre-treatment. As expected given the focus on children's behavioural problems, 70% of children were male.

Measures

Treatment dropout and session attendance. Negative treatment outcome measures included dropout, counts of sessions provided, and the number of sessions not attended or cancelled. First, *dropout* was defined as any family who completed the pre-treatment phase but did not complete a 12-week assessment. Second, the total number of PCIT sessions and total number of Relationship Enhancement phase sessions (the first phase of PCIT) were documented. The number of additional individual sessions also was recorded. These sessions were provided when caregivers had significant concerns other than child behavioural problems that were regarded as too important to neglect. Last, the number of sessions not attended and/or cancelled by the client (DNA/CC) was recorded.

Maternal depressive symptomatology. The BDI-II, a clinical interview, and the Measure of Observed Depressive Symptoms (MOODS) were used to measure caregivers' depressive symptomatology. The MOODS is an observational coding system developed for use in the current study. After extensive examinations and comparisons of these measures (see Scholes, 2005), caregivers were classified as depressed and nondepressed based on the BDI-II and clinical interview. Caregivers who were diagnosed as depressed on the clinical interview *or* scored 20 and above on the BDI-II were classified as depressed. Caregivers who were not diagnosed as depressed on the clinical interview *and* scored below 20 on the BDI-II were classified as nondepressed. Because the MOODS assessment was not used to identify depressed caregivers, it was used as an outcome measure when depressed and nondepressed caregivers were compared.

The BDI-II is a 21-item self-report measure of depressive symptoms. It was developed for the assessment of symptoms corresponding to criteria for diagnosing depressive disorders listed in the DSM-IV (APA, 2001). The BDI-II has a score range from 0 to 63, with high scores indicating more depressive symptomatology. For example, a score of 10 on the BDI-II would be classified in the minimally depressed range. Whereas, a score of 20 would be classified as moderately depressed (Beck, et al., 1996). The BDI-II was measured three times; prior to assignment to PCIT or waitlist conditions, after 6 weeks of participation, and after 12 weeks of participation. The interitem correlation was adequate at all three assessments; Cronbach's α ranged from .61 to .87.

A semi-structured clinical interview also was conducted prior to treatment to assess current depression, among other factors. The length of the interview was usually 20 minutes and included questions about symptoms based on the DSM-IV criteria for depressed affect (e.g., worthlessness, loss of energy, concentration problems, sleeping irregularities, weight change). Symptoms were characteristic of a major depressive disorder, and participants responded to questions about chronicity of symptoms, past/present medication and other diagnosed disorders (e.g., bipolar disorder).

Finally, the MOODS measure was used to measure observed depressive symptoms. The MOODS was developed after reviewing the DSM-IV criteria and descriptions of depressed affect found in the literature (e.g., mental status examination). Caregivers were videotaped in the clinic therapy room for 10-minutes (a portion of the DPICS III measure) while playing with the accompanying child at pre- and 12-week assessment periods. Using a set of toys selected by the child, each caregiver was instructed to play with her child, while also allowing the child to direct the play and following the child's lead. To allow caregivers to relax and become more natural in their play prior to coding, observational coding was completed while observing the second 5 minutes of this videotaped interaction. Scores were assigned after observing caregivers' emotional expression, speech quality, and body posture. Each rating was made on a scale from 1 to 5. Response options included 1 (*no signs of depression*), 2 (*minimal signs*), 3 (*moderate signs*), 4 (*moderate-significant signs*), and 5 (*significant signs of depression*).

The coding system was initially developed, tested and revised by viewing and assessing five videos, along with comparing the observation and rating of the five videos with the clinical interview and BDI-II scores. This investigation was aimed at assessing the accuracy of the behavioural characteristics as indicators of depressive symptoms and allowed for necessary adjustments. Once the coding system was revised and appeared accurate in comparison to the clinical interview and self-report of depression, the coding system was shown to three registered clinical psychologists to assess the face validity of the observational characteristics of depressed affect. After discussions, small modifications were made.

One female and one male undergraduate psychology student were trained and coded videotapes. The initial training involved 5 hours of teaching the coders about the system, and practicing with videos of caregivers. Interrater reliability checks were completed before assigning videos for independent coding. An interrater reliability (i.e., the intra-class correlation) of .90 was found between the two coders and the first author. Coders did not watch more than one video of a caregiver (i.e., if they watched a pre-assessment video, they would not watch a 12-week assessment video). After they completed half the list of videos, another five randomly selected videos were used to reassess interrater reliability.

Observed parent-child interactions. The Dyadic Parent-Child Interaction Coding System – Third Edition (DPICS III) was used to assess a number of features of parent-child social interactions. DPICS III allows therapists to assess observed behaviours of caregivers when interacting with their children in the clinic setting (Eyberg, Duke, McDiarmind & Boggs, 2004). Generally, coding of observed interactions is in the form of counts of the frequency of skills that a caregiver uses with her child. The principle scales in DPICS III include praise, descriptions (information and behavioural), reflections (referred to as positive maternal behaviours) and instructions (direct and indirect) negative talk and questions (referred to as negative maternal behaviours).

Independent coders completed DPICS III coding while watching the videotapes of 5-minutes of parent-child interactions in the clinic. Assistants were blind to group membership, other measures, and had no previous contact with families. Five undergraduate psychology students were trained in the DPICS III and viewed all videotapes. After extensive training, high interrater reliability (i.e., the intraclass correlation) was found for praises, descriptions/reflections, negative talk, questions, and instructions, .99, .89, .78, .94, .94, respectively.

Procedure

Prior to randomisation, families attended a psychology clinic for two sessions. First, the primary therapist assigned to the family conducted an interview with the caregiver. This interview included gathering a complete history of depressive symptoms. In a second assessment session at the clinic, a 25-minute play interaction between the caregiver and child was videotaped.

Parent-Child Interaction Therapy condition. Eight therapists with more than one year of training and practice in PCIT provided the intervention. All were registered psychologists who also were postgraduate students under supervision. PCIT was provided at a university psychology clinic and sessions were held weekly. The intervention was not time-limited, so that families involved had a range of 1 to 47 sessions prior to attrition or completing treatment. For most sessions, the caregiver and child were situated in one room with up to three sets of play toys, while the therapist was in an observation room coaching the caregiver during her play with the child. Coaching occurred through an earpiece and microphone device.

Supported waitlist condition. Families allocated to the 12-week supported waitlist received weekly telephone contact from a PCIT therapist, in order to provide supportive counselling with personal issues and parenting-related stressors. To attempt some control over the services available to waitlist families and to reduce the likelihood of access to parenting interventions during this 12-weeks, family therapy and child behavioural management assistance were not recommended to the waitlist families. However, if they had individual concerns that seemed to require immediate assistance, the waitlist families were referred to community services for individual therapy or other support services.

RESULTS

Distributions of Measures and Examination of Analytic Assumptions

All continuous measures were assessed to determine if scores were normally distributed. Some distributions (the number of DNA/CC, the number of additional sessions, depression self-report scores, and three of the measures of observed parent-child interactions) were positively or negatively skewed and a few outliers were identified. Outliers were continually assessed throughout the following analyses, but removal of the participants with extreme scores did not significantly impact any of the results.

The assumption of equality of variance was assessed throughout the analyses using Box's M test. The test was never found to be significant, therefore the variability of measures and the covariance did not differ considerably when the treatment and waitlist groups were compared, $p > .001$. Mauchley's test of sphericity examined whether the correlation between treatment and waitlist was the same when more than two levels were used (i.e., BDI-II scores for pre-treatment, 6-week, 12-week). This assumption was violated and consequently, the Huynh-Feldt correction was used. Additionally, the Levene's test of homogeneity of variance revealed no significant problems with measures of depression.

Descriptive Information

As some data were only collected from participants in treatment (session attendance) and observation data were missing for eight participants due to poor video or sound quality, sample sizes ranged from 52 to 87. Means and standard deviations for all dependent variables are summarised in Table 1.

Treatment Attendance of Depressed and Nondepressed Caregivers

Dropout. It was predicted that the dropout rate for depressed caregivers in PCIT treatment would be higher than for nondepressed caregivers. This was not found. There was no significant difference in the dropout rate between depressed and nondepressed caregivers in PCIT, $\chi 2 = .16$, $p = .69$. About 32% of nondepressed caregivers did not complete the 12-week assessment, whereas about 36% of depressed caregivers did not complete this assessment. This finding was similar when only nondepressed and depressed participants in the treatment condition were compared.

Survival analysis was conducted to further describe dropout patterns of depressed and nondepressed caregivers, and to compare the groups. Results are illustrated in Figure 1. The vertical axis shows 100% survival (i.e., 0% attrition) on the left which declines as the number of scheduled sessions increased and families dropped out of the intervention (see Riegelman & Hirsch, 1996). Taking into account the timing of dropout, depressed caregivers tended to dropout slightly, but not significantly, earlier than nondepressed caregivers. However, depressed caregivers also had a slightly higher, but not significantly higher, final survival rate (around 56%) than nondepressed caregivers (50%), Wilcoxen $\chi 2 = .21$, $p = .64$.

Table 1. Means and Standard Deviations for All Continuous Dependent Variables

Dependent variable	*N*	*M*	*SD*
Observed depressive symptoms, pre	87	2.9	1.3
Observed depressive symptoms, 12-weeks	57	2.6	1.4
Number of total sessions	38	18.1	8.0
Number of additional sessions	38	0.9	1.2
Number of did not attend/cancellations	38	4.6	4.2
Number of relationship enhance sessions	38	10.1	4.4
Observed praises, pre, %	87	4.0	5.5
Observed praises, 12-weeks, %	57	11.1	11.0
Observed reflections/descriptions, pre, %	87	49.2	13.5
Observed reflections/descriptions, 12-weeks, %	57	58.0	15.5
Observed questions, pre, %	87	31.9	13.4
Observed questions, 12-weeks, %	57	21.7	17.2
Observed instructions, pre, %	87	12.5	10.1
Observed instructions, 12-weeks, %	57	7.8	6.8
Observed negative talk, pre, %	87	1.2	3.5
Observed negative talk, 12-weeks, %	57	1.4	3.3

Session attendance. It was expected that depressed compared to nondepressed caregivers assigned to PCIT treatment would have a greater number of additional sessions, DNA/CC, a greater number of relationship enhancement phase sessions, and a greater number of total sessions. To compare the two groups, three analyses of covariance (ANCOVA) models were estimated with depression status (depressed/nondepressed) as the independent variable. The number of total sessions was included as a covariate to adjust for differential time in treatment. Providing no support for our hypotheses, depressed caregivers did not differ from nondepressed caregivers in the numbers of additional sessions, DNA/CC, and relationship enhancement phase sessions, $F(1,54) = 1.6$, $F(1,53) = 0.1$, and $F(1,54) = 1.6$, respectively.

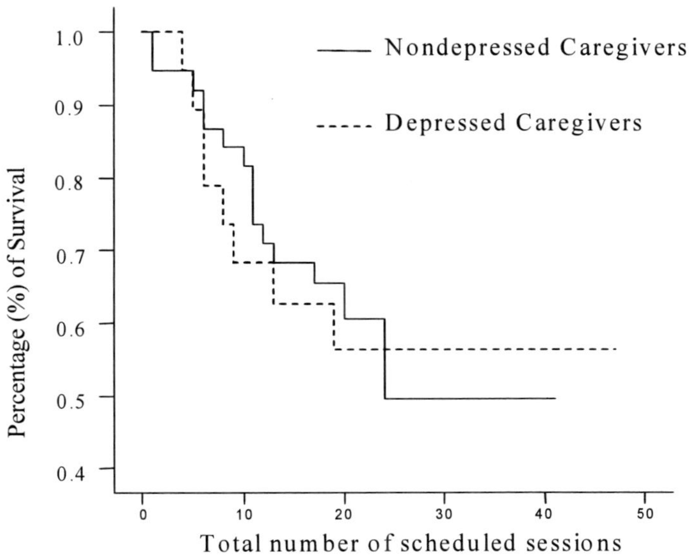

Note. Depressed $N = 19$, Nondepressed $N = 38$.

Figure 1. Survival of depressed and nondepressed caregivers during treatment.

Observed Parent-Child Interactions, Depression, and Treatment Versus Waitlist

Pre-assessment differences. Five t-tests were used to compare depressed and nondepressed caregivers on observed behaviours when interacting with their children prior to the start of treatment or the supported waitlist. No support for hypothesised group differences was found; there were no group differences in observed praises, reflections/descriptions, questions, instructions, and negative talk of depressed and nondepressed caregivers when assessed prior to treatment or waitlist (see Table 2).

Patterns of observed positive behaviours. It was predicted that the percentage of praises and reflections/descriptions would have increased less for depressed caregivers than nondepressed caregivers in treatment, but no changes were expected among nondepressed or depressed caregivers in the waitlist comparison group. Two repeated measures ANOVAs were estimated to test these predictions. The models had two between group factors (treatment condition and depression status), and one within group factor. In the first model, the dependent variable was observed parental praises of their children. In the second model the dependent variable was observed parental reflections and descriptions when interacting with their children.

Of most importance here, no significant 3-way interaction and no significant depression group x time interaction were found when observed praise was the dependent variable. Yet, a significant 2-way interaction was found between treatment group and time, $F(1, 46) = 17.0$, $p < .05$. Caregivers in PCIT treatment had a significant increase in observed praise, pre-treatment $M = 4.1$; $SE = 1.1$; 12-week $M = 14.5$; $SE = 1.9$; paired $t(1, 30) = 6.0$, $p < .05$. Caregivers on the waitlist showed no change in observed praise, pre-treatment $M = 5.8$; $SE = 1.4$; 12-week $M = 4.2$; $SE = 2.2$; paired $t(1, 18) = -.87$, $p = .40$.

Table 2. Comparisons of Pre-Assessment Parent-Child Interactions between Depressed and Nondepressed Female Caregivers

	Depressed caregivers		Nondepressed caregivers		
Dependent variable	*M*	*SD*	*M*	*SD*	*t*
Observed praises, pre, %	4.7	1.2	3.6	0.6	-0.9
Observed reflections/descriptions, pre, %	48.2	2.8	49.8	1.7	0.5
Observed questions, pre, %	29.0	2.4	33.4	1.8	1.5
Observed instructions, pre, %	12.9	2.0	12.4	1.8	-0.2
Observed negative talk, pre, %	2.0	0.9	0.8	0.3	-1.5

When observed reflections/descriptions was the dependent variable, a significant 3-way interaction was found, F (1, 46) = 4.8, p < .05. As shown in Figure 2, opposite to our expectation, depressed as compared to nondepressed caregivers receiving PCIT appeared to have a steeper incline in reflections/description, pre-treatment M = 47.6; SE = 4.9; 12-week M = 72.2; SE = 3.4, compared to nondepressed caregivers in treatment, pre-treatment M = 51.2; SE = 3.2; 12-week M = 65.5; SE = 2.2. In addition, there was a significant 2-way interaction between treatment condition and time, F(1, 46) = 21.6, p < .05. Caregivers in treatment were observed to increase in reflections/descriptions, pre- M = 50.1; SE = 2.9; 12-week M = 67.4; SE = 1.8; paired t(1, 30) = 5.9, p < .05, whereas caregivers on the waitlist showed no significant change with a mean of about 48.5 at both the pre- and 12-week assessments.

Patterns of observed negative behaviours. We predicted that observed parental instructions, questions, and negative talk when interacting with their children would decrease less for depressed caregivers than nondepressed caregivers in treatment; no changes in the waitlist were expected. Three repeated measures ANOVAs were performed with two between group factors (treatment condition and depression status), and one within group factor. The dependent variables were observed parental instructions, questions, and negative talk.

There were no significant 3-way interactions for observed instructions and questions, and no significant 2-way interactions between depression group and time. Yet, there was a significant 2-way interaction between the treatment condition and time for observed instructions, F(1, 46) = 4.4, p < .05. Instructions among caregivers in treatment decreased, pre- M = 10.2; SE = 1.9; 12-week assessment M = 5.3; SE = 1.2; paired t(1, 30) = -2.8, p < .05, whereas instructions among caregivers on the waitlist did not significantly change over time, pre- M = 9.7; SE = 2.3; 12-week M = 11.5; SE = 1.5; t(1, 18) = .53, p = .60. There also was a significant 2-way interaction between the treatment condition and time for caregiver questions, F(1, 46) = 12.2, p < .05. Questions among caregivers in treatment decreased, pre- M = 29.6; SE = 2.9; 12-week M = 10.9; SE = 2.3; paired t(1, 30) = -6.2, p < .05, but the questions among caregivers on the waitlist did not significantly change over time, pre- M = 35.7; SE = 3.5; 12-week M = 35.9; SE = 2.8; paired t(1, 18) = -.04, p = .97.

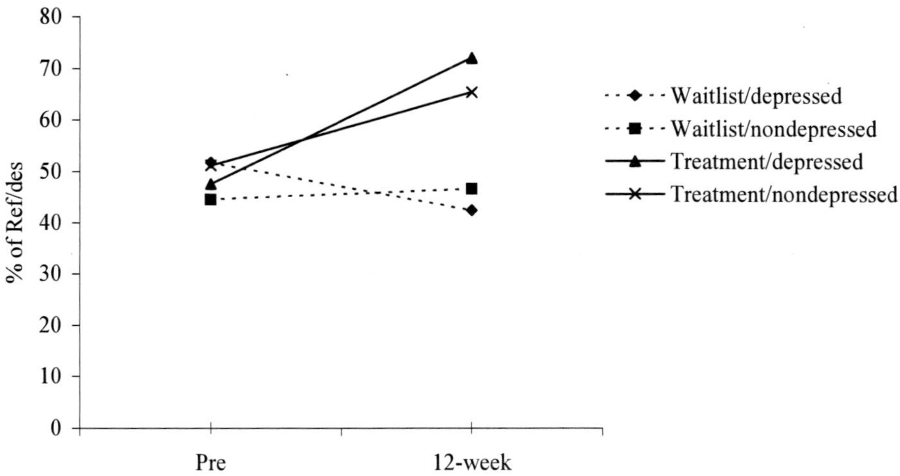

Note. Waitlist/Nondepressed N = 12, Waitlist/Depressed N = 7, Treatment/Nondepressed N = 22, Treatment/Depressed N = 9.

Figure 2. The 3-way interaction between depression status, treatment condition and time for reflections/descriptions.

Although the base rate of caregiver negative talk was quite low, a significant 3-way interaction was found, $F(1, 46) = 4.2, p < .05$. Yet, the results were not exactly as predicted. As shown in Figure 3, there was a trend for depressed caregivers on the waitlist to use more negative talk over time, pre- $M = 1.1$, $SE = .90$; 12-week $M = 6.1$, $SE = 1.1$; paired $t(1, 6) = 2.3$, $p = .06$. The other three groups of caregivers had levels of negative talk that were low and stayed very low between the pre- and 12-week assessments.

Treatment, Waitlist and Differences in Depressive Symptoms

It was hypothesised that caregivers' self-report of depressive symptoms would decline during participation in PCIT, whereas there would be no significant change in depressive symptoms among caregivers on the waitlist. A repeated measures ANOVA was used to test this hypothesis. The between-subject variable was treatment condition (treatment/waitlist). The within-subject variable was time (pre-assessment/12-week). The dependent variable was depressive symptomatology as measured by the BDI-II.

This hypothesis was not supported. There was no significant main effect for treatment condition, $F\ (1, 47) = .44$, and no significant interaction between time and treatment condition, $F\ (2, 46) = 1.7$. However, results revealed a main effect for time, $F\ (2, 47) = 5.0$, $p < .05$. Planned contrasts showed that, on average, the depressive symptoms of caregivers in both the treatment group and the waitlist group declined from the pre- to the 6-week assessment, but no significant change was found between the 6-week and 12-week assessments for either group (see Figure 4). More specifically, there was a difference between the pre-treatment BDI-II score and 6-week BDI-II score, $F\ (1, 71) = 4.7$, $p < .05$. Caregivers were highest in depressive symptoms at pre-assessment, $M = 13.6$; $SD = 12.1$, with significantly lower levels of depressive symptoms by the 6-week, $M = 10.1$; $SD = 9.4$, and 12-week assessments, $M = 10.0$; $SD = 9.9$. However, there was no significant change in depressive symptoms from the 6-week to the 12-week assessment, $F(1, 47) = .51$.

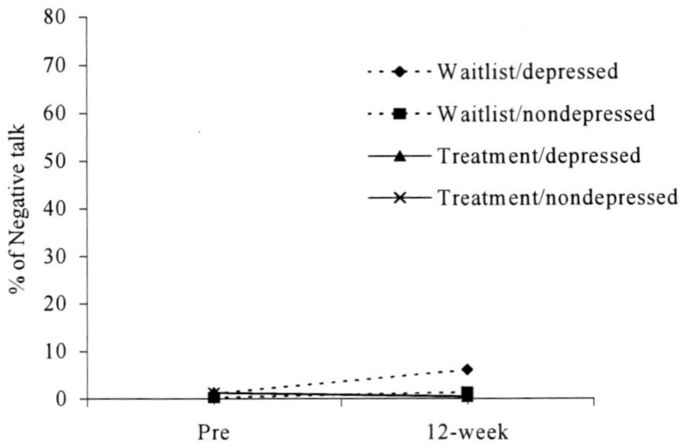

Note. Waitlist/Nondepressed $N = 12$, Waitlist/Depressed $N = 7$, Treatment/Nondepressed $N = 22$, Treatment/Depressed $N = 9$.

Figure 3. The 3-way interaction between depression status, treatment condition and time for negative talk.

A repeated measure ANOVA was used to test the prediction that observed maternal depressive symptoms (measured by the MOODS) would decrease from the pre- to the 12-week assessment among caregivers in treatment more than among caregivers on the waitlist. In support of this hypothesis, a significant two-way interaction was found between treatment condition and time, $F(1, 48) = 4.9$, $p < .05$ (see Figure 5). Caregivers in treatment displayed fewer depressive symptoms from the pre-assessment to the 12-week assessment, pre- $M = 2.9$; $SE = .3$; 12-week $M = 2.3$; $SE = .3$; paired $t(1, 33) = -2.7$, $p < .05$. There was no significant change in observed depressive displays among caregivers on the waitlist, pre- $M = 2.9$; $SE = .3$, 12-week $M = 3.2$; $SE = .3$, paired $t(1, 17) = .75$, $p = .46$.

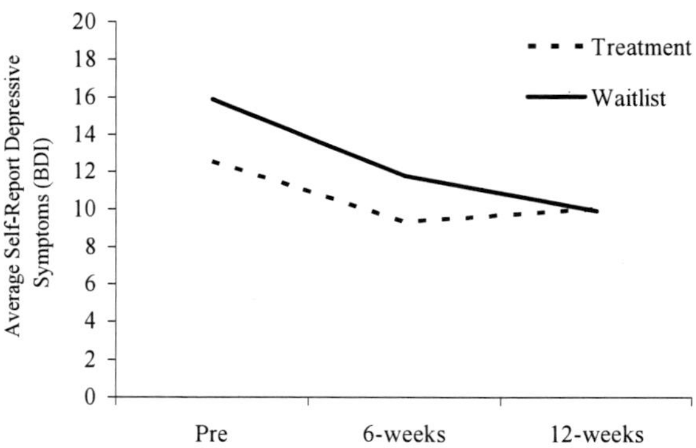

Note. Treatment $N = 34$, Waitlist $N = 18$.

Figure 4. The 2-way interaction between treatment condition and time for self-report of depressive symptoms (Beck Depression Inventory scores).

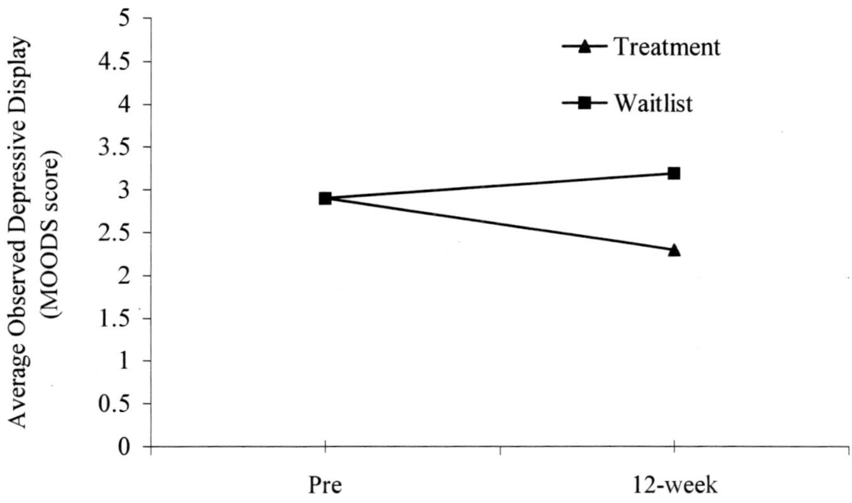

Note. Treatment $N = 34$, Waitlist $N = 18$.

Figure 5. The 2-way interaction between treatment condition and time for observed displays of depressive affect (MOODS scores).

CONCLUSION

There were three primary aims in the current study of Parent-Child Interaction Therapy (PCIT) and caregiver depression. The first aim was to examine the association between maternal depression and treatment retention/dropout after using a multimethod approach to identify caregivers who were or were not depressed. The second aim was to investigate whether there was a moderating effect of caregiver depression on intervention effectiveness, with effectiveness measured by repeated observations of caregiver verbalisations when interacting with their young children. Finally, the third aim was to test whether the parenting intervention had an influence on caregiver depressive symptoms when compared to a supported waitlist.

Caregiver Depression, Dropout, and Treatment Attendance

The first study aim was to examine the impact of caregiver depression on treatment attrition and attendance in a parenting intervention. Our findings support evidence from other studies that have reported no significant associations between maternal depression and negative treatment outcomes (Kazdin et al., 1994; Webster-Stratton & Hammond, 1990). Yet, a number of other researchers have reported associations between maternal depression and such negative treatment outcomes as dropout rates (Forehand, Furey, & McMahon, 1984; Griest et al., 1981; Kazdin, 1995; Kazdin & Wassell, 1999; McMahon, Forehand, Griest, & Wells, 1981). Much past research has been limited by methodological problems, such as a lack of diagnostic tools for depression classification and low pre-treatment questionnaire scores that were used to assess depression (see also Kazdin et al., 1997 who outlines some limitations of past research on negative treatment outcomes). We overcame this by using three measures of depression, including self-report, clinical interview and observational methods, and the self-report and clinical interview assessments were used to better identify depressed caregivers.

Overall, many authors have described the possibility of a link between maternal depression and negative treatment outcomes (e.g., dropout, disengagement, and lack of maintenance of treatment gains), but there has been little supporting empirical evidence for these hypotheses. Concern over caregiver depression interfering with treatment outcomes may not be completely justified, at least among mostly socioeconomically disadvantaged families who were referred to or self-referred to a parenting intervention and had children with behavioural problems. Some researchers have noted that no single factor is sufficient for establishing risk for negative treatment outcomes, but a range of characteristics accumulate as risk factors (e.g., socioeconomic disadvantage, maternal depression, severity of child conduct problems; Assemany & McIntosh, 2002; Kazdin, 1995; Serketich & Dumas, 1996). However, our isolation of depression shows that this caregiver characteristic has limited association with negative treatment outcomes in a parenting intervention when provided to socioeconomically disadvantaged female caregivers and their young children with behavioural problems.

Caregiver Depression and Parent-Child Interactions

Our second aim was to determine whether caregiver depression moderated parent-child interactions, measured at pre-assessment and following the intervention or waitlist condition. Overall, there was very little evidence of depression as a moderator. There were no significant differences in parent-child interactions (i.e., praises, reflections/descriptions, instructions, questions, and negative talk) between depressed and nondepressed caregivers at pre-assessment. Furthermore, depressed and nondepressed caregivers did not significantly differ in the amount of change in parent-child interactions from pre- to the 12-week assessments. Instead, improvements in parent-child interactions were found among all treatment participants when compared to those on the waitlist.

There is currently mixed evidence in the literature surrounding the link between maternal depression and observed parent-child interactions. Our findings of no initial differences in parent-child interactions of depressed and nondepressed caregivers are consistent with some previous literature (e.g., Chi & Hinshaw, 2002; Frankel & Harmon, 1996), but contradict other studies (e.g., Downey & Coyne, 1990; Lovejoy et al., 2000). Clearly, this is an area of research that warrants further attention.

Some research has shown that depressed and nondepressed caregivers only differ in their negative interactions, but do not differ with regard to positive interactions with their children (Lovejoy et al., 2000). Therefore, the percentage of praises and positive attention (assessed via reflections and descriptions) during caregiver-child interactions supports this proposition by showing that positive behaviours of depressed and nondepressed caregivers did not differ at pre-assessment and depression did not moderate the effect of treatment on these positive treatment outcomes.

Yet, the finding of little group difference and low rates of negative talk in both depressed and nondepressed caregivers is still perplexing. The low rates of negative talk made it difficult to be confident in our analyses of pre-assessment group differences and change in negative talk over time. It could be that the laboratory and play setting had the effect of minimising the frequency of negative talk. Observations in the home or other more natural settings should be considered in future research, but other work from our group has shown low levels of negative behaviours in home settings as well (McCarthy, 2006), and previous research has failed to find difference in behaviours observed in the laboratory and in home settings (Lovejoy et al., 2000).

There also were no differences between depressed and nondepressed caregivers when pre-assessment instructions and questions were compared, and there were no differences when the treatment outcomes of depressed and nondepressed caregivers were compared. Instructions and questions were considered to be negative aspects of caregivers' interactions with children during play. In PCIT, these are construed as negative, because caregivers who have children with behaviour problems are encouraged to reduce their use of questions and instructions during play, while increasing their praise and reflections of children's behaviours (Hembree-Kigin & McNeil, 1995). However, these behaviours cannot always be construed as negative outside the context of PCIT, and it is less surprising that these forms of female caregiver interactions with their children did not differ between depressed and nondepressed caregivers.

Depressive Symptoms During PCIT and Supported Waitlist Participation

When analyses were completed to investigate our third study aim (i.e., whether there was an association between treatment participation and depressive affect or observed depressive displays), improvements in self-reported depressive symptoms were found. On average, improvements in self-reported depression occurred early – between the pre-assessment and the assessment 6 weeks into PCIT or the waitlist condition; depression levels did not significantly differ between the 6-week and the 12-week assessments. Additionally, these early improvements were similar among female caregivers in treatment *and* on the supported waitlist, suggesting that decreased depression was not necessarily a by-product of participation in PCIT. These findings are consistent with some studies (Cunningham, Bremner, & Boyle, 1995; Irvine et al., 1999; McGillicuddy, Rychtarik, Duquette, & Morsheimer, 2001; Taylor, Schmidt, Pepler, & Hodgins, 1998), while conflicting with a few others (Barlow & Coren, 2005; Dadds & McHugh, 1992; Hutchings et al., 2002). For example, Irvine et al. found no significant changes in depressive symptoms, while Hutchings et al. found significant improvements in depressive symptoms through the course of a parenting intervention. These decreases in self-reported depressive symptoms that were found here were comparable to those reported in another study of PCIT with high risk families (Chaffin et al., 2004).

There are many possible explanations for the decrease in depressive symptoms when reported by caregivers, especially depressed caregivers. First, the waitlist condition was designed to be supportive in that caregivers were contacted each week in order to discuss concerns unrelated to parenting, along with gaining supportive counselling and referrals, when necessary. The regular contact with a supportive presence may have been associated with changes in caregivers' depressive symptoms. Second and related to this, the change in self-reported depressive symptoms may have been tapping a decrease in parental distress, rather than clinical depression, as has been suggested by others (Tennen et al., 1995). Caregiver distress may have been reduced by even a small amount of regular contact with a parenting intervention. These findings raise the issue that the presence of any kind of therapeutic support may be enough to reduce caregivers' depressive symptoms, and these symptoms will decline rather rapidly. The participation in a parenting intervention (e.g., PCIT), individual counselling, or even a combination of a parenting intervention with a depression component may be equally as effective in reducing caregivers' depressive symptoms. This is further supported by research that has found parenting interventions versus parenting interventions with enhanced components to directly focus on reducing depressive symptoms are similarly effective in reducing depressive symptoms of caregivers. For example, Chaffin et al., 2004 compared three different treatments (PCIT, PCIT plus individualised enhanced services, and a standard community-based parenting group) and found equally significant improvements in depressive symptoms (see also Sanders & McFarland, 2000).

Somewhat in contrast, however, when our measure of observed depressive displays by female caregivers (i.e., the MOODS observational measure) was used in a similar analysis, results were somewhat inconsistent with those found with self-reported depressive symptoms, and provide some support for an effect of PCIT on depressive displays. All caregivers in treatment were observed to improve on the MOODS from the pre-assessment to the 12-week assessment, whereas there was no significant change among caregivers on the supported waitlist. It is difficult to interpret this finding as showing only improvements in depressive symptom, however, because MOODS scores only had modest (but significant) correlations with other depression measures (self-report or clinical interview). The changes in positive parent-child interactions from pre- to post-treatment were similar to the changes seen in depressive displays among caregivers in treatment. Because the MOODS was coded by viewing caregivers interacting with their children, it is likely that the focus on promoting positive parent-child interactions had an influence on both parent-child interactions and MOODS scores, with caregivers reducing their depressive displays over time as they increased positive interactions with their children over time.

Limitations and Strengths of the Study

Similar to other empirical studies, depressed and nondepressed caregivers who initiated and at least completed the two pre-assessment sessions were included in the current study. This sample may not have been representative of all depressed caregivers with young children in the community. We were unable to gather information about the families who contacted the service, but did not attend at least the first session. It is possible that the individuals who attended the parenting intervention may have been unrepresentative in some way. For example, depressed caregivers in the study may have differed from other depressed caregivers on their level of motivation, level of initiative, willingness to receive help, or other factors that helped them commit to the intervention and display improvements in interactions with their children and reductions in their depressive displays.

Along with this limitation, there were a number of strengths to mention. First, a variety of assessments methods were used, including self-report (e.g., BDI-II), observations (e.g., DPICS-III), and therapist-reported attendance details. Thus, the findings were not dependant on only one reporter or type of assessment method. Second, this use of multiple methods also extended to the measure of depression. Third, a supported waitlist group was used to allow comparisons between caregivers participating in the treatment and those that were not. Due to the supported waitlist, it can be concluded that it was not PCIT that was associated with improvement in self-reported depressive symptoms. Fourth, the depressed caregivers in the study had fairly high levels of depression making this study more generalisable to a sample of female caregivers with clinical levels of depression.

SUMMARY

In summary, caregiver depression has been often described as having a negative impact on parenting behaviour, child adjustment and outcomes of treatment for parenting and child problems (Brent et al., 1998; Downey & Coyne, 1990; Goodwin & Gotlib, 2002; Lovejoy et al., 2000; Southam-Gerow, Kendall, & Weersing, 2001; Stoolmiller, Duncan, Bank, & Patterson, 1993). Our findings suggest that this may not be the case among low socioeconomic status, female caregivers who attend an intensive intervention focusing on parenting behaviours for their young children with behaviour problems. With the high prevalence rate of depression among women (Chaffin, Kelleher, & Hollenberg, 1996; Lovejoy et al., 2000; Nolen-Hoeksema, 2001) and the negative long-term outcomes associated with child behavioural problems (Bor, Sanders & Markie-Dadds, 2002), it is critical that therapeutic attention focuses on intervening early when there are parenting and child behaviour problems in order to decrease problems or, at the least, undermine escalation. However, it may be difficult to simultaneously intervene in all areas of concern. This is where the current results may be useful. Parenting interventions have been found to be effective for parents with children who have significant behaviour problems (Webster-Stratton & Taylor, *h*impact on attendance and length of an intervention, and outcomes in terms of observed parent-child interactions. These findings should reduce concern that depressive symptoms might interfere with attendance and outcomes in a parenting intervention for female caregivers and their young children. Additionally, contact with an intervention, whether with weekly session or via a supportive phone call, is associated with declining caregiver depressive symptoms. This should alleviate some concern about the lack of effectiveness of parenting intervention when caregivers are found to have high levels of depressive symptomatology.

ACKNOWLEDGMENTS

A portion of this work was included in the Professional Doctoral Dissertation of Dr. Mark Scholes. We are grateful for financial support from the Future Directions Prevention and Early Intervention Trial funded by the Queensland Department of Child Safety, Australia. We extend a personal thanks to all the children and parents for their time and cooperation in this study, and our appreciation for therapeutic, and data collection and entry assistance from Dr. Angela Anthonysamy, Elbina Avdagic, Michelle Hanisch, Dr. Kate McCarthy, Leanne McGregor, Dr. Anne Stuksrud, and Judith Warner.

REFERENCES

American Psychiatric Association. (2001). *Diagnostic and statistical manual of mental disorders (4th ed.)*. Washington, DC: Author.

Assemany, A., & Mclntosh, D. (2002). Negative treatment outcomes of behavioral parent training programs. *Psychology in the Schools, 39*, 209-219.

Barlow, J., & Coren, E. (2005). Parental-training for improving maternal psychosocial health (Review). *Cochrane Library, Issue 2.*

Beck, A. T., Steer, R. A., & Brown, G. K. (1996). *Beck Depression Inventory Manual* (2nd Edition). San Antonio, TX: The Psychological Corporation.

Bor, W., Sanders, M. R., & Markie-Dadds, C. (2002). The effects of the Triple P- Positive Parenting Program on preschool children with co-occurring disruptive behavior and attentional/hyperactive difficulties. *Journal of Abnormal Child Psychology, 30*, 571-587.

Brent, D. A., Kolko, D. J., Birmaher, B., Baugher, M., Bridge, J., Roth, C., & Holder, D. (1998). Predictors of treatment efficacy in a clinical trial of three psychosocial treatments for adolescent depression. *Journal of the American Academy of Child and Adolescent Psychiatry, 37*, 906-916.

Chaffin, M., Kelleher, K., & Hollenberg, J. (1996). Onset of physical abuse and neglect: Psychiatric, substance abuse, and social risk factors from prospective community data. *Child Abuse and Neglect, 20,* 191-203.

Chaffin, M., Silovsky, J. F., Funderburk, B., Valle, L. A., Brestan, E. V., Balachova, T., Jackson, S., Lensgraf, J., & Bonner, B. L. (2004). Parent-child interaction therapy with physically abusive parents: Efficacy for reducing future abuse reports. *Journal of Consulting and Clinical Psychology, 72*, 500-510.

Chambless, D. L., & Ollendick, T. H. (2000). Empirically supported psychological interventions: Controversies and evidence. *Annual Review of Psychology, 52*, 685-716.

Chi, T., & Hinshaw, S. (2002). Mother-child relationships of children with ADHD: The role of maternal depressive symptoms and depression-related distortions. *Journal of Abnormal Psychology, 30*, 287-400.

Cunningham, C. E., Bremner, R., & Boyle, M. (1995). Large group community-based parenting programs for families of preschoolers at risk for disruptive behavior disorders: Utilization, cost-effectiveness, and outcome. *Journal of Child Psychology and Psychiatry and Allied Disciplines, 36*, 1141-1159.

Dadds, M. R., & McHugh, T. A. (1992). Social support and treatment outcome in behavioral family therapy for child conduct problems. *Journal of Consulting and Clinical Psychology, 60*, 252-259.

Downey, G., & Coyne, J. (1990). Children of depressed parents: An integrative review. *Psychological Bulletin, 108*, 50-76.

Eyberg, S. M., Boggs, S., & Algina, J. (1995). Parent-child interaction therapy: A psychosocial model for the treatment of young children with conduct problem behavior and their families. *Psychopharmacology Bulletin, 31*, 83-91.

Eyberg, S.M., Duke, M., McDiarmid, M., Boggs, S., Robinson, E., & Washington, E. (2004). *Dyadic Parent-Child Interaction Coding System Third Edition.* Unpublished manuscript. University of Florida.

Eyberg, S. M., & Robinson, E. (1983). Parent-child interaction training. Effects on family functioning. *Journal of Clinical Child Psychology, 11*, 130-137.

Foote, R. C., Eyberg, S. M., & Schuhmann, E. M. (1998). Parent-child interaction approaches to the treatment of child behavior problems. In T. H. Ollendick, & Prinz, R. J. (Eds.), *Advances in Clinical Child Psychology* (pp. 125-151). New York and London: Plenum Press.

Forehand, R., Furey, W. M., & McMahon, R. J. (1984). The role of maternal distress in a parent training program to modify child non-compliance. *Behavioral Psychotherapy, 12*, 93-108.

Frankel, K., & Harmon, R. (1996). Depressed mothers: They don't always look as bad as they feel. *Journal of the American Academy of Child and Adolescent Psychiatry, 35*, 289-309.

Goodman, S., & Gotlib, I. (1999). Risk for psychopathology in the children of depressed mothers: A developmental model for understanding mechanisms of transmission. *Psychological Review, 106*, 458-490.

Goodwin, S., & Gotlib, I. (2002). *Children of depressed parents: Mechanisms of risk and implications for treatment*. American Psychological Association: Washington, DC.

Griest, D. L., Forehand, R., & Wells, K. C. (1981). Follow-up assessment of parent behavioral training: An analysis of who will participate. *Child Study Journal, 11*, 221-229.

Hembree-Kigin, T. L., & McNeil, C. B. (1995). *Parent-child interaction therapy*. New York: Plenum Press.

Hops, H., Biglan, A., Sherman, L., Arthur, J., Friedman, L., & Osteen, V. (1987). Home observations of family interactions of depressed women. *Journal of Consulting and Clinical Psychology, 55*, 341-346.

Hutchings, J., Appleton, P., Smith, M., Lane, E., & Nash, S. (2002). Evaluation of two treatments for children with severe behavior problems: Child behavior and maternal mental health outcomes. *Behavioral and Cognitive Psychotherapy, 30*, 279-295.

Irvine, A. B., Biglan, A., Smolkowski, K., Metzler, C. W., & Ary, D. V. (1999). The effectiveness of a parenting skills program for parents of middle school students in small communities. *Journal of Consulting and Clinical Psychology, 67*, 811-825.

Kazdin, A. E. (1995). Child, parent and family dysfunction as predictors of outcome in cognitive-behavioral treatment of antisocial children. *Behavior Research and Therapy, 33*, 271-281.

Kazdin, A., Holland, L., & Crowley, M. (1997). Family experience of barriers to treatment and premature termination from child therapy. *Journal of Consulting and Clinical Psychology, 65*, 453-463.

Kazdin, A. E., Mazurick, J. L., & Siegel, T. C. (1994). Treatment outcome among children with externalizing disorder who terminate prematurely versus those who complete psychotherapy. *Journal of American Academy of Child and Adolescent Psychiatry, 33*, 549-557.

Kazdin, A. E., & Wassell, G. (1999). Barriers to treatment participation and therapeutic change among children referred for conduct disorder. *Journal of Clinical Child Psychology, 28*, 160-172.

Lovejoy, M., O'Hare, G., & Neuman, G. (2000). Maternal depression and parenting behavior: A meta-analytic review. *Clinical Psychology Review, 20*, 561-592.

McCarthy, K. (2006). *An observational study of high-risk mothers and children during a frustrating task*. unpublished dissertation, Department of Psychology, Griffith University, Gold Coast, Australia.

McGillicuddy, N. B., Rychtarik, R. G., Duquette, J. A., & Morsheimer, T. (2001). Development of a skill training program for parents of substance-abusing adolescents. *Journal of Substance Abuse Treatment, 20*, 59-68.

McMahon, R. J., Forehand, R., Griest, D. L., & Wells, K. C. (1981). Who drops out of therapy during parent behavioral training? *Behavioral Counselling Quarterly, 1*, 79-85.

Nolen-Hoeksema, S. (2001). Gender differences in depression. *Current Directions in Psychological Science, 10*, 173-176.

Querido, J. G., Eyberg, S. M., & Boggs, S. R. (2001). Revisiting the accuracy hypothesis in families of young children with conduct problems. *Journal of Clinical Child Psychology, 30*, 253-261.

Radke-Yarrow, M., Nottelmann, E., Belmont, B., & Welsh, J. D. (1993). Affective interactions of depressed and nondepressed mothers and their children. *Journal of Abnormal Child Psychology, 21*, 683-696.

Riegelman, R. K., & Hirsch, R. P. (1996). *Studying a study and testing a test: How to read the health science literature (Third Edition).* New York: Little, Brown and Company.

Sameroff, A. J. (2004). Ports of entry and the dynamics of mother-infant interactions. In A. J. Sameroff, S. C. McDonough, & K. L. Rosenblum (Eds.), *Treating parent-infant relationship problems: Strategies for intervention* (pp. 3-28). New York: Guilford.

Sanders, M. R., & McFarland, M. (2000). Treatment of depressed mothers with disruptive children: A controlled evaluation of cognitive behavioral family intervention. *Behavior Therapy, 31*, 89-112.

Scholes, M. A. (2005). *Female caregiver depression in Parent-Child Interaction Therapy: Identification, change, and moderation of treatment outcomes*. unpublished dissertation, Department of Psychology, Griffith University, Gold Coast, Australia.

Serketich, W. J., & Dumas, J. E. (1996). The effectiveness of behavioral parent training to modify antisocial behavior in children: A meta-analysis. *Behavior Therapy, 27*, 171-186.

Southam-Gerow, M. A., Kendall, P. C., & Weersing, V. R. (2001). Examining outcome variability: Correlates of treatment response in a child and adolescent anxiety clinic. *Journal of Clinical Child Psychology, 30*, 422-436.

Stoolmiller, M., Duncan, T., Bank, L., & Patterson, G. R. (1993). Some problems and solutions in the study of change: Significant patterns in client resistance. *Journal of Consulting and Clinical Psychology, 61*, 920-928.

Taylor, T. K., Schmidt, F., Pepler, D., & Hodgins, C. A. (1998). A comparison of eclectic treatment with Webster-Stratton's parents and children series in a children's mental health centre: A randomized controlled trial. *Behavior Therapy, 29*, 221-240.

Tennen, H., Hall, J. A., & Affleck, G. (1995). Depression research methodologies in *Journal of Personality and Social Psychology*: A review and critique. *Journal of Personality and Social Psychology, 68*, 870-884.

Thomas, R., & Zimmer-Gembeck, M. J. (2007). Behavioral outcomes of Parent-Child Interaction Therapy and Triple P - Positive Parenting Program: A review and meta-analysis. *Journal of Abnormal Child Psychology, 35,* 475-495.

Webster-Stratton, C., & Hammond, M. (1990). Predictors of treatment outcome in parent training for families with conduct problem children. *Behavior Therapy, 21*, 319-337.

Webster-Stratton, C., & Taylor, T. (2001). Nipping early risk factors in the bud: Preventing substance abuse, delinquency, and violence in adolescence through interventions targeted at young children (0-8 years). *Prevention Science, 2*, 165-192.

In: Abnormal Psychology: New Research
Editor: Helen D. Friedman and Paulina K. Revera
ISBN: 978-1-60692-636-9

Chapter 5

THE ROLE OF NEGATIVE AFFECTIVE VALENCE IN RETURN OF FEAR

Inneke Kerkhof*[1]*, Debora Vansteenwegen, Tom Beckers, Trinette Dirikx, Frank Baeyens, Rudi D'Hooge and Dirk Hermans
University of Leuven, Belgium

ABSTRACT

Epidemiological research shows that about 30 percent of the general population will develop an anxiety disorder at some point in life (Kessler, Koretz, Merikangas, & Wang, 2004). Unsurprisingly, much research is invested in unveiling the processes that are responsible for the origin and maintenance of anxiety disorders, as well as in the principles that constitute the core of successful treatment. The general efficacy of exposure-based treatments for these disorders is irrefutable. Nevertheless, return of fear after successful exposure is a common finding and constitutes a challenge for clinical practice and fear research.

According to contemporary learning theories, fear can be acquired through an associative learning process. In a fear conditioning procedure a neutral stimulus (the Conditioned Stimulus or CS) comes to evoke fear after it was repeatedly paired with an aversive stimulus (the Unconditioned Stimulus or US). From this perspective extinction – a decrease in conditioned responding to the CS due to repeated presentations of the CS alone – can be viewed as an experimental model for exposure therapy. Return of conditioned responses after extinction then can be seen as a model for relapse after treatment. Experimental research suggests that during a fear acquisition procedure the reinforced CS (CS+) does not only become a valid predictor for the US but also acquires a negative connotation that is resistant to extinction. This is in line with the clinical observation that even after avoidance behavior has been drastically reduced through exposure, spider fearful individuals continue to consider spiders as negative animals (Baeyens, Eelen, Van den Berg, & Crombez, 1989). This remaining negative valence

[1] Department of Psychology, University of Leuven, Tiensestraat 102, 3000 Leuven, Belgium
Tel : ++32 - (0)16 - 32.58.67
Fax : ++32 - (0)16 - 32.60.99
Email : Inneke.Kerkhof@psy.kuleuven.be

after extinction/exposure might function as an affective-motivational source for return of fear. Procedures that alter the valence of the fear eliciting stimulus after extinction/exposure (e.g., counterconditioning procedures) might then be effective in diminishing return of fear.

In this chapter, we will give an overview of the research literature on the role of affective valence in (return of) fear. In addition, we discuss results of an animal (mice) study that was designed to investigate the impact of a counterconditioning procedure after extinction on return of conditioned responding.

INTRODUCTION

The Possible Role of Negative Affective Stimulus Valence in Return of Fear

Epidemiological research shows that about 30 percent of the general population will develop an anxiety disorder at some point in life (Kessler, Koretz, Merikangas, & Wang, 2004). Not surprisingly, a lot of research is invested in unveiling the processes that are responsible for the origin and maintenance of fear, as well as in the principles that constitute the core of successful treatment. In this context, there have been a lot of developments during the last four decades. The general efficacy of exposure-based treatments for anxiety disorders is now irrefutable. For some anxiety disorders like simple phobia, treatment success is so high that it is almost unequalled in our health services in general (e.g., Öst, 1989). Also for disorders like panic disorder, agoraphobia, post-traumatic stress disorder and social phobia, treatment outcome of exposure-based treatments is generally good (e.g., Van Balkom et al., 1997). These positive developments have led to a shift in research goals. Because of the successes at the curative level, more attention has been devoted to primary and secondary prevention. Concerning the latter (secondary or relapse prevention) it is important to acknowledge that a number of patients – in spite of apparently successful treatment – experience a return of symptoms of fear and anxiety. For some this is a source for complete relapse. This return of symptoms of fear and anxiety after successful treatment is known as 'return of fear' (ROF, Rachman, 1989) and constitutes a challenge for clinical practice and fear research.

Contemporary models of human classical conditioning and more specifically of fear conditioning, provide a rich conceptual framework for the understanding of the etiology, maintenance and treatment of human fears and phobias (Craske, Hermans, & Vansteenwegen, 2006). The essence of these models is that they view classical conditioning as the acquisition of associations between memory representations. For instance, being repeatedly confronted with a panic attack (referred to as the Unconditioned Stimulus or US) in the context of a supermarket (referred to as the Conditioned Stimulus or CS), can lead to the formation of an association between the memory representations of both stimuli/events. Later confrontation with the CS will activate the representation of the US, as well as the fear that is associated with it. From this perspective, exposure therapy can be viewed as the clinical analogue of extinction (i.e., unreinforced presentations of the CS after acquisition that result in a decrease in conditioned responding). ROF after treatment then can be seen as the clinical analogue of return of conditioned responses after extinction.

In the context of the current chapter, two recent insights from fear research are important. First, during the last decennia it became clear that extinction does not reflect an 'unlearning' of the underlying CS-US association (Bouton, 2004). Instead, extinction reflects new (inhibitory) learning, leaving the initial CS-US association intact. This original association can be activated by several 'post-extinction events', resulting in a return of the extinguished responses. Examples of such post-extinction events are the mere passage of time ('spontaneous recovery'), a change of context ('renewal') or the presentation of US-only trials after extinction ('reinstatement').

A second relevant insight is that during a fear acquisition procedure the meaning of the CS alters in two important ways. The CS not only becomes a valid predictor for the US (which results in its presentation being accompanied by increasing levels of fear as the CS activates the expectation of US occurrence), but also acquires a negative connotation through evaluative conditioning (De Houwer, Thomas, & Baeyens, 2001). Hence, two types of learning co-occur in a fear conditioning procedure: expectancy or predictive learning (i.e., participants learn that the CS predicts US occurrence, they expect the US to follow when they see the CS) and evaluative learning (Hermans, Crombez, Vansteenwegen, Baeyens, & Eelen, 2002). Importantly, several studies found the acquired negative connotation of the CS – in contrast to its acquired signal-value – to be (rather) unaffected by an extinction procedure (Dirikx, Hermans, Vansteenwegen, Baeyens, & Eelen, 2004; Hermans et al., 2002; Vansteenwegen, Francken, Vervliet, De Clercq, & Eelen, 2006). Significant levels of negative valence can still be observed for the CS, even if extinction reduces the US-expectancy to pre-acquisition level (Hermans et al., 2002; Vansteenwegen et al., 2006). If we translate this to a clinical situation, these findings suggest that to the extent that the acquisition of clinical anxiety (e.g., agoraphobia) is based on the contingent presentation of an originally neutral stimulus (e.g., supermarket) and an aversive event (e.g., a panic attack), this might not only result in the supermarket becoming a valid predictor for a panic attack, but also in an affective shift for supermarkets. Moreover, the findings concerning the relative resistance to extinction of this acquired evaluative meaning suggest that exposure treatment for clinical fear might successfully reduce the expectancy component in clinical fear (and therefore might lead to diminished fear reactions), but might leave the acquired affective meaning relatively unaltered. In our example, this would mean that the patient no longer expects a panic attack when entering a large supermarket, and after successful exposure treatment again frequents these superstores, but still somehow dislikes them. Clinical experience indicates that this differential outcome can indeed be observed (Marks, 1987).

In addition to the fact that the CS-US association can survive extinction and hence form the basis for ROF, we consider the evaluatively conditioned, but extinction-resistant negative valence of the CS as a second possible source for the re-emergence of the original phobic fear. There are several ways in which residual negative associations could increase the risk of relapse. In general, negative stimuli are more easily associated with aversive outcomes than are neutral or positive stimuli (e.g., Hamm, Vaitl, & Lang, 1989). Moreover, negative valence is associated with action tendencies of escape and avoidance (e.g., Chen & Bargh, 1999). Encounters with the previously phobic object are therefore more likely to reinstate phobic fear if the object elicits negative affect then when it would elicit neutral or positive affect. An alternative route may follow from the emotion theory proposed by Lang (1995). According to Lang, all emotions can be situated in a two-dimensional space, with affective valence (positive/negative) and arousal (high/low) as crucial dimensions. These dimensions interact to constitute different emotions. Against this background, fear can be considered as an emotion characterized by a combination of negative valence and high levels of arousal. Extinction/exposure will lead to a significant decrease in arousal, but leaves the negative stimulus valence intact (cf. Hermans et al., 2002). Following this, fear for the CS may re-emerge relatively easily if this still negatively valenced CS is encountered in an arousing context and negative valence and a higher level of arousal are thus recombined. A reinstatement procedure, for example, that comprises presenting US-only trials after extinction, could be considered as a procedure that essentially endows the context with a higher level of arousal. Importantly, re-emergence of fear might even occur if the experienced arousal is in fact unrelated to the US. In our example this would imply that if after his/her treatment the patient enters a supermarket that is still endowed with negative valence, and he/she is aroused for reasons that are unrelated to this situation (e.g., bad news, too much coffee), this combination might lead to enhanced fear or even a new panic attack.

The findings concerning return of conditioned fear responses after extinction and extinction-resistant stimulus valence are both theoretically and clinically relevant. They suggest that simple extinction/exposure might not be sufficient and raise the possibility that procedures that alter the valence of the fear-eliciting stimulus could function as an adjunct to mere CS-only presentations and might be effective in diminishing ROF. Up till now, however, research on the role of negative affective stimulus valence in ROF is rather sparse, both in humans and animals. In line with our hypothesis two laboratory studies on reinstatement in humans found the remaining negative valence of the reinforced CS (CS+) after extinction to be predictive for the return of fear for this CS+ after reinstatement (Dirikx et al., 2004; Hermans et al., 2005). The more negative the CS+, the more reinstatement was observed. Further evidence comes from a study in spider phobics by Huijding and de Jong (2005), who found residual negative associations after exposure treatment to be predictive for symptom return (i.e., return of overt avoidance behavior) at two-month follow-up. The findings of these studies are, however, post-hoc and correlational. In the present chapter a study in laboratory rodents will be presented in which the role of negative affective valence in ROF was investigated *experimentally* by manipulating the valence of the CS+ after extinction through a counterconditioning (CC) procedure. Before we go into this study, we will first take a look at the literature on CC. In a typical CC procedure a CS is paired with a US of one affective sign (positive/negative) in a first phase and with a US of the opposite sign (negative/positive) in a subsequent phase (generally referred to as the CC phase). As explained above, two outcomes can co-occur when a CS is paired with a valenced US: expectancy-learning (the CS acquires signal-value, the US is expected to follow after the CS) and evaluative learning (the valence of the CS shifts in the direction of the valence of the US). Because in a CC phase a CS is paired with a new US, CC might affect both types of learning. In the next section we will look at studies that investigated the impact of CC on indices of evaluative learning. In human studies typical indices of evaluative learning are valence ratings and indirect reaction time tasks (e.g., the Affective Priming Paradigm of Fazio, Sanbonmatsu, Powell, & Kardes, 1986 or Greenwald, McGhee, & Schwartz's (1998) Implicit Association Test). In animal studies, evaluative learning is generally inferred from preference choice tests (e.g., two-bottle preference tests, Scalera, 2000). Subsequently, we will focus on CC in relation to expectancy-learning. Two indices commonly used to assess expectancy-learning in humans are electrodermal activity and US-expectancy ratings. In animals, expectancy-learning is often assessed with a suppression index (see further) or by scoring US-specific anticipatory behavior (e.g., defensive or appetitive responses).

The Influence of Counterconditioning on Indices of Evaluative Learning

As mentioned in the introduction, several studies provide evidence for evaluative learning to be resistant to extinction (see De Houwer, Baeyens, & Field, 2005 for an overview). It appears to be the case that once a stimulus has acquired a valence as the result of being paired with a liked or disliked stimulus, this acquired valence cannot readily be changed by repeatedly presenting this stimulus on its own. In a CC procedure a CS is not presented without US, but is paired with a new oppositely valenced US. Research on evaluative conditioning suggests that the new CS-US pairings in the second phase of a CC experiment have an impact on the evaluative value the CS acquired in the first phase. We will now give an overview of this research.

Several studies in humans looked at the effect of a CC procedure on evaluative learning. Baeyens, Eelen, and Van den Berg (1989) were the first to demonstrate that the conditioned valence of a CS can be eliminated and even changed into an opposite evaluation by a CC procedure. Baeyens et al. (1989) conducted a picture-picture evaluative conditioning study that started with a baseline measurement of valence followed by an acquisition phase in which neutral faces (CSs) were paired with liked, disliked or other neutral faces (USs). Following this acquisition phase, some of the CSs were involved in a CC treatment, which entailed that those CSs were paired with a new US of a valence opposite to the valence of the US with which they were previously paired. Other CSs were presented on their own during the second phase (extinction treatment), whereas still other CSs were not presented during the second phase (control treatment). After the second phase, participants were required to rerate the valence of all CSs (test). Results showed that the liking of extinction CSs and control CSs increased from baseline to test if they were paired with a positive US during acquisition, but decreased if they were paired with a negative US. Hence, the extinction procedure did not abolish the influence of the acquisition contingencies. In contrast, the liking of CSs that were submitted to a CC treatment was the same on baseline and test, with a trend towards a shift in valence in the direction of the US with which these CSs were paired in the second phase. The influence of the acquisition contingencies was thus eliminated by the CC treatment. Since this first study, successful CC effects were obtained in several other human studies using different evaluative conditioning paradigms (e.g., flavor-taste conditioning, Baeyens, Crombez, De Houwer, & Eelen, 1996; picture-picture conditioning, Lipp & Purkis, 2006), and different direct and indirect measures (e.g., ratings, Baeyens et al., 1996; the Implicit Association Test, Rydell & McConnell, 2006; Rydell, McConnel, Strain, Claypool, & Hugenberg, 2007; the Initial-Preference Task, Dijksterhuis 2004). A number of studies even succeeded in changing pre-existing (rather than recently acquired) attitudes through CC (e.g., the negative attitude towards spiders of spider phobics, Eifert, Craill, Carey, & O'Conner, 1988; implicit self-esteem, Dijksterhuis, 2004; racial prejudice, Olson & Fazio, 2006).

We are unaware of any animal study that looked at the impact of CC on evaluative learning (i.e., on the valence of the CS). Most likely this is related to the fact that adequate valence measures for animals are difficult to develop.

The Influence of Counterconditioning on Indices of Expectancy-Learning

In this section we will look at studies that investigated the impact of CC on indices of expectancy-learning. We are unaware of any experimental studies in humans that looked at the influence on expectancy-learning of pairing a CS with differently valenced USs in successive phases. Several studies in rats, however, have addressed this issue and looked at the impact of presenting CS-food pairings after CS-shock pairings or the reverse (Bouton & Peck, 1992; Brooks, Hale, Nelson, & Bouton, 1995; Delprato & Jackson, 1973; Peck & Bouton, 1990). In all these studies, the CS was found to evoke responding appropriate to the second US by the end of the second phase. Bouton and Peck (1992), for example, observed strong freezing responses (which are natural defensive responses of rats indicative of fear) towards a tone that was initially paired with shock. These freezing responses were, however, gradually replaced by head-jerk responses (which are appetitive responses a rat makes to auditory stimuli that have been associated with food) in a second phase in which the tone was paired with food. Hence, CC resulted in a shift in expectancy-learning; performance corresponding to the second association replaced performance to the first. An important note to make here is that even though CC was effective in establishing a new conditioned response towards the CS, this does not imply that the initially learned CS-shock association was destroyed. Similar to what was found for extinction, several studies found CC to be incapable of destroying the previously acquired association. In several studies by Bouton and colleagues (Bouton & Peck, 1992; Brooks et al., 1995; Peck & Bouton, 1990) rats received CS-shock pairings followed by CS-food pairings. Even though appetitive responses were observed at the end of the second phase, a return of the original fear response towards the CS was observed after the mere passage of time (i.e., spontaneous recovery, Bouton & Peck, 1992), after a change of context (i.e., renewal, Peck & Bouton, 1990) and after the presentation of a number of unsignaled shocks (i.e., reinstatement, Brooks et al., 1995). According to Bouton (2002, 2004), both extinction and CC reflect new context-dependent learning rather than unlearning. Hence, ROF can still occur after CC.

Counterconditioning as a Technique to Reduce Return of Fear?

Based on the aforementioned research, we can conclude that whereas extinction only seems to have an influence on expectancy-learning, CC seems to be capable of influencing both expectancy-learning and evaluative learning. Previous studies further suggest that ROF can still be observed after a CC procedure. These studies, however, do not exclude the possibility that ROF can be *reduced* by CC as in those studies the amount of ROF after CC was never compared to a control group that received no CC trials. Therefore, in the present mice study, we wanted to examine if CC can have a beneficial effect on ROF when a group that undergoes extinction and CC is compared to a group that only receives extinction trials. We expected to find less ROF after CC, based on the idea that the remaining negative valence of the CS+ after extinction can form an affective-motivational source for ROF and that this negative connotation can be changed through CC (and not through extinction).

Despite the fact that evaluative CC techniques are sometimes applied in clinical practice (e.g., Korrelboom, van der Gaag, Hendriks, Huijbrechts, & Berretty, 2008), experimental research on the effectiveness of applying such techniques to reduce (return of) fear is scarce.

There is only one experimental study we are aware of that has looked at the impact of changing valence through CC on fear. De Jong, Vorage and Van den Hout (2000) compared a group of spider phobics that received a standard one-session exposure treatment to a group that received an equally long treatment that consisted of exposure and CC. In the CC group, tasty food-items were used during the standard exposure exercises and the participants' favorite music was played. In contrast to what was expected, no difference in treatment efficacy was observed between both groups when tested immediately after treatment and at 1 year follow-up. Moreover, CC was not found to be more effective in altering the affective valence of spiders than regular exposure treatment; both procedures resulted in a significant reduction in the negative evaluation of spiders. There are, however, some important limitations to the De Jong and al. (2000) study. A first limitation is that the standard exposure sessions probably included several ingredients that may have helped to undermine the negative affective valence of spiders and can be conceptualized as forms of CC (e.g., accepting expressions by the therapist towards spiders, information about spiders that portrays them as tender, fragile and timid animals). A second remark is that both procedures altered the affective evaluations of spiders in a positive direction, but did not lead to the abolishment of spiders' negative valence; an important amount of negative valence remained after both treatments. Perhaps the CC procedure was too brief in duration or not of sufficient strength to neutralize the spiders' negative valence.

In the present study we wanted to further investigate the possible impact on ROF of a CC procedure aimed at changing the negative valence of the CS+. Therefore, a reinstatement study was set up in laboratory rodents (mice). In previous research in our lab (Dirikx et al., 2007), ROF after reinstatement was assessed in mice using a differential conditioned suppression paradigm. In a first phase, one CS was consistently paired with a US (foot shock) while another CS was not, resulting in selective suppression of previously trained instrumental behavior during the CS+. After the extinction phase, half of the animals (reinstatement group) received unsignaled USs while the other half (control group) did not. A differential return of conditioned responding was observed in the reinstatement group only. In the present study the same differential conditioned suppression paradigm was used, but with an extra phase added in between the extinction and reinstatement phase. During this phase, half of the mice (counterconditioning group; CC group) received CC trials during which the CS+ was paired with food pellets, while the other half (further extinction group; FE group) received additional extinction trials. We expected to find less reinstatement (i.e., ROF) for the CS+ in the CC group as compared to the FE group.

METHOD

Subjects

The subjects were 49 experimentally naïve female C57BL mice from Elevage Janvier, Le Genest St. Isle, France. All animals were kept under standard laboratory conditions on a 12h/12h dark-light schedule, with constant room temperature and humidity, standard lab chow and water ad libitum. The animals were between 91 and 105 days old at the start of shaping. The animals were food-deprived prior to the start of the study and maintained on 80 to 90% of their initial body weight.

Apparatus and Stimuli

Eight operant soundproof chambers (Coulbourn Instruments, Allentown, PA) were used for shaping and classical conditioning. The conditioned stimuli were 30 s tones (4000 Hz or 1000 Hz). Due to a procedural error the assignment of tones to CS-type was not fully counterbalanced across subjects; for 31 subjects the 1000 Hz tone was used as the CS+ and the 4000 Hz tone as the CS-, while for the remaining 18 subjects the reverse was true. A 200 ms foot shock (0.2 mA) was used as the US. Sucrose pellets (Noyes Precision Pellets, Formula F from Research Diets Inc., New Brunswick, USA) were used for shaping and classical conditioning. During the CC phase grain pellets (Noyes Precision Pellets, Formula A/I) were used because preference tests administered before the start of the experiment had indicated that the mice preferred these pellets over sucrose pellets[2]. All stimulus presentations and response registrations were programmed with Graphic State 3.0 software (Coulbourn Instruments, Allentown, PA).

Procedure

In the present study fear conditioning was assessed using a conditioned suppression paradigm. In a typical conditioned suppression paradigm animals are first shaped to emit an operant response (e.g., lever pressing, nose poking) to obtain a positive reinforcer (e.g., food pellets) until a stable response rate is reached. Following this pre-training a Pavlovian conditioning procedure (e.g., a tone followed by a shock) is superimposed on this ongoing operant responding. The conditioned effect is a disruption of the operant responding. If the animal is scared of the CS, it will probably freeze and emit fewer operant responses during the CS than in the immediately preceding pre-CS interval. Hence, learning of the Pavlovian associations can be derived from the amount of suppression of the operant response. This amount of suppression is measured by calculating a suppression ratio (A/A+B) with A and B representing response rates during the CS and during equal periods of time immediately before CS onset, respectively. A suppression ratio of .50 indicates an equal response rate in the presence of the CS versus in the absence of the CS, thus complete lack of suppression (i.e., no fear). Complete suppression of responding during the CS (i.e., strong fear) is represented by a ratio of 0. In the current study suppression of previously trained nose poking behavior was used as an index of fear conditioning.

The experiment consisted of six phases: shaping of instrumental responding, acquisition, extinction, CC or further extinction, reinstatement and test of conditioned emotional

---

[2] During the preference tests, mice had access to two different kinds of pellets (20 g of each kind) in their home cage for 14 hours. After this period, the intake weight for each type of pellet was calculated by subtracting the weight of the remaining pellets from the original weight. Three types of pellets were compared: standard purified pellets (Noyes Precision Pellets, Formula P), sucrose pellets (Formula F) and grain pellets (Formula A/I). A significant difference in intake weight was only observed between sucrose and grain pellets with mice eating more grain pellets ($M = 14$ g) than sucrose pellets ($M = 10$ g), $t(7) = -10.40$, $p < .0001$.

responding. The first three phases and the last phase were identical for all animals. The experiment took 116 days in total. One training or test session was scheduled per day and every session took approximately 30 minutes. The 49 mice were housed in seven groups of six animals and one group of seven animals that were initially tested together. On day 18 of the extinction phase, the mice were assigned to one of the four experimental groups. Thirteen mice (8 with the 1000 Hz tone and 5 with the 4000 Hz tone as CS+) were assigned to the CC-reinstatement group, 12 (1000 Hz: 8, 4000 Hz: 4) were assigned to the CC-control group, 12 (1000 Hz: 7, 4000 Hz: 5) to the FE-reinstatement group and 12 (1000 Hz: 8, 4000 Hz: 4) to the FE-control group. The mice were also rehoused so that reinstatement and control animals were in separate home cages. We did this to avoid that control mice would notice fear reactions in the mice of the reinstatement groups during and after the reinstatement phase.

Shaping. In an operant shaping procedure, all mice were gradually trained to use a nose poke device to obtain sucrose pellets. During the first six sessions, a CRF schedule (Continuous Reinforcement) was applied, implying that every nose poke was reinforced by delivery of a food pellet. In the first three CRF sessions additional food pellets were given every two minutes regardless of nose poking behavior to alert the animals to the very possibility of food pellet delivery, and to demonstrate the contingency between the mechanical sound of the food pellet dispenser and food pellet delivery. Subsequently, two FR5 (Fixed Ratio, 5 nose pokes) and two FR10 sessions were programmed, in which every fifth or tenth nose poke was reinforced, respectively. The FR sessions were followed by nine VR10 (Variable Ratio, 10 nose pokes) sessions, in which reinforcement occurred after a mean of 10 nose pokes (range 4-16). Subsequently, the mice received five sessions of VI 30 s (Variable Interval with a mean of 30 s) training during which a nose poke was reinforced after mean intervals of 30 s (range 15-45). Additional shaping sessions followed after these VI 30 s sessions because shaping was interrupted for a week and because we wanted to achieve high and stable response rates. These additional sessions consisted of two FR10 sessions, 10 VR10 and 11 VI 30 s sessions.

Habituation. Before the start of acquisition, one habituation session was scheduled. During this session both CSs were presented six times without US, superimposed on the VI 30 s schedule (i.e., superimposed on the ongoing operant nose poke response). Suppression of this nose poking response constituted the index of fear for the CSs in this and the following phases.

Acquisition. During acquisition a Pavlovian fear conditioning procedure was superimposed on the VI 30 s reinforcement schedule. One 30 s tone (CS+) co-terminated with a 200 ms foot shock. The second CS (CS-) never co-terminated with foot shock. Each of the 17 acquisition sessions contained 6 presentations of every CS with a mean inter-trial interval (ITI) of approximately 80 s.

Extinction. None of the tone CSs was followed by the US during the extinction phase. Otherwise presentation parameters were the same as during acquisition. There were 20 extinction sessions in total.

Counterconditioning or further extinction. After the extinction phase, half of the mice (CC group) received 17 CC sessions during which the CS+ was followed by delivery of a grain pellet, while the CS- was not. The other half of the mice (FE group) received further extinction sessions. For both groups the nose poke devices were removed from the chambers. We did this because pellets could only be delivered through one feeder hole in the chamber and we wanted to make sure that the mice of the CC group would notice the new contingencies (i.e., pellet deliverance is related to the presentation of the CS+ and not merely to nose poking like in the previous phases). For a similar reason (i.e., because the mice would learn that pellet deliverance is only related to CS+ and not to CS- presentations), the CS+ and CS- were presented blocked in this phase of the experiment. Each 30 minutes session consisted of 15 minutes during which the CS+ was presented six times with an ITI of approximately 100 s and 15 minutes during which the CS- was presented six times with an ITI of approximately 100 s.

Nose poke retraining. After the CC / FE phase, the nose poke devices were placed back in the chambers and all mice were retrained to nose poke at a stable rate. The mice received one FR5 session, five FR10 sessions and six VI 30 s sessions.

Reinstatement. During the reinstatement session, half of the mice of the CC group (CC-reinstatement group) and half of the mice of the FE group (FE-reinstatement group) received four unsignaled USs. The USs were administered at approximately 6 min, 10 min, 18 min and 23 min after the onset of the session. In the control groups (CC-control group and FE-control group) no USs were presented during the reinstatement session.

Test. Twenty-four hours after the reinstatement treatment a test session took place. During this test session both CSs were tested six times, without reinforcement.

RESULTS

Figure 1 provides an overview of the mean suppression ratios for the CS+ and CS- during the habituation, acquisition and extinction phase.

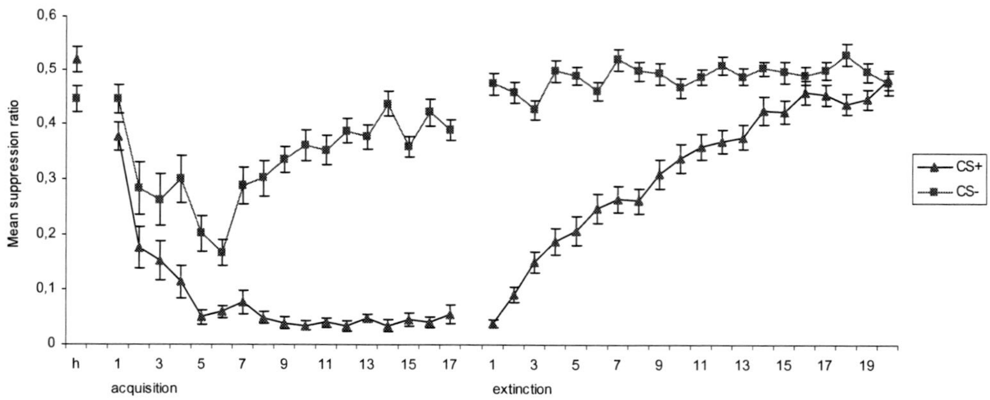

Figure 1. Mean suppression ratios for the total group during the habituation (h), acquisition (1-17) and extinction (1-20) sessions. Lower values represent stronger conditioned responding. Error bars represent standard errors of means.

Scoring and Statistics

The degree of fear conditioning was assessed by determining if the normally ongoing nose poking behavior was disrupted by the CS presentations. To measure suppression to the tones, for each session a suppression ratio (A/A+B) was calculated with A and B representing response rates during the CSs and during equal periods of time immediately before CS onset, respectively. As explained earlier, a suppression ratio of .50 indicates complete lack of suppression and thus no fear, while complete suppression of responding (i.e., strong fear) during the CS is represented by a ratio of 0. An alpha level of .05 was used for all statistical tests.

Habituation and Acquisition

We expected to observe a similar low or absent amount of fear for both CSs during the habituation phase and at the very beginning of acquisition as both tones are initially new and neutral for the mice. An increase in fear throughout the acquisition phase was expected for the reinforced CS, while little or no change in fear was expected for the CS-. In terms of suppression ratios this implies that we expected high suppression ratios during habituation and at the beginning of acquisition. Throughout acquisition, we expected to observe a decrease in the suppression ratio for the CS+ and little or no change in the suppression ratio for the CS-. In addition, we expected to find no differences between the four experimental groups as all groups received the same stimulus presentations and contingencies in the habituation and acquisition phase.

As shown in Figure 1, the CS+ and the CS- elicited similar low amounts of suppression (i.e., low amounts of conditioned fear) during the habituation phase. The 2 (condition: reinstatement vs. control) x 2 (treatment: CC vs. FE) x 2 (CS-type: CS+ vs. CS-) analysis of variance (ANOVA) showed neither a main effect of CS-type, $F(1, 45) = 3.28$, $MSE = .04$, $p = .08$, nor a significant interaction with condition or treatment, both with $F < 1$. The mean suppression ratios for the CS+ and CS- were .52 and .44, respectively. The absence of a main effect of CS-type indicates that, in line with what we expected, the CS+ and CS- did not differ in the extent to which they elicited suppression (i.e., fear) before the start of the acquisition phase. The absence of an interaction with condition and treatment signifies that this effect is the same in the different experimental groups.

In comparison with the first acquisition session, suppression to the CS+ was much stronger by the end of acquisition, while for the CS- little change in suppression was observed. The mean suppression ratios for all 17 acquisition sessions are depicted in Figure 1. A 2 x 2 x 2 x 2 ANOVA with condition and treatment as between-subjects variables and CS-type and moment (first acquisition session vs. last acquisition session) as within-subjects variables confirmed the differential acquisition of conditioned suppression. The moment by CS-type interaction proved to be highly significant, $F(1, 44) = 37.50$, $MSE = .02$, $p < .001$, clearly showing differential acquisition of fear. There was a significant increase in suppression and thus in conditioned fear for the CS+, $F(1, 44) = 120.73$, $MSE = .02$, $p < .001$, with mean suppression ratios of .38 and .05 during the first and last acquisition session, respectively. For the CS-, on the other hand, no significant change in suppression (i.e., in conditioned fear) was observed from the first to the last acquisition session, $F(1, 44) = 3.32$, $MSE = .02$, $p = .08$, with mean suppression ratios of .45 and .39, respectively. None of these effects interacted with the condition or treatment variables. A similar pattern of data was thus observed in the different experimental groups.

In conclusion we can say that the results of the habituation and acquisition phase were fully in line with expectations. Similar low amounts of conditioned fear were observed for the

CS+ and CS- during habituation and at the beginning of acquisition. Throughout the acquisition phase the mice gradually acquired the differential contingencies between the CSs and the US and showed an increase in conditioned fear for the CS+ but not for the CS-.

Extinction

During the extinction phase, we expected to observe a gradual diminishment of the conditioned fear for the CS+. By the end of extinction we expected the CS+ to elicit similar low amounts of fear as the CS-. In terms of suppression ratios we thus expected to see an increase in the suppression ratio for the CS+ during extinction and high suppression ratios for both the CS+ and CS- at the end of extinction. Also for the extinction phase, no differences were expected between the four experimental groups as the extinction procedure was the same in all groups.

As shown in Figure 1, as predicted, the mean suppression ratio for the CS+ increased substantially from the end of acquisition to the end of the extinction phase. The difference in suppression elicited by the CS+ and CS- by the end of extinction was much smaller than the difference observed at the end of the acquisition phase. To test for extinction, the mean suppression ratios of the last acquisition session and the last extinction session were compared in a 2 (condition) x 2 (treatment) x 2 (CS-type) x 2 (moment) ANOVA. As expected, the moment by CS-type interaction was highly significant, $F(1, 45) = 89.75$, $MSE = .02$, $p < .001$. A significant decrease in suppression was observed both for the CS+ and CS-, with respectively $F(1, 45) = 299$, $MSE = .01$, $p < .001$ and $F(1, 45) = 10.81$, $MSE = .02$, $p < .01$, but this decrease was larger for the CS+ than for the CS-. In terms of conditioned fear this means that a reduction in fear was observed throughout extinction for both CSs with a particularly strong decrease in fear for the CS+. In addition, the analysis yielded significant main effects of moment, $F(1, 45) = 211.70$, $MSE = .01$, $p < .001$, and CS-type, $F(1, 45) = 80.34$, $MSE = .02$, $p < .001$. Overall, less suppression (i.e., less conditioned fear) was observed at the end of extinction in comparison with the end of acquisition and the CS+ elicited more suppression/fear than the CS-. At the end of extinction there was no significant difference between the mean suppression ratios for the CS+ ($M = .48$) and CS- ($M = .47$), $F < 1$. Hence, the CS+ and CS- no longer differed with respect to the amount of conditioned fear they elicited. None of the effects interacted with condition or treatment.

We can conclude that extinction has clearly taken place. In line with our predictions, a strong decrease in conditioned fear for the CS+ was observed throughout extinction. At the end of extinction both CSs elicited similar and low amounts of fear. The preconditions for investigating reinstatement (i.e., successful differential acquisition and extinction in all groups) were thus met.

Test of Reinstatement

The reinstatement manipulation was expected to lead to a return of conditioned fear for the CS+ but not for the CS- in the reinstatement groups, while the control groups were not expected to show any changes in comparison with responding during the extinction phase. Importantly, we expected to observe less return of fear for the CS+ in the CC-reinstatement group as compared to the FE-reinstatement group. In terms of suppression ratios this means that we expected a decrease in the suppression ratio for the CS+ in the reinstatement groups, with a stronger decrease for the FE-reinstatement group as compared to the CC-reinstatement group.

To test for reinstatement, the mean suppression ratio of the last extinction session was compared with that of the test session. Figure 2 shows the mean suppression ratios of the last extinction session and the test session per group. A strong return of conditioned responding for the CS+ was observed in the reinstatement groups. Contrary to what we expected, increased suppression (i.e., fear) was also observed for the control groups. Moreover, and also in contrast to our expectations, a similarly strong return of fear was observed for the CC groups as compared to the FE groups. A 2 (condition) x 2 (treatment) x 2 (CS-type) x 2 (moment) ANOVA confirmed this description of the data. The crucial test for differential reinstatement, the Moment x CS-type x Condition interaction failed to approach significance, $F(1, 45) = 2.03$, $MSE = .02$, $p = .16$. Importantly, the Condition x Moment interaction was significant, $F(1, 45) = 9.30$, $MSE = .03$, $p < .01$, indicating that the increase in fear was stronger in the reinstatement groups than in the control groups. The ANOVA revealed main effects of all three variables. Overall, the CS+ elicited more suppression/fear than the CS-, $F(1, 45) = 20.38$, $MSE = .02$, $p < .001$. More suppression/fear was observed during the test session in comparison with the end of extinction, $F(1, 45) = 60.56$, $MSE = .03$, $p < .001$, and more suppression/fear occurred in the reinstatement groups as compared to the control groups, $F(1, 45) = 12.56$, $MSE = .02$, $p < .001$. Further, a significant Moment x CS-type interaction was observed, $F(1, 45) = 20.36$, $MSE = .02$, $p < .001$, that indicated a stronger increase in suppression from the end of extinction to test for the CS+ as compared to the CS-. In other words, a stronger return of conditioned fear was observed for the CS+ than for the CS-. The fact that this interaction was not only significant in the reinstatement groups, $F(1, 45) = 17.99$, $MSE = .02$, $p < .001$, but also in the control groups, $F(1, 45) = 4.67$, $MSE = .02$, $p < .05$, signifies that differential spontaneous recovery of conditioned fear occurred in those last groups. Next, we analyzed the data separately for the CS+ and CS-. A significant Moment x Condition interaction was observed for the CS+, $F(1, 45) = 10.47$, $MSE = .02$, $p < .01$, with a stronger increase in suppression/fear for the CS+ in the reinstatement groups than in the control groups. This interaction was not significant for the CS-, $F(1, 45) = 2.00$, $MSE = .02$, $p = .16$. Hence, even though a differential ROF was observed both in the reinstatement groups and the control groups, the unsignaled USs in the reinstatement groups resulted in a stronger ROF for the CS+.

Next, we looked at whether this reinstatement effect was modulated by our CC manipulation. The Treatment x Condition x Moment interaction was, however, not significant for the CS+, $F(1, 45) = 1.14$, $MSE = .02$, $p = .29$. Hence, contrary to what we predicted, a similar amount of return of fear for the CS+ after reinstatement was observed in the CC-reinstatement group and the FE-reinstatement group. As we hypothesized that CC might also be effective in reducing return of fear due to spontaneous recovery, we compared the control groups to see if less spontaneous recovery for the CS+ alone or for the CS+ as compared to the CS- could be observed in the CC-control group as compared to the FE-control group. This was, however, not the case, both $F < 1$. Thus, in contrast to what we hypothesized, no effect was found of the CC treatment on ROF due to reinstatement or spontaneous recovery.

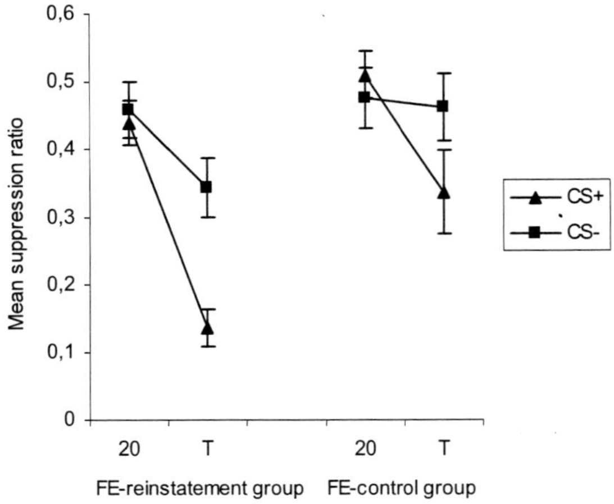

a

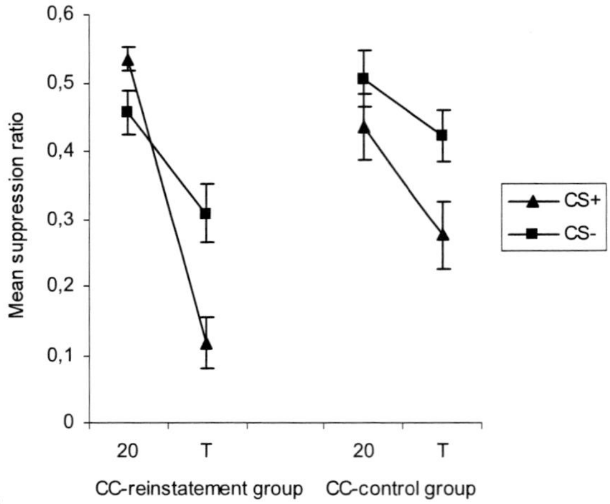

b

Figure 2. Mean suppression ratios for the last (20) extinction session and the test session (T) for the FE-reinstatement group (left hand side of a), the FE-control group (right hand side of a), the CC-reinstatement group (left hand side of b) and the CC-control group (right hand side of b). Lower values represent stronger conditioned responding. Error bars represent standard errors of means.

Conclusion

In the present study we wanted to investigate the impact on ROF of applying a CC procedure to diminish the negative valence of the CS+ after extinction. In a differential conditioned suppression paradigm in mice, successful differential acquisition and extinction of conditioned suppression were observed. Low amounts of fear were observed for the CS+ and CS- at the beginning of acquisition. Throughout the acquisition phase the mice gradually acquired the differential contingencies between the CSs and the US and showed an increase in conditioned fear for the CS+ but not for the CS-. The repeated presentation of the CSs in absence of the US led to the extinction of this differential fear. The preconditions for investigating reinstatement were thus met.

We failed, however, to replicate the differential reinstatement effect found by Dirikx et al. (2007). This was mainly due to the fact that a differential ROF (with a stronger return of conditioned responding for the CS+ as compared to the CS-) was not only observed in the reinstatement groups, but also in the control groups that had received no unsignaled USs. This phenomenon of a return of extinguished conditioned responding merely through the passage of time is known in the literature as 'spontaneous recovery' (for a review see Rescorla, 2004). In general, stronger spontaneous recovery effects are observed when the time delay between extinction treatment and test becomes longer (e.g., Quirk, 2002). The spontaneous recovery effect in the control groups of the current study is then probably due to the 12 sessions nose poke retraining that took place (and hence formed a delay period) in between the CC/FE phase and the reinstatement phase and during which no CS tones were presented. Future research could add a short extinction reminder phase (consisting of a few extinction sessions) before the test phase to prevent the occurrence of spontaneous recovery in the control groups. When the data were analyzed separately for the CS+ and CS- a stronger ROF for the CS+ was observed in the reinstatement groups than in the control groups. Hence, we can say that our reinstatement manipulation was effective and resulted in additional ROF for the CS+ in the reinstatement groups as compared to the control groups.

In contrast to what we predicted, no beneficial effect was found of the CC treatment on ROF due to reinstatement. An equally strong return of conditioned responding after the reinstatement manipulation was observed both in the FE-reinstatement group and in the CC-reinstatement group. As we hypothesized that CC might also be effective in reducing ROF due to spontaneous recovery, we compared the control groups to see if less spontaneous recovery could be observed in the CC-control group as compared to the FE-control group. This was not the case. Hence, we can conclude that our CC treatment was ineffective in reducing ROF due to reinstatement or spontaneous recovery.

Taken together, the data of the present study support previous studies that found that ROF can still be observed after applying a CC procedure (Bouton & Peck, 1992; Brooks et al., 1995, Peck & Bouton, 1990). In addition, the present data suggest that CC is also ineffective in *reducing* ROF by changing the negative valence of the CS+ after extinction. One possible interpretation of this finding is that the hypothesis that the extinction-resistant negative valence of the CS+ forms a source for ROF should be rejected. If we translate this to the clinical practice, our findings then suggest that combining standard exposure techniques with procedures which are specifically designed to reduce the negative valence of the fear-eliciting stimulus, not necessarily results in a lower relapse rate. An alternative explanation of our null finding, however, is that the valence of the CS+ was perhaps not (sufficiently) altered by our CC procedure. Since the valence of the CSs was not measured during the experiment, this alternative explanation cannot be excluded. The CC phase of the present experiment was longer than in other animal studies (e.g., Bouton & Peck, 1992; Brook et al., 1995; Delprato & Jackson, 1973; Peck & Bouton, 1990). Nevertheless, the 17 sessions of CC might still have been insufficient to alter the negative valence of the CS+. Although there is evidence that very short contingent presentations are already sufficient to change the affective valence of neutral stimuli (e.g., Baeyens, Eelen, Crombez, & Van den Bergh, 1992) or to neutralize the valence of previously conditioned stimuli (e.g., Baeyens et al., 1989), it may well be that a longer CC procedure or the contingent presentation of more intense or several positively valenced stimuli are necessary in case of stimuli with a very strong negative valence. In order to learn more about the role of stimulus valence in fear conditioning in animals, it will be important for further research to develop a valence/preference measure that can be administered during the experiment. Finding a good index for evaluative learning (certainly in the case of tone-CSs) is, however, not a simple task as it is often difficult to disentangle evaluative learning from expectancy-learning.

To conclude, the present results showed that ROF was not reduced by applying a CC procedure to diminish the negative valence of the CS+ after extinction. However, as we cannot definitely conclude that our CC procedure succeeded in changing the valence of the CS+, more research is needed to verify this conclusion.

References

Baeyens, F., Crombez, G., De Houwer, J., & Eelen, P. (1996) No evidence for modulation of evaluative flavor-flavor associations in humans. *Learning and Motivation, 27*, 200-241.

Baeyens, F., Eelen, P., Crombez, G., & Van den Bergh, O. (1992). Human evaluative conditioning: Acquisition trials, presentation schedule, evaluative style, and contingency awareness. *Behaviour Research and Therapy, 30,* 133-142.

Baeyens, F., Eelen, P., Van den Bergh, O., & Crombez, G. (1989). Acquired affective evaluative value - conservative but not unchangeable. *Behaviour Research and Therapy, 27*, 279-287.

Bouton, M. E. (2002). Context, ambiguity, and unlearning: Sources of relapse after behavioral extinction. *Biological Psychiatry, 52*, 976-986.

Bouton, M. E. (2004). Context and behavioral processes in extinction. *Learning & Memory, 11*, 485-494.

Bouton, M. E., & Peck, C. A. (1992). Spontaneous-recovery in cross-motivational transfer (counterconditioning). *Animal Learning & Behavior, 20*, 313-321.

Brooks, D. C., Hale, B., Nelson, J. B., & Bouton, M. E. (1995). Reinstatement after counterconditioning. *Animal Learning & Behavior, 23*, 383-390.

Chen, M., & Bargh, J. A. (1999). Consequences of automatic evaluation: Immediate behavioral predispositions to approach or avoid the stimulus. *Personality and Social Psychology Bulletin, 25,* 215-224.

Craske, M. G., Hermans, D., & Vansteenwegen, D. (Eds.) (2006). *Fear and learning: Basic science to clinical application.* Washington, DC: American Psychological Association.

De Houwer, J., Baeyens, F., & Field, A. P. (2005). Associative learning of likes and dislikes: some current controversies and possible ways forward. *Cognition & Emotion, 19*, 161-174.

De Houwer, J., Thomas, S., & Baeyens, F. (2001). Associative learning of likes and dislikes: A review of 25 years of research on human evaluative conditioning. *Psychological Bulletin, 127,* 853–869.

de Jong, P. J., Vorage, I., & van den Hout, M. A. (2000). Counterconditioning in the treatment of spider phobia: effects on disgust, fear, and valence. *Behaviour Research and Therapy, 11*, 1055-1069.

Delprato, D. J., & Jackson, D. E. (1973). Counterconditioning and exposure-only in treatment of specific (conditioned suppression) and generalized fear in rats. *Behaviour Research and Therapy, 11*, 453-461.

Dijksterhuis, A. (2004). I like myself but I don't know why: Enhancing implicit self-esteem by subliminal evaluative conditioning. *Journal of Personality and Social Psychology, 86*, 345-355.

Dirikx, T., Beckers, T., Muyls, C., Eelen, P., Vansteenwegen, D., Hermans, D., & D'Hooge, R. (2007) Differential acquisition, extinction and reinstatement of conditioned suppression in mice. *The Quarterly Journal of Experimental Psychology, 60*, 1313-1320.

Dirikx, T., Hermans, D., Vansteenwegen, D., Baeyens, F., & Eelen, P. (2004). Reinstatement of extinguished conditioned responses and negative stimulus valence as a pathway to return of fear in humans. *Learning & Memory, 11*, 549-554.

Eifert, G. H., Craill, L., Carey, E., & O'Connor, C. (1988). Affect modification through evaluative conditioning with music. *Behaviour Research and Therapy, 26,* 321–330.

Fazio, R. H., Sanbonmatsu, D. M., Powell, M. C., & Kardes, F. R. (1986). On the automatic activation of attitudes. *Journal of Personality and Social Psychology, 50*, 229-238.

Greenwald, A. G., McGhee, D. E., & Schwartz, J. L. K. (1998). Measuring individual differences in implicit cognition: The implicit association test. *Journal of Personality and Social Psychology, 74*, 1464-1480.

Hamm, A. O., Vaitl, D., & Lang, P. J. (1989). Fear conditioning, meaning, and belongingness – a selective association analysis. *Journal of Abnormal Psychology, 98,* 395-406.

Hermans, D., Crombez, G., Vansteenwegen, D., Baeyens, F., & Eelen, P. (2002). Expectancy-learning and evaluative learning in human classical conditioning: Differential effects of extinction. In S. P. Shohov (Ed.), *Advances in Psychology Research, Vol. 12* (pp.17-41). New York: Nova Science.

Hermans, D., Dirikx, T., Vansteenwegen, D., Baeyens, F., Van den Bergh, O., & Eelen, P. (2005). Reinstatement of fear responses in human aversive conditioning. *Behaviour Research and Therapy, 43*, 533-551.

Huijding, J., & de Jong, P. J. (2005). Changes of automatic and self-reported spider phobia-related affective associations following treatment and the prediction of symptom return. Unpublished doctoral dissertation, Rijksuniversiteit Groningen, 2005.

Kessler, R. C., Koretz, D., Merikangas, K. R., & Wang, P. S. (2004). The epidemiology of adult mental disorders. In B. L. Levin, J. Petrilia, & K. D. Hennessy (Eds.), *Mental health services: A public health perspective, Second Edition.* New York: Oxford University Press.

Korrelboom, C. W., van der Gaag, M., Hendriks, V. M., Huijbrechts, I. P. A. M., & Berretty, E. W. (2008). Treating obsessions with Competitive Memory Training: a pilot study. *The Behavior Therapist, 31*, 29-36.

Lang, P. J. (1995). The emotion probe – studies of motivation and attention. *American Psychologist, 50,* 372-385.

Lipp, O. V., & Purkis, H. M. (2006). The effects of assessment type on verbal ratings of conditional stimulus valence and contingency judgments: Implications for the extinction of evaluative learning. *Journal of Experimental Psychology – Animal Behavior Processes, 32*, 431-440.

Marks, I. M. (1987). *Fears, phobias, and rituals: Panic, anxiety and their disorders.* Oxford: Oxford University Press.

Olson, M. A., & Fazio, R. H. (2006). Reducing automatically activated racial prejudice through implicit evaluative conditioning. *Personality and Social Psychology Bulletin, 32*, 421-433.

Öst, L. G. (1989). One-session treatment for specific phobias. *Behaviour Research and Therapy, 27,* 1-7.

Peck, C. A. & Bouton, M. E. (1990). Context and performance in aversive-to-appetitive and appetitive-to-aversive transfer. *Learning and Motivation, 21,* 1-31.

Quirk, G. J. (2002). Memory for extinction of conditioned fear is long-lasting and persists following spontaneous recovery. *Learning and Memory, 9,* 402-407.

Rachman, S. (1989). The return of fear: Review and prospect. *Clinical Psychology Review, 9,* 147-168.

Rescorla, R. A. (2004). Spontaneous recovery. *Learning and Memory, 11,* 501-509.

Rydell, R. J., & McConnell, A. R. (2006). Understanding implicit and explicit attitude change: A systems of reasoning analysis. *Journal of Personality and Social Psychology, 91,* 995-1008.

Rydell, R. J., McConnell, A. R., Strain, L. M., Claypool, H. M., & Hugenberg, K. (2007). Implicit and explicit attitudes respond differently to increasing amounts of counterattitudinal information. *European Journal of Social Psychology, 37*, 867-878.

Scalera, G. (2000). Taste preference and acceptance in thirsty and dehydrated rats. *Physiology and Behavior, 71*, 457-468.

van Balkom, A. J. L. M., Bakker, A., Spinhoven, P., Blaauw, B. M. J. W., Smeenk, S., & Ruesink, B. (1997). A meta-analysis of the treatment of panic disorder with or without agoraphobia: A comparison of psychopharmacological, cognitive-behavioral, and combination treatments. *Journal of Nervous and Mental Disease, 185,* 510-517.

Vansteenwegen, D., Francken, G., Vervliet, B., De Clercq, A., & Eelen, P. (2006). Resistance to extinction in evaluative conditioning. *Journal of Experimental Psychology-Animal Behavior Processes, 32*, 71-79.

ACKNOWLEDGMENTS

This research was supported by Grant G.0268.06 of the Fund for Scientific Research, Flanders, Belgium and by a University of Leuven grant GOA/2007/03.

In: Abnormal Psychology: New Research
Editor: Helen D. Friedman and Paulina K. Revera
ISBN: 978-1-60692-636-9

Chapter 6

THE NEUROPSYCHOLOGY OF ALCOHOLISM

J. Uekermann and I. Daum
Institute of Cognitive Neuroscience, Department of Neuropsychology,
Ruhr-University of Bochum, Germany

ABSTRACT

Studies on neuropsychological functions in alcoholism have reported a range of impairments including visuo-spatial abilities, attention, memory, executive functions and social cognition. On the basis of neuropsychological studies as well as imaging data different models have been proposed for the interpretation of these deficits. The present chapter aims to give an overview of findings concerning the neuropsychology of alcoholism by reviewing investigations on cognitive functions as well as imaging and electrophysiological data. In addition, the potential contribution of drinking variables, family history of alcoholism, gender and affective variables as well as the presumable relevance of cognitive deficits for the treatment of alcoholism will be discussed.

1. INTRODUCTION

Alcoholism is associated with a consumption of dangerous quantities of alcohol despite knowledge of adverse effects on health, social life and/or work. Chronic alcoholism results in progressive brain changes, which are proposed to underlie neuropsychological deficits including visuo-spatial abilities, attention, memory and executive functions. Social cognition such as affect perception and theory of mind may also be affected.

The reported brain changes and cognitive dysfunction in turn may influence further progression and treatment of the disease. In this context the spiral distress model of addiction by Koob and Le Moal (1997) is of importance. Koob and Le Moal (1997) and Koob et al. (2004) assume that repeated failures of self-regulation may lead to chronic drug use, which is associated with progressive dysregulation of the brain reward system. In a modification of this model Crews et al. (2005) postulate that neurodegenerative processes in alcoholism result in impairments of attention and executive function and thus contribute to the progression of alcoholism by increasing loss of control and cognitive inflexibility.

The present chapter focuses on the brain changes as well as the cognitive impairments in alcoholism. In the first section structural, diffusion tensor imaging studies as well as electrophysiological data will be discussed. Cognitive impairments are summarized in the second section by reviewing neuropsychological and functional imaging data. On the basis of imaging and neuropsychological findings different neuropsychological models have been developed, which will be discussed in the third section. Eventually, variables contributing to the neuropsychological impairment pattern (e.g. drinking variables, family history of alcoholism, gender and affective variables) and the implications of brain changes and cognitive dysfunction for the treatment of alcoholism will be discussed.

2. Brain Changes in Alcoholism

The nature of brain dysfunction in alcoholism has been elucidated by electrophysiological investigations. In studies using resting electroencephalogram reduced alpha power, increased beta and theta power have been observed (see Porjesz et al., 2005). Event-related potential analyses have revealed changes of the P50, P300, brain-stem auditory-evoked potentials and mismatch negativity. The P50 refers to the reduction of P50 amplitude to the second stimulus when a pair of identical stimuli is presented (Adler et al., 1982). This so called sensory gating effect is thought to reflect a filtering mechanism of redundant information (Freedman et al., 1991). Marco et al. (2005) presented repeated tones to alcoholic patients and found a reduced P50 sensory gating effect. This finding was interpreted as reflecting an inhibitory deficit in early pre-attentive auditory sensory gating in alcoholism. The P300 is thought to reflect stimulus evaluation and attentional allcocation processes (Donchin et al., 1986; Polich, 1986) and is typically investigated using the 'oddball paradigm', in which an infrequent tone is presented within a series of frequent tones. Participants are required to respond to the infrequent tone. Alcoholic patients show a reduced P300 amplitude (Costa et al., 2000; Hada et al., 2000), which has been interpreted as a deficit in inhibitory mechanisms. To measure brain-stem auditory-evoked potentials auditory click stimuli are presented. Significantly delayed latencies have been reported in alcoholism (Cadaveira et al., 1994). The mismatch negativity, which is elicited when infrequent sounds are presented in a sequence of frequent sounds reflects auditory discrimination and sensory memory (Näätänen, 1992). Results from different investigations have shown larger mismatch negativity in chronic alcoholism (see Ahveninen et al., 2000) indicating attentional deficits in alcoholism.

Whereas the observed electrophysiological changes have been attributed to the neurotoxic effects of alcohol in early studies, more recent data suggest that at least some of the electrophysiological alterations may reflect a predisposition toward the development of alcoholism and thus can be found in individuals with a high risk to develop alcoholism such as children of alcoholics (see Porjesz et al., 2005).

Several structural and diffusion tensor imaging studies have been carried out in the last decades to characterize the effects of chronic alcohol intake on the brain in more detail. These investigations have shown that chronic alcohol consumption results in significant structural, physiological as well as functional changes of distinct neural systems (see Sullivan and Pfefferbaum, 2005). Approximately 50-70% of alcoholics show signs of brain abnormalities (Mann et al., 1995). The changes are more severe in alcoholism associated neuropsychiatric syndromes such as Korsakoff's syndrome or Marchiafava-Bignami disease. However, even in alcoholic patients without these syndromes a range of cortical and subcortical alterations as well as changes of brainstem structures may occurr.

Cortical changes in alcoholism include volume loss of gray and white matter in the frontal, parietal and temporal cortex (Pfefferbaum et al. 1992; Jernigan et al., 1991) as well as larger sulci and ventricle volumes (Agartz et al., 1991; Pfefferbaum et al., 1995). The loss of white matter is more pronounced than gray matter loss. Larger sulci and ventricle volumes can also be found in heavy drinkers without alcohol dependence (Ding et al., 2004; Kubota et al., 2001). The frontal lobes are particularly affected (Kril and Halliday, 1999) and volume shrinkage is related to the amount of consumed alcohol (Pfefferbaum et al., 1998). In this context the recency-frequency index seems to be a better predictor for brain shrinkage than the amount of alcohol over the lifetime (see Sullivan and Pfefferbaum, 2005). The specific vulnerability of the frontal lobes is also supported by Harper et al. (1987), who reported a reduced number of cortical neurons in the superior frontal cortex. Volume loss has also been reported in the thalamus, putamen, caudate (Sullivan et al., 2003), nucleus accumbens (Sullivan et al., 2005), mammillary body (Sullivan et al., 1999), hippocampus (Nagel et al., 2005), corpus callosum (Estruch et al., 1997; Oishi et al., 1999) and cerebellar vermis (Sullivan et al., 2000).

Several investigations have shown that the observed brain changes are partly reversible in abstinence. Mann et al. (1992) carried out CT density measures and found a significant reduction of CSF volume and an increase in CT density measures suggesting that abstinence effects are not due to rehydration (Mann, 1993). Shear et al. (1994) investigated alcoholics 1 and 3 months after the last drink. Alcoholics who were still abstinent after 3 months showed reduced cerebrospinal fluid and white matter increases. However, reversibility of brain shrinkage is not complete, and abnormalities can be observed even after years of abstinence (see Moselhy et al., 2001).

The extent of brain damage, electrophysiological changes and neuropsychological dysfunction are presumably influenced by several factors (e.g. family history of alcoholism, gender, concurrent smoking), which will be discussed in further detail in section 5.

3. Cognitive Functions in Alcoholism

3.1. Intellectual Functioning

Intellectual function is not a single ability, but refers to many discrete cognitive abilities that work together (Lezak, 1995). Patients suffering from alcoholism may have deficits of one or more of these subcomponents (Hambidge, 1990). Early investigations concerning cognitive functions in alcoholism indicated visual-spatial and learning deficits (Tarter, 1980; Guthrie and Elliott, 1980). Visuo-spatial impairments were revealed by significantly lower scores in the performance subscale of the Wechsler Adult Intelligence Scales (Tarter, 1980; Smith and Smith, 1977). In a later study by Hambidge (1990), 58% of alcoholics showed impairments on the performance subscale of the Wechsler Adult Intelligence Scales, whereas only 3% had verbal deficits. The impairment pattern of alcoholics in the Wechsler Intelligence Scales of alcoholics was also supported in a study by Barron and Russell (1992), who interpreted their findings in terms of the fluidity theory. Fluid intelligence refers to abilities required in tasks, for which familiar solutions are not available (Lezak, 1995). Crystallized intelligence on the other hand involves well-practiced and familiar skills. Concerning this distinction, deficits on fluid tasks are expected, whereas crystallized intelligence is thought to remain intact. The results, however, may also be interpreted in terms of task complexity. Deficits might thus be expected on unfamiliar tasks that require integration and manipulation of stimuli, whereas intact performance would be expected for routine abilities (see also 3.5).

3.2. Visuo-Spatial Functions

Early investigations have revealed visuo-spatial deficits in alcoholism, whereas verbal performance has been suggested to remain relatively intact (see 3.1). These studies were mainly based on standardized neuropsychological tests including group comparisons. According to Fox et al. (2000), potential functional dissociations might explain why estimates of the proportion of individual alcoholics who show impairments in these tests vary between 30 and 75% (Tarter and Edwards, 1986; Parsons, 1989). Fox et al. (2000) carried out an investigation using a single-case approach. A double-dissociation between organizational memory and visuo-spatial functions was observed, suggesting that both abilities may be independently affected. Basic visual functions were investigated by Wegener et al. (2001). Speed discrimination problems and impairments in the perception of slowly coherently moving dots were reported. No differences were found for faster speed stimuli. Since it has been previously shown that a pathway including the parvocellular layers of the lateral geniculate nucleus, the primary visual cortex and the prestriate cortex is involved in the processing of slow speed motion (Ffytche et al., 1995) it was argued that this stream may be particularly affected in alcoholism.

3.3. Attention

Attention does not include a single function, but rather refers to capacities involved in the way an organism becomes receptive to stimuli and may begin processing incoming information (Lezak. 1995). Studies investigating attentional functions in alcoholism have revealed impairments of divided and selective attention (Stormark et al., 2000; Smith and Oscar-Berman, 1992). Divided attention refers to the ability to divide attention between two concurrent tasks, whereas selective attention includes the ability to ignore irrelevant stimuli while selectively attending to relevant stimuli. In a more recent investigation, Tedstone et al. (2004) administered a test battery including different attentional tasks. Alcoholics showed deficits on all tasks. Concerning divided attention alcoholics showed slower reaction times as well as a higher number of errors. In addition, alcoholics demonstrated increased interference on the Stroop task, but not on the flanker task. On the basis of these results, Tedstone et al. (2004) concluded that impairments are restricted to “late” selection, whereas tasks requiring "early" selection remain intact. However, both tasks may have also differed on the degree of executive control requirements (see 3.5).

Attentional processes may be also of relevance for the treatment of alcoholism. In this context the cognitive-motivational theory by Finn and Hall (2004) and Finn et al. (2002) is of importance. The key question being addressed by this model is how a specific personality risk for alcoholism (e.g. impulsive behaviour) is related to cognitive functions, such as short-term memory capacity. According to this model, a high short-term memory capacity is associated with the ability to use low-salient information and it facilitates to shift the influence on decisions from high-salient stimuli to less salient stimuli. Delayed consequences of behaviour are assumed to be less salient and immediate contingencies are more salient for impulsive people. On the basis of these assumptions, Finn et al. (1999) administered a neuropsychological test battery, including assessments of inhibition and short-term memory capacity to alcoholic patients. They observed that patients with low short-term memory capacity had difficulty learning response inhibition after contingency reversal supporting the view that a low short-term capacity may be associated with impulsive behaviour and thus may contribute to maintenance of alcoholism.

3.4. Memory

Learning and memory deficits are a prominent characteristic of alcoholism (Parson and Nixon, 1993). Tivis et al. (1995) reported verbal and non verbal memory deficits in 94 % of investigated alcoholics. The observed memory deficits have been associated with hippocampal dysfunction (see Farr et al., 2005), which is presumably due to alterations of the hypothalamic-puitary-adrenal (HPA) regulation. Errico et al. (2002) investigated the association between cortisol dysregulation and memory impairment. Cortisol measures were carried out during withdrawal, neuropsychological testing as well as after exposure to cold pressor and mental arithmetic stress.

Alcoholics showed significant deficits of immediate and delayed verbal memory and delayed visual reproduction. A significant increase of cortisol during withdrawal in comparison with the baseline morning cortisol sample on the subsequent session was observed. The cortisol difference score, however, did not correlate with memory measures. After stress exposure alcoholics showed lower cortisol levels in comparison with controls. In the control group higher cortisol levels were associated with worse memory performance. In the alcoholic group attenuated cortisol levels were related to worse delayed verbal memory suggesting that altered HPA function may contribute to memory problems in alcoholics.

The observed memory impairments in alcoholism may also be at least partially due to the use of different strategies to perform a task. This view is supported by Fama et al. (2004), who assessed visuoperception, perceptual learning, declarative memory and executive functions. The results suggested that whereas healthy controls used visuospatial processes to perform a perceptual learning task, alcoholics used executive processes (see 3.5). Thus memory impairments could also result from high executive demands involved in memory processing.

3.5. Executive Functions

Executive functions refer to a range of processes, engaged in cognitive control and coordination of information processing (see Heyder et al., 2004). One prominent feature of the neuropsychological pattern in alcoholism are executive deficits including cognitive flexibility, problem solving, verbal and non-verbal abstraction and decision making (see Moselhy et al., 2001; Mitchell et al., 2005). Ihara et al. (2000) administered the Behavioral Assessment of the Dysexecutive Syndrome, a battery aimed to assess everyday executive functions. On the basis of a profile analysis, Ihara et al. (2000) reported four different impairment patterns: One group included patients with dissociations between impaired executive functions and preserved intelligence and memory. The second group consisted of patients with executive and memory deficits but without intellectual impairments. The third group showed a general intellectual deterioration and the fourth group included patients with intact cognitive performance. The first two groups included about two third of the patients. Executive deficits have been interpreted in terms of the 'frontal lobe hypothesis' of alcoholism, which asserts a specific vulnerability of the prefrontal cortex to the toxic effects of alcohol (see 4.).

Evidence for the 'frontal lobe hypothesis' also comes from imaging studies. Samson et al. (1986) reported a reduced regional distribution index in the medial frontal cortex. Dao-Castellana et al. (1998) reported that the mediofrontal cortex was in particular affected by metabolic dysfunction. Further studies have observed correlations between metabolism in the prefrontal cortex and anterior cingulate and performance in the Wisconsin Card Sorting Test, Halstead Category Test, Stroop Test and verbal fluency tasks (Adams et al., 1993; Adams et al., 1995; Dao-Castellana et al., 1998). Executive deficits in alcoholism may be of particular relevance for the therapy of alcoholism (see 6).

3.6. Social Cognition

Whereas executive functions and memory in alcoholism have been extensively studied, only few neuropsychological investigations have adressed social cognition in alcoholism. In an early study Cermak et al. (1989) investigated the perception of affective faces in alcoholism. No significant differences between alcoholics and healthy controls were observed. However, later investigations have shown significant impairments in the perception of affective faces and emotional prosody in alcoholism (Phillippot et al., 1999; Monnot et al., 2001). In the study by Uekermann et al. (2005) no deficits were found on simple tasks, which required linguistic and affective prosody perception, whereas significant mpairments were observed on tasks, in which the semantic content and prosody did not match. On the basis of the impairment pattern it was concluded that deficits of affect perception occur in "ambiguous situation, in which no additional cues could be used simultaneously for the interpretation of emotional prosody". Affect perception deficits are of particular relevance in the light of the study by Kornreich et al. (2002), who reported significant associations between affect perception deficits and interpersonal social problems.

Investigations of complex social cognition situations such as interpersonal problem solving, humour processing and theory of mind are sparse. Patterson et al. (1988) administered the Adaptive Skills Battery, in which interpersonal situations are presented and participants are instructed to give their best and their typical response. Alcoholics showed reduced competency scores for the typical, but not best responses suggesting that alcoholics show deficits concerning the execution of skills whereas knowledge of these skills is intact.

In an early investigation by Cermak et al. (1989) humour processing in alcoholism was investigated. In this investigation cartoons with two alternative endings were presented and participants were instructed to choose the correct funny ending. Alcoholics did no differ significantly from healthy controls concerning the number of correct punchlines, but they showed a qualitatively different error pattern. In a recent investigation by Uekermann et al. (submitted) the association between humour processing, theory of mind, and executive functions was investigated. The authors reported significant humour processing deficits, which were related to theory of mind and executive function. Since deficits of theory of mind and affect perception may contribute to interpersonal problems these impairments may be highly relevant for the therapy of alcoholism. Thus further studies are desirable, in which these issues are investigated in further detail.

4. Neuropsychological Models

The cognitive impairments in alcoholism have been interpreted in the light of different neuropsychological models (see Uekermann et al., 2003). According to the 'Premature Aging Hypothesis' alcoholism leads to a premature aging of the brain resulting in neuropsychological impairments that can also be observed in the course of normal aging (see Cermak, 1990).

The 'Right Hemisphere Hypothesis' postulates a specific vulnerability of the right hemisphere to the neurotoxic effects of alcohol leading to neuropsychological impairments on tasks depending on the functional integrity of the right hemisphere (see Cermak, 1990). Ellis (1990) investigated the 'Premature Aging Hypothesis' and the 'Right Hemisphere Hypothesis' using a dichotic listening procedure and neuropsychological measures. Alcoholic patients and older participants showed a decline in nonverbal abilities, which was similar to that observed in patients with damage to the right hemisphere suggesting right hemisphere dysfunction in aging and alcoholism. However, this assumption was not supported by laterality testing. In addition, verbal and non-verbal tests did probably differ on task difficulty and/or executive demands (see 3.1 and 3.5).

Results from other investigations have also failed to provide strong support for the 'Premature Aging' and the 'Right Hemisphere Hypothesis'. Oscar-Berman et al. (1990) presented faces expressing a particular emotion to alcoholic patients and non-alcoholic controls. No significant interaction between age and alcoholism was observed. Kramer et al. (1989) observed different patterns of verbal memory deficits in aging and alcoholism. Cermak et al. (1989) reported that the performance of alcoholic patients differed from that of patients with damage to the right hemisphere on all administered tasks. Uekermann et al. (2003) observed spared abilities on tasks that depend on the functional integrity of the right hemisphere. In summary, there is little support for the 'Premature Aging' and the 'Right Hemisphere Hypothesis'.

A more diffuse, generalized dysfunction of the brain is postulated by the 'Hypothesis of Mild Generalized Dysfunction' resulting in a variable impairment pattern (de Obaldia et al.,

1981). The 'Frontal Lobe Hypothesis' suggests a specific vulnerability of the prefrontal cortex leading to executive deficits (see 3.5). Ratti et al. (1999) investigated the validity of the different neuropsychological models. The 'Right Hemisphere Hypothesis' and the 'Hypothesis of Mild Generalized Dysfunction' did not receive firm support. The observed impairment pattern and frontal atrophy was consistent with the frontal lobe hypothesis.

Noel et al. (2001) reported executive deficits in alcoholism, whereas non-executive functions were intact. Investigations using computed tomography studies have also reported frontal lobe changes. In addition, neurophysiological investigations found reduced cerebral blood flow as well as dcreased frontal lobe glucose utilisation (see Moselhy et al., 2001), supporting the 'frontal lobe hypothesis' of alcoholism. However, the question whether these deficits are causally linked to alcohol consumption or reflect a predisposition to develop alcoholism remains a matter of debate (see 6.).

5. Variables Contributing to Cognitive Impairments in Alcoholism

Several variables such as autobiographical drinking history, liver status, smoking, affective as well as personality variables presumably influence cognitive impairments in alcoholism.

The relation between autobiographical drinking history and neuropsychological impairments has been a subject of controversity. Ryback (1971) postulated a continuum between abstinent individuals and heavy drinkers. According to the continuity hypothesis alcoholics cognitive abilities appear along a continuum between social drinkers and patients with Korsakoff's syndrome. However, results from different studies concerning the influence of drinking variables are inconsistent. Sinha et al. (1989) did not find any significant associations between drinking variables and neuropsychological performance. Eckardt et al. (1998) hypothesized that cognitive deficits in alcoholism only occur after a minimum of 10 years. In the investigation by Beatty (2000) this assumption was not supported. Alcoholic patients with disease duration of 4-9 years and alcoholics with disease duration of more than 10 years did not differ significantly. Recent investigations have suggested that the recent alcohol consumption may be a better predictor for cognitive dysfunction than lifetime alcohol consumption. Horner et al. (1999) reported that whereas duration of drinking history was not associated with poorer performance, significant associations were found between amount of recent alcohol consumption and cognitive measures. The influence of recent quantity of consumed alcohol was also confirmed in a more recent investigation by Zinn et al. (2004). In addition to the quantity of consumed alcohol, the number of detoxification and concurrent smoking may be of relevance. Duka et al. (2003) reported more severe impairments in alcoholic patients with two or more detoxifications in comparison with alcoholics with no or one detoxification. However, since the number of detoxifications was confounded with other autobiographical drinking variables further investigations are necessary to investigate the influence of the number of detoxifications in more detail. The influence of concurrent cigarette smoking was investigated in a recent study by Gazdzinski et al. (2005). The results implied that alcoholism with concurrent cigarette smoking has stronger detrimental effects than alcoholism or cigarette smoking alone.

Other important variables are duration of abstinence and number of detoxifications. Imaging studies have shown that brain changes are reversible, although reversibility is not complete and brain alterations can bee seen even after years of abstinence (see 2.)

Cognitive improvements may occur immediately after withdrawal (Mann et al., 1999). Bates et al. (2005) found a medium effect size improvement of memory functions after six weeks of abstinence. Johnson-Greene et al. (1997) investigated the influence of abstinence using positron emission tomography and neuropsychological measures reporting recovery of cerebral metabolic rates for glucose as well as cognitive improvement in abstinent patients in comparison with patients who relapsed. Results from other studies, in which the influence of abstinence on cognitive functions was investigated also suggest that recovery is not complete (e.g. Brandt et al., 1983).

Family history of alcoholism may also be of importance. In early investigations compounded neuropsychological impairments have been suggested (Yohman and Parsons, 1987; Schaeffer et al., 1988). Tapert and Brown (2000) compared alcohol and drug dependent adolescents with and without a positive history of alcoholism. The results supported the view that family history and substance use are separate risk factors for poorer cognitive performance in adolescence. The potential influence of a positive family history of alcoholism is also supported by imaging studies. Cardenas et al. (2005) reported that a positive family history of problem drinking was associated with smaller CSF volumes. In addition, a less inhibitory frontal response during a go/no go-task was observed in youths with positive family history of alcoholism in comparison with a negative family history (Schweinsburg et al., 2004). However, given the fact that perinatal complications and head trauma are more likely in children of alcoholics the data should be interpreted with caution (see Giancola and Moss, 1998).

Another important confounding variable may be liver function. The available evidence is inconsistent. In early investigations significant correlations between liver function and cognitive performance was observed (see Schafer et al, 1991), but more recent data did not replicate these effects (O'Mahony, 2005).

Gender may also be of relevance. Mann et al. (1992) reported comparable brain shrinkage in male and female alcoholics, although women had significantly shorter ethanol expositions. In addition, Hommer et al. (1999) observed larger brain volume differences between female alcoholics and nonalcoholics than those in male alcoholics and nonalcoholics. A more pronounced vulnerability of the female CNS to the neurotoxic effects of alcohol was also confirmed in a recent study by Mann et al. (2005). Neuropsychological investigations showing more severe cognitive impairments in females also suggest a greater vulnerability to the deleterious effects of alcohol (e.g. Acker, 1986).

Depression is the most frequent disorder in alcoholism with 15-18% suffering from major depression (Driessen et al., 1998). Depression as such is associated with cognitive impairments (Burt et al., 1995; Veiel, 1997), which are presumably related to reduced cerebral activation in the prefrontal cortex (Rajkowska, 2000; Sheline, 2000). Results from studies, in which the potential cumulative effect of depression on cognitive functions has been investigated are inconsistent. In an early study by Sinha et al. (1989) depressive symptoms correlated with overall cognitive impairments. Depression was a significant predictor of cognitive measures at admission and follow-up in the investigation by Schafer et al. (1991). In other studies no significant relations were observed. In a more recent study by Uekermann et al. (2003) alcoholic patients with and without depressive symptoms as well as depressed patients were compared. The results implied that cognitive impairments in alcoholism are not generally exacerbated by depressive symptoms. However, further studies are desirable to investigate the association between alcoholism, depressive symptoms and cognitive impairments in further detail.

6. Summary and Conclusion

As outlined above alcoholism is associated with a range of neuropsychological deficits including attention, memory, executive deficits and social cognition. These deficits are presumably related to dysfunction of the prefrontal cortex. Several investigations have shown that the cognitive deficits in alcoholism may contribute to the maintenance of alcoholism. Maintenance of alcoholism results in more pronounced cerebral changes, which may then be associated with more severe cognitive dysfunction leading to a worse prognosis concerning rehabilitation. Crews et al. (2005) assumes that neurodegenerative processes in alcoholism result in impairments of attention and executive function and thus contribute to the progression of alcoholism by increasing loss of control and cognitive inflexibility (see 1.).

In this context the heuristic frontostriatal alcohol addicition model by Giancola and Moss (1998) may be important. According to this model alcohol and alcohol associated stimuli lead to activation of the ventral striatum and ventral tegmentum resulting in stereotypic and overlearned behaviours (e.g. alcohol taking). In addition, the prefrontal cortex is inhibited by dopaminergic innervation from the ventral tegmentum and direct pharmacological actions of alcohol. With prolonged chronic alcohol consumption dysfunction of the prefrontal cortex occurs as reflected by neuron loss, reduced cerebral blood flow and diminished metabolism (see 2). These processes may be associated with a reduced capacity to use novel adaptive behaviour in response to alcohol related stimuli and thus contribute to negative outcome of therapeutic interventions.

Results from several investigations support this model. Bowden-Jones et al. (2005) reported an association between early relapse and impulsivity as reflected by choices governed by immediate gain irrespective of later outcome. Results in executive tests predicted alcohol consumption in a study by Deckel and Hesselbrock (1996). Rinn et al. (2002) administered a comprehensive neuropsychological test-battery. In addition, a denial measure was used, which was defined as the percentage of the patient's denial-related treatment goals that remained unachieved at the time of discharge. Impairments on planning, problem solving and concept formation were associated with higher denial. In addition to executive functions memory has shown to be significanty associated with outcome measures in alcoholism (Blume et al., 2005).

However, it should be noted again that the question whether the observed deficits are a consequence or a predisposition of the disease is still a matter of controversity. The assumption that inhibition deficits may at least reflect a predisposition to the development of alcohol and drug addiction is supported by Nigg et al. (2006), in which an association between poor response inhibition, problem drinking and drug use in adolescents at risk for the development of alcoholism and other substance use disorders was shown.

Despite the fact that alcoholics show affect perception and theory of mind deficits, only little work has done concerning the influence of social cognition on outcome measures in alcoholism. This is of particular relevance in the light of the study by Kornreich et al. (2002), in which correlations between affect perception deficits and interpersonal problems have been observed. In future, studies are desirable investigating the association between cognitive dysfunction, affect perception deficits and outcome in further detail.

REFERENCES

Acker, C. (1986). Neuropsychological deficits in alcoholics: the relative contributions of gender and drinking history. *British Journal of Addiction,* 81(3), 395-403.

Adams, K.M., Gilman, S., Koeppe, R.A., Brunberg, J.A., Dede, D., Barent, S., and Kroll. P.D. (1993). Neuropsychological deficits are correlated with frontal hypometabolism in positron emission tomography studies of older alcoholic patients. *Alcoholism: Clinical and Experimental Research,* 17, 205-210.

Adams, K.M., Gilman, S., Koeppe, R., and Kluim, K.J. (1995). Correlation of neuropsychological function with cerebral metabolic rate in subdivisions of frontal lobes of older alcoholic patients measured with (sup-1-sup-8F) fluorodeoxyclucose and positron emission tomography. *Neuropsychology,* 9, 275-280.

Adler, L.E., Pachtman, E., Franks, R.D., Pecevich, M., Waldo, M.C., and Freedman, R. (1982). Neurophysiological evidence for a defect in neuronal mechanisms involved in sensory gating in schizophrenia. *Biological Psychiatry,* 17(6), 639-54.

Agartz, I., Saaf, J., Wahlund ,L.O., and Wetterberg, L. (1991). T1 and T2 relaxation time estimates and brain measures during withdrawal in alcoholic men. *Drug and Alcohol Dependence,* 29(2), 57-69.

Ahveninen, J., Jaaskelainen, I.P., Pekkonen, E., Hallberg, A., Hietanen, M., Naatanen, R., Schroger, E., and Sillanaukee, P. (2000). Increased distractibility by task-irrelevant sound changes in abstinent alcoholics. *Alcoholism: Clinical and Experimental Research,* 24(12), 1850-4.

Barron, J.H., and Russell, E.W. (1992). Fluidity theory and neuropsychological impairment in alcoholism. *Archives of Clinical Neuropsychology,* 7(2), 175-88.

Bates, ME., Voelbel, G.T., Buckman, J.F., Labouvie, E.W., and Barry, D. (2005). Short-term neuropsychological recovery in clients with substance use disorders. *Alcoholism: Clinical and Experimental Research,* 29(3), 367-77.

Beatty, W.W., Tivis, R., Stott, H.D., Nixon, S.J., and Parsons, O.A. (2000). Neuropsychological deficits in sober alcoholics: influences of chronicity and recent alcohol consumption. *Alcoholism: Clinical and Experimental Research,* 24(2), 149-54.

Blume, A.W., Schmaling, K.B., and Marlatt, G.A. (2005). Memory, executive cognitive function, and readiness to change drinking behavior. *Addictive Behaviours,* 30(2), 301-14.

Bowden-Jones, H., McPhillips, M., Rogers, R., Hutton, S., and Joyce, E. (2005). Risk-taking on tests sensitive to ventromedial prefrontal cortex dysfunction predicts early relapse in alcohol dependency: a pilot study. *Journal of Neuropsychiatry and Clinical Neuroscience,* 17(3),17-20.

Brandt, J., Butters, N., Ryan, C., and Bayog, R. (1983). Cognitive loss and recovery in long-term alcohol abusers. *Archives of General Psychiatry,* 40(4), 435-42.

Burt, D.B., Zembar, M.J., and Niederehe, G. (1995). Depression and memory impairment: a meta-analysis of the association, its pattern, and specificity. *Psychological Bulletin,* 117(2), 285-305.

Cadaveira, F., Corominas, M., Rodriguez Holguin, S., Sanchez-Turet, M., and Grau, C. (1994). Reversibility of brain-stem evoked potential abnormalities in abstinent chronic alcoholics: one year follow-up. *Electroencephalogram and Clinical Neurophysiology,* 90(6), 450-5.

Cardenas, V.A., Studholme, C., Meyerhoff, D.J., Song, E., and Weiner, M.W. (2005). Chronic active heavy drinking and family history of problem drinking modulate regional brain tissue volumes. *Psychiatry Research,* 138(2), 115-30.

Cermak, L.S. (1990). Cognitive-processing deficits in chronic alcohol abusers. *Alcohol Health and Research World,* 14 (2), 130-137.

Cermak, L.S., Verfaellie, M., Letourneau, L., Blackford, S., Weiss, S., and Numan, B. (1989). Verbal and nonverbal right hemisphere processing by chronic alcoholics. *Alcoholism: Clinical and Experimental Research*, 13, 611-6.

Costa, L., Bauer, L., Kuperman, S., Porjesz, B., O'Connor, S., Hesselbrock, V., Rohrbaugh, J., and Begleiter, H. (2000). Frontal P300 decrements, alcohol dependence, and antisocial personality disorder. *Biological Psychiatry,* 47(12), 1064-71.

Crews, F.T., Buckley, T., Dodd, P.R., Ende, G., Foley, N., Harper, C., He, J., Innes, D., Loh, el-W., Pfefferbaum, A., Zou, J., and Sullivan, E.V. (2005). Alcoholic neurobiology: changes in dependence and recovery. *Alcoholism: Clinical and Experimental Research,* 29(8), 1504-13.

de Obaldia, R., Leber, W.R., and Parsons, O.A. (1981). Assessment of neuropsychological functions in chronic alcoholics using a standardized version of Luria's Neuropsychological Technique. *International Journal of Neuroscience,* 14(1-2), 85-93.

Dao-Castellana, M.H., Samson, Y., Legault, F., Martinot, J.L., Aubin, H.J., Crouzel, C., Feldman, L., Barrucand, D., Rancurel, G., Feline, A., and Syrota, A. (1998). Frontal dysfunction in neurologically normal chronic alcoholic subjects: metabolic and neuropsychological findings. *Psychological Medicine,* 28(5), 1039-48.

Deckel, A.W., and Hesselbrock, V. (!996). Behavioral and cognitive measurements predict scores on the MAST: a 3-year prospective study. *Alcoholism: Clinical and Experimental Research,* 20(7), 1173-8.

Ding, J., Eigenbrodt, M.L., Mosley, T.H. Jr., Hutchinson, R.G., Folsom, A.R., Harris, T.B., and Nieto, F.J. (2004). Alcohol intake and cerebral abnormalities on magnetic resonance imaging in a community-based population of middle-aged adults: the Atherosclerosis Risk in Communities (ARIC) study. *Stroke*, 35(1), 16-21.

Donchin, E., Miller, G.A., and Farwell, L.A. (1986). The endogenous components of the event-related potential--a diagnostic tool? *Progressions in Brain Research,* 70, 87-102.

Driessen, M., Veltrup, C., Wetterling, T., John, U., and Dilling, H. (1998). Axis I and axis II comorbidity in alcohol dependence and the two types of alcoholism. *Alcoholism: Clinical and Experimental Research,* 22(1), 77-86.

Duka, T., Townshend, J.M., Collier, K., and Stephens, D.N. (2003). Impairment in cognitive functions after multiple detoxifications in alcoholic inpatients. *Alcoholism: Clinical and Experimental Research,* 27(10), 1563-72.

Eckardt, M.J., File, S.E., Gessa, G.L., Grant, K.A., Guerri, C., Hoffman, P.L., Kalant, H., Koob, G.F., Li, T.K., and Tabakoff, B. (1998). Effects of moderate alcohol consumption on the central nervous system. *Alcoholism: Clinical and Experimental Research,* 22(5), 998-1040.

Ellis, R.J. (1990). Dichotic asymmetries in aging and alcoholic subjects. *Alcoholism: Clinical and Experimental Research,* 114(6), 863-71.

Errico, A.L., King, A.C., Lovallo, W.R., and Parsons, O.A. (2002). Cortisol dysregulation and cognitive impairment in abstinent male alcoholics. *Alcoholism: Clinical and Experimental Research,* 26(8), 1198-204.

Estruch, R., Nicolas, J.M., Salamero, M., Aragon, C., Sacanella, E., Fernandez-Sola, J., and Urbano-Marquez, A. (1997). Atrophy of the corpus callosum in chronic alcoholism. *Journal of Neurological Science,* 146(2),145-51.

Fama, R., Pfefferbaum, A., and Sullivan, E.V. (2004). Perceptual learning in detoxified alcoholic men: contributions from explicit memory, executive function, and age. *Alcoholism: Clinical and Experimental Research,* 28(11), 1657-65.

Farr, S.A., Scherrer J.F, Banks, W.A., Flood, J.F., and Morley, J.E. (2005). Chronic ethanol consumption impairs learning and memory after cessation of ethanol. *Alcoholism: Clinical and Experimental Research,* 29(6), 971-82.

Ffytche, D.H., Skidmore, B.D., and Zeki, S. (1995). Motion-from-hue activates area V5 of human visual cortex. *Proceedings: Biological Science,.* 260(1359), 353-8.

Finn, P.R., and Hall, J. (2004). Cognitive ability and risk for alcoholism: short-term memory capacity and intelligence moderate personality risk for alcohol problems. *Journal of Abnormal Psychology,* 113(4), 569-81.

Finn, P.R., Justus, A., Mazas, C., and Steinmetz, J.E. (1999). Working memory, executive processes and the effects of alcohol on Go/No-Go learning: testing a model of behavioral regulation and impulsivity. *Psychopharmacology,* 146(4), 465-72.

Finn, P.R., Mazas, C.A., Justus, A.N., and Steinmetz, J. (2002). Early-onset alcoholism with conduct disorder: go/no go learning deficits, working memory capacity, and personality. *Alcoholism: Clinical and Experimental Research,* 26(2), 186-206.

Freedman, R., Waldo, M., Bickford-Wimer, P., and Nagamoto, H. (1991). Elementary neuronal dysfunctions in schizophrenia. *Schizophrenia Research,* 4(2), 233-43.

Fox, A.M., Coltheart, M., Solowij, N., Mitchie, P.T., and Fox, G.A. (2000). Dissociable cognitive impairments in problem drinkers. *Alcohol and Alcoholism,* 35, 1, 52-54.

Gazdzinski, S., Durazzo, T.C., Studholme, C., Song, E., Banys, P., and Meyerhoff, D.J. (2005). Quantitative brain MRI in alcohol dependence: preliminary evidence for effects of concurrent chronic cigarette smoking on regional brain volumes. *Alcoholism: Clinical and Exprimental Research,* 29(8),1484-95.

Giancola, P.R., and Moss, H.B. (1998). Executive cognitive functionng in alcohol use disorders. *Recent Developments in Alcoholism,* 14, 227-51.

Guthrie, J., and Elliott, W.A. (1980). The nature and reversibility of cerebral impairment in alcoholism. *Journal of Studies in Alcoholism,* 41, 147-155.

Hada, M., Porjesz, B., Begleiter, H., and Polich, J. (2000). Auditory P3a assessment of male alcoholics. *Biological Psychiatry,* 48(4), 276-86.

Hambidge, D.M. (1990). Intellectual impairment in male alcoholics. *Alcohol and Alcoholism,* 25(5), 555-9.

Harper, C., Kril, J., and Daly, J. (1987). Are we drinking our neurones away? *British Medical Journal (Clinical Research Edition),* 294(6571), 534-6.

Heyder, K., Suchan, B., and Daum, I. (2004) Cortico-subcortical contributions to executive control. *Acta Psychologica,* 115(2-3), 271-89.

Hommer, D., Momenan, R., Kaiser, E., and Rawlings, R. (1999). Evidence for a gender-related effect of alcoholism on brain volumes. *American Journal of Psychiatry,* 158(2), 198-204.

Horner, M.D., Waid, L.R., Johnson, D.E., Latham, P.K., and Anton, R.F. (1999). The relationship of cognitive functioning to amount of recent and lifetime alcohol consumption in outpatient alcoholics. *Addictive Behaviours,* 24(3), 449-53.

Ihara, H., Berrios, G.E., and London, M. (2000). Group and case study of the dysexecutive syndrome in alcoholism without amnesia. *Journal of Neurology, Neurosurgery and Psychiatry,* 68(6), 731-7.

Jernigan, T.L., Butters, N., DiTraglia, G., Schafer, K., Smith, T., Irwin, M., Grant, I., Schuckit, M., and Cermak, L.S. (1991). Reduced cerebral grey matter observed in alcoholics using magnetic resonance imaging. *Alcoholism: Clinical and Experimental Research,* 5(3), 418-27.

Johnson-Greene, D., Adams, K.M., Gilman, S., Koeppe, R.A., Junck, L., Kluin, K.J., Martorello, S., and Heumann, M. (1997). Effects of abstinence and relapse upon neuropsychological function and cerebral glucose metabolism in severe chronic alcoholism. *Journal of Clinical and Experimental Neuropsychology,* 19(3), 378-85.

Koob, G.F., Ahmed, S.H., Boutrel, B., Chen, S.A., Kenny, P.J., Markou, A., O'Dell, L.E., Parsons, L.H., and Sanna, P.P. (2004). Neurobiological mechanisms in the transition from drug use to drug dependence. *Neuroscience and Biobehavioral Reviews,* 27(8), 739-49.

Koob, G.F., and Le Moal, M. (1997). Drug abuse: hedonic homeostatic dysregulation. *Science*, 278(5335), 52-8.

Kornreich, C., Philippot, P., Foisy, M.L., Blairy, S., Raynaud, E., Dan, B., Hess, U., Noel, X., Pelc, I., and Verbanck, P. (2002). Impaired emotional facial expression recognition is associated with interpersonal problems in alcoholism. *Alcohol and Alcoholism,* 37(4), 394-400.

Kramer, J.H., Blusewicz, M.J., and Preston, K.A. (1989). The premature aging hypothesis: old before its time? *Journal of Consultant and Clinical Psychology,* 57(2), 257-62.

Kril, J.J., and Halliday, G.M. (1999). Brain shrinkage in alcoholics: a decade on and what have we learned? *Progress in Neurobiology,* 58(4), 381-7.

Kubota, M., Nakazaki, S., Hirai, S., Saeki, N., Yamaura, A., and Kusaka, T. (2001). Alcohol consumption and frontal lobe shrinkage: study of 1432 non-alcoholic subjects. *Journal of Neurology, Neurosurgery and Psychiatry*, 71(1), 104-6.

Lezak, M.D. (1995). Neuropsychological Assessment. New York: Oxford University Press.

Mann, K., Ackermann, K., Croissant, B., Mundle, G., Nakovics, H., Diehl, A. (2005). Neuroimaging of gender differences in alcohol dependence: are women more vulnerable? *Alcoholism: Clinical and Experimental Research,* 29(5), 896-901.

Mann, K., Batra, A., Gunthner, A., and Schroth, G. (1992). Do women develop alcoholic brain damage more readily than men? *Alcoholism: Clinical and Experimental Research,* 16(6), 1052-6.

Mann, K., Gunther, A., Stetter, F., and Ackermann, K. (1999). Rapid recovery from cognitive Deficits in abstinent alcoholics: a controlled test-retest study. *Alcohol and Alcoholism,* 34(4), 567-74.

Mann, K., Mundle, G., Langle, G., and Petersen, D. (1993). The reversibility of alcoholic brain damage is not due to rehydration: a CT study. *Addiction,* 88(5), 649-53.

Mann, K., Mundle, G., Strayle, M. and Wakat, P. (1995). Neuroimaging in alcoholism: CT and MRI results and clinical correlates. *Journal of Neural Transmission (General Section),* 99(1- 3), 145-55.

Marco, J., Fuentemilla, L. and Grau, C. (2005). Auditory sensory gating deficit in abstinent chronic alcoholics. *Neuroscience Letters,* 375(3), 174-7.

Mitchell, J.M., Fields, H.L., D'Esposito, M. and Boettiger, C.A. (2005). Impulsive responding in alcoholics. *Alcoholism: Clinical and Experimental Research,* 29(12), 2158-69.

Monnot, M., Nixon, S., Lovallo, W. and Ross, E. (2001). Altered emotional perception in alcoholics: deficits in affective prosody comprehension. *Alcoholism: Clinical and Experimental Research,* 25(3), 362-9.

Moselhy, H.F., Georgiou, G. and Kahn, A. (2001). Frontal lobe changes in alcoholism: a review of the literature. *Alcohol and Alcoholism,* 36(5), 357-68.

Näätänen, R. (1992). Attention and Brain Funtion. Hillsdale: Erlbaum.

Nagel, B.J., Schweinsburg, A.D., Phan, V. and Tapert, S.F. (2005). Reduced hippocampal volume among adolescents with alcohol use disorders without psychiatric comorbidity. *Psychiatry Research,* 139(3),181-90.

Nigg, J.T., Wong, M.M., Martel, M.M., Jester, J.M., Puttler, L.I., Glass, J.M., Adams, K.M., Fitzgerald, H.E. and Zucker, R.A. (2006). Poor response inhibition as a predictor of problem drinking and illicit drug use in adolescents at risk for alcoholism and other substance use disorders. *Journal of the American Academy of Child and Adolescent Psychiatry.* 45(4), 468-75.

Noel, X., Van der Linden, M., Schmidt, N., Sferrazza, R., Hanak, C., Le Bon, O., De Mol, J., Kornreich, C., Pelc, I. and Verbanck, P. (2001). Supervisory attentional system in nonamnesic alcoholic men. *Archives of General Psychiatry,* 58(12), 1152-8.

Oishi, M., Mochizukmi, Y. and Shikata, E. (1999). Corpus callosum atrophy and cerebral blood flow in chronic alcoholics. *Journal of Neurological Science,* 162(1), 51-5.

O'Mahony, J.F. (2005).Cognitive performance and liver function among recently abstinent alcohol abusers. *Addictive Behaviours,* 30(2), 369-73.

Oscar-Berman, M., Hancock, M., Mildworf, B., Hutner, N., and Weber, D.A. (1990). Emotional perception and memory in alcoholism and aging. *Alcoholism: Clinical and Experimental Research,* 14(3), 383-93.

Parsons, O.A. (1989). Impairments of sober alcoholics' cognitive functioning: the search for determinants. In T. Lober, W.R. Miller, P.E. Nathan and G.A. Marlatt (Eds*.), Addictive Behaviours: Prevention and Early Intervention* (pp. 101-116). Amsterdam: Swets and Zeitlinger.

Parsons, O.A., and Nixon, S.J. (1993). Neurobehavioral sequelae of alcoholism. *Neurologic Clinics*, 11(1), 205-18.

Patterson, B.W., Parsons, O.A., Schaeffer, K.W., and Errico, A.L. (1988). Interpersonal problem solving in alcoholics. *Journal of the Nervous and Mental Diseases,* 176(12), 707-13.

Pfefferbaum, A., Sullivan, E.V., Rosenbloom, M.J., Mathalon, D.H., and Lim, K.O. (1998). A controlled study of cortical gray matter and ventricular changes in alcoholic men over a 5-year interval. *Archives of General Psychiatry, 55*(10), 905-12.

Pfefferbaum, A., Sullivan, E.V., Mathalon, D.H., Shear, P.K., Rosenbloom, M.J., and Lim, K.O. (1995). Longitudinal changes in magnetic resonance imaging brain volumes in abstinent and relapsed alcoholics. *Alcoholism: Clinical and Experimental Research,* 19(5), 1177-91.

Pfefferbaum, A., Lim, K.O., Zipursky, R.B., Mathalon, D.H., Rosenbloom, M.J., Lane, B, Ha, C.N., and Sullivan, E.V. (1992). Brain gray and white matter volume loss accelerates with aging in chronic alcoholics: a quantitative MRI study. *Alcoholism: Clinical and Experimental Research,* 16(6), 1078-89.

Philippot, P., Kornreich, C., Blairy, S., Baert, I., Den Dulk, A., Le Bon, O.,Streel, E., Hess, U., Pelc, I., and Verbanck, P. (1999). Alcoholics' deficits in the decoding of emotional facial expression. *Alcoholism: Clinical and Experimental Research,* 23,1031-8.

Polich, J. (1986). Attention, probability, and task demands as determinants of P300 latency from auditory stimuli. *Electroencephalogram and Clinical Neurophysiology,* 63(3), 251-9.

Porjesz, B., Rangaswamy, M., Kamarajan, C., Jones, K.A., Padmanabhapillai, A., and Begleiter, H. (2005). The utility of neurophysiological markers in the study of alcoholism. *Clinical Neurophysiology,* 116(5), 993-1018.

Rajkowska, G. (2000). Postmortem studies in mood disorders indicate altered numbers of neurons and glial cells. *Biological Psychiatry,* 48(8), 766-77.

Ratti, M.T., Soragna, D., Sibilla, L., Giardini, A., Albergati, A., Savoldi, F., and Bo, P (1999). Cognitive impairment and cerebral atrophy in "heavy drinkers". *Progress in Neuropsychopharmacology and Biological Psychiatry,* 23(2), 243-58.

Rinn, W., Desai, N., Rosenblatt, H., and Gastfriend, D.R. (2002). Addiction denial and cognitive dysfunction: a preliminary investigation. *Journal of Neuropsychiatry and Clinical Neuroscience,* 14(1), 52-7.

Ryback, R.S. (1971). The continuum and specificity of the effects of alcohol on memory. A review. *Quarterly Journals of Studies on Alcohol,* 32(4), 995-1016.

Samson, Y., Baron, J.C., Feline, A., Bories, J., and Crouzel, C. (1986). Local cerebral glucose utilisation in chronic alcoholics: a positron tomographic study. *Journal of Neurology, Neurosurgery and Psychiatry,* 49(10), 1165-70.

Schaeffer, K.W., Parsons, O.A., and Errico, A.L. (1988). Abstracting deficits and childhood conduct disorder as a function of familial alcoholism. *Alcoholism: Clinical and Experimental Research,* 12(5), 617-8.

Schafer, K., Butters, N., Smith, T., Irwin, M., Brown, S., Hanger, P., Grant, I., and Schuckit, M. (1991). Cognitive performance of alcoholics: a longitudinal evaluation of the role of drinking history, depression, liver function, nutrition, and family history. Alcoholism: *Clinical and Experimental Research,* 15(4), 653-60.

Schweinsburg, A.D., Paulus, M.P., Barlett, V.C., Killeen, L.A., Caldwell, L.C., Pulido, C., Brown, S.A., and Tapert, S.F. (2004). An FMRI study of response inhibition in youths with a family history of alcoholism. *Annals of the New York Academy of Science,* 1021, 391-4.

Shear, P.K., Jernigan, T.L., and Butters, N. (1994). Volumetric magnetic resonance imaging quantification of longitudinal brain changes in abstinent alcoholics. *Alcoholism: Clinical and Experimental Research,* 18(1), 172-6.

Sheline, Y.I. (2000). 3D MRI studies of neuroanatomic changes in unipolar major depression: The role of stress and medical comorbidity. *Biological Psychiatry,* 48(8), 791-800.

Sinha, R., Parsons, O.A., and Glenn, S.W. (1989). Drinking variables, affective measures and neuropsychological performance: familial alcoholism and gender correlates. *Alcohol*, 6(1), 77-85.

Smith, M.E., and Oscar-Berman, M. (1992). Resource-limited information processing in alcoholism. *Journal of Studies on Alcohol,* 53(5), 514-8.

Smith, H.H. Jr, and Smith, L.S. (1977). WAIS functioning of cirrhotic and non-cirrhotic alcoholics. *Journal of Clinical Psychology,* 33(1), 309-13.

Stormark, K.M., Laberg, J.C., Nordby, H., and Hugdahl, K. (2000). Alcoholics' selective attention to alcohol stimuli: automated processing? *Journal of Studies on Alcohol,* 61(1), 18-23.

Sullivan, E.V., Deshmukh, A., De Rosa, E., Rosenbloom, M.J., and Pfefferbaum, A. (2005). Striatal and forebrain nuclei volumes: contribution to motor function and working memory deficits in alcoholism. *Biological Psychiatry,* 57(7), 768-76.

Sullivan, E.V., Deshmukh, A., Desmond, J.E., Lim, K.O., and Pfefferbaum, A. (2000). Cerebellar volume decline in normal aging, alcoholism, and Korsakoff's syndrome: relation to ataxia. *Neuropsychology*, 14(3), 341-52.

Sullivan, E.V., Lane, B., Deshmukh, A., Rosenbloom, M.J., Desmond, J.E., Lim, K.O., and Pfefferbaum, A. (1999). In vivo mammillary body volume deficits in amnesic and nonamnesic alcoholics. *Alcoholism: Clinical and Experimental Research,* 23(10), 1629-36.

Sullivan, E.V., and Pfefferbaum, A. (2005) Neurocircuitry in alcoholism: a substrate of disruption and repair. *Psychopharmacology* (Berl), 180(4), 583-94.

Sullivan, E.V., Rosenbloom, M.J., Serventi, K.L., Deshmukh, A., and Pfefferbaum, A. (2003). Effects of alcohol dependence comorbidity and antipsychotic medication on volumes of the thalamus and pons in schizophrenia. *American Journal of Psychiatry,* 160(6), 1110-6.

Tapert, S.F., and Brown, S.A. (2000). Substance dependence, family history of alcohol dependence and neuropsychological functioning in adolescence. *Addiction*, 95(7), 1043-53.

Tarter, R.E. (1980). Brain damage in chronic alcoholism. A review of the psychological evidence. In D. Richer (Ed.), *Addiction and Brain Damage* (pp. 267-297). London: Croom-Helm.

Tarter, R.E., and Edwards, K.L. (1986). Multifactorial etiology of neuropsychological impairment in alcoholics. *Alcoholism: Clinical and Experimental Research,* 10(2), 128-35.

Tedstone, D., and Coyle. K. (2004). Cognitive performance in sober alcoholics: performance on selected and divided attention tasks. *Drug and Alcohol Dependence*, 75(3), 277-286.

Tivis, R., Beatty, W.W., Nixon, S.J., and Parsons, O.A. (1995). Patterns of cognitive impairment among alcoholics: are there subtypes? *Alcoholism: Clinical and Experimental Research,* 19(2), 496-500.

Uekermann, J., Channon, S., Winkel, K., Schlebusch, P., Trenckmann, U., and Daum, I. (submitted). Theory of mind, humour processing and executive functioning in alcoholism.

Uekermann, J., Daum, I., Schlebusch, P., and Trenckmann, U. (2005). Processing of affective stimuli in alcoholism. *Cortex*, 41(2), 189-94.

Uekermann, J., Daum, I., Schlebusch, P., Wiebel, B., and Trenckmann, U. (2003). Depression and cognitive functioning in alcoholism. *Addiction*, 98(11), 1521-9.

Veiel, H.O. (1997). A preliminary profile of neuropsychological deficits associated with major depression. *Journal of Clinical and Experimental Neuropsychology*, 19(4), 587-603.

Wegner, A.J., Gunthner, A., and Fahle, M. (2001). Visual performance and recovery in recently detoxified alcoholics. *Alcohol and Alcoholism,* 36(2), 171-9.

Yohman, J.R., and Parsons, O.A. (1987). Verbal reasoning deficits in alcoholics. *Journal of Nervous and Mental Diseases,* 175(4), 219-23.

Zinn, S., Stein, R., and Swartzwelder, H.S. (2004). Executive functioning early in abstinence from alcohol. *Alcoholism: Clinical and Experimental Research,* 28(9), 1338-46.

In: Abnormal Psychology: New Research
Editor: Helen D. Friedman and Paulina K. Revera
ISBN: 978-1-60692-636-9

Chapter 7

PERCEPTION WITHOUT AWARENESS: THE QUALITATIVE DIFFERENCES APPROACH

Juan J. Ortells [1], ***María T. Daza*** [1], ***Carmen Noguera*** [1], ***Encarna Carmona*** [1], ***Elaine Fox*** [2] ***and María J. F. Abad*** [3]

1 University of Almería , Spain
2 University of Essex , England
3 University of Jaén, Spain

Is it possible to perceive stimulus information even when there is no awareness of perceiving? This question has been the focus of considerable research and discussion for more than 100 years (see Adams, 1957, for a review of earlier studies). However, despite the numerous experimental reports suggesting that our behavior and thoughts may be influenced by unconscious processes, research on perception without awareness has usually been plagued by continual controversy (Merikle, 1992). Much of this controversy stems directly from the logic underlying the task-*dissociation paradigm*, which has traditionally been the most widely followed approach to address that issue.

Although various versions of this paradigm have been used, the basic assumption underlying all versions is that unconscious perception can be demonstrated via a dissociation between two different indices or measures of perception. One *direct* measure (e. g., stimulus recognition) would reflect the effect of a perceived stimulus on the instructed responses to that stimulus (which is typically assessed by a measure of accuracy at the instructed task). Such a direct effect is assumed to indicate whether any relevant stimulus information is consciously perceived. A second *indirect* measure of stimulus perception would be an uninstructed effect of the task stimulus on behavior, which is assumed to be also sensitive to unconsciously perceived information. As an illustration, a well-known indirect effect is semantic priming (see also the Stroop's (1935) interference effect), which consists of a facilitation of responses (in terms of speed and/or accuracy) to a target stimulus (e.g., CAT) when it is preceded by a semantically related (prime) word (e.g., DOG), than when the preceding prime word is unrelated to the target (e.g., ARM). A dissociation is demonstrated whenever there is a reliable indirect effect by a stimulus that is unaccompanied by any direct effect of that stimulus. In other words, perception without awareness would be demonstrated whenever the indirect measure of perception (e.g., semantic priming) shows some sensitivity to stimuli under conditions on which the direct measure shows null sensitivity.

In spite of this relatively straightforward logic underlying the dissociation paradigm, it has proven difficult to design experiments that provide compelling, uncontroversial evidence for perception without awareness. On the one hand, there usually has been a lack of agreement about what constitutes an adequate direct measure of conscious perception. On the other hand, the means of using dissociation data to draw conclusions about unconscious perception have remained controversial. As noted by some authors (e.g., Holender, 1986; Reingold & Merikle, 1988), this is because the interpretation of a dissociation pattern mainly depends on assumptions being made about the relation of conscious and unconscious perception to performance on direct and indirect tasks. In an influential review, Holender (1986) suggested that in order that the occurrence of an indirect effect in the absence of a direct effect (i.e., an *indirect-without-direct-effect pattern*) provides compelling evidence for unconscious perception, the direct measure must be assumed to be sensitive to all relevant conscious effects of stimuli, and such a measure must exhibits null sensitivity. If this *exhaustiveness assumption* (as labelled by Reingold & Merikle, 1988) cannot be justified, then any dissociation between measures may simply indicate that the direct and indirect indices are sensitive to different aspects of consciously perceived stimuli. In addition, the direct measure should *exclusively* be influenced by conscious processes (i.e., an *exclusiveness assumption*). If a direct effect is sensitive to both consciously and unconsciously perceived information, then the attempt to establish null sensitivity for the direct measure could eliminate or underestimate any evidence for unconscious perception.

1. The Traditional Dissociation Paradigm: Subjective Versus Objective Measures of Awareness

In efforts to find satisfactory exhaustive measures of conscious perception and to demonstrate that perception occurs even when these measures exhibit null sensitivity, two general classes of direct indices have been used, *subjective* and *objective*. With subjective measures, stimulus awareness is indexed by participants' self-reports of their conscious perceptual experiences. When these subjective reports show that participants do not believe any useful stimulus information was perceived, it is assumed that they did not have any relevant conscious experiences (i.e., a phenomenal lack of stimulus awareness). As an example of the general approach consider the classic experiment reported by Sidis (1898). He presented observers a series of cards containing single printed letters or digits. Participants saw the cards at a distance such that they informed all that they could see on each card was a dim, blurred spot or nothing at all. Yet, despite participants' reports indicated that they were unaware of perceiving either letter or digits, they were able to guess both the category (i.e., letter vs. digit) and the identity of the stimulus at a considerable better than chance level of performance (67% correct responses). On the basis of this dissociation between verbal self-reports and forced-choice guessing (i.e., direct vs. indirect measures of stimulus perception, respectively), Sidis concluded that he had found evidence for perception without awareness.

In general, the pattern of data obtained by these early studies indicate that relatively simple visual stimuli such as horizontal, vertical, and diagonal lines (e.g. Baker, 1937;

Dunlap, 1900), circles, triangles, and squares (e.g. Miller, 1942; Williams, 1938), and letter and digits (e.g. Sidis, 1898; Stroh, Shaw & Washburn, 1908), can be perceived even when there is no awareness of perceiving. Likewise, latter studies using both behavioural and neuroimaging techniques (e.g., functional magnetic resonance imaging, positron emission tomography) have reported evidence that more complex information such as the lexical or semantic status or verbal stimuli (e.g. Cheesman & Merikle, 1986; Forster & Davis, 1984; Forster & Veres, 1998; Merikle, Joordens & Stolz, 1995), or the emotions expressed in faces (e.g. Esteves, Dimberg & Öhman, 1994; Esteves & Öhman, 1993; Whalen, Rauch, Etcoff, Mclnerney, Lee & Jenike, 1998), can be perceived even though participants' introspective reports indicated that they were unaware of critical stimuli.

If one accepts participants' verbal reports as valid indicators of awareness, then there is considerable evidence for unconscious perception. However, a number of investigators (e.g., Eriksen, 1960; Holender, 1986) have suggested that when awareness is assessed by subjective measures, there is always the concern that observers′ descriptions of their conscious experiences are influenced by many factors other than their awareness of the critical stimuli (cf. Eriksen, 1960). For example, statements or comments indicating an absence of relevant conscious experiences may simply reflect biases introduced by either the experimental setting or the participants' preconceived ideas concerning the value of particular types of conscious experiences for guiding decisions, rather a true absence of relevant conscious experiences. It this was actually the case, the studies using subjective measures may provide nothing more than additional demonstrations of the unreliability of introspective reports (cf. Merikle, 1992).

Because of these interpretative problems with introspective reports, a number of investigators have preferred to use objective behavioural measures of perceptual discrimination to distinguish between conscious and unconscious perception. Examples of objective measures are: forced-choice, presence-absence decisions and forced-choice decisions among a small set of stimulus alternatives. When an objective measure is used to index conscious awareness, a failure to discriminate between alternative stimulus states, such as the presence or absence of a stimulus (i.e., a forced-choice performance at chance), would indicate an absence of relevant, consciously perceived information.

At first sight, measures of discriminative capacities have both intuitive appeal and some methodological advantages relative to introspective self-reports. As noted by Merikle (1992), if a stimulus is presented under conditions such that observers are unable to distinguish between its presence or absence, then it seems reasonable to assume that presentation of this stimulus did not lead to conscious awareness. Additionally, unlike introspective reports, with an objective measure perceptual sensitivity can be measured independent of the influence of preconceived biases (e.g., Eriksen, 1960; Holender, 1986).

Anthony Marcel (1980; 1983a; 1983b) was the first investigator to report that visually degraded stimuli can be perceived even when they are presented below an objectively defined threshold for awareness. For example, Marcel (1983a, Experiment 1) presented a display containing either a word or a blank field followed by a masking display, with perception of the masked words being assessed by both direct and indirect measures. The direct task consisted of a forced-choice presence vs. absence detection, such that on each trial the participants should decide whether the mask was preceded or not by a word. Participants were also required to select between two different words, what was more similar (either in semantic or in grapheme characteristics) to the masked word (the indirect task). The critical finding was that participants performed above chance in the similarity judgment (indirect) task, even at a word-mask stimulus onset asynchrony (SOA) such that it was impossible for them to discriminate better than chance when a word was present from when a word was absent. Further evidence for semantic encoding of words presented below an objective threshold for awareness was reported by Marcel using other indirect measures of word perception, such as semantic priming or the Stroop interference effect. In the variant of the Stroop (1935) color-word task used by Marcel (1983a, Experiment 3), participants named the color (red vs. green) of a central patch that was preceded by a masked prime word, which consisted of either a congruent color word, an incongruent color word or a control letter string. Previous research indicates that color-naming latencies in this task increase (i.e., interference effect) when the color patch is preceded by an incongruent color word, and decrease (i.e., facilitation effect) when it is preceded by a congruent color word (e.g., Dalrymple-Alford, 1972). The word-mask SOA was either of 400 ms, such that all participants were able to consciously perceive the word's identity, or a much shorter time. This latter SOA was for each participant 5 ms lesser than a previously established awareness threshold, which was defined by Marcel as the SOA interval at which presence/absence decisions were no better than chance. Marcel found reliable facilitation and interference effects at both SOA conditions, that is, even when participants were unable to discriminate between the presence or absence of the color words (see also Marcel, 1983b).

Whereas further studies have replicated and extended Marcel's findings (e.g. Balota, 1983; Bar & Biederman, 1998; Dagenbach, Carr & Wihelmsen, 1989; Dehaene, Naccache, Le Clec'H, Koechlin, Mueller, Dehaene-Lambertz, van de Moortele, & Le Bihan, 1998; Kemp-Wheeler & Hill, 1988; McCauley, Parmelee, Sperber & Carr, 1980), other investigators have been unable to successfully replicate the results reported y Marcel (e.g. Cheesman and Merikle, 1984). And more important, the results of studies using objective measures of awareness have been critized on the basis of several methodological concerns, which call into question whether the critical stimuli were actually presented below the participants' awareness thresholds (e.g., Cheesman & Merikle; 1984; 1985; Holender, 1986; Merikle, 1982; Nolan & Caramazza, 1982; Purcell, Stewart & Stanovich, 1983). For example, it has been argued that the participants' thresholds are usually based on such a small number of trials that it is not possible to obtain a reliable estimate of each participant's response distribution. Thus a non-discriminative responding (i.e., a 50% correct in a two-choice task) could not necessarily be attributed to a genuine inability to utilize the available perceptual information. It could, for example, be the case that participants performing a presence/absence detection on visually degraded stimuli showed a bias to say "no" on most trials, regardless of the stimulus was present or absent. On the other hand, the masking conditions used in some studies (e.g. McCauley et al., 1980) were less effective on the priming (indirect) trials than on the threshold (direct) trials, and hence, stimulus perception on the former trials could have occurred with, instead without, awareness. Furthermore, in some previous studies (e.g., Marcel, 1983a) the actual criterion for threshold performance was defined as "a performance less than 60% correct" (instead of 50%) in a two-choice task. Under these circumstances, some conscious detection of the masked stimuli could have occurred. In support of that argument, Cheesman & Merikle (1984; see also Nolan and Caramazza, 1982; Purcell et al., 1983) used the Marcel's Stroop task methodology but introducing two modifications. First, participants' ability to identify the color words was measured using a forced-choice discrimination procedure involving four response alternatives (i.e., four possible color words). This method tried to avoid possible individual differences in the willingness to guess a response. Secondly, different word-mask SOAs were manipulated to estimate different levels of efficiency in word identification task: 25% (random performance because the existence of *four* response alternatives), 55%, 90% and 100% (in this latter case, the word was followed by no mask). Results showed reliable facilitation and interference effects at all the SOA conditions that allowed a word identification better than chance (i.e., 55%, 90%, and 100%), but not at the SOA interval inducing a non-discriminative responding (25% correct). Against Marcel's findings, this last result suggests that there is no semantic encoding for stimuli presented below an objective threshold for awareness. Interestingly, participants' self-reports indicated that they were unaware of word identity not only at the SOA condition associated with a random identification, but also at those SOA conditions producing identification scores reliably better than chance (i.e., 55% and 90% correct responses). Accordingly, Cheesman and Merikle suggest that there is compelling and consistent evidence for perception without awareness only when subjective, rather than objective, thresholds are used to define stimulus awareness.

2. Alternative Approaches to the Study of Unconscious Perception

Overall, traditional studies using objective direct measures of stimulus perception have not provided evidence, either for or against perception without awareness, that is any more definitive and convincing that has been provided by studies using subjective measures (Merikle, 1992). In fact, empirical approaches using the dissociation paradigm present a series of limitations, which make any data pattern difficult to interpret.

Firstly, it should be noted that studies of perception without awareness have traditionally used any kind of *facilitation paradigm*, whereby effects on unconscious perception of a stimulus produced the same data pattern as did conscious perception. According to Debner and Jacoby (1994), because both types of processes can contribute to performance in a similar vein (i.e., facilitating), it is difficult to determine whether the supposedly unconscious influences might partly or completely be attributed to any residual conscious perception. On the other hand, it has been argued that requiring direct measures that reflect both exclusively and exhaustively all relevant consciously perceived information (e.g. Holender, 1986) may be too stringent requirements for demonstrating unconscious influences. Reingold and Merikle (1988; 1990; see also Merikle & Reingold, 1998) point out that it appears unrealistic to expect that any particular direct measure of perception could actually be sensitive to all conscious stimulus effects. As stated by these authors, "...no matter what direct measure is selected, there is no way to demonstrate conclusively that this measure is a completely satisfactory measure of all relevant conscious experiences" (Merikle & Reingold, 1998, p. 305). Reingold and Merikle also considered implausible that unconscious stimulus effects should be excluded from contributing to performance on direct measures. It could rather be the case that any direct (like indirect) effect might include both conscious and unconscious contributions (see also Jacoby, Lindsay & Toth, 1992).

Finally, irrespective of either subjective or objective direct measures of conscious perception are used, traditional studies aimed to find an indirect effect in the complete absence of a direct effect (i.e., an *indirect-without-direct-effect* data pattern) would require accepting a null hypothesis (i.e., the hypothesis of no direct effect), and this is statistically problematic. As noted by Merikle and Joordens (1997a), it is impossible to demonstrate in a completely convincing fashion that null sensitivity necessarily indicates no relevant information was consciously perceived. There is the possibility that some amount of stimulus information was detected on at least some occasions that eluded detection by conventional direct tasks. Thus, claiming a null result on a direct measure is always susceptible to the familiar criticisms of inappropriately asserting the truth of a null hypothesis (e.g., the methodology may have been inadequate to reveal the true sensitivity of the measure).

Because of these limitations, an increasingly number of researchers abandoned the research strategy of establishing dissociations to demonstrate unconscious perception, and moved the methodology forward. On the assumption that it may just be impossible to design experiments that satisfy the logical requirements of the dissociation paradigm, a series of alternative approaches have been developed. These approaches provide different methods for studying perception without awareness that do not require a convincing demonstration of a null effect.

2.1. The Relative Sensitivity Approach

Reingold and Merikle (1988; 1990; Merikle & Reingold, 1991) proposed an alternative strategy in which, rather than searching an indirect-without-direct effect pattern, they advocate the search of an indirect effect that is statistically stronger (i.e., *more sensitive*) than a direct effect, when the two effects are comparable. This relative sensitivity approach is based on a relaxation of Holender's assumptions about direct measures. Firstly, Reingold and Merikle propose to replace the Holender's exclusiveness assumption with an "*inclusiveness*" assumption, according to which any direct (or indirect) measure of perception is potentially sensitive to both conscious and unconscious influences. In order to interpret any pattern of data from direct and indirect measures in terms of unconscious cognition, Reingold and Merikle introduced an additional *minimal* assumption, which replaced the exhaustiveness assumption. According to such a *relative sensitivity* assumption, the sensitivity of a direct measure to task-relevant information should be greater or at least equal that the sensitivity of the indirect measure to the same information. The rationale underlying this assumption is that consciously perceived information relevant to a particular discrimination (e.g., an old-new judgment), if exists, it should be used equally or more efficiently when participants are instructed explicitly to make the discrimination, than when they are instructed to judge the stimuli on some other basis (i.e., an indirect effect). Based on this relative sensitivity assumption, an unconscious influence is demonstrated whenever an indirect effect is statistically stronger than a comparable direct effect from the same stimulus information, irrespective of the direct measure exhibits a true null sensitivity or it does not. This is the case because the relative sensitivity assumption rules out the possibility that superior performance on the indirect task is attributable to conscious, task-relevant information.

It is important to note that the interpretation of an indirect-greater-than-direct pattern as evidence for unconscious cognition is only warranted if both direct and indirect measures are truly comparable. That is, both measures must be described on the same measurement scales and obtained in response to the same task stimuli. Otherwise, the greater sensitivity of an indirect measure might simply reflect a methodological artefact (e.g., differences in measurement scales, or in response bias across the two tasks), rather than an unconscious influence. As an example of this approach consider the now-classic study by Kunst-Wilson and Zajonc (1980; see also Mandler, Nakamura & Van Zandt, 1987). In a first phase of the experiment, they presented 10 meaningless, irregular geometric shapes, with each shape being presented five times for a 1-ms duration each time, such that no participants reported seeing any of the shapes. Following this initial presentation, the participants were shown 10 pairs of shapes, with each pair consisting of an "old" shape (which had been presented during the previous phase) and a "new" (not previously presented) shape. On each pair of shapes, participants were required to make two forced-choice tasks, namely, a recognition task and a preference task. For the recognition (direct) task, participants had to select the member of the pair that had been presented previously. For the preference (indirect) task, participants were told to choose the shape of each pair that they preferred. Whereas participants' performance in the recognition task was not better than chance (i.e., 50% correct), they performed significantly above chance in the preference task (i.e., 60%), thus suggesting that this latter (indirect) task was a more sensitive measure of the old-new discrimination than the recognition task. What makes the Kunst-Wilson and Zajonc's data a so compelling evidence for unconscious influence is that their direct (recognition) and indirect (preference) measures of memory were matched on all characteristics except the task's instructions. Thus, both measures were based on the same study and test conditions, the same pairs of stimuli and the same response metric. Another good example of the relative sensitivity approach is the study by Merikle and Reingold (1991), which examined the effects that allocation of visual attention may have on the relative sensitivity of direct and indirect measures of memory for words. Their experiments consisted on two phases. During a first study phase, participants were presented with pairs of words and were required to name one cued word in each pair. During the test phase, new words and either the previously cued words (Experiment 1) or the previously uncued words (Experiments 2a and 2b) were presented against a background mask. Participants were required to judge whether a word was old or new (a direct recognition task), or whether the contrast between a word and the background was high or low (an indirect task). Merikle and Reingold found that for the attended (cued) words, the direct task was much more sensitive than the indirect task. Yet, for the uncued (ignored) words the indirect task was initially more sensitive than the direct task, thus suggesting unconscious processing underlying memory for the ignored words.

An important advantage of using comparable direct and indirect measures to study unconscious processes, is that the methodological requirements are less stringent and *a priori* assumptions more minimal than those required by the traditional dissociation paradigm. As pointed by Greenwald, Klinger and Schuh (1995), by avoiding any need to justify an exhaustiveness assumption and to demonstrate a null direct effect, the relative sensitivity approach appeared to have it easier to develop more convincing evidence for unconscious cognition. However, it should be noted that the indirect-greater-than direct pattern has demonstrated to be replicable only in research using memory-based measures, in which both direct and indirect effects are measured at a substantial delay after stimulus presentation. But this is not the case in research aimed to study perception without awareness, mainly because it has proven difficult to find direct and indirect measures of perception that can be truly comparable (cf. Greenwald et al., 1995).

2.2. The Regression Analysis Method

Greenwald and colleagues (Draine & Greenwald, 1998; Greenwald & Draine, 1997; Greenwald, Draine & Abrams, 1996; Greenwald et al., 1995) have recently developed a new methodology for studying perception without awareness, which is based on a mixture of ideas taken from both the relative sensitivity approach and the classic dissociation paradigm. As already noted, an usual criticism to the traditional dissociation paradigm is that any convincing demonstration of an indirect effect in the absence of a direct effect requires the acceptance of a null hypothesis (i.e., a null result on the direct measure has been achieved). To bypass the statistical problems associated with asserting the truth of a null hypothesis, Greenwald et al. use a regression analysis strategy. The major innovation of this method is to analyse data using tests of the regression relation between direct and indirect measures of responses to near-threshold stimuli. In the regression analysis, the amount of semantic priming (an indirect effect) produced by near-threshold stimuli is plotted against a direct objective measure of the prime stimuli. In the priming task, participants perform a binary categorization judgment either for affectively polarized words (i.e., pleasant vs. unpleasant) or for common first names (to be categorized as male or female). The target word is preceded (by a variable time interval, depending on the experiment) by a briefly presented and masked prime word, which could be either related (i.e., belonging to the same category) or unrelated to the target. To increase the sensitivity to priming, Greenwald and colleagues (e.g., Draine & Greenwald, 1998; Greenwald et al., 1996) have recently used a "response-window procedure" in which participants are always required to respond to the target item within a moderately early response window (i.e., 250 ms ± 133 ms). This forced-responding method substantially controls response time and moves the priming effect into response accuracy (e.g., d' units of discriminability). Direct (objective) measures of prime perceptibility are obtained in separate (later) blocks of trials, in which participants make various discriminations of content for the masked primes, for example, deciding whether the prime stimulus was a word or a XGXG string. As occurred with the priming measures, the index of direct processing is also measured in terms of d' units (i.e., accuracy), such that both indirect and direct measures have rational zero points. Participants' performance on both tasks is then analysed as regression functions that relate priming scores to direct measures of perceptibility of the primes (where zero values on indirect and direct tasks indicate absence of priming and perceptibility, respectively). The height at which the regression function crosses the vertical axis (the *regression intercept*) provides a critical test for the hypothesis that priming has occurred unconsciously (Greenwald et al., 1996). This is because the intercept of the regression equation is an estimation of the level of performance on the indirect measure (i.e., the magnitude of semantic priming) associated with a zero value on the direct measure (i.e., d' = 0). Under these circumstances, the finding of a significant (i.e., a nonzero effect) regression intercept effect would indicate an unconscious contribution to the indirect measure. Note that with this regression method, evidence for unconscious perception (i.e., the indirect-without-direct effect pattern) occurs in the form of a null hypothesis rejection (i.e., an intercept effect significantly greater than zero), rather than the null hypothesis acceptance that characterized the traditional dissociation paradigm (Greenwald et al., 1995).

The approach developed by Greenwald and colleagues represents one of the most rigorous applications of the dissociation paradigm for studying perception without awareness, in that it reverses the usual difficulty associated with asserting the truth of a null hypothesis.

However, their regression methodology relies on a series of assumptions, which must be satisfied to interpret a regression data pattern as providing compelling evidence for unconscious perception. For example, given that the exact value of the intercept parameter is a key issue in the Greenwald et al.'s application of the regression method, it is necessary to consider whether there is measurement variability (i.e., participant-to-participant response variation) in the direct (predictor) measure. Thus, the presence of a substantial variability in such a measure might lead to inflated intercepts even in the absence of any unconscious effect (Dosher, 1998). As already noted, in experiments by Greenwald et al. the predictor score is usually an objective direct measure of perceptual sensitivity (d') based on two-alternative forced-choice tasks, where a d' score = 0 is assumed to reflect stimulus unawareness. Yet, in some of their experiments (e.g., Draine & Greenwald, 1998) there is a noticeable d' variability for the direct task, including d' values below zero. As noted by Dosher (1998), such a values theoretically should arise because of measurement error, which could produce contaminated intercept values. It still remains unclear whether a d' score above zero in forced-choice tasks necessarily reflects a conscious perception of critical stimuli. In fact, neuropsychological research has consistently showed that brain-damaged (e.g. cortically blind) patients can perform significantly better than chance (e.g. d' > 0) when they are encouraged to make forced-choice discriminations on several attributes of stimuli (e.g., spatial location, movement, orientation, shape, or meaning) about which they report to be completely unaware (see Farah, 2001, for a recent review on neuropsychological research about consciousness). On the other hand, in a number of experiments examining the influence of different attentional instructions on semantic processing of parafoveally presented words (e.g., Ortells & Tudela, 1996; see also Ortells, Abad, Noguera & Lupiáñez, 2001), we found that the to-be-attended words produced facilitatory priming. Conversely, the words that participants were instructed to ignore produced an opposite pattern of negative priming, thus suggesting that these latter stimuli were truly ignored. But whereas participants' self-reports indicated no awareness about the ignored words' identity (unlike the attended words), their performance in a further recognition test about the unattended (and the attended) words yielded d' scores significantly greater than zero for those words.

Another implied assumption of the regression method by Greenwald et al. is that, in order that an *indirect-without-direct-effect pattern* provides evidence for unconscious processing, is also necessary that direct and indirect measures were comparable. That is, both measures should reflect some similar processing of the stimuli, and comparability requires at least a modest correlation between the direct and indirect measures. As argued by Dosher (1998; see also Merikle & Reingold, 1998), in the absence of a correlation between measures, the regression intercept may simply reveal the *overall mean* sensitivity of the indirect measure (with a number of the indirect data likely having associated direct scores above-zero). In order to justify the comparability of direct and indirect tasks, a number of criteria must be satisfied, such as the fact that both measures index the same perceptual discrimination, are based on the same response metric, and the experimental conditions for administering both tasks are completely matched. But this does not seem to be the case in some of Greenwald et al.'s experiments. For example, the semantic categorization (e.g., pleasant vs. unpleasant) indirect task used by Draine and Greenwald (1998) appears a quite different task that discriminating a word from a XGs string, with this latter task likely inducing no-semantic processing strategies. In addition, direct and indirect measures were assessed under considerably different conditions. Whereas the direct task did not impose time pressure on the participants' response (which could result in a substantial amount of variability across participants), the response-window procedure used in the indirect task required all the participants to respond within an experimenter-defined temporal interval. All of these differences in task quality, time testing and time pressure would call into question the comparability and appropriateness of the direct task, and contribute to the lack of a correlation between measures. To sum up, if the validity of the assumptions underlying an appropriate application of the regression method is not carefully considered (with each of the potential artefacts being rule out), then the regression strategy may be not any more informative than other previous approaches based on the dissociation paradigm (Dosher, 1998; Merikle & Reingold, 1998).

2.3. Qualitative Differences between Conscious and Unconscious Perception

It should be noted that the absence of a strong relationship between the direct and indirect measures, might reflect the fact that conscious and unconscious cognitive processes in certain domains can be independent. Based on that assumption and rather than to simply ask whether a stimulus can be unconsciously perceived, many investigators have addressed the question of how does unconscious perception differ from conscious perception (e.g. Dixon, 1981; Merikle & Daneman, 1998; Merikle, Smilek & Eastwood, 2001). Basically, the experimental logic is to contrast perception with and without awareness in order to determine whether a stimulus can have qualitatively different consequences on cognitive and affective reactions depending on whether it was either consciously or unconsciously perceived. Throughout the present section we describe a series of different approaches, which have consistently demonstrated that perception with and without awareness does lead to qualitatively different behavioural effects[7].

On the one hand, a series of studies have showed that a word is coded differently depending on whether is either consciously or unconsciously perceived. For example, Groeger (1984) presented visually (for a variable exposure time, depending on the group of participants) single target words and required participants to identify and select that stimulus from a subsequently presented matrix of 24 different words. The target word was never presented in the matrix, although this contained words that were either structurally (i.e., orthographically) or semantically similar to the target. When the target words were briefly presented such that participants experienced no awareness of them, they tended to select the semantically related words. But when the target words were presented for longer durations, thus allowing that they were perceived with a low level of awareness, participants tended to select the visually similar words. Groeger (1988) obtained a similar result pattern when words were presented auditorily. Namely, participants selected from the matrix either phonologically similar or semantically related foils, depending on whether the target words had been perceived with or without awareness, respectively.

Other interesting series of studies have demonstrated that the influence of context in perception is limited to information that is consciously perceived. In contrast, unconscious

---

7 It is interesting to note that in most of approaches examining qualitative differences between conscious and unconscious perceptual processes, subjective measures of awareness are assumed to provide an adequate indication of the presence (or absence) of relevant conscious experiences.

perception would induce more automatic reactions, which would not be constrained by contextual information. To illustrate, Marcel (1980) presented sequences of three words (e.g. *hand – palm – wrist*) as follows: (a) A clearly visible context word (e.g., hand) aimed to bias interpretation of (b) an upcoming polysemus word with two different meanings (e.g., palm), and (c) a clearly visible target word related to one of the two possible meanings of the polysemous word (e.g., wrist). Unlike both the context and the target words, the polysemous word was presented under conditions so that they were either consciously or unconsciously perceived. In the former condition (conscious perception), time to respond to the target word was faster if it was preceded by a meaning-related context word (i.e., a semantic priming effect). Thus reaction times to the target "wrist" were faster for the sequence *hand-palm-wrist*, relative to the sequence *tree-palm-wrist*, as the target and the context were related to the same meaning of the polysemus word in the former, but not in the latter condition. However, when the polysemous word was not consciously perceived, time to respond to the target word was facilitated if it was preceded by a polysemous word with a related meaning (e.g., wrist preceded by palm, relative to wrist preceded by river), regardless of the meaning of the preceding biasing context word (e.g., palm vs. tree). As hypothesized by Marcel, it appears then that selective context-driven perception requires conscious awareness, as the context word biased interpretation of the polysemus word only when it was consciously perceived. But in the absence of conscious awareness the multiple meanings of a stimulus would automatically be activated.

On the other hand, there are several findings suggesting that affective reactions are more likely to be influenced by unconsciously perceived than by consciously perceived stimuli (e.g., Kunst-Wilson & Zajonc, 1980; Murphy & Zajonc, 1993). For example, Murphy and Zajonc (1993) required participants to indicate on a five-point scale whether each of a series of clearly visible Chinese ideographs represented a "good" or a "bad" concept. Each ideograph was preceded by a picture of a human face expressing either happiness (e.g., a smile) or anger (e.g., a scowl). The presentation duration of the faces was manipulated between-participants at two levels: 4ms and 1000 ms, such that participants reported either no awareness (4 ms) or a complete awareness (1000 ms) of the faces. Participants in the 1000-ms group were instructed to completely ignore the faces and to concentrate exclusively on rating the ideographs. Murphy and Zajonc observed that participants' ratings of the ideographs were reliably influenced by the emotion expressed by the preceding faces (i.e., an ideograph was more likely rated as representing a "good" concept if it was preceded by a smiling face). But such an influence only occurred when the faces were presented for 4 ms, such that participants reported no awareness of them, thus suggesting an important qualitative difference between conscious and unconscious perception.

In a series of recent experiments, Fox and colleagues have also used emotional stimuli to investigate possible attentional biases in subclinical anxiety (e.g., Correa, Fox, Carmona, Noguera, Lupiáñez & Tudela, 2002; Fox, 1996; Fox, Russo, Bowles & Dutton, 2001). To illustrate, Correa et al. (2002) have reported that high anxious people can show a faster shifting of spatial attention to threatening stimuli (e.g., angry faces), as these stimuli had advantage over positive or neutral stimuli in attracting attention to their own location. Interestingly, such attention orienting biases occurred only when the faces were masked and participants were unaware of them. When the faces were consciously perceived, there was a delayed disengagement of attention in anxious people (see also Fox et al., 2001), but no evidence for enhanced cueing was found.

Several particularly interesting approaches to the study of unconscious perception have developed measures of perception that are influenced in opposite ways by consciously and unconsciously perceived information. The logic underlying to these studies is based on the assumption that conscious perception enables individuals to act intentionally on the world (e.g., they are able to follow instructions) and to produce effects on it. In contrast, information perceived without awareness leads to much more automatic reactions that cannot be controlled by individuals (e.g. Marcel, 1988; Searle, 1992). A good example is the stem completion task administered under *exclusion* instructions. The distinguishing characteristic of that measure, which was originally developed by Jacoby (1991; see also Debner & Jacoby, 1994; Jacoby, Toth & Yonelinas, 1993; Merikle & Joordens, 1997a; Merikle et al., 1995; Smith & Merikle, 1999), is that participants are instructed not to use particular responses when completing word stems. Consider, for example, the study by Debner and Jacoby (1994), in which, the likelihood that words were perceived with or without awareness was controlled by varying the stimulus duration. On each trial, a single word (e.g., *table*) was presented for either a short (i.e., 50 ms) or a somewhat longer (i.e., 150 ms) duration (depending on the experiment), and followed by a mask. Immediately following the mask offset, a three-letter stem consisting of the first three letters from the preceding word (e.g. *tab*_ _) was presented, and the participants were required to complete the word stem with any word that came to mind *except* the word that had just been presented (e.g. they could complete the word stem with *taboo*, but not *table*). Debner and Jacoby found that participants were able to follow these "*exclusion*" instructions when the words were presented for the longer 150-ms duration. Namely, target words were used to complete the word stems much less often than occurred in a baseline condition. Yet, when the words were presented for 50-ms, participants had difficulty following the exclusion instructions, as they used these words to complete the stems much more often than the baseline level, despite the explicit instructions not to use those words. These findings showed that the target words were always perceived, irrespective of they were presented for either 150 or 50 ms, but they influenced the participants' completions in opposite ways (relative to the baseline level), depending on its presentation duration. If, as already noted, an assumption is made that a stimulus must be consciously perceived in order that it can guide our actions in the world, then the results reported by Debner and Jacoby suggest that participants were generally aware of the words presented for 150 ms (i.e., a lower exclusion performance relative to the baseline level in the stem completion task), and generally unaware of those presented for the shorter 50-ms duration (i.e., higher than baseline exclusion performance). Debner and Jacoby (1994, Experiment 3) found a similar pattern of qualitative differences in the consequences of perception, when stimulus awareness was controlled instructing participants on how to focus or distribute their attention (see also Smith & Merikle, 1999). An important advantage of the exclusion procedure by Debner and Jacoby (1994; see also Merikle & Joordens, 1997a), as compared to traditional approaches using "facilitation" paradigms, is that conscious and unconscious influences are placed "in opposition". Under these circumstances, evidence of unconscious perception cannot be explained as truly resulting from conscious perception, as the latter would produce an opposite result pattern.

Converging evidence that unconscious perception leads to automatic reactions whereas conscious perception allows individuals to modify their reactions, comes from an elegant series of Stroop-priming studies by Merikle and colleagues, which showed that individuals can use predictive strategies based on stimulus redundancy only when the predictive stimuli are consciously perceived (e.g. Cheesman & Merikle, 1986; Merikle & Cheesman, 1987; Merikle and Joordens, 1997a; 1997b; Merikle et al., 1995). Their experiments are based on a variant of the Stroop (1935) color-word interference task, in which two color words (RED or GREEN) are used to prime responses to a probe target consisting of a color patch (or a series of ampersands) that was also *red* or *green*. The standard result found with this task is that responses to the probe target (e.g. *red*) are slower when it follows an incongruent color word (e.g. GREEN) that when it follows a congruent color word (e.g. RED). This interference effect presumably occurs because participants cannot avoid reading the word even if they are not required to read it, and reading a word that refers to a conflicting color concept interferes with responding to the color target. However, the typical Stroop interference is *reversed* whenever incongruent prime-target pairings (GREEN – *red*) occurred more frequently than congruent (RED- *red*) prime-target pairings. Namely, the reaction times are faster on incongruent than on congruent trials. One explanation of that reversed Stroop effect is that participants capitalize on the predictive information provided by the prime words (e.g., Merikle et al., 1995). Given that there are only two possible colors, participants learn to expect that the target color on each trial will be the color not named by the preceding prime word. Such a predictive strategy would facilitate performance on the incongruent trials and slow performance on the congruent trials, thus leading to a reversal of the typical Stroop interference. Interestingly, Merikle and colleagues have consistently reported that the predictive strategy in the two-color variant of the Stroop task is adopted by participants only when the prime words are consciously perceived. In contrast, when the words are not consciously perceived, the standard interference effect is rather found. For example, Merikle and Joordens (1997b, Experiment 1A) presented a single central prime word (RED or GREEN in grey color) for 33 ms, which was followed either immediately or after a delay of 134 ms (depending on the group of participants) by a pattern-mask (seven ampersands in grey color), thus resulting in a prime-mask stimulus onset asynchrony –SOA- of either 33 ms[8] or 167 ms, respectively. The masked prime word was always followed by a central target, which consisted of seven ampersands displayed –until response- in either red or green, with participants being required to make a button-press response to indicate the target color as quickly as possible. For both groups of participants, the prime-target SOA remained fixed at 300 ms. On 75% of the trials, the prime and the target were incongruent (RED-green), whereas on the remaining 25% of the trials, the prime and the target were congruent (RED-red). Merikle and Joordens found a significant crossover interaction between masking condition and prime-target congruency: With a delayed mask (i.e., a prime-mask SOA of 167 ms) the reaction times (RTs) were *faster* on incongruent than on congruent trials. Such a reversed (i.e., facilitatory) Stroop effect suggests that participants consciously identified the prime word followed by a delayed mask, and then used the predictive information provided by the word to anticipate the target color (see also Logan, Zbrodoff & Williamson, 1984). On the contrary, with an immediate mask (i.e., a prime-mask SOA of 33 ms), a typical Stroop

[8] In a number of previous studies, Merikle and colleagues (e.g., Cheesman & Merikle, 1985; 1986; Merikle et al., 1995) have consistently found that a prime-mask SOA of 33 ms is below most participants' threshold for subjective awareness. This result has been confirmed in a series of recent experiments in our labs. Thus, when we required participants to make forced-choice binary tasks (e.g. an animate/inanimate judgment) on words presented for 33 ms and immediately masked, their performance was reliably better than chance (i.e., d' > 0). Yet, they reported a complete phenomenal lack of stimulus awareness, thus suggesting that words presented under immediate masking conditions were *below* a subjective threshold, but *under* an objective threshold for stimulus awareness.

interference effect emerged, thus suggesting that participants experienced no awareness of the primes when they were presented for 33 ms and immediately followed by a mask. This crossover in performance (i.e., reversed Stroop vs. interference effect) provides an additional qualitative difference that distinguishes conscious from unconscious perception.

In a series of recent experiments (e.g., Daza & Ortells, 2000a; Daza, Ortells, & Fox, in press) using the Merikle and Joordens' task, we have replicated and extended the findings by these authors. We have consistently shown that behavioural consequences of perceiving a stimulus with or without phenomenological awareness are qualitatively different not only by the sign (i.e. interference vs. facilitation) of the corresponding Stroop priming effect, but also by the time course of each priming effect (see Figure 1).

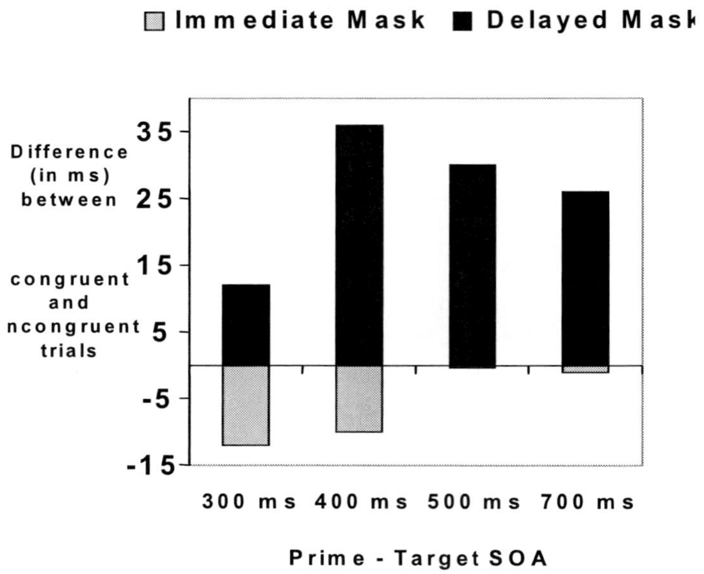

Figure 1. Stroop-priming effects from color words presented under immediate vs. delayed mask conditions as a function of the prime-target SOA
(Daza, Ortells & Fox, in press).

When the prime word was immediately masked, such that participants reported a complete absence of conscious awareness of word's identity, a reliable Stroop interference was consistently found at a prime-target SOA of 300 ms, thus replicating the Merikle and Joordens' findings. Additionally, whereas such an interference effect was still significant at a prime-target SOA of 400 ms, it declined to zero at longer SOA intervals of 500 ms and 700 ms (Daza et al., in press, Experiments 2 and 3), thus suggesting a relatively fast decay over time for that supposedly "automatic" Stroop-priming effect. Regarding the prime words that were followed by a delayed mask, an opposite facilitation (i.e., reversed Stroop) effect was found, although this effect reached significance at prime-target SOAs of 400 ms or longer. At a SOA interval of 300 ms, we consistently failed to replicate the reversed Stroop reported by Merikle and Joordens, regardless of whether our participants were either more or less actively encouraged for relying on the predictive information provided by the word to optimize their performance. The fact that participants' self-reports in all our experiments indicated that they were aware of the word's identity on most (or many) of trials under the delayed masking condition, suggests that consciously perceiving a stimulus constitutes a necessary, though not sufficient condition, in order to that stimulus guides intentional actions. To the extent that a reversed Stroop mainly reflects the contribution of strategic processes, and on the basis of the literature suggesting that controlled (strategic) processes build up much more slowly (and are often more sustained) than automatic processes (e.g. De Groot, 1984; Neely, 1977; Ortells et al., 2001; Posner & Snyder, 1975a; 1975b; Shenaut & Ober, 1996; Shiffrin & Schneider, 1977), the Daza et al.' findings (see Figure 1) suggest that a prime-target SOA of 300 ms would not give most observers sufficient time to use the prime word in a strategic manner to anticipate the target color.[9]

How to explain, then, the fact that Merikle and Joordens (1997b) we able to observe a significant reversed Stroop with a delayed mask using a short SOA of 300 ms? The reasons for the discrepancies between their results and those by Daza et al. (in press) remain unclear. But an inspection of Figure 1 in their paper (p. 224) suggests that the overall reaction times in their study were faster (i.e., lower than 400 ms) than those reported by Daza et al. (i.e., greater than 400 ms). Whereas all participants in our experiments had no prior experience with this kind of task, it could be the case that some (or many) of the subjects in Merikle and Joordens' study had previously participated in other similar studies. If this were actually the case[10], and on the basis of prior evidence showing that the time necessary to implement strategic processes can be shortened by practice (e.g., Logan & Zbrodoff, 1982; see also Logan, 1985), it remains possible that in Merikle and Joordens' study, a seemingly "short" SOA of 300 ms could still represent enough time for strategy development for a great proportion of their participants.

In either case, the Daza et al.' findings of differential SOA functions for the "automatic" versus "strategic" components of the two-color word Stroop effects, provide further strength for the claim that these two Stroop effects observed under the immediate vs. delayed mask conditions, would indeed reflect different underlying processes.

In a number of additional experiments in our labs using other priming procedures, we have found a fairly similar differential time-course of effects stemming from conscious vs. unconsciously perceived stimuli (e.g., Daza & Ortells, 2000b; Daza, Ortells & Noguera, 2001). The basic procedure used in these experiments was as follows: On each trial an uppercase prime word (e.g. CAT) was displayed at the centre of the screen for 33 ms, and was followed either immediately or after a variable delay of either 34, 134, 234 or 334 ms (depending on the experiment) by a pattern mask. The mask offset was followed by a central (lowercase) target word (e.g., hand) on which participants made a semantic categorization (animals vs. body parts) task (see Figure 2). On the 80% of the trials (unrelated condition) the prime and target words belonged to different semantic categories (e.g., CAT – mouth; NOSE – dog), whereas on the remaining 20% of the trials (related condition) the prime-target pairs were highly -associated words of the same semantic category (e.g. CAT – dog; NOSE – mouth).

---

[9] Note, in fact, that less than one half of participants in each of the Daza et al.'s experiments did show a reversed (facilitatory) Stroop from consciously perceived stimuli at the shortest prime-target SOA (300 ms).

[10] We have recently known by both Phil Merikle (personal communication, July 16th, 2001) and Steve Joordens (personal communication, October 25th, 2001) that some of their participants were given considerable training to use the prime word to anticipate the target color. Furthermore, some of the participants in their study could have been in other "perception without awareness" experiments, experiments that gave them experience with briefly presented and masked items.

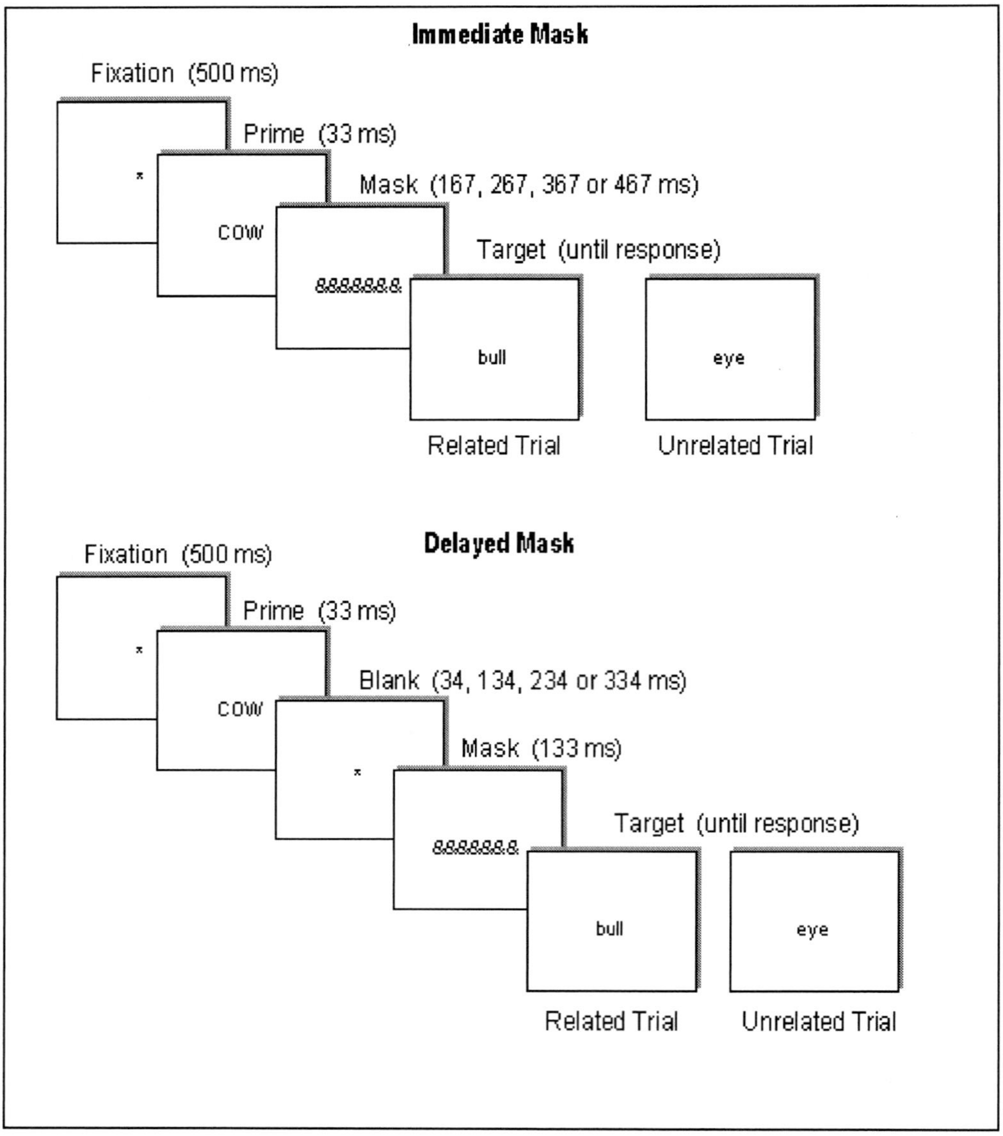

Figure 2. Sequence of events for trials in the priming procedure used by Daza & Ortells (2000b; see also Daza, Ortells & Noguera, 2001).

As in our Stroop-priming studies, irrespective of whether participants were either aware (delayed mask) or unaware (immediate mask) of the prime word, they were encouraged to use the predictive information provided by the prime word to optimise their categorization performance. So, given a particular prime word, they should expect that the upcoming target would belong to a different semantic category, as the unrelated trials were much more frequent than the related trials (see also Neely, 1977). The prime-target SOA was again manipulated at four levels: 200, 300, 400 and 500 ms.

The overall pattern of results mirrored to that found with the Stroop-priming task. Namely, when participants experienced no awareness of the prime word's identity (immediate mask), we obtained facilitatory semantic priming (i.e., faster reaction times on related than on unrelated trials). Such a supposedly "automatic" priming effect was significant at prime-target SOAs of 200, 300 and 400 ms, but it completely disappeared at the longer SOA of 500 ms (see Figure 3).

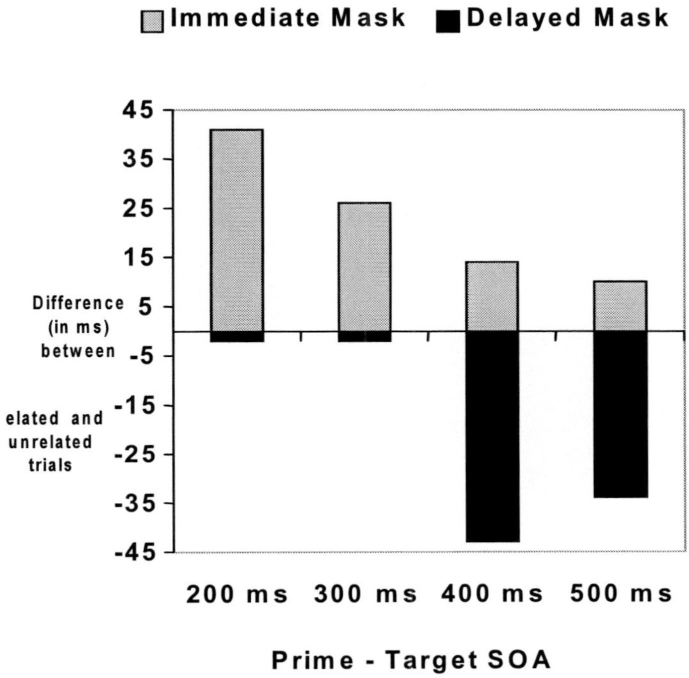

Figure 3. Semantic priming effects from masked words as a function of the masking (immediate vs. delayed) condition and the prime-target SOA (Daza & Ortells, 2000b).

On the other hand, when the prime word was followed by a delayed mask, such that participants were able to consciously perceive the word, a reversed semantic priming (i.e., interference) was rather found: reaction times were slower for related than for unrelated trials. Yet, as depicted in Figure 3, this strategic reversed priming was only found at SOAs of 400 ms or longer, with no priming effect being observed at the shorter SOAs of 200 and 300 ms. This latter result is clearly consistent with prior evidence from priming studies suggesting that obtaining a reliable strategy-dependent effect would usually require the use of time intervals of 400 ms or longer (e.g., De Groot, 1984; Di Pace, Longoni & Zoccolotti. 1991; Fuentes & Tudela, 1992; Neely, 1977; Ortells et al, 2001; Posner & Snyder, 1975a; 1975b; Shenaut & Ober, 1996).

One could argue that the lack of reversed priming effects in the delayed masking condition at the shorter SOAs (see also Daza et al., in press) it does not necessarily reflect the absence of strategic influences at that time intervals. Rather, it could be the case that the strategic processes contribute also immediately, but such an influence was overridden by an equally large automatic influence. As the automatic influence subsides (i.e., as the SOA interval is lengthened), the strategic influences would then predominate. To examine whether the reversed priming effects in our task mainly reflects the contribution of strategic (controlled) processes, or rather a combination of both, strategic and automatic influences, we have conducted an experiment in which the level of practice with the priming task (using a fixed prime-target SOA of 400 ms) was manipulated (Daza et al, 2001). If this last factor could influence to a greater extent the implementation of strategic (controlled) processes than that of automatic processes, and to the extent that the reversed priming from consciously perceived words mainly reflects the contribution of strategic influences, then we expected that such a priming effect was significant only when participants reached some level of practice with the task. In contrast, an unconsciously perceived prime word (immediate masking) should produce reliable automatic (facilitatory) priming even when participants have not enough practice with the task, with such a priming effect remaining similar across trial blocks. In other words, we expected that priming effects interacted with trial block with a delayed, but not with an immediate mask. The results were clearly consistent with our predictions (see Figure 4). Thus, an unconsciously perceived prime produced facilitatory priming, which reached significance since the first trial block. Conversely, with a delayed mask, the reversed priming effect started to be significant since the second block of trials, with no reliable priming being observed at the first trial block.

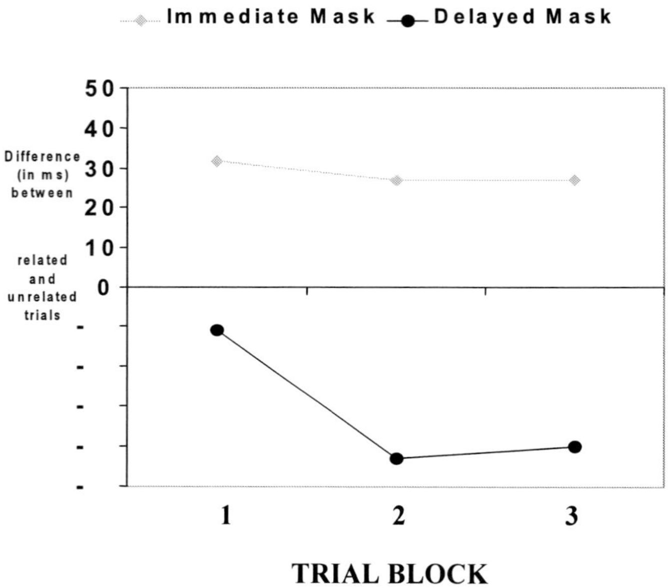

Figure 4. Semantic priming effects from words presented under immediate vs. delayed mask conditions as a function of the trial block (Daza, Ortells, & Noguera, 2001).

3. Conclusions

The question of whether perception can occur without awareness has been the focus of much research and controversy for many years. Traditional empirical approaches have generally aimed to find dissociations between performance on direct and indirect tests of perception. With the dissociation paradigm, perception without awareness is demonstrated whenever the indirect test shows sensitive to stimulus information on which the direct test shows null sensitivity. A weakness of studies using this dissociation paradigm, however, is that the conclusiveness of findings presumed to provide evidence for unconscious perception, depends entirely upon the adequacy of the measures used to define consciousness. Regardless of whether introspective (subjective) or behavioural (objective) measures of awareness are used, it is always possible to question whether that measure is actually successful (i.e., exhaustive) in guaranteeing a complete absence of *all* relevant conscious experiences. This would explain why traditional studies have not led to completely convincing evidence for unconscious perception, with the reported findings being open to alternative interpretations.

However, over the last two decades a number of alternative research strategies have been developed, which provide new methodologies for studying perception without awareness that do not require either the use of exhaustive measures of awareness or a convincing demonstration of a null direct effect. One particularly useful way of approaching to the study of unconscious perception is to focus on its distinction from conscious perception. That is, how do conscious and unconscious perceptual processes differ? As pointed out by Merikle and Daneman (1998; see also Merikle, 1992), the distinction between conscious and unconscious cognition is much more significant if both kinds of processes lead to qualitatively different consequences than if unconscious perception is simply a quantitatively weaker form of conscious perception.

Throughout the present review we have summarized a series of interesting qualitative differences in the behavioural consequences (e.g., cognitive and affective reactions) of perceiving a stimulus with or without awareness. The demonstration of qualitative differences in performance across aware and unaware conditions has considerable potential for at least two reasons. First, it constrains alternative interpretation of data (i.e., validating measures of awareness), thus providing more compelling evidence for the existence of unconscious perception than dissociations reported by traditional approaches. Secondly, the suggestion that conscious and unconscious perception can involve qualitatively different operations raises interesting questions about the nature of unconscious processing, and points to new insights and understandings regarding human cognition.

ACKNOWLEDGMENTS

The writing of this chapter was supported by a Grant BSO2000-1411-C02-02 from Ministerio de Ciencia y Tecnología (Dirección General de Investigación) of Spain, to Juan J. Ortells, María T. Daza, Carmen Noguera and María J.F. Abad. Correspondence could be sent to Juan J. Ortells, Departamento de Neurociencia y Ciencias de la Salud. Facultad de Humanidades y Ciencias de la Educación. Universidad de Almería. 04120. Almería. Spain (E-mail: *jortells@ual.es*).

REFERENCES

Adams, J.K. (1957). Laboratory studies of behavior without awareness. *Psychological Bulletin*, *54*, 383-405.

Baker, L.E. (1937). The influence of subliminal stimuli on verbal behavior. *Journal of Experimental Psychology*, *20*, 84-100.

Balota, D.A. (1983). Automatic semantic activation and episodic memory. *Journal of Verbal Learning and Verbal Behavior*, *22*, 88-104.

Bar, M., & Biederman, I. (1998). Subliminal visual priming. *Psychological Science*, 9, 464-469.

Cheesman, J., & Merikle, P.M. (1984). Priming with and without awareness. *Perception and Psychophysics*, *36*, 387-395.

Cheesman, J., & Merikle, P.M. (1985). Word recognition and consciousness. In D. Besner, T.G. Waller, & G.E. McKinnon (Eds.). *Reading research: Advances in theory and practice*. New York: Academic Press.

Cheesman, J., & Merikle, P.M. (1986). Distinguishing Conscious from Unconscious Perceptual Processes. *Canadian Journal of Psychology*, *40*, 343-367.

Correa, A., Fox, E., Carmona, E., Noguera, C., Lupiáñez J. & Tudela P. (2002, April). The processing of emotional faces at two levels of awareness in subclinical anxiety. *Poster presented at the IV Conference of the Spanish Society for Experimental Psychology*, Oviedo, Spain.

Dagenbach, D., Carr, T.H., & Wihelmsen, A. (1989). Task-induced strategies and near-threshold priming: conscious influences on unconscious perception. *Journal of Memory and Language*, *28*, 412-443.

Dalrymple-Alford, E.C. (1972). Associative facilitation and interference in the Stroop color-wprd task. *Journal of Experimental Psychology*, *98*, 274-276.

Daza, M.T., & Ortells, J.J. (2000a, March). Procesamiento automático vs. controlado de palabras: relación entre atención y conciencia. [Automatic vs. controlled word processing: Relations between attention and consciousness]. *Paper presented at the III Conference of the Spanish Society for Experimental Psychology,* Barcelona, Spain.

Daza, M.T., & Ortells, J.J. (2000b, September). Curso temporal del procesamiento semántico automático (no-consciente) vs. controlado (consciente) de estímulos lingüísticos. [Time-course of automatic (unconscious) vs. controlled (conscious) semantic processing of verbal stimuli]. *Paper presented at the XII Conference of the Spanish Society for Comparative Psychology*, Granada, Spain.

Daza, M.T., Ortells, J.J., & Fox, E. (in press). Perception without awareness: Further evidence from a Stroop priming task. *Perception and Psychophysics*.

Daza, M.T., Ortells, J.J., & Noguera, C. (2001, September). Priming semántico consciente vs. no-consciente producido por palabras enmascaradas parafoveales. [Conscious vs. unconscious semantic priming from parafoveal masked words]. *Paper presented at the III Attention Meeting (RECA3)*, Almería, Spain.

Debner, J.A., & Jacoby, L.L. (1994). Unconscious perception: Attention, awareness, and control. *Journal of Experimental Psychology: Learning, Memory, and Cognition*, *20*, 304-317.

De Groot, A.M.B. (1984). Primed lexical decision: combined effects of the proportion of related prime-target pairs and the stimulus-onset asynchrony of prime and target. *Quarterly Journal of Experimental Psychology, 36A*, 253-280.

Dehaene, S., Naccache, L., Le Clec'H, G., Koechlin, E., Mueller, M., Dehaene-Lambertz, G., van de Moortele, P.F., & Le Bihan, D. (1998). Imaging unconsious semantic priming. *Nature, 395*, 597-600.

Di Pace, E., Longoni, A.M. & Zoccoloti, P. (1991). Semantic processing of unattended parafoveal words. *Acta Psychologica, 77*, 21-34.

Dixon, N.F. (1981). *Preconscious processing*. London: Wiley.

Dosher, B.A. (1998). The response-window regression method--some problematic assumptions: comment on Draine and Greenwald (1998). *Journal of Experimental Psychology: General, 127*, 311-317.

Draine, S.C., & Greenwald, A.G. (1998). Replicable unconscious semantic priming. *Journal of Experimental Psychology: General, 127*, 286-303.

Dunlap, K. (1900). The effect of imperceptible shadows on the judgment of distance. *Psychological Review, 7*, 435-453.

Eriksen, C.W. (1960). Discrimination and learning without awareness: A methodological survey and evaluation. *Psychology Review, 67*, 279-300.

Esteves, F., Dimberg, U., & Öhman, A. (1994). Automatically elicited fear: conditioned skin conductance responses to masked facial expressions. *Cognition and Emotion, 8*, 393-413.

Esteves, F., & Öhman, A. (1993). Masking the face: recognition of emotional facial expressions as a function of the parameters of backward masking. *Scandinavian Journal of Psychology, 34*, 1-18.

Farah, M. J. (2001). Consciousness. In B. Rapp (Ed.), *The Handbook of Cognitive Neuropsychology* (pp. 159-182). Psychology Press, UK.

Forster, K.I., & Davis, C. (1984). Repetition priming and frequency attenuation in lexical access. *Journal of Experimental Psychology: Learning, Memory and Cognition, 10*, 680-698.

Forster, K.I., & Veres, C. (1998). The prime lexicality effect: form-priming as a function of prime awareness, lexical status and discrimination difficulty. *Journal of Experimental Psychology: Learning, Memory and Cognition, 24*, 498-514.

Fox, E. (1996). Selective processing of threatening words in anxiety: The role of awareness. *Cognition and Emotion, 10*, 449-480.

Fox, E., Russo, R., Bowles, R., & Dutton, K. (2001). Do threatening stimuli draw or hold visual attention in subclinical anxiety? *Journal of Experimental Psychology: General, 130,* 681-700.

Fuentes, L.J., & Tudela, P. (1992). Semantic processing of foveally and parafoveally presented words in a lexical decision task. *Quarterly Journal of Experimental Psychology, 45A*, 299-322.

Greenwald, A.G., & Draine, S. (1997). Do subliminal stimuli enter the mind unnoticed?. Tests with a new method. In J. Cohen & J. Schooler (Eds.). *Scientific approaches to consciousness* (pp. 83-108). Mahwah, NJ: Erlbaum.

Greenwald, A.G., Draine, S., & Abrams, R.L. (1996). Three cognitive markers of unconscious semantic activation. *Science, 273*, 1699-1702.

Greenwald, A.G., Klinger, M.R., & Schuh, E.S. (1995). Activation by marginally perceptible ("subliminal") stimuli: Dissociation of unconscious from conscious cognition. *Journal of Experimental Psychology: General, 124*, 22-42.

Groeger, J.A. (1984). Evidence of unconscious semantic processing from a forced-error situation. *British Journal of Psychology, 75*, 305-314.

Groeger, J.A. (1988). Qualitatively different effects of undetected and unidentified auditory primes. *Quarterly Journal of Experimental Psychology, 40A*, 323-339.

Holender, D. (1986). Semantic activation without conscious identification in dichotic listening, parafoveal vision, and visual masking: A survey and appraisal. *The Behavioral and Brain Sciences, 9*, 1-66.

Jacoby, L.L. (1991). A process dissociation framework: Separating automatic from intentional uses of memory. *Journal of Memory and Language, 30*, 513-541.

Jacoby, L.L., Lindsay, D.S., & Toth, J.P. (1992). Unconscious influences revealed: Attention, awareness, and control. *American Psychologist, 47*, 802-809.

Jacoby, L.L., Toth, J.P., & Yonelinas, A.P. (1993). Separating conscious and unconscious influences of memory: Measuring recollection. *Journal of Experimental Psychology General*, Vol 122(2): 139-154.

Kemp-Wheeler, S.M., & Hill, A.B. (1988). Semantic priming without awareness: some methodological considerations and replications. *Quarterly Journal of Experimental Psychology, 40A*, 671-692.

Kunst-Wilson, W.R., & Zajonc, R.B. (1980). Affective discrimination of stimuli that cannot be recognized. *Science, 207*, 557-558.

Logan, G.D. (1985). Executive control of thought and action. *Acta Psychologica, 60*, 193-210.

Logan, G.D., & Zbrodoff, N.J. (1982). Constraints on strategy construction in a speeded discrimination task. *Journal of Experimental Psychology: Human Perception and Performance, 8*, 502-520.

Logan, G.D., Zbrodoff, N.J., & Williamson, J. (1984). Strategies in the color-word Stroop task. *Bulletin of the Psychonomic Society, 22*,135-138.

Mandler, G., Nakamura, Y., & Van Zandt, B.J.S. (1987). Nonspecific effects of exposure on stimuli that cannot be recognized. *Journal of Experimental Psychology: Learning, Memory, and Cognition, 13*, 646-648.

Marcel, A.J. (1980). Conscious and preconscious recognition of polisemous words: locating the selective effect of prior verbal context. In R.S. Nickerson (Ed.). *Attention and performance VIII.* Hillsdale, New Jersey: Erlbaum.

Marcel, A.J. (1983a). Conscious and unconscious perception: Experiments on visual masking and word recognition. *Cognitive Psychology, 15*, 197-237.

Marcel, A.J. (1983b). Conscious and unconscious perception: An approach to the relation between phenomenal experience and perceptual processes. *Cognitive Psychology, 15*, 238-300.

McCauley, C., Parmelee, C.M., Sperber, C.D., & Carr, T.H. (1980). Early extraction of meaning from pictures and its relation to conscious identification. *Journal of Experimental Psychology: Human Perception and Performance, 6*, 265-276.

Merikle, P.M. (1982). Unconscious perception revisited. *Perception and Psychophysics, 31*, 298-301.

Merikle, P.M. (1992). Perception without awareness: Critical issues. *American Psychologist, 47*, 792-795.

Merikle, P.M., & Cheesman, J. (1987). Current status of research on subliminal perception. In M. Wallendorf & P.F. Anderson (Eds.). *Advantages in Consumer Research, Vol. XIV*. Provo, UT: Association for Consumer Research.

Merikle, P.M., & Daneman, M. (1998). Psychological investigations of unconscious perception. *Journal of Consciousness Studies, 5*, 5-18.

Merikle, P.M., & Joordens, S. (1997a). Measuring unconscious influences. In J.D. Cohen, & J.W. Schooler (Eds.), *Scientific approaches to consciousness* (pp.109-123). Mahwah, NJ: Erlbaum.

Merikle, P.M., & Joordens, S. (1997b). Parallels between perception without attention and perception without awareness. *Consciousness and Cognition, 6*, 219-236.

Merikle, P.M., Joordens, S., & Stolz, J.A. (1995). Measuring the relative magnitude of unconscious influences. *Consciousness and Cognition, 4*, 422-439.

Merikle, P. M., & Reingold, E.M. (1991). Comparing direct (explicit) and indirect (implicit) measures to study unconscious memory. *Journal of Experimental Psychology: Learning, Memory and Cognition, 17*, 224-233.

Merikle, P.M., & Reingold, E.M. (1998). On demonstrating unconscious perception: comment on Draine and Greenwald (1998). *Journal of Experimental Psychology: General, 127*, 304-310.

Merikle, P.M., Smilek, D., & Eastwood, J. (2001). Perception without awareness: perspectives from cognitive psychology. *Cognition, 79*,115-134.

Miller, J.G. (1942). *Unconsciousness*. New York: Wiley.

Murphy, S.T., & Zajonc, R.B. (1993). Affect, cognition, and awareness: Affective priming with optimal and suboptimal stimulus exposures. *Journal of Personality and Social Psychology, 64*, 723-739.

Neely, J.H. (1977). Semantic priming and retrieval from lexical memory: Roles of inhibitionless spreading activation and limited-capacity attention. *Journal of Experimental Psychology: General, 106*, 226-254.

Nolan, K.A., & Caramazza, A. (1982). Unconscious perception of meaning: A failure to replicate. *Bulletin of the Psychonomic Society, 20*, 23-26.

Ortells, J.J., Abad, M.J.F., Noguera, C., & Lupiáñez,J. (2001). Influence of prime-probe stimulus onset asynchrony and prime precuing manipulations on semantic priming effects with words in a lexical decision task. *Journal of Experimental Psychology: Human Perception and Performance, 27*, 75-91.

Ortells, J.J., & Tudela, P. (1996). Positive and negative semantic priming of attended and unattended parafoveal words in a lexical decision task. *Acta Psychologica, 94*, 209-226.

Posner, M.I., & Snyder, C.R.R. (1975a). Attention and cognitive control. In R. Solso (Ed.). *Information Processing and Cognition: The Loyola Symposium*. Hillsdale. New Jersey: Erlbaum.

Posner, M.I., & Snyder, C.R.R. (1975b). Facilitation and inhibition in the processing of signals. In P.M.A. Rabbitt y S. Dornic (Eds.). *Attention and performance V*. New York: Academic Press.

Purcell, D.G., Stewart, A.L., & Stanovich, K.E. (1983). Another look at semantic priming without awareness. *Perception and Psychophysics, 34*, 65-71.

Reingold, E.M., & Merikle, P.M. (1988). Using direct and indirect measures to study perception without awareness. *Perception and Psychophysics*, *44*, 563-575.

Reingold, E.M., & Merikle, P.M. (1990). On the inter-relatedness of theory and measurement in the study of unconscious processes. *Mind and Language*, *5*, 9-28.

Searle, J.R. (1992). *The rediscovery of the mind.* Cambridge, MA: MIT Press.

Shenaut, G.K., & Ober, B.A.. (1996). Methodological control for semantic priming in Alzheimer's disease. *Psychology and Aging*, *11*, 443-448.

Shiffrin, R.M., & Schneider, W. (1977). Controlled and automatic human information processing: II. Perceptual learning, automatic attending and a general theory. *Psychological Review*, *84*, 127-190.

Sidis, B. (1898). *The psychology of suggestion.* New York: Appleton.

Smith, S.D., & Merikle, P.M. (1999, June). Assessing the duration of memory for information perceived without awareness. *Poster presented at the 3rd annual meeting of the Association for the Scientific Study of Consciousness*, Canada.

Stroh, M., Shaw, A.M., & Washburn, M.F. (1908). A study in guessing. *American Journal Psychology*, *51*, 243-245.

Stroop, J.R. (1935). Studies of interference in serial verbal reactions. *Journal of Experimental Psychology*, *18,* 643-662.

Whalen, P.J., Rauch, S.L., Etcoff, N.L., Mclnerney, S.C., Lee, M.B., & Jenike, M.A. (1998). Masked presentations of emotional facial expressions modulate amygdala activity without explicit knowledge. *Journal of Neuroscience*, *18*, 411-418.

Williams, A.C. (1938). Perception of subliminal visual stimuli. *Journal of Psychology*, *6*, 187-199.

In: Abnormal Psychology: New Research
Editor: Helen D. Friedman and Paulina K. Revera
ISBN: 978-1-60692-636-9

Chapter 8

INTRAPSYCHIC FACTORS CONTRIBUTING TO ADOLESCENT DEPRESSION

***Lisa C. Milne*[11] *and Philip Greenway*[2]**
[1]Australian Catholic University, Fitzroy, Victoria, Australia
[2]Monash University, Clayton, Victoria, Australia

ABSTRACT

Depression during adolescence is both a normal phenomena and cause for concern, with the sequelae sometimes including poorer academic and occupational outcomes, social withdrawal, and suicide. The etiology of depression, especially during adolescence has been associated with a number of factors, including biological factors (Riddle and Cho, 1989), early physiological and psychological trauma (Toolan, 1981), psychological and psychosocial factors (National Institute of Mental Health, 1981). There have also been attempts to understand depression as a result of intrapsychic factors, such as a failure to individuate (Blos, 1968), insecure attachments (Armsden, McCauley, Greenberg, Burke and Mitchell, 1990) negative parental representations, and object relations that lack self-other differentiation (Blatt, Wein, Chevron, and Quinlan, 1979).

The separation-individuation process, where adolescents attempt to let go of their dependence on their parents, in a process similar to that which occurs in infancy, is central to adolescent development. The quality of attachment to the primary caregiver also impacts upon the ability of adolescents to re-negotiate the changes in these attachments. Parental representations both conscious and unconscious are also related to adjustment in adolescence. Self-report measures of perceptions of maternal care as being either over-protective or uncaring; have also been related to depression, suicidal thoughts and disrupted interpersonal relationships (Blatt, Wein, Chevron, and Quinlan, 1979).

During childhood the estimates of rates of depression do not tend to show gender differences, yet by adolescence females are diagnosed with depression at twice the rate that males are – and this gender difference in epidemiology remains throughout adulthood (Angold and Worthman, 1993). This would suggest that the causal and maintaining factors are in some way related to gender. The present study examines from

[11] Correspondence: Dr. Lisa Milne, 266 Middleborough Rd Blackburn South, Victoria, Australia, 3168. EMAIL: lcmilne@netspace.net.au

a psychoanalytic perspective, the intrapsychic factors associated with symptoms of depression in adolescents, and in particular gender differences are examined.

A non-clinical sample of 81 adolescents was assessed on a number of theoretically related measures: separation-individuation; anaclitic depression; introjective depression; attachment style; parental representations, and symptoms of depression. The aim of this study was to analyse the factors that mediate the relationship between parenting variables and symptoms of depression in adolescent males and females.

INTRODUCTION

About 3% of pre-pubertal children, aged six to eleven years, and 9% of adolescents, aged 12 to 16 years receive a diagnosis of major depression (Cooper and Goodyer, 1993; Fleming and Offord, 1990; Garrison, Addy, Jackson, McKeown, and Waller, 1992; Whitaker et al., 1990). Research using self-rating scales suggests that between 25 to 40% of adolescents admit to being depressed (Ehrenberg, Cox, and Koopman, 1990; Berganza and Aguilar, 1992; Swanson, Linskey, Quintero-Salinas, Pumariega, and Holzer, 1992). The rates for females exceed those for males by a ratio of approximately 2:1, a difference which emerges by the age of 14 (Culbertson, 1997). The etiology of depression, especially during adolescence implicates a number of factors, including biological factors (Riddle and Cho, 1989), genetic and environmental factors (Silberg et al., 1999), early physiological and psychological trauma (Toolan, 1981), psychological and psychosocial factors (National Institute of Mental Health, 1981).

Pubertal maturation (Gore, Aseltine, and Colton, 1992), low parental education, and sexuality, (Kaltiala-Heino, Rimpelä, Rantanen, and Laippala, 2001; Rubin, et al., 1992), often occur in girls who are depressed. Girls are more likely to use ruminative coping techniques (e.g., Nolen-Hoeksema, 1994) and have negative a body image (Simmons and Blyth, 1987) both of which contribute to depression (Nolen-Hoeksema, Morrow, and Fredrickson, 1993). Girls are also more likely than boys to have negative perceptions of themselves (Ohannessian, Lerner, von Eye, and Lerner, 1996). Stress and social support have also been associated with depression in girls (Schraedley, Gotlib, and Hayward, 1999). For boys, several factors are frequently noted, high parental education, being at a higher level at school, the incidence of suicides in families and among friends, sexual abuse. For both genders, social support protects against depression, as well as achievement pressures (Rubin et al., 1992). These authors suggested that boys find effective support in their peers and girls in family members. Physical and sexual abuses are strongly associated with depression for both boys and girls, although sexual abuse had a stronger impact upon boys (Schraedley et al., 1999). Uncontrollable negative events, such as parental divorce or moving to another area, generally result in depression, especially if children and adolescents blame themselves, as researchers have often reported (Harrington, 1994) as did perceived lack of social support (Kaltiala-Heino, et al., 2001).

Biological factors also contribute to vulnerability to depression (Brage, 1995; Riddle and Cho, 1989). In a study examining possible causes of depression, Silberg et al. (1999) looked at the influence of genetic and environmental risk factors for depression in pre-pubertal and pubertal male and female monozygotic and dizygotic twins as part of the Virginia Twin Study of Adolescent Behavioral Development. They found that depression, over early to mid adolescent years, increased only in those boys who experienced negative life events. However, depressive symptoms did increase in all girls, even in those who had not experienced negative life events. Their findings indicated that latent genetic factors explained some 28-30% in overall variance for depressive symptoms. One of these might be the association between hormonal concentrations and negative affect, reported previously by Nottelmann, et al. (1987). A second suggested by the researchers, was a predisposition to experience particular stressful events which may account for some of the increase in depression in adolescent girls. The two factors seem to interact in a complex way.

The pathways to depression begin at a very early age. Of inhibited children in the Dunedin longitudinal study of 1037 children assessed at intervals from birth to 21 years, Caspi (2000) concluded:

> When observed at age 3, children classified as inhibited (8% of the sample) were notably shy, fearful, and socially ill-at-ease. As adolescents they suffered from internalizing problems of distress. At age 18, they were characterized by overcontrolled, cautious, and nonassertive personality styles, expressing little desire to take on leadership roles or to exert influence over others. By age 21, they reported lower levels of social support, and their mental health was compromised by depression. (p. 168)

Temperament observed as early as three years old seems to have a pervasive effect on development in terms of personality, which together with interpersonal factors predispose some individuals to depression (Caspi, 2000).

Against this background of genetic factors and external events, the attachment styles acquired by adolescents contribute to their developmental paths and the liability of their becoming depressed. For each individual a predominant pattern emerges which endures into adulthood, unless interpersonal relationships intervene to effect it (Stein et al., 2002). Four categories of attachment have been described, initially by Ainsworth, Blehar, Waters, and Wall (1989), in their categorization of infants, and later by others. Bartholomew (1997), for example, categorized the four as follows. *Securely* attached individuals have a consistently positive image of themselves and others, are high on autonomy and are able to use others as a source of support. *Preoccupied* individuals have a negative self-image but a positive view of others, are overly concerned with their attachment needs, are dependent and continually seek validation through gaining the approval of others. *Fearfully* attached individuals have a negative view of themselves and others, and despite wanting acceptance, avoid closeness to protect themselves from rejection. Individuals with a *Dismissing* attachment style have a positive view of themselves, but a negative view of others, use distancing strategies to defend themselves against rejection, and are self-reliant. These styles lead to the construction of internal representations of one's self and others, and act as internal working models, which help individuals to understand their environment, survive in it and feel secure (Pietromonaco and Barrett, 2000).

The transition from childhood to adulthood involves change across all areas of development, including physical, sexual, cognitive, and psychological changes. The process of separating from one's family, and becoming a unique, autonomous adult, can be traumatic. The emotional upheaval often experienced during this transition period means that some degree of psychological disturbance is normal. Moreover, behaviour considered unacceptable, such as rebelliousness, defiance, moodiness, and withdrawal, during adolescence, may not only be considered typical, but in fact, to some degree an essential feature of the adolescence (A. Freud, 1958; Steinwand, 1984).

Significantly however, psychological disturbance frequently emerges during adolescence. Psychiatric illnesses, such as psychosis, delinquency, promiscuity, depression, and suicidal behaviour, are among the disturbances, which become evident during adolescence, even if the precipitating trauma occurred much earlier (Laufer, 1997). There is abundant literature relating to environmental and social factors, which contribute to breakdown at adolescence (e.g., Deming, 1989; Heaven, 2001; Irwin and Millstein, 1986; Way and Robinson, 2003). There is also literature, which deals with individual intrapsychic factors associated with poor outcomes for adolescents. Some of these include: underlying disturbances in the process of separation-individuation (e.g., Steinwand, 1984); the capacity for relatedness to others i.e., object relations (e.g., Levine, Tuber, Slade, and Ward, 1991); attachment to significant others, including peers (e.g., Armsden et al., 1990); and internal representations of parents (e.g., Ross, Clayer, and Campbell, 1983). Although the contribution of each of these factors individually to adolescent psychological adjustment has been partially addressed by the existing literature, there has been very little research which examines the relationship between contributing variables, and their combined effect on adolescent adjustment.

The psychological tasks of adolescence include the development of a unique ego identity, effective and constructive separation from one's parents, the capacity to develop satisfying sexual and other social relationships with peers and adults outside of the family. During adolescence, development can be erratic, the girl or boy striving to move forward, and only to regress to earlier positions. This waxing and waning continues throughout adolescence making it difficult to predict, at any point in time, the level of development achieved by a particular adolescent.

Psychological, biological, social, and cognitive changes create anxiety for the adolescent. The degree to which previous stages of development have been managed, in particular the infantile stage of separation-individuation, strongly influences the parallel stage in adolescence. Those who are able to rely on their parents, and who have internalised a sense of self worth, are better equipped to handle separation, individuation and other changes required.

The Basic Tasks of Adolescence

Commonly agreed tasks of adolescence include: developing a unique identity, managing psychosexual development; and separating from one's parents and developing intimate relationships with people outside the family. According to traditional psychoanalytic theory, the biological and psychological changes, which mark puberty, awaken the adolescent's sexual drive and allow for the establishment of heterosexuality and of a masculine or feminine identity. These changes bring with them a need to balance the demands of the sexual drive and those of conscious agencies of repression. Other psychoanalytic theorists, such as Otto Rank, moved away from the sexual emphasis of the original theory, recognising the adolescent's need to establish independence (Ausubel, 1954). Corey (1946) summarised the developmental tasks of adolescence as being: to learn to accept one's body image; adopt appropriate sex roles; establish independence from adult, especially parental domination; achieve economic independence; and develop a system of values. Sarnoff (1987) cited three factors which initiate and shape the move from latency to adolescence: (i) the psychological/emotional, characterised in psychoanalytic terms, by the return of pre-latency fantasy, the decline of the structure of latency, and a shift from a dependence on a reality defined by the parental environment to one can feel to one based on relationships outside the family; (ii) pubertal influences, such as the physical changes and the psychological impact of menarche or the first ejaculation; (iii) social and parental pressures toward social behaviour with appropriate sexual partners , including dating and parental encouragement of sexual differentiated social behaviour. Similarly, Friedman and Laufer (1997) regarded the main areas of change for adolescents as being: their relationship with parents; with peers and their attitude to their sexually maturing bodies. In like vein, Blos (1962) described the psychological development of adolescents as being characterised by object relations directed towards finding a heterosexual object, made possible by giving up the bisexual positions of the previous phase. Breaking away from the infantile love objects, adolescents were disturbed by the new, unknown territory in which they find themselves. Children who have been overly gratified by a parent, on whom they came to depend, often find that on entering adolescence they are disillusioned with themselves and their limited attainments in reality (Blos, 1967).

Necessary Modifications in the Adolescent's Relationship to Parents

At the end of childhood adolescents feel the impulse to change the quality of family ties, and to develop close relationships, not only with same age peers, but also with other adults. Giving up their dependence on a parent, however, creates anxiety and feelings of emptiness for them. In adolescents who have been securely attached to their parents, sufficient, inner love for themselves, first laid down in constructive childhood relationships, enables them to strive for greater autonomy (Laufer, 1997). From this perspective, the rebelliousness seen frequently in adolescents appears to originate partly in maladaptive attachment relationships with their parents. If one accepts this proposition, rebelliousness may, for some adolescents, be a symptom of a parental attachment, which has and still does create feelings of being overprotected, conditionally loved, or of being dismissed by seemingly cold and distant parents. Such maladaptive attachments generate various forms of anxiety, psychopathology and behavioural reactions as maturing adolescents strive to separate from their parents. Since adolescence is a time of the reorganization of identity, the confusion often accompanying it, requires flexibility on the part of the parent. The securely attached adolescent can usually draw on parental support, so that what might, in the insecurely attached seem like rebellion, appears to the understanding and supporting parent only as an attempt at self assertion. Likewise, efforts to distance themselves from parents are taken to be an expression of a natural need for adolescents to have their own life and not as rejection. The flexibility of both parent and adolescent in a mutually secure relationship allows for seemingly contradictory behavioural expressions, such as dependence in one context and distancing and autonomy in another. Attachments, which do not have this flexibility, lack effective avenues for negotiation between parent and adolescent. As Anna Freud pointed out, the task of the mother (or significant caregiver) is to be there to be left, as the only way that an adolescent can disengage from parental internalisations (Kroger, 1996). This process of separating, while maintaining the capacity for constructive closeness, requires parental confidence in the adolescent's capacity for autonomy, shown by a relaxing of control and an insistence on the dependent closeness of earlier stages of development.

SEPARATION-INDIVIDUATION PROCESS

The adolescent process of separation-individuation reflects that of infancy, in important ways. As infants gradually gain psychological separateness from their mothers, they and their caregivers learn specific habits of mutual interacting which as they mature become stable attachment styles, that is, more or less firm ways of perceiving and relating to the interpersonal world. Initially, the child in the separation-individuation process begins to discover and accept the existence of the external world, as distinct and apart from them selves. Mahler (1968), and later Mahler, Pine, and Bergman (1975) described in detail the stages of the infant's psychological development. Infants move from a stage of perceiving their source of need satisfaction as belonging solely to themselves ("normal autism"), and, because of a symbiotic relationship with their caregiver, view the outside world only dimly as external and as meeting their needs. During this phase, however, mothers do not always meet their babies' needs on demand, while at the same time ensuring that this does not cause too much frustration or engulfment by anxiety. From about 9 months of age onwards, coinciding with much greater mobility, infants move into their own physical and psychological space and begin to differentiate themselves from their mother. In this stage, they present a variety of cues about their internal states and mothers respond selectively leading infants to vary their behaviours according to her responses. Through this process, the child reflects the unconscious needs of the mother. Following this stage, infants move into a period of rapprochement. Their self-esteem becomes vulnerable, as the realization dawns on them that they are not as omnipotent as they have previously assumed. Sensing separateness from mother, they now want her around. They begin discover and master increasing segments of their physical surroundings, provided they feel mother's encouragement and availability (Mahler and Gosliner, 1955). Cognitive development is the focus of the final sub-phase, involving the acquisition of verbal communication, use of fantasy and reality testing. Infants establish mental representations of the self as separate from others, object constancy enabling them to survive without the continual presence of the mother (Mahler and La Perriere, 1965).

Later researchers were not all in total agreement with Mahler's theory (e.g., Horner, 1985; Lichtenberg, 1983; Stern, 1985), especially over the concept of symbiosis. Mahler used this term metaphorically, to describe the state of un-differentiation, or fusion, between infant and mother. She recognised the child's awareness of inside and outside as separate but not his or her ability to differentiate between 'I' and 'not-I'. This is not symbiosis in the biological sense of the word, as infants depends absolutely on the mother, while her need for the infant is relative (Benedek, 1959). The main critics of Mahler's theory included Horner, Stern, Blanck and Blanck, and even her colleague Fred Pine.

SEPARATION-INDIVIDUATION EXPERIENCE IN INFANCY AND ADOLESCENCE

Attachment style forms the interlink between both phases of separation-individuation in infancy and adolescence. Blos (1967) saw the relevance of Mahler's work to adolescence, and described the internal changes in adolescents as a second individuation phase. He suggested that everyone experiences some emotional injury, and that childhood trauma is a relative term, its impact varying in its severity and the vulnerability of the individual child and that mastering childhood psychological trauma is a lifelong process (Blos, 1962). Adolescence, he thought, was a time offering opportunities for the resolution of trauma, and that, although its effects could never be removed completely, at the end of adolescence, traumatic experiences could optimally be integrated into the ego (Kroger, 1996). Blos (1967) reported that he had observed, in his analytic work with adolescents, the re-involvement of the ego and superego functions of infantile object relations. He concluded that the danger to ego integrity did not derive alone from the strengths of the pubertal drives, but in equal measure, from the strength of a regressive pull, which made the struggle for individuation harder. For example, children separated from their mothers, due perhaps to maternal psychiatric illness, experience not only physical separation, but also apparent rejection by their mother, who is likely to be emotionally unavailable. Unable to predict their mothers' behaviour, these children are unable to form a secure attachments, and not likely to develop the inner resources necessary to cope with separations. At adolescence, where separating from the family becomes a major task, these children are likely to feel again the disturbances of their early childhood now in the form of adolescent insecurities.

Blos (1968) argued that being able to withstand and master the regressive pull was a central feature of normal adolescence, and various forms of psychopathology, such as psychosis, suicide attempts, drug use, and depressive disorders resulted from failure to do so. To some extent, he was reflecting the traditional view of adolescence, which failed to explain normal adolescence adequately, but emphasized psychopathology (Steinwand, 1984). At the time Blos was writing, emotional upheaval had began to seem to researchers to be an essential part of a normal adolescence. Anna Freud (1958) had even suggested that the absence of the emotional upheaval might signal a developmental delay resulting from excessive defense against drive. Steinwand (1984) argued that severe personality disorganisation in hospitalised adolescents frequently illustrates inadequacies that had occurred previously during infantile separation-individuation, and were not caused by the process of adolescence.

Erikson (1963) asserted in similar vein that in attempting to define and integrate their identity, adolescents feel independent and able to develop intimate relationships, as well as to re-experience the infantile process of separation-individuation. Blos (1967) pointed out how both periods bring a heightened vulnerability in personality organisation along with urgency for change consonant with the maturational forward surge. Along with increased instinctual drives and physical development of an adult body image, the process of individuation is also cognitive. On attaining formal operations, a system of logic, in which judgments and arguments inseparable from their content, no longer constrain adolescents. They achieve an ability to view the world from the perspective of others and to deal with problems beyond their immediate experience (Steinwand, 1984) and to evaluate events and attitudes critically, even those of their parents, with the result that they begin to see them more realistically.

Blos (1967) described ego weakness in adolescents as resulting from both their lessening dependence on parents and partially from the effect of newly felt, overwhelming drives. He argued that acting out, learning disorders, lack of purpose, moodiness and negativism were common symptoms of failures of individuation. The attempt to 'stamp out' their parents' influence was central to adolescents' separation individuation difficulties. Consciously they turned away from their parents, but unconsciously feared them because several factors stirred anxiety, namely renewed oedipal strivings, which triggered defensive regression, an unconscious wish not to separate, and lastly a tendency to inflate their parents with grandiose, infantile conceptions (Schafer, 1973). This unconscious situation made it difficult for adolescents to detach from their parents until they could transform their inner, infantile world to a stable adult one. As a result, adolescents were vulnerable to feeling that they controlled, over-stimulated or hurt by others. The challenge for them was to preserve the attachment with their parents, while at the same time developing a sense of self.

What Mahler (1963) called 'a hatching from the symbiotic membrane to become an individuated toddler', in adolescence becomes the shedding of family dependencies, and the loosening of infantile object ties fostering the move into adulthood (Blos, 1979). This development maturing over time, eventually becomes stable and marks the end of adolescence. Parents help to preserve adolescents' attachment during individuation by acknowledging, respecting and supporting their developing individuality (Quintana and Lapsley, 1990). Adolescents, who can rely on their original attachment, are more likely to find the transition to individuation to be smoother than those who cannot. More recently, therapists have realised that attachment is not the opposite of separation-individuation, but essential to its development (e.g. Armsden and Greenberg, 1987; Josselson, 1988; Quintana and Lapsley, 1990).

Esman (1980), like Blos, drew the analogy between the infants' development of motor skills accompanying their emergence from a symbiotic relationship with their mother and adolescents' attempts at self-assertion and independence as they separate themselves from their family. As infants practice their new found independence, adolescents also experiment with a new body image, greater competencies and more freedom, providing the parents allow these things to happen. The adolescent's moodiness is akin to the toddler's "low keyedness" described by Mahler, and results from their struggle to deal with loss experienced as a consequence of their efforts at detachment. They may also demonstrate rapprochement, approaching their parents for support and moving away when the closeness generates anxiety.

Quintana and Kerr (1993) concurred that separation-individuation theory accounts for key developmental tasks of late adolescence (17-21 years) but made the criticism that researchers have tended to emphasise the work of Blos (1962, 1979), without taking into account that of others such as Grotevant and Cooper (1985) and Josselson (1980). Josselson in particular, stressed the importance of the rapprochement phase in which individuals integrate connectedness and separateness. Others have emphasised the importance of the parent-adolescent attachment to adolescents' later adjustment (e.g. Lapsley, Rice and Fitzgerald, 1990; Quintana and Lapsley, 1987, 1990). Clearly, adolescents need their familial attachments and support in their growth towards individuality (Quintana and Kerr, 1993). However, some forms of both connectedness and separateness have been associated with adaptiveness and others with distress.

As in infancy, parents must achieve a sensitive if not paradoxical balance between being nurturing and supportive, while allowing greater responsibility, and facilitating the adolescent's gradual relinquishment of the ego-dependencies of the latency period. Unstable or too intense attachments complicate this process. An individual's failure to negotiate the analogous process in infancy puts him or her at risk when facing the task in adolescence. Poor attachments are likely to create a greater risk of inadequate adjustment or psychopathology, even though sub-clinical feelings of loss and depression are normal in adolescence.

Attachment Theory

Mahler (1968) had connected the separation-individuation process of infancy with the security of the mother-child bond. If the mother is not available as a secure base, from which the child can begin to explore the world, he or she will have trouble negotiating the separation-individuation phase of development. Ainsworth et al. (1978) identified varying patterns of attachment, secure, and three insecure attachments: avoidant; resistant; and disorganised/disoriented. Securely attached infants and their mothers interact positively with each other. These infants cooperate and are willing to comply with their mothers' requests, tend to cry less and show less separation disturbance than the insecurely attached groups (Ainsworth et al., 1978). They appear to be positive and accepting of close bodily contact with the mother and seem able to use her as a secure base from which to explore, consequently spending a lot of time in exploratory play. Avoidant infants do not show distress upon mother's departure, and explore actively in her absence and appear friendly to an unfamiliar adult in the room, nor do they immediately acknowledge their mother's return, averting their gaze from her or moving away if she approaches (Lyons-Ruth, 1991). When observed at home avoidant infants are more angry and distressed around their mother than secure infants (Ainsworth et al., 1978). Main and Weston (1982) suggested that this avoidant behaviour is a defensive strategy to cope with distress related to mother's departure. This enables the child to displace their anger by focusing attention on inanimate features of their environment. In the resistant pattern of attachment, infants alternate between clinging and angrily resistant behaviour. Distressed when their mother leaves, they seek contact on her return, but are often angry and difficult to comfort (Lyons-Ruth, 1991). They manifest more separation-anxiety and do not have confident expectations of the mother's accessibility and responsiveness. They are unable to use her as a secure base from which to explore (Ainsworth et al., 1978), are slower to be soothed than securely attached infants. They are also angry when their mothers do not pick them up, but try to play with them instead, and even when they are picked up, they seem both angry and clinging. These reactions may be an exaggerated attempt to elicit comfort from a poorly responsive caregiver (Main and Hesse, 1990). Main and Solomon (1990) described a third pattern of insecure attachment, disorganised/disoriented. These infants are inconsistent in reaction to the distress of their mother leaving. They show both approach and avoidance tendencies, having failed to develop a consistent strategy for managing stress related to the need for comfort and security (Lyons-Ruth, 1991). Lyons-Ruth, (1991) reported that mothers who are depressed, maltreating or alcoholic, are more likely to have infants with ambivalent behaviours. She also suggested that such avoidant, distressed and angry behaviour reflects a deep-seated disturbance in their relationship with their mother.

The quality of the initial attachment between mother and child sets the scene for the child's social and cognitive development and self-confidence. Without a secure base and a consistent, reliable relationship with the mother the infant lacks the necessary skills to approach later developmental tasks. Similarly adolescents need to experience their parents as a secure base in order that they can being to move away from home, and into the world (Ainsworth, 1989).

Kobak and Sceery (1988) pointed out that attachment theory deals with affect regulation, the different patterns of attachment providing individuals with rules or habits for reacting to emotionally distressing situations. They investigated three types: secure; dismissing; and preoccupied, in a sample of college students, with an average age of about 18 years. Their findings indicated that securely attached individuals represented their parents as loving and available through distressing events. Although these participants reported some negative childhood experiences, the absence of idealisation and good recall of attachment experiences characterised their representations. Those with a dismissing style reported having experienced considerable rejection from parents. However, they had difficulty in actually recalling distressing experiences in childhood, which the authors interpreted as a defensive attempt to minimise the painful affect associated with rejection. Individuals with a preoccupied style represented parents as loving, but as role reversing, they recalled distressing events, but often in a confused manner. These adolescents modulated their feelings of by continuing their efforts to gain support from parents. Peers rated securely attached individuals as more ego-resilient (using the Q-sort), less anxious and hostile. They rated individuals with a dismissing style as low on ego-resilience. These individuals reported themselves as feeling lonely and having less social support from their families. Peers rated individuals with a pre-occupied style as less ego-resilient and more anxious and they themselves reported higher levels of personal distress, at the same time viewing their family as giving them more support than the dismissive group.

Quintana and Lapsley (1990) showed that the two aspects of adolescent ego development: attachment and differentiation could be meaningfully combined into a single separation-individuation construct. They concluded that a multidimensional individuation construct that includes both attachment and psychological differentiation was a better predictor of ego identity than was parental control. De Jong (1992) found that students with a history of suicidality exhibited the lowest security of attachment and the least degree of individuation in their current relationship with their parents.

Parental Representations, Gender and Depression

Attachment styles shed light on adolescent depression and suicide. Armsden et al. (1990) examined the security of parent and peer attachment, using the Inventory of Parent and Peer Attachment (IPPA) among four groups of early adolescents: clinically depressed; non-depressed psychiatric controls; non-psychiatric controls; and adolescents with resolved depression. They found that the depressed adolescent reported significantly less secure parent attachment than either of the control groups and less secure peer attachment than the psychiatric control group.

Milne and Greenway (2001) studied those aspects of the adolescents' relationships with their parents, which predict strong peer attachments. We demonstrated that adolescents attachment their peers is more likely to be strong, when: first, they have a strong attachment to their parents; second, there is affection, emotional warmth, and empathy from their mother, and third, there were fewer problems in the separation-individuation process.

Adolescents' emotional states seem to influence their perceptions of their parents strongly, and to affect their relationships with parents in ways that either enhance or hinder their transition from childhood to adulthood. Perceptions tend to become enduring internal representations of parents, which in turn become part of the adolescents' way of thinking about themselves and others. For example, these images can become involved in suicidal thoughts and feelings of depression. Suicidal adolescents have been found to think that their parents are lacking in care and over-protective, (Adam, Keller, West, Larose and Goszer, 1994; Goldney, 1985; Parker, 1979). Both males and females with suicidal thoughts have reported parents who favoured siblings rather, were un-stimulating, guilt engendering, rejecting and unaffectionate (Ross et al., 1983). Moreover, parental mood can have a significant effect on adolescent adjustment. Thomas and Forehand (1996) reported that the relationship between fathers and adolescents influenced adjustment to divorce, and that the relationships within couples and paternal emotional mood predicted adolescent adjustment in married families. They also found that although lack of parent support negatively affected both genders, females were more likely to compensate for this by establishing relationships outside the family.

Other studies have found a significant relationship between perception of poor maternal care and both depression (e.g. Blatt et al., 1979; Lamont, Fischoff and Gottlieb, 1976; Rey, 1995) and disrupted interpersonal relations in the childhood experiences of depressed patients (e.g. Beck, 1967; Blatt, 1974; Fenichel, 1945). Blatt et al., (1979) studied the relationship of descriptions of parents to aspects of depression in a sample of normal young adults. They found that negative ratings of parents, significantly correlated with depression. Kirkcaldy, Siefen, and Furnham (2003) found that females also reported more problems related to self-image (physical appearance, self-acceptance and relationship with peers), and lower levels of acceptance by their fathers but not their mothers. The researchers implied that females get the conflicting messages from their culture, mostly through parental expectations, that "young women are expected to be more assertive and competitive in their attitudes, whilst maintaining their physical appeal and femininity."(p.56). Silverstein and Lynch (1998) made the interesting suggestion that their findings of inferior self-image, lower paternal acceptance, higher maternal rejection, together with higher gastro-intestinal disorders may partly explain the higher incidence of eating disorders in females than in males.

As a basic requirement, caregivers need to provide a secure base and to encourage the child to move gradually away from it Bowlby (1977). Parents being either over protective or providing insufficient care become problematic for their children (Blatt et al., 1979; Parker, 1979). Parker, Kiloh and Hayward (1987), using the Parental Bonding Index (PBI) found that parental uncaring and overprotective attachment styles played a significant role in conditions like dysthymia and reactive depression, with an imputed psychosocial aetiology, but not in endogenously depressed individuals with psychopathology such as bipolar disorder or melancholia, disorders with imputed genetic and biochemical bases. The results were not conclusive, as the researchers could not determine whether anomalous parenting was irrelevant in endogenous depressives or whether the two groups of depressives differed in terms of a personality dimension, which induce neurotic depressives to judge interpersonal relationships negatively. However, they concluded that the PBI was able to discriminate between depressive groups. Type of depression appears to be a relevant factor when considering associations with other variables. Silverstein and Lynch (1998) compared depression in females, with and without anxious, somatically related problems, such as sleep disorders, headaches, fatigue and appetite disturbances. They observed that father's attitude influenced these symptoms, as did achievement related issues. With regard to mothers, they found that, those who emphasized career success, were likely to have daughters with anxious somatic depression. Fathers who assumed males to be superior to females likewise had daughters with anxious somatic depression. On a similar theme, Egger, Costello, Erkanli, and Angold (1999) found that, in the age range 9-16 years, somatic complaints were strongly associated with emotional disorders in girls and disruptive behaviours in boys. Interestingly, abdominal complaints were related to oppositional defiant disorders and ADHD in boys and stomach pains and headaches were related to anxiety disorders in girls. For both boys and girls musculoskeletal pains were related to depression.

Acklin, Bibb, Boyer, and Jain, (1991) used a modified version of Mayman's (1968) Early Memory Questionnaire which elicits a narrative of an early memory and questions clarifying several aspects, such as, the age at which the incident described occurred, the clearest parts of it, the feelings associated with it, and which details the respondent would chose to change. In a non-clinical sample, they found that the technique reliably described the different attachment styles. Fowler, Hilsenroth and Handler (1994) also used Mayman's (1968) procedure in both clinical and non-clinical samples. They found that the early memories of the clinical sample contained more negative affect, and a characterisation of 'self' and 'other' that tended to be flat, one-dimensional and simplistic, in comparison to the non-clinical group whose early memories tended to richer, more complex and more life-like. They concluded that from the data collected and case vignettes that the EM procedure is a unique and powerful projective tool.

Parental representations, measured by both self-report and projective measures, have been associated with attachment, levels of object relations, depression, interpersonal relations, and the development of ego identity. Parental representations appear to hold information about the quality of the parent-child relationship. It is likely that parental representations are not only associated with symptoms of depression, but may also with the process of separation-individuation.

Blatt's Theory of Anaclitic and Introjective Depression

Depression in adolescence is associated with a failure in individuation (Blos, 1968), insecure attachments (Armsden et al., 1990) negative parental representation and internal objects which lack self-other differentiation (Blatt et al., 1979). Blatt (1974) saw depression as a normal affect state, varying in intensity. Blatt and Shichman (1983) proposed that two primary tasks of adolescences were: the formation of stable, enduring, mutually satisfying interpersonal relationships; and the achievement of a differentiated, consolidated, stable, realistic, essentially positive identity. They delineated two primary developmental lines, the anaclitic and introjective, respectively, which interact as development proceeds. Disruptions result in one or other dominating, and lead to psychopathological distortion.

Depression has been defined in a variety of ways, as a clinical disorder, as a normal and necessary affect state (Bibring, 1953; Freud, 1914; Zetzel, 1960), as a reaction to extreme deprivation in infancy (Spitz and Wolf, 1946); a developmental stage (Winnicott, 1954), as being concerned with restoring past pleasures (Rubenfine, 1968), a character style (Blatt, 1966), as characterized by a fundamental loss of self-esteem, (Fenichel 1945), and as including cognitive dysfunction consisting of negative thought patterns and attitudes (Barnett and Gotlib,1988).

According to Bibring (1953), depression originated in three possible sources: in the oral stage in the experience of not being loved; at the anal level in feelings of failure to achieve mastery over one's body, and at the phallic level in which the oedipal struggle results in feelings of helplessness about being defeated or punished. Blatt (1974) elaborated on Fenichel's description of the loss of self-esteem, suggesting two distinct pathways to depression, both beginning with marked loss of self-esteem. The first, which he referred to as anaclitic, began very early in life, when the caregiver's absence or unavailability triggered abandonment anxiety in a child. The second, which he referred to as introjective, began at a later stage in childhood and was marked by criticism and negative judgments about a child's behaviours or abilities. The first he saw as primarily oral in nature and the second as involving issues around the Oedipal conflict. Blatt suggested that the two types of depression probably exist on a continuum. He also thought that depression was partly a function of impairments in the development of object relations. Both types of depression originate in the developmental stages in infancy in which self and object representations are still being established, but after boundary between them has been established as constant.

Anaclitic Depression

Anaclitic depression, also referred to as simple or primary depression is primarily oral in nature and originates in childhood reactions to narcissistic injury and loss of love (Blatt, 1974). It brings feelings of helplessness, weakness, depletion, and fears of abandonment out of which begins a desperate struggle to maintain direct physical contact with the need-gratifying object. These individuals are usually free from guilt but are slower in their cognitive and psychomotor reactions, they feel dejected, detached weary, inferior, worthless, empty and report numerous physical and psychosomatic complaints (Jacobson, 1971). Often they show a desperate need to deny object loss and seek immediate direct replacement (Blatt et al., 1979). Object relations, for them, are mainly incorporative (Freud, 1917; Klein, 1934; Fenichel, 1945). The concept of 'anaclitic depression' also corresponds with Mahler's symbiotic and early separation-individuation phase of development (Mahler, 1968). They feel a constant demand for the visible and physical presence of significant others, but do not seem to internalise gratifying experiences. Further, they meet separation with primitive defences such as denial (Blatt, 1974).

Introjective Depression

Blatt describes introjective depression as being 'developmentally more advanced' where individuals have feelings of being unworthy, unlovable, in contrast to unloved, guilty and failing to live up to expectations (Blatt, 1974). They have attained a higher level of development as indicated by the predominance of guilt, which requires an ability to be self-reflective and to assume responsibility. They seek love and approval by striving and perfection (Blatt et al., 1979) but mostly without lasting satisfaction (Blatt, 1974). They find it difficult to express aggressive feelings towards people they love, because of fear of losing them (Blatt, 1974). Object relations are at a later stage of separation-individuation, and are concerned with securing the object's approval and love. They mostly use the major defence of introjection or identification with the aggressor, and turning against the self. They base their internal representations on aggressive aspects of relationships with the result that they internalize feelings of guilt doubt and self-criticism (Blatt, 1974).

Developmental Lines for Depression

Blatt and Shichman (1983) proposed that separate but interdependent developmental lines for the two kinds of depression, the anaclitic involving a focus on satisfying interpersonal relationships; the introjective involving an internal focus on developing a stable, independent sense of self. In normal development, the two lines overlap extensively and psychopathology results from an exaggeration of either line, depression emphasizing dependence and histrionic behaviours from the anaclitic and depression emphasizing deficiencies in the self, paranoia, obsessive-compulsiveness, and narcissism from the introjective. Both types of depression range in intensity from mild to psychotic, and involve different types of impairments in object relations. In both types individuals struggle to maintain contact with people significant to them.

During adolescence, individuals experience a revival of the conflicts of an earlier stage of development, about age 5-8 years, in which children learn to interact effectively with their parents, and depression results as a normal experience. Disturbances in how others are represented internally may then become apparent, as they may not be as readily available to provide support in the way they were before. The more successfully children were able to relate to others in the earlier stage, the more likely they are to deal effectively later in adolescence with separating themselves from their family, and achieving emotional equilibrium, motivation and satisfaction of their needs. The more advanced their level of development, the greater their capacity to feel in touch with significant others symbolically rather than through direct contact, and to deal more effectively with feelings of loss. A predisposition to depression results from two types of disturbances in the internal representations of others. Distortions in how available and caring they are set up the conditions for anaclitic depression. Deficiencies in self-concept associated with guilt predispose individuals to introjective depression. Blatt, D'Afflitti, and Quinlan (1976) suggested that the two were often compounded, especially so in clinical samples. Blatt et al., (1979) examined descriptions of parents in a sample of normal young adults finding that depression was related to parents perceived as lacking in nurturance, affection and support rather than to parents seen as striving, harsh and judgmental.

ARE FEMALES MORE PRONE TO ANACLITIC DEPRESSION AND MALES MORE PRONE TO INTROJECTIVE DEPRESSION?

Girls report more negative life events than boys. These mostly involve family incidents around dependency and interpersonal problems to do with peers, both of which lead to depression (Davies and Windle, 1997). Likewise, Laursen (1996) found that girls are aware of conflict in friendships, conflict which increases a throughout adolescence. Ge, Conger, and Elder (1996) found that early maturing girls associated with more deviant peers than later or normally maturing girls and that this association lead to an increase in depression. Hankin and Abramson (2001) argued that when inferential style is measured accurately it reveals a connection with depression, with girls showing more rumination than boys. Since their rumination is mostly about negative life events to do with interpersonal matters, such as family or friendships problems or sexual abuse, girls would be likely to show symptoms of an anaclitic type. In line with this, Davis (1999) found that girls reported more emotional memories than boys and that they did so more quickly, and lastly, that the genders did not differ for non-emotional memories. Reviewing these studies, Hankin and Abramson (2001) concluded that "girls are more cognitively vulnerable in the interpersonal domain than boys." (p786). If this conclusion is accurate girls should show greater vulnerability to anaclitic factors in depression than boys.

With regard to introjective depression, the evidence available is sparse and unclear as to whether gender differences play an active role. Boys report more negative academic, school based problems than girls, which might suggest introjective problems, but the study in question did not include that in its focus (Rudolph and Hammen, 1999). In a study on college students, Reis and Grenyer (2002) found that although there were gender differences for anaclitic depression, females scoring higher, there were none for introjective depression. With regard to the latter it correlated with fearful attachment and self-oriented perfectionism, a scale which measured the inner motivation to be successful. Contemporary theories about women's development emphasize that women adopt a primary relational orientation, while men assume a central focus on agency, emphasizing aspects of experience of self as independent and autonomous (Chodorow, 1978; Gilligan, 1982; Surrey, 1993). This theoretical position might lead one to hypothesize that women might worry less about introjective problems than men. Shahar, Blatt, and Ford (2003) comparing anaclitic, introjective and mixed category, treatment resistant inpatients on a number clinical measures found the effects of gender too complex to interpret with confidence. However, they did assert:

> The intense preoccupations of anaclitic and introjective individuals either with issues of interpersonal relatedness or self-definition suggests that these two types of personality organization reflect a capacity to construct a relatively coherent mode of adaptation. (p. 98).

The two personality tendencies interact with other factors, such as negative life events, genetic predispositions, family structure and general gender role socialization, leading in a variety of ways to different forms of depression.

RATIONALE FOR THE PRESENT STUDY

This study examines the gender differences in the factors which mediate the relationship between perceptions of parenting and symptoms of depression in adolescents. Five "parenting variables" were selected: maternal care, maternal control, paternal care, paternal control and parental attachment and four possible mediating factors were selected: peer attachment, separation-individuation; introjective depression; and anaclitic depression.

It is well established that aspects of the way one is parented may lead to or protect against depression at different stages of the life span. People who report perceptions of parents as not caring are more likely to be depressed (e.g., Rey, 1995), and young adults who rate their parents negatively are also more likely to be depressed (Blatt et al., 1979). Adolescents who perceive their parents as not caring, and as over-protective are more likely to be suicidal than those who report having caring parents who are not controlling (Adam et al., 1994; Goldney, 1985; Parker, 1979), and more likely to have conditions with a psychological basis such as dysthymia or reactive depression (Parker et al., 1987). Adolescents with less secure attachments to their parents are more likely to be depressed (Armsden et al., 1990) and conversely securely attached adolescents and young adults tend to represent their parents as loving and available in times of need (Kobak and Sceery, 1988).

The relationship between parenting and depression in adolescents is not solely a direct one, due to both situational and intra-personal factors. With regard to external factors, Leinonen, Solantaus, and Punamaki (2003) listed factors affecting parenting style, such as daily hassles, economic hardship, work-related stress, and unemployment. They cited evidence showing that such economic pressures lead both mothers and fathers to be more punitive, coercive inconsistent and less authoritative in their parenting behaviours. Poor parenting, whatever its causes, negatively and directly affects the attachment styles of children, and has a flow-on effect on related processes, such as peer attachment, separation-individuation, introjective depression, and anaclitic depression. These in turn relate in complex ways to depressive affect. This study has its focus on the parent-child attachment process and does not take into account external pressures on parents. It should be noted that external pressures occur unpredictably in a child's development and what was before an adequately caring and supportive environment, might change into one which is inconsistent and punitive.

The process may be illustrated in a simplified way by examining how a child's insecure attachment to his or her parents might lead to depression. The initial attachment to the parent during infancy forms the basic blueprint for subsequent relationships. It fosters within the child insecurities and anxieties which foster dysfunctional emotional processes which affect his or her interpersonal relationships (Ainsworth, 1989). A repertoire of poor social experiences then begins, that results in depression in adolescence, and beyond.

Adolescents with stronger attachments to parents are more likely to have good peer relationships (Milne and Greenway, 2001), furthermore those with good peer relationships, are less likely to be depressed (Armsden et al., 1990). Gender differences probably play a role. Rubin et al., (1992) suggested that while social support buffers both boys and girls against depression, for boys effective support comes from their peers and for girls from family members. Schwartz, Dodge, Pettit and Bates (2000) showed as previous authors, that friendships play a crucial role in adolescents' development of social competence, self esteem and school adjustment. They also found that children exposed to a harsh home environment are likely to show dysfunctional emotional behaviours which lead to their being victimized. As Schwartz et al. comment "these problematic developmental trajectories can be altered by the positive influence of early friendships". Findings such as these strongly suggest that peer attachments may act as mediators between factors operating in the parent child attachment process and depression.

Similarly, the separation-individuation process, like that of peer attachment, may mediate the relationship between parental influence on a child and depression. Separation-individuation occurs more or less smoothly in the context of a secure attachment relationship. Insecurely attached have problems in separation-individuation both in infancy and adolescence (Blos, 1967). An adolescent ambivalent and insecure in their individuality is likely to function in less than optimal ways in areas like school achievement, satisfying recreational pursuits and interpersonal relationships. Failures in these areas are then likely to generate the conditions in which depression takes hold.

An exaggeration of either of the two developmental lines, described by Blatt as introjective and anaclitic are also set up in the child's initial relationship with parents. Introjective depression results from criticism and negative judgements about a child's behaviours or abilities, and anaclitic depression due to parental absence or unavailability (Blatt, 1974). Both developmental styles may lead to depression, albeit of different kinds. We included them because we were examining possible gender differences and anaclitic depression is more common in females than males.

We expected depression in girls to be more strongly associated with interpersonal problems: family and friends (Hankin and Abramson, 2001) and to be anaclitic (Reis and Grenyer, 2002). Fathers who have negative parenting attribute may effect girls more than boys (Kirkcaldy et al., 2003). The research was less clear for boys, but they are perhaps more vulnerable to depression when they have problems with peers (Kaltiala-Heino et al., 2001).

METHODOLOGY

Sample

Participants were 82 (30 male and 52 female) secondary school students aged between 14 and 16 years. There was no significant age difference between males (M=15.03, SD=.78) and females (M=15.25 years, SD=.68 years). Subjects were recruited from government secondary schools in Melbourne suburbs. All subjects volunteered to participate in the project after parental consent to participate in the project was given.

Measures

The instruments used were: the Parental Bonding Instrument - adolescent version (PBI; Pedersen, 1994); the Inventory of Parent and Peer Attachment (IPPA; Armsden and Greenberg, 1987); the Separation-Individuation Inventory (SII; Christenson and Wilson, 1985), the shortened version of the Depressive Experiences Questionnaire – Adolescent version (DEQ-A; Fichman, Koestner, and Zuroff , 1994) to measure anaclitic and introjective styles, and The Self-Rating Depression Scale (SDS; Zung, 1965) was used to measure symptoms of clinical depression (American Psychiatric Association; *DSM-IV*, 1994).

The Parental Bonding Instrument (Parker, Tupling, and Brown, 1979) is a self-report scale measuring subjects' perception of care from their mother (MCARE) and their father (PCARE), and protection from their mother (MCONTROL) and their father (PCONTROL) they received in childhood. The dimensions of care and control were identified as underlying parental attitudes and behaviours (Parker et al., 1979). Pedersen (1994) developed a shortened version of the PBI, suitable for use with adolescents. From the results of a pilot study, five "care" items and five "protection" items were selected on the basis of how well they were understood by students (Pedersen, 1994). The instrument's validity was supported by its capacity to discriminate between controls, anxious/depressed and delinquent subjects.

The Inventory of Parent and Peer Attachment (Armsden and Greenberg, 1987), a 53-item, self-report inventory for use with adolescents, measures the security of attachment to parent (IPPA-PA) and peers (IPPA-PE). The inventory, derived from attachment theory, measures behavioural and affective-cognitive dimensions of adolescents' attachment to their parents and peers (Armsden and Greenberg, 1987). Armsden and Greenberg (1987) reported good three-week test-retest reliability of the IPPA for both the parent (.93) and peer scales (.86). Armsden and Greenberg (1987) reported significant correlations between peer attachment scores and the Tennessee Self-Concept Scale (TSCS), Social Self-Concept subscale ($r=.57$, $p<.001$) and between parent attachment and Family Self-Concept subscale as measured by the TSCS ($r=.78$), thus supporting the inventory's validity.

The Separation-Individuation Inventory (SII; Christenson and Wilson, 1985) is a 39-item true-false, self-report inventory that assesses manifestations of disturbances in the separation and individuation process. The reliability and validity of the instrument has been supported (Dolan, Evans, and Norton, 1992; Gunderson, 1983). Christenson and Wilson (1985) suggested that the instrument could be used to separate those with borderline symptomatology from those without. They found that scores of 190 or higher detected 70% of people with a DSM-III diagnosis of borderline personality disorder. In the present study the wording of items 10, 21, 24, and 38 was altered slightly to account for possible low levels of reading comprehension among the subjects, e.g., the word "intoxicated" was substituted with "drunk".

Blatt, et al. (1992) developed the Depressive Experiences Questionnaire for Adolescents (DEQ-A). The present study used a shortened version of the DEQ-A (Fichman et al., 1994), which is composed of 20 items. Fichman et al. (1994) concluded that the shortened version of the DEQ-A had acceptable psychometric properties, demonstrated good predictive validity and was thought to be appropriate for use when the researcher had a limited time period to conduct research with children or adolescents.

The Self-Rating Depression Scale (SDS; Zung, 1965) is a 20 item self-report inventory assessing symptoms of depression, using a 4-point Likert scale. An SDS score of 50 is considered the morbidity cut-off score, scores above which are indicative of depression (Zung, 1973).

Procedure

Potential subjects and their parents were given a written statement explaining the researcher was interested in investigating the opinions of normal adolescents. Parental consent was required for subjects to participate. Once potential subjects were identified, the project was verbally explained to them and consent gained before proceeding. The data were collected from class groups of about 10 subjects in each session, which was held during school hours, within their school. Each subject was given a package containing the questionnaires described above. The questionnaires were presented in a counterbalanced order. The questionnaires were administered by a registered psychologist.

RESULTS

Variables Used in the Analysis

Table 1 lists the variables used in the analysis and the instrument from which they were derived.

Table 1. Variable Used in the Analysis

Variable	Description	Instrument
1. MCARE	Maternal Care	PBI
2. MCONTROL	Maternal Control	PBI
3. PCARE	Paternal Care	PBI
4. PCONTROL	Paternal Control	PBI
5. IPPA-PA	Parent Attachment	IPPA
6. IPPA-PE	Peer Attachment	IPPA
7. SEP-IND	Separation-Individuation	SII
8. ANACLITIC	Anaclitic Depression	DEQ-A
9. INTROJECTIVE	Introjective Depression	DEQ-A
10. SDS	SDS Score	SDS

Descriptive Statistics

Table 2 shows the means and standard deviations of the continuous variables used in the analysis, for males and females. An SDS score of 50 is considered the morbidity cut-off score, for depression (Zung, 1973). Nine males (30%) and 12 females (23%) obtained SDS scores above 50, suggesting that these subjects are depressed. This is not consistent with previous findings that more females than males are depressed.

Table 3 shows the results of the t-tests for independent samples between males and females on the variables used in the analysis. The only variables on which males and females differed significantly were peer attachment (IPPA-PE) and anaclitic depression (ANACLITIC). The mean scores on both IPPA-PE and ANACLITIC were higher for females, suggesting that they have higher levels of attachment to peers and are more inclined to report symptoms consistent with anaclitic depression.

Table 2. Mean and Standard Deviation of Variables used in the Analysisfor Males and Females

Variable	Males (n=30)		Females (n=52)	
	M	SD	M	SD
1. MCARE	9.33	3.59	9.65	3.13
2. MCONTROL	5.30	3.36	6.60	4.01
3. PCARE	8.00	3.40	8.35	3.41
4. PCONTROL	5.10	3.60	5.65	3.61
5. IPPA-PA	91.83	22.04	90.38	19.96
6. IPPA-PE	74.33	17.07	87.60	20.34
7. SEP-IND	206.82	73.20	180.89	59.24
8. ANACLITIC	32.78	8.52	38.40	7.83
9. INTROJECTIVE	29.18	7.42	32.08	9.88
10. SDS	44.07	15.11	42.98	9.52

Table 3. Results of Independent Samples t-Test between Males and Females on Variables used in the Analysis

Variable	*t*	*Df*	*P* (2-Tailed)
1. MCARE	-.423	80	.674
2. MCONTROL	-1.493	80	.139
3. PCARE	-.450	79	.654
4. PCONTROL	-.657	79	.512
5. IPPA-PA	.305	80	.761
6. IPPA-PE	-3.010	80	.003
7. SEP-IND	1.669	72	.100
8. ANACLITIC	-2.945	76	.004
9. INTROJECTIVE	-1.353	76	.180
10. SDS	.399	80	.691

Tables 4a and 4b shows the Pearson product-moment correlations for the independent variables (MCARE, MCONTROL, PCARE, PCONTROL, IPPA-PA) the mediating variables (IPPA-PE, SEP-IND, ANACLITIC, INTROJECTIVE) and the dependent variable (SDS) for both males and females. Many of the variables are highly correlated, indicating that they share a substantial amount of variance.

Table 4a. Intercorrelations of Variables used in the Analysis for Females

Variable	1	2	3	4	5	6	7	8	9
1. MCARE									
2. MCONTROL	-.49†								
3. PCARE	.38†	-.04*							
4. PCONTROL	.01*	.44†	-.12*						
5. IPPA-PA	.64†	-.56†	.39†	-.39†					
6. IPPA-PE	.64†	-.60†	.14*	-.32*	.63†				
7. SEP-IND	-.30*	.51†	-.14*	.52†	-.57†	-.69†			
8. ANACLITIC	-.12*	-.010	-.19*	-.09*	-.080	-.060	.32*		
9. INTROJECTIVE	-.49†	.220	-.29*	.02*	-.49†	-.45†	.43†	.20*	
10. SDS	-.40†	.38†	-.34*	.34*	-.71†	-.59†	.72†	.28*	.55†

* *p*<.05† *p* <.05

Table 4b. Intercorrelations of Variables used in the Analysis for Males

Variable	1	2	3	4	5	6	7	8	9
1. MCARE									
2. MCONTROL	-.47†								
3. PCARE	.76†	-.45*							
4. PCONTROL	-.64†	.71†	-.67†						
5. IPPA-PA	.61†	-.59†	.57†	-.60†					
6. IPPA-PE	.40*	-.08	.26	-.29	.58†				
7. SEP-IND	-.36	.19	-.13	.31	-.30	-.62†			
8. ANACLITIC	.22	-.15	.26	-.45*	.52†	.41*	-.34		
9. INTROJECTIVE	-.61†	.05	-.37	.16	-.27	-.27	.29	.06	
10. SDS	-.67†	.39*	-.53†	.65†	-.69†	-.63†	.79†	-.47*	.35

p<.05 † p <.05

Relationship of Perceived Levels of Parental Care and Control to Depression

To assess the relative contribution of each parent to depression, MCARE, PCARE, MCONTROL and PCONTROL were regressed onto to SDS for each gender, results are shown in tables 5a and 5b for males and females respectively. For both females and males, PCONTROL and MCARE were included in the final regression equation, while PCARE and MCONTROL were excluded. For females the model accounted for about 28% of the variance, while for males the model accounted for 53% of the variance.

Table 5a. Summary of Stepwise Regression Analyses - Main Effects – Females

Model	B	*SE B*	β	*T*	P
Constant	49.566	4.204		11.789	<.001
MCARE	-1.220	.373	-.402	-3.271	.002
PCONTROL	.909	.327	.342	2.782	.008

Note: R2=.276

Table 5a. Summary of Stepwise Regression Analyses - Main Effects – Males

Model	B	*SE B*	β	*T*	*p*
Constant	53.689	9.719		5.524	<.001
MCARE	-1.859	.722	-.442	-.2.575	.016
PCONTROL	1.515	.720	.361	2.105	.045

Note: R^2=.531

Mediation Analysis

We hypothesised first, that there would be significant relationships between depression (SDS) and MCARE, MCONTROL, PCARE, PCONTROL and IPPA-PA, and second, that these relationships would be mediated by IPPA-PE, SEP-IND, INTROJECTIVE and ANACLITIC. IPPA-PA was added to obtain a direct measure of parental attachment.

A series of regressions in which each of the parenting variables (MCARE, PCARE, MCONTROL, PCONTROL and IPPA-PA) was the IV and depression as measured by the SDS was the DV. Tables 6a and 6b are a summary of the regression analyses for the main effects for females and males, respectively. There is a highly significant relationship between each of the parenting variables and symptoms of depression in both females and males. Low levels of MCARE and PCARE (care) contributed to higher scores on the SDS, while higher levels of MCONTROL and PCONTROL (over-protection) were associated with higher levels of depressive symptoms. Higher scores on IPPA-PA were related to lower SDS scores.

Table 6a. Summary of Regression Analyses - Main Effects – Females

Model	**B**	*SE B*	β	*P*	R^2
MCARE→Depression	-1.217	.394	-.400	.003	.160
MCONTROL→Depression	.895	.311	.377	.006	.142
PCARE→Depression	-.956	.378	-.340	.015	.115
PCONTROL→Depression	.901	.357	.339	.015	.115
IPPA-PA→Depression	-.338	.048	-.708	<.001	.501

Table 6b. Summary of Regression Analyses - Main Effects - Males

Model	B	*SE B*	β	*P*	R^2
MCARE→Depression	-2.834	.587	-.674	<.001	.454
MCONTROL→Depression	1.744	.782	.388	.034	.151
PCARE→Depression	-2.360	.710	-.532	.002	.283
PCONTROL→Depression	2.705	.605	.645	<.001	.416
IPPA-PA→Depression	-.473	.094	-.690	<.001	.477

In order to test whether the mediating variables: peer attachment (IPPA-PE); separation-individuation (SEP-IND); introjective depression (INTROJECTIVE); and anaclitic depression (ANACLITIC) influenced the relationship between the independent variables: maternal care (MCARE); Maternal Over-control (MCONTROL); Paternal Care (PCARE); Paternal Over-control (PCONTROL); parent attachment (IPPA-PA) and the DV, SDS, a series of regression analyses were conducted between the IV and the mediator variable, then the dependent variable was regressed on both the independent and mediator variables. Mediation was substantiated following Newsom's (2002) suggestion to use Sobel's (1982) approach where a z-score is calculated for the product of the two regression equations. The *z*-score is then divided by the standard error of the indirect path. The z-score was then tested for significance using the Goodman (I) test equation, (Goodman, 1960), as suggested by Preacher and Leonardelli (2003), and using their online calculation tool. Figure 1 is the generic model tested.

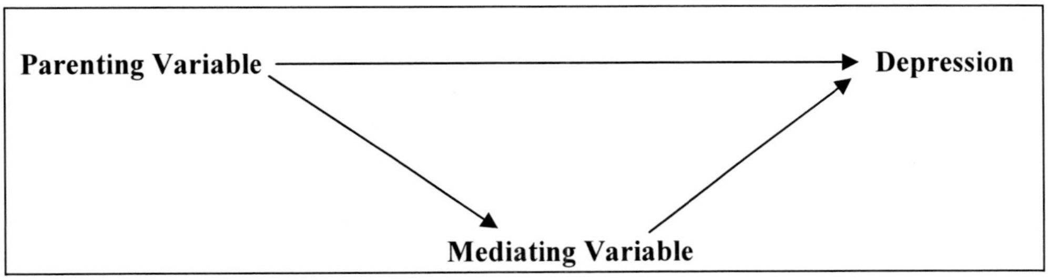

Figure 1. Generic Model of Mediational Analysis.

The Relationship between Maternal Care (MCARE) as a Predictor of Depression

Females

IPPA-PE acted as a mediating variable between MCARE and SDS (β=-.570, p<.001; R^2=.353, $F(2, 49)$=13.382, p<.001). When simultaneously entered into the regression equation with IPPA-PE, MCARE was not a significant predictor. The Goodman (I) version of the Sobel test was used to test for significance of the mediating variable. Results of the *z*-test were z=-3.162 (p=.002), indicating the effect of the mediating variable, IPPA-PE was significant.

SEP-IND also acted as a mediator variable between MCARE and SDS (β=.669, p<.001; R^2=.544, F(2, 43)=25.697, p<.001). When simultaneously entered into the regression equation with SEP-IND, MCARE was not a significant predictor. The result of the Goodman (I) Sobel test was z=-1.969 (p=.049), indicating the effect of the mediating variable, SEP-IND was marginally significant.

INTROJECTIVE acted as a mediator variable between MCARE and SDS (β=.480, p=.001; R^2=.321, F(2, 47)=11.131, p<.001). When simultaneously entered into the regression equation with INTROJECTIVE, MCARE was not a significant predictor. The result of the Goodman (I) Sobel test was z=-2.546 (p=.011), indicating the effect of the mediating variable, INTROJECTIVE was significant.

ANACLITIC did not act as a mediator variable between MCARE and SDS. The result of the Goodman (I) Sobel test was z=-0.658 (p=.511), indicating the effect of the mediating variable, ANACLITIC was not significant. While both ANACLITIC and MCARE were separately significant predictors of SDS, MCARE did not predict ANACLITIC. When simultaneously entered into the regression equation MCARE was a significant predictor, but ANACLITIC was not, (β=.233, p=.082; R^2=.199, F(2, 47)=5.855, p=.005).

Males

For males, the picture was quite different. The relationship between MCARE and SDS was not mediated by any of the mediating variables. The regression equating predicting SDS directly from MCARE was significant (β=-.674, p<.001; R^2=.454, F(1, 28)=23.324, p<.001). IPPA-PE was predicted by MCARE (β=.396, p=.030; R^2=.157, F(1, 28)=5.205, p=.030). When entered simultaneously into the regression equation with MCARE, IPPA-PE was a significant predictor of SDS, (β=-.435, p=.002; R^2=.614, F(2, 27)=21.461, p<.001), and MCARE was also a significant predictor (β=-.502, p=.001). The Goodman (I) Sobel test result was z=-1.831 (p=.067), indicating the IPPA-PE was not acting was a mediating variable. This suggests that both IPPA-PE and MCARE both independently contribute to SDS in adolescent males.

SEP-IND, for males did not mediate the relationship between MCARE and SDS. The Goodman (I) Sobel test result was z=-1.829 (p=.067). SEP-IND was not predicated by MCARE (β=-.363, p=.058; R^2=.132, F(1, 26)=3.942, p=.058), but it did predict SDS in males, independently of MCARE (β=.758, p<.001; R^2=.574, F(1, 26)=35.053, p<.001). When entered simultaneously into the regression equation both MCARE (β=-.343, p=.010) and SEP-IND (β=.633, p<.001; R^2=.676, F(2, 25)=26.104, p<.001) were independently significant predictors of SDS.

INTROJECTIVE did not mediate relationship between MCARE and SDS. The Goodman (I) Sobel test result was z=-0.015 (p=.988). While INTROJECTIVE was predicted by MCARE (β=-.611, p<.001), INTROJECTIVE on its own did not predict SDS(β=.352, p=.066; R^2=.124, F(1, 26)=3.676, p=.066). When simultaneously entered into the regression equation with MCARE, INTROJECTIVE (β=.003, p=.988; R^2=..328, F(2, 25)=6.098, p=.007) was not a significant predictor of SDS in adolescent males, and MCARE remained significant (β=-.571, p=.011).

Similarly, ANACLITIC did not mediate the relationship between MCARE and SDS. The Goodman (I) Sobel test result was z=-0.972 (p=.331). ANACLITIC was not predicted by MCARE (β=.221, p=.259; R^2=.049, F(1, 26)=1.331, p=.259), yet it was a significant predictor of SDS (β=-.472, p=.011; R^2=.223, F(1, 26)=7.442, p<.011). When simultaneously entered into the regression equation with MCARE, ANACLITIC remained a significant predictor of SDS (β=-.363, p=.024; R^2=.453, F(2, 25)=10.364, p=.001), as did MCARE (β=-.492, p=.003).

The Relationship between Maternal Control (MCONTROL) as Predictor of Depression

Females

IPPA-PE acted as a mediator of the relationship between MCONTROL and SDS (β=.-.576, p<.001; R^2=.353, F(2, 49)=13.367, p<.001). When simultaneously entered into the regression equation with IPPA-PE, MCONTROL (β=.029, p=.840) was not a significant predictor. The result of the Goodman (I) Sobel test was z=3.181 (p=.001), indicating the effect of the mediating variable, IPPA-PE was significant.

SEP-IND also acted as a mediator variable between MCONTROL and SDS (β=.734, p<.001; R^2=.519, F(2, 43)=23.191, p<.001). When simultaneously entered into the regression equation with SEP-IND, MCONTROL (β=-.027, p=.829; was not a significant predictor. The result of the Goodman (I) Sobel test was z=3.232 (p<.001), indicating the effect of the mediating variable, SEP-IND was significant.

For females, INTROJECTIVE did not fully mediate the relationship between MCONTROL and SDS. The regression equation with MCONTROL predicting INTROJECTIVE was not significant. When entered simultaneously into the regression equation with MCONTROL, INTROJECTIVE predicted SDS (β=.497, p<.001; R^2=.363, F(2, 47)=13.403, p<.001), as did MCONTROL (β=.248, p=.044). The result of the Goodman (I) Sobel test was z=1.443 (p=0.149).

Similarly, ANACLITIC mediated the relationship between MCONTROL and SDS. The Goodman (I) Sobel test result was z=0.029 (p=.977). ANACLITIC was not predicted by MCONTROL (β=-.005, p=.975; R^2<.001, F(1, 48)=0.001, p=.975), yet it was a significant predictor of SDS. When simultaneously entered into the regression equation with MCONTROL, ANACLITIC remained a significant predictor of SDS, (β=.276, p=.039; R^2=.205, F(2, 47)=6.044, p=.005), and MCONTROL was also significant (β=.359, p=.008) hence both ANACLITIC and MCONTROL independently contribute to SDS in adolescent females.

Males

For males, as was the case with MCARE, no variables were found to mediate the relationship between MCONTROL and SDS. The regression equation predicting SDS directly from MCONTROL was significant (β=.388, p=.034; R^2=.151, F(1, 28)=4.971, p=.034). IPPA-PE was not predicted by MCONTROL (β=-.083, p=.663). The Goodman (I)

Sobel test result was z=.4270 (p=.6694), indicating that IPPA-PE was not acting as a mediating variable. Both MCONTROL (β=.338, p=.018) and IPPA-PE (β=-.606, p<.001; R^2=.515, F(2, 27)=14.330, p<.001), remained significant predictors when entered into the regression equation simultaneously.

SEP-IND, for males did not act as a mediating variable between MCONTROL and SDS. The Goodman (I) Sobel test result was z=0.943 (p=.345). SEP-IND was not predicated by MCONTROL (β=.187, p=.340; R^2=.035, F(1, 26)=.946, p=.340). However, when entered simultaneously into the regression equation, SEPIND was a significant predictor of SDS (β=.731, p<.001; R^2=.594, F(2, 25)=18.314, p<.001), but MCONTROL was not (β=.145, p=.275).

INTROJECTIVE did not mediate relationship between MCONTROL and SDS. The Goodman (I) Sobel test result was z=0.239 (p=.811). INTROJECTIVE was not predicted by MCONTROL (β=.054, p=.787; R^2=.003, F(1, 26)=0.075, p=.787), and as previously mentioned, INTROJECTIVE on its own did not predict SDS. When simultaneously entered into the regression equation with MCONTROL, INTROJECTIVE was not a significant predictor of SDS in adolescent males (β=.338, p=.072; R^2=.193, F(2, 25)=2.991, p=.072), and MCONTROL also lost significance (β=.263, p=.156). It would appear that INTROJECTIVE has accounted for some of the variance between MCONTROL and SDS, even though it was not significant, but enough to make MCONTROL lose its predictive power.

Similarly, ANACLITIC did not act as mediating variable between MCONTROL and SDS. The Goodman (I) Sobel test result was z=0.7047 (p=.481). ANACLITIC was not predicted by MCONTROL (β=-.153, p=.437; R^2=.023, F(1, 26)=0.622, p=.437), yet it was a significant of SDS. When entered simultaneously into the regression equation MCONTROL was no longer a predictor of SDS (β=.214, p=.227), but ANACLITIC was (β=.284, p=.018; R^2=.267, F(2, 25)=4.564, p=.020). Again this is a complicated finding, with some of the predictive power of MCONTROL being removed, but the mediation effect still not reaching significance.

The Relationship Between Paternal Care (PCARE) as a Predictor of Depression

Females

For females, none of IPPA-PE, SEP-IND, INTROJECTIVE, or ANACLITIC mediated the relationship between PCARE (PCARE) and SDS, which was in itself significant (β=-.340, p=.015; R^2=.115, F(1, 49)=6.394, p=.015). IPPA-PE was not significant as a mediating variable: z=-0.927 (p=.355). When simultaneously entered into the regression equation with PCARE, IPPA-PE was a significant predictor (β=-.566, p<.001; R^2=.429, F(2, 48)=18.061, p<.001), as was PCARE (β=-.263, p=.021), so both independently seem to contribute to SDS.

SEP-IND had no significant indirect effect upon the relationship between PCARE and SDS, z=-0.297 (p=.354). SEP-IND was not predicted by PCARE (β=-.143, p=.349; R^2=.020, F(1, 43)=0.895, p=.349). When both PCARE and SEP-IND were simultaneously entered into the regression equation, both remained significant predictors of SDS:, PCARE (β=-.221, p=.037; R^2=.567, F(2, 42)=27.460, p<.001); SEP-IND (β=.689, p<.001).

INTROJECTIVE had no significant indirect effect upon the relationship between PCARE and SDS: z=-1.987 (p=.074), although it approached significance. Yet, PCARE significantly predicted INTROJECTIVE (β=-.288, p=.045; R^2=.083, F(1, 47)=4.252, p=.045); and INTROJECTIVE significantly predicted SDS, as already mentioned. When entered simultaneously into the regression equation, PCARE no longer predicted SDS:, PCARE (β=-.185, p=.148; R^2=.335, F(2, 46)=11.586, p<.001); and INTROJECTIVE remained significant (β=.498, p<.001). This finding probably indicates that INTROJECTIVE was most likely having some indirect effected upon the relationship between PCARE and SDS, but the effect was not large enough to reach significance in this sample.

ANACLITIC did not mediate the relationship between PCARE and SDS in adolescent girls: z=-0.936 (p=.349). There was no significant direct relationship between PCARE and ANACLITIC, though ANACLITIC independently predicted SDS. Interestingly, when entered simultaneously entered into the regression equation, PCARE remained a significant predictor of SDS (β=-.285, p=.045; R^2=.156, F(2, 46)=4.262, p=.020) but ANACLITIC was no longer significant (β=.225, p=.110) possibly suggesting that the variance that ANACLITIC contributes to depression, can be accounted for by PCARE, that PCARE mediates the relationship between ANACLITIC and SDS in girls.

Males

Males showed a similar pattern, where the proposed mediating variables did not show a significant indirect effect upon the relationship between PCARE and SDS. IPPA-PE was not significant as a mediating variable: z=-1.293 (p=.196). PCARE was not a significant predictor of IPPA-PE (β=.257, p=.170; R^2=.066, F(1, 28)=1.988, p=.170). When simultaneously entered into the regression equation with PCARE, IPPA-PE was a significant predictor (β=-.532, p<.001; R^2=.547, F(2, 27)=16.293, p<.001), as was PCARE (β=-.395, p=.007), so both independently seem to contribute to SDS.

As for females, SEP-IND had no significant indirect effect upon the relationship between PCARE and SDS, z=-0.0654 (p=.948) for males. SEP-IND was not predicted by PCARE (β=-.129, p=.514; R^2=.017, F(1, 26)=0.439, p=.514). When both PCARE and SEP-IND were simultaneously entered into the regression equation, both remained significant predictors of depression:, PCARE (β=-.336, p=.007; R^2=.685, F(2, 25)=27.172, p<.001); SEP-IND (β=.714, p<.001).

INTROJECTIVE had no significant indirect effect upon the relationship between PCARE and SDS z=-0.9403 (p=.347). PCARE did not significantly predict INTROJECTIVE (β=-.370, p=.052; R^2=.137, F(1, 26)=4.132, p=.052); and as already mentioned, INTROJECTIVE did not significantly predict SDS. When entered simultaneously entered into the regression equation neither PCARE nor INTROJECTIVE predicted SDS: PCARE (β=-.345, p=.081; R^2=.226, F(2, 25)=3.656, p=.040); and INTROJECTIVE (β=.224, p=.247), even though on its own, PCARE predicted SDS.

ANACLITIC did not mediate the relationship between PCARE and SDS in adolescent boys: z=-1.101 (p=.271). There was no significant direct relationship between PCARE and ANACLITIC, though ANACLITIC independently predicted SDS. Interestingly, when entered simultaneously entered into the regression equation, PCARE was no longer a significant predictor of SDS (β=-.327, p=.067; R^2=.322, F(2, 25)=5.938, p=.008) but ANACLITIC remained a significant predictor (β=-.386, p=.032). This suggests that ANALCLITIC may mediate the relationship between PCARE and SDS in boys, even though it is not at the level of statistical significance.

The Relationship Between Paternal Control (PCONTROL) as a Predictor of Depression

Females

For girls, IPPA-PE had an indirect effect on the relationship between PCONTROL and SDS: z=2.081 (p=.037). PCONTROL predicted IPPA-PE (β=-.323, p=.021; R^2=.104, F(1, 49)=5.704, p=.021). When entered simultaneously into the regression equation, PCONTROL was no longer a significant predictor of SDS: (β=.162, p=.183; R^2=.385, F(2, 48)=15.026, p<.001); and IPPA-PE remained significant (β=-.549, p<.001).

SEP-IND also had an indirect effect on the relationship between PCONTROL and depression: z=3.245 (p=.001). PCONTROL predicted SEP-IND (β=.519, p<.001; R^2=.270, F(1, 43)=15.889, p<.001). When entered simultaneously into the regression equation, PCONTROL was no longer a significant predictor of SDS: (β=-0.009, p=.944; R^2=.519, F(2, 42)=22.636, p<.001); and SEP-IND remained significant (β=.725, p<.001).

INTROJECTIVE did not have a significant indirect effect on the relationship between PCONTROL and SDS: z=0.143 (p=.886). PCONTROL did not predict INTROJECTIVE (β=.021, p=.885; R^2<.001, F(1, 47)=.021, p=.885). When entered simultaneously into the regression equation both PCONTROL and INTROJECTIVE were significant predictors of SDS: PCONTROL (β=.345, p=.003; R^2=.423, F(2, 46)=16.842, p<.001); INTROJECTIVE (β=.544, p<.001), hence both appear to be independently important in accounting for the variance of SDS.

Similarly, ANACLITIC did not have a significant indirect effect on the relationship between PCONTROL and SDS: z=-0.529 (p=.597). PCONTROL did not predict ANACLITIC (β=-0.85, p=.559; R^2=.007, F(1, 47)=.346, p=.559). When entered simultaneously into the regression equation both PCONTROL and ANACLITIC were significant predictors of SDS: PCONTROL (β=.383, p=.005; R^2=.224, F(2, 46)=6.643, p=.003); ANACLITIC (β=.312, p=.021), hence both appear to be independently important in accounting for the variance of depression.

Males

For boys, IPPA-PE did not have an indirect effect on the relationship between PCONTROL and SDS: z=1.456 (p=.145). PCONTROL did not predict IPPA-PE (β=-.291, p=.118; R^2=.085, F(1, 28)=2.598, p=.118). When entered simultaneously into the regression equation, both PCONTROL and IPPA-PE remained significant predictors of SDS: PCONTROL (β=.503, p<.001; R^2=.633, F(2, 27)=23.302, p<.001); and IPPA-PE (β=-.487, p<.001).

Similarly, for SEP-IND, there was no indirect effect on the relationship between PCONTROL and depression: z=1.559 (p=.119). PCONTROL did not predict SEP-IND (β=.308, p=.111; R^2=.095, F(1, 26)=2.718, p=.111). When entered simultaneously into the regression equation, PCONTROL and SEP-IND remained significant predictors of SDS: PCONTROL (β=.373, p=.003; R^2=.700, F(2, 25)=29.150, p<.001); and SEP-IND (β=.643, p<.001), suggesting both independently contribute to levels of SDS.

INTROJECTIVE had no significant indirect effect upon the relationship between PCONTROL and SDS, z=0.670 (p=.503). PCONTROL did not significantly predict INTROJECTIVE (β=.164, p=.403; R^2=.027, F(1, 26)=0.722, p=.403). When entered simultaneously entered into the regression equation PCONTROL remained a significant predictor of SDS: (β=.527, p=.003; R^2=.394, F(2, 25)=8.127, p=.002); and INTROJECTIVE did not significantly contribute to levels of SDS: INTROJECTIVE (β=.265, p=.105).

ANACLITIC did not have a significant indirect effect on the relationship between PCONTROL and SDS: z=1.254 (p=.210). PCONTROL predicted ANACLITIC (β=-.446, p=.017; R^2=.199, F(1, 26)=6.442, p=.017). When entered simultaneously into the regression equation, PCONTROL was a significant predictor of SDS (β=.450, p=.017; R^2=.385, F(2, 25)=7.810, p=.002); but ANACLITIC was not significant in the regression equation: ANACLITIC (β=-.271, p=.134).

THE RELATIONSHIP BETWEEN PARENTAL ATTACHMENT (IPPA-PA) AS A PREDICTOR OF DEPRESSION

Females

For girls, IPPA-PE had no indirect effect on the relationship between IPPA-PA and SDS: z=-1.862 (p=.063). IPPA-PA predicted IPPA-PE (β=.626, p<.001; R^2=.392, F(1, 50)=32.297, p<.001). When entered simultaneously into the regression equation, IPPA-PA remained a significant predictor, but IPPA-PE just missed being statistically significant: IPPA-PA (β=-.553, p<.001; R^2=.539, F(2, 49)=29.590, p<.001); and IPPA-PE (β=-.247, p=.053). This suggests that some mediation was occurring, even thought it was not at the level of statistical significance, as supported by the Sobel test result.

SEP-IND also had an indirect effect on the relationship between IPPA-PA and depression: z=-3.126 (p=.002). IPPA-PA predicted SEP-IND (β=-.567, p<.001; R^2=.322, F(1, 44)=20.899, p<.001). When entered simultaneously into the regression equation, IPPA-PA and SEP-IND remained strong predictors of SDS: IPPA-PA (β=-.434, p<.001; R^2=.646, F(2, 43)=39.280, p<.001); and SEP-IND (β=.474, p<.001). This indicates that while SEP-IND mediates the relationship between IPPA-PA and SDS, it is only a partial mediation, with IPPA-PA contributing variance independently of SEP-IND.

INTROJECTIVE also acted as a mediating variable on the relationship between IPPA-PA and SDS: z=-2.013 (p=.044). IPPA-PA predicted INTROJECTIVE (β=-.489, p<.001; R^2=.239, F(1, 48)=15.049, p<.001). When entered simultaneously into the regression equation both IPPA-PA and INTROJECTIVE were significant predictors of SDS: IPPA-PA (β=-.578, p<.001; R^2=.559, F(2, 47)=29.844, p<.001); INTROJECTIVE (β=.270, p=.019). As with IPPA-PE, and SEP-IND, this indicates that while INTROJECTIVE mediates the relationship between IPPA-PA and SDS, it is only a partial mediation, with IPPA-PA contributing variance independently of SEP-IND.

ANACLITIC did not have a significant indirect effect on the relationship between IPPA-PA and SDS: z=-0.496 (p=.620). IPPA-PA did not significantly predict ANACLITIC (β=-0.079, p=.583; R^2=.006, F(1, 48)=0.305, p=.583). When entered simultaneously into the regression equation both IPPA-PA and ANACLITIC were significant predictors of depression: IPPA-PA (β=-.693, p<.001; R^2=.552, F(2, 47)=28.950, p<.001); ANACLITIC (β=.219, p=.030). Hence IPPA-PA and ANACLITIC independently contribute to the variance of SDS.

Males

IPPA-PE did not have an indirect effect on the relationship between IPPA-PA and SDS: z=-1.886 (p=.059). IPPA-PA predicted IPPA-PE (β=.575, p=.001; R^2=.330, F(1, 28)=13.822, p=.001). When entered simultaneously into the regression equation, both IPPA-PE and IPPA-PA remained significant predictors of SDS: IPPA-PA (β=-.487, p=.004; R^2=.560, F(2, 27)=17.208, p<.001); and IPPA-PE (β=-.353, p=.032).

SEP-IND did not have an indirect effect on the relationship between IPPA-PA and SDS: z=-1.539 (p=.124). IPPA-PA was not a significant predictor of SEP-IND (β=-.302, p=.119; R^2=.091, F(1, 26)=2.600, p=.119). When entered simultaneously into the regression equation, IPPA-PA and SEP-IND were strong predictors of SDS: IPPA-PA (β=-.425, p=.001; R^2=.738, F(2, 25)=35.259, p=.001); and SEP-IND (β=.630, p<.001).

INTROJECTIVE did not act as a mediating variable on the relationship between IPPA-PA and SDS: z=-0.837 (p=.402). IPPA-PA did not predict INTROJECTIVE (β=-.268, p=.168; R^2=.072, F(1, 26)=2.007, p=.168). When entered simultaneously into the regression equation, IPPA-PA was a significant predictor of SDS, (β=-.561, p=.002; R^2=.416, F(2, 25)=8.894, p=.001); but INTROJECTIVE was not significant (β=.202, p=.215).

ANACLITIC did not have a significant indirect effect on the relationship between IPPA-PA and SDS: z=-1.052 (p=.293). IPPA-PA significantly predicted ANACLITIC (β=-.515, p=.005; R^2=.265, F(1, 26)=9.386, p=.005). When entered simultaneously into the regression equation IPPA-PA was a significant predictor of SDS: (β=-.506, p=.009; R^2=.411, F(2,25)=8.710, p<.001); but ANACLITIC was not significant (β=-.211, p=.250).

Table 9a. Summary of Mediation Effects - Females

Relationship Indirectly Effected	Mediating Variables
MCARE→Depression	IPPA-PE SEP-IND INTROJECTIVE
MCONTROL→Depression	IPPA-PE SEP-IND
PCARE→Depression	no mediators
PCONTROL→Depression	IPPA-PE SEP-IND
IPPA-PA→Depression	SEP-IND INTROJECTIVE

Table 9b. Summary of Mediation Effects – Males

Relationship Indirectly Effected	Mediating Variables
MCARE→Depression	no mediators
MCONTROL→Depression	no mediators
PCARE→Depression	no mediators
PCONTROL→Depression	no mediators
IPPA-PA→Depression	no mediators

DISCUSSION

We demonstrated that higher levels of perceived maternal care, paternal care, and parent attachment were negatively correlated with depression, and maternal control, paternal control were positively correlated with depression for both boys and girls. When the relative contribution of maternal care and control, and paternal care and control were analysed, we found that for both boys and girls, it was the combination of low levels of maternal care with high levels of paternal control that best predicated depression. Interestingly, the resulting regression equation explained 53% of the variance in boys compared with only 28% of the variance in girls. Suggesting for girls in particular, that the direct relationship between lack of care from the mother, and over-protection from the father only is only a small part of the picture and that something else must be accounting for their depression too.

We then sought to determine whether these relationships were direct or whether the way adolescents experience their parents influences subsequent development stage (peer attachment, separation-individuation; introjective depressive style and anaclitic depressive style) which in turn contribute to depression. In analysing the role of the mediating variables, we found, as expected dramatic gender differences. In general, the relationship between perceived parenting and symptoms of depression in males was direct, but in females was mediated by other psychological factors.

The relationship between maternal care and depression was mediated by peer attachment, separation-individuation, and introjective depression for girls, but there was no mediation of the same relationship for boys. That is while the lower levels of maternal care was apparently directly related to depression for boys, in girls, lack of maternal care had flow-on effects, which in turn were associated with depression. Similarly, maternal control was directly related to depression in boys, but in girls was mediated by both peer attachment and separation-individuation. It appears that the mother has a more widespread, effect upon the girl's psychological development than boys'. This supports the findings of Rubin et al. (1992) who indicated that girls rely on social support from their family more so than their peers, so when this is absent, one can expect girls may have problems. We demonstrated that poor peer attachments in boys was also associated with depression, as suggested by Schwartz, Dodge, Pettit and Bates (2000), but that poor peer attachments were not the result of negative parenting, to the extent that they are with girls.

The level of perceived care form the father was more directly related to depression in girls, as well as for boys. In boys the relationship between paternal care and depression was not mediated by, and in fact not related to peer attachment, separation-individuation, introjective depression, or anaclitic depression. For girls, the relationship between paternal care and depression was not fully mediated by any of the proposed mediators, although the introjective depression seemed to be acted as a partial mediator. However, the relationship between paternal control and depression mirrored that of maternal control and depression. As suggested by Kirkcaldy, Siefen, and Furhan (2000), a negative father may have more of an impact upon girls than boys. Paternal control was mediated by peer attachment and separation-individuation, as suggested by Blos (1967) but for girls only, there were no mediating effects for boys. Again suggesting that perhaps girls are more vulnerable than boys to the wider implications of negative aspects of parenting, that is, they cause more problems for girls than for boys.

Finally, the relationship between parent attachment and depression in girls was mediated by separation-individuation, and introjective depression in girls, with no mediators for boys.

Our hypothesis that females would be more vulnerable to an exaggeration in the anaclitic line of depression was supported by the finding of significantly higher mean scores on anaclitic depression for girls compared with boys. However, anaclitic depression did not act as a mediating variable between depression and any of the parenting variables, for girls or boys. While girls did not obtain higher mean scores on introjective depression, introjective depression did act as a mediator between maternal care and depression and parent attachment and depression. Hence for the girl, an impact of negative parenting may be that she is more self-critical, which in turn contributes to her higher level of depression.

The Role of the Mother

Maternal care refers how caring the mother is perceived by the adolescent to be, with high scores reflecting perceived higher levels of care. Maternal care for both males and females was negatively associated with depression. Girls who perceived their mothers as caring were able to form strong attachments to peers which then protected them from higher levels of depression. In males the same pattern occurred but did not reach statistical significance. This relationship makes sense in terms of attachment theory and object relations – that is, that early significant relationships, particularly with the primary caregiver, become internalised, and forms the blueprint for subsequent relationships. So it makes sense that if one feels cared for, that the internal working model for relationships would be positive, and allow potentially positive attachments to peers to be formed.

Even though disturbances in the separation-individuation process contributed to depression in both males and females, the role of maternal care varied. In females, lower levels of maternal care contributed to disturbances in the separation-individuation process, which in turn was related to levels of depression. But in males the two phenomena – maternal care and separation-individuation were not related. This suggests that for females the relationship with the mother is more complex, than it is with males. For an adolescent male to individuate he must separate (usually) from a female, his mother, in order to develop heterosexual relationships outside of the family. So while a caring mother may facilitate this process for the boy, at some level, he is going to separate from her, whether she is caring or not. This may be why there was no association between maternal care and levels of disturbance in separation-individuation in males. For girls the story is a bit different. Not only does she *not* have to separate from the mother, in order to form heterosexual relationships outside of the family, her primary figure of identity is usually the mother. So at a time where her identity as a woman is developing, she is trying to psychologically individuate, a seemingly paradoxical situation. A caring mother, who understands the girl's variable needs' will facilitate the separation-individuation process, whereas a mother who is less caring may create disturbances in the separation-individuation process, which in turn lead to depression. Gender differences are also observable in the separation-individuation process of infancy. Infant boys are oriented toward activity more so than girls, and mother's of boys tend to be more allowing of freedom of movement, and longer elation of mood in their infant boys. Boys are much more determined to escape from the mother, than girls. Their greatest anxiety for the infant boy is merging with the mother, which would result in loss of a sense of self, and his masculine identity (Kaplan, 1978). The infant girl's relationship with her mother is more complex. She is less inclined to separate, and finds separations more anxiety provoking when they occur. She longs for closeness yet pushes her mother away, at a time when she is becoming aware of gender differences. Her temporary angry response to her mother is her unconscious blaming of the mother for the little girl's anatomical shortcomings (Kaplan, 1978. The little girl has to resolve this by beginning to see her mother not as someone who wants to dominate her, but as someone who is supportive and someone with whom she identifies. Hence, a mother who is not able to do this for her daughter creates ongoing problems for the girl's developing identity. Although the idea that there is something wrong with her body, is only an unconscious temporary position for the infant girl, it remerges, in a conscious form at adolescence, with the adolescent girl much more prone to disturbances on bogy image, eating disorders (DSM-IV), and resulting depression (Nolen-Hoeksema et al., 1993).

Females who reported having caring mothers were less likely to have problems involving the development of a stable, independent sense of self (introjective depression), which in turn lead to lower levels of symptoms of depression. So again, some of the effects of maternal care on depression are indirect, perhaps because the development of an independent sense of self, for a girl, is intrinsically linked to the mother, as the primary role model. Whereas for males, maternal care was related to having a stable independent sense of self, but that boys' sense of self did not manifest as actual depressive symptoms. This may indicate that males and females have experiences different of depression.

A surprising finding was that maternal care was not related to anaclitic depression in either males or females. Anaclitic depression refers to an exaggeration of the developmental line concerned with getting one's dependency needs met, and manifests as fears of being abandoned and a struggle to maintain contact with the need-gratifying object. This would seem to come directly from the infant's relationship with the mother. A mother that is, in Winnicott's terms, 'good-enough' supports the infant so that he or she comes to feel that the mother is a reliable source of love and food and can makes fears disappear, and that this can be relied upon. A mother that is preoccupied, uncaring or inconsistent creates for the infant overwhelming anxiety. Perhaps this feeling is so primitive that it does not directly manifest as symptoms of depression in conventional terms, but rather as anxieties in relationships and an unconscious depression.

A mother who is perceived as being overly-protective was for both males and females associated with symptoms of depression. This relationship was, for females but not males, mediated by attachment to peers and disturbances in separation-individuation. Maybe the pathway for females is that an over-protective mother disallows experiences with the peer group, or in some way undermines the girl's confidence that she is unable to form stronger peer attachments, leaving her vulnerable to depression. Similarly, an over-protective mother may become anxious at the girl's attempts to individuate, and somehow sabotage her normal development, causing disturbances in the girl's separation-individuation that lead to depression.

Why is it that boys' don't show this same pattern? Perhaps the over-protective mother has a more pragmatic impact upon the boy to prevent him from behaving in certain ways, but that because of his greater psychological need to separate from her, she has less of an impact upon his individuation and relationships with peers, even though his perception that she is over-protective may manifest directly as depression. As already discussed infant boys are more inclined to separate from their mother, and seemingly mothers' differentiate from infant boys and girls in their permissiveness of the separation. At adolescence the boy of the over-controlling mother has probably already negotiate a form of separation, which she has less control over. Boys with an over-protective mother may be buffered by having father as an ally, someone with whom he can identify, and importantly develop an awareness of his masculinity. It is possible that sons of the controlling mother who has some 'success' end up with more severe psychological problems, so studying a clinical population may be warranted.

The Role of the Father

The father has a very different role to the mother, and he initially takes a less direct role, compared with the intensity of the mother-baby relationship. As the infant emerges as a social being, he provides a bridge between the mother and home and the outside world (Raphael-Leff, 1991). Even the young infant knows that the father is a more exciting, stimulating playmate (Karen, 1994), but that his authority is to be feared (Raphael-Leff, 1991).

Not surprisingly, the role of the father for boys and girls differed. The level of perceived care from fathers', while directly associated with depression, was not mediated by any of the psychological variables, for either girls or boys. So seemingly the association is direct, if the adolescent feels father does not care, they are more likely to feel depressed. For girls, there was no relationship between feeling cared for by her father and peer attachment, separation-individuation or anaclitic depression. The father, who generally is not the primary care-giver, has a less psychologically complex role, particularly during infancy. So at adolescence it is easier for the girl to psychologically separate from him. Seemingly, she forms her blueprint for attachments from her mother which then determines the quality of her peer relationships. While paternal care is not related to the girl developing an anaclitic style of depression – problems being able to form stable, enduring, mutually satisfying interpersonal relationships; it is related to introjective depression – problems achieving a differentiated, consolidated, stable, realistic, essentially positive identity. While INTROJECTIVE did not act as a mediating variable (it approached significance), for girls, perceived level of paternal care was related to levels of introjective depression. Hence the father also has a role in helping the girl feel that she competent and good enough. In infancy, the father provides for his daughter an experience other than mother. As she grows to become aware of gender differences, she experiences the possibilities of her feminine identity outside her relationship with her mother, and a positive relationship with her father gives her a sense that she is valued as a woman (Kaplan, 1978).

For boys perceived level of paternal care was not related to peer attachment, separation-individuation, introjective depression or anaclitic depression. It is apparent that the boy does not have a similar pattern of relationship with his father, that the girl has with her mother. As the primary care giver, her relationship is unique, and even though care from the father is essential, it does not have the same impact on subsequent psychological tasks for the adolescent.

Perceived levels of paternal control, were however important in a number of ways. Firstly, when maternal care, maternal control, paternal care and paternal control were all entered into a regression equation to predict depression (refer to tables 5a and 5b) the final predictors for both boys and girls were maternal care and paternal control. For girls this equation accounted for about 28% of the variance, but for boys it accounted a very large 53% of the variance. So, to varying degrees, for boys and girls, it is the perception that mother is not caring and father is controlling that is associated with symptoms of depression. For girls, peer attachment mediates the relationship between paternal control and symptoms of depression, although this relationship does not exist for boys. Perhaps the controlling father exerts his influence over his daughter in a way that prevents her from forming good peer attachments, and potentially finding a sexual partner, but he does not do the same to his son - typical of the 'double standards' of gender politics seen in many families.

The relationship between perceived levels of paternal control and symptoms of depression was, for girls, also mediated by separation-individuation. The controlling, over-protective father may prohibit the girls push to individuate disallowing her the necessary experiences outside of the family, and not being aware of her variable needs for distance and closeness during this time. Again, this pattern was not seen for boys.

It is also possible that the level of control the father has influences the family unit more generally. The father, who traditionally has the role of psychologically containing and supporting the mother while she is carrying and caring for the baby (Raphael-Leff, 1991). A father who is overly protective or unable to be flexible for the changing needs of the family, may effect a change in the mother, either via his lack of support, or her feeling she needs to compensate for him, which in turn could affect the family system. Further, it has been found that marital satisfaction influences the quality of the child's relationship with the mother (Belsky, 1984).

Limitations of the Study

The present study explored the gender differences in the relative contribution of parenting variables to symptoms of depression in adolescents. Some qualifications should be made. First, we were really only concerned with the contribution of parental variable to subsequent depressive symptoms in adolescents. There is of course the possibility that other factors contribute to some of the variance in symptoms of depression, such as environmental, genetic or social factors. The relative contribution of all possible factors producing depressive symptoms in adolescents requires further research. Second, the sample was of adolescents from the normal population, rather than the clinical population. Further research would be needed to see whether the same trends hold for adolescents who are classified as clinically depressed or who have other forms of psychopathology. Third, we suggested only a few possible mediating factors. There are many other potential factors that may be influenced by parenting variables and either contribute to or protect against depressive symptoms of adolescence. Fourth, the sample of boys was small compared with girls. While this in itself is an important finding, as it demonstrates that fewer boys are willing to participate in psychological tasks, it does limit the statistical power of the tests. Fifth, is the problem of actually defining 'adolescence'. Other researchers (e.g., Angold and Worthman, 1993) have highlighted the difficulties of studying adolescent populations. They suggest that studies should more carefully consider the pubertal status of adolescents, through the assessment of endocrine changes, rather than less accurate means, such as self-report. However such a requirement would severely limit research. We attempted to overcome this problem by using a narrow age range (14-16 years). However, there would still undoubtedly be developmental variations in the present sample, and hence, the results cannot be generalised to different aged adolescents.

Future research may consider the role of mother and father separately and develop assessments that adequately capture the differences in these parenting roles for both boys and girls. It would also be important to examine a clinical population to see whether the same conclusions can be drawn.

References

Acklin, M.W., Bibb, J.L., Boyer, P., and Jain, V. (1991). Early memories as expressions of relationship paradigms: A preliminary investigation. *Journal of Personality Assessment, 57*, 177-192.

Adam, K.S., Keller, A., West, M., Larose, S., and Goszer L.B. (1994). Parental representation in suicidal adolescents: A controlled study. *Australian and New Zealand Journal of Psychiatry, 28*, 418-425.

Ainsworth, M.D.S. (1989). Attachments beyond infancy. *American Psychologist, 4*, 709-716.

Ainsworth, M. D. S., Blehar, M. C., Waters, E., and Wall, S. (1978). *Patterns of attachment: A psychological study of the strange situation.* Hillsdale, New Jersey: Lawrence Erlbaum Associates, Inc.

American Psychiatric Association. (1994). *Diagnostic and statistical manual of mental disorders.* (4th ed.). Washington, DC: Author.

Armsden, G.C., and Greenberg, M. (1987). The inventory of parent and peer attachment: Individual differences and their relationship to psychological well-being in adolescence. *Journal of Youth and Adolescence, 16*, 427-454.

Armsden, G.C., McCauley, E., Greenberg, M.T., Burke, P.M., and Mitchell, J.R. (1990). Parent and peer attachment in early adolescent depression. *Journal of Abnormal Child Psychology, 18*, 683-697.

Angold, A., Worthman, C.W. (1993). Puberty onset of gender differences in rates of depression: A developmental, epidemiologic and neuroendocrine perspective. *Journal of Affective Disorders, 29*, 145-158.

Ausubel, D.P. (1954). *Theory and problems of adolescent development.* New York: Grune and Stratton.

Barnett, P. A. and Gotlib, I. H. (1988). Psychosocial functioning and depression: Distinguishing among antecedents, concomitants and consequences. *Psychological Bulletin, 104, 97-126.*

Bartholomew, K. (1997). Adult attachment perspectives. *British Journal of Medical Psychology, 70*, 249-263.

Beck, A.T. (1967). *Depression: Clinical, experimental and theoretical aspects.* New York: Harper and Row.

Belsky, J. (1984). The determinant of parenting: A process model. *Child Development,55*, 83-96.

Benedek, T. (1959). Parenthood as a developmental phase: A contribution to the libido theory. *Journal of the American Psychoanalytic Association, 7*, 389-417.

Berganza, C.E., and Aguilar, G. (1992). Depression in Guatemalan adolescents. *Adolescence, 27*, 771-782.

Bibring, E. (1953). The mechanism of depression. In P. Greenacre (Ed.) *Affective disorders.* (pp. 13-48). New York: International Universities Press, 1966.

Blatt, S.J. (1966). Review of *Neurotic Styles* by D. Shapiro. *Psychiatry, 29*, 426-427.

Blatt, S.J. (1974). Levels of object representation in anaclitic and introjective depression. *Psychoanalytic Study of the Child, 29*, 107-157.

Blatt, S.J., D'Alfflitti, J.P., and Quinlan, D.M. (1976). Experiences of depression in normal young adults. *Journal of Abnormal Psychology, 85*, 383-389.

Blatt, S.J., Schaffer, C.E., Bers, S.A., and Quinlan, D.M. (1992). Psychometric properties of the Depressive Experiences Questionnaire for adolescents. *Journal of Personality Assessment, 59*, 82-98.

Blatt, S.J., and Shichman, S. (1983). Two primary configurations of psychopathology. *Psychoanalysis and Contemporary Thought, 6*, 187-254.

Blatt, S. J., Wein, S. J., Chevron, E., and Quinlan, D. M. (1979). Parental representation and depression in normal young adults. *Journal of Abnormal Psychology, 88*, 388-397.

Blos, P. (1962). *On Adolescence: A Psychoanalytic Interpretation.* Collier-MacMillan Limited: London.

Blos, P. (1967). The second individuation process of adolescence. *Psychoanalytic Study of the Child, 22*, 162-186.

Blos, P. (1968). Character formation in adolescence. *Psychoanalytic Study of the Child, 23*, 245-263.

Blos, P. (1979). *The Adolescent Passage*. International Universities Press, Inc.: New York.

Bowlby, J. (1977). The making and breaking of affectional bonds. I. Aetiology and psychopathology in the light of attachment theory, *British Journal of Psychiatry, 130*, 201-210.

Brage, D.G. (1995). Adolescent depression: A review of the literature. *Archives of Psychiatric Nursing, 9*, 45-55.

Caspi, A. (2000). The child is father of the man: Personality continues from childhood to adulthood. *Journal of Personality and Social Psychology, 78*, 158-172.

Chodorow, N. (1978). Mothering, object relations, and the female oedipal configurations. *Feminist Studies, 4*, 137-158.

Christenson, R.M., and Wilson, W.P. (1985). Assessing pathology in the separation-individuation process by an inventory. *The Journal of Nervous and Mental Disease, 173*, 561-565.

Cooper, P.J., and Goodyer, I.A., (1993). Community study of depression in adolescent girls, *British Journal of Psychiatry, 163*, 369-380.

Corey, S. M. (1946). Developmental Tasks of Youth. In *John and Society Year Book.* New York: Harper.

Crick, N.R., Werner, N.E., Casas, J.F., O'Brien, K.M., Nelson, D.A., Grotpeter, J.K., and Markon, K. (1999). Childhood aggression and gender: A new look at an old problem. In D. Bernstein (Ed.). *Gender and motivation: Nebraska Symposium on Motivation* (pp. 75-141). Lincoln: University of Nebrraska Press.

Culbertson, F.M. (1997). Gender and depression: An international review. *American Psychologist, 52*, 25-31.

Davies, P.T., and Windle, M. (1997). Gender-specific pathways between maternal depressive symptoms, family discord, and adolescent adjustment, *Developmental Psychology, 33*, 657-668.

Davis, P.J. (1999). Gender differences in autobiographical memory for childhood emotional experiences. *Journal of Personality and Social Psychology, 76*, 498-510.

De Jong, M.L. (1992). Attachment, individuation, and risk of suicide in late adolescence. *Journal of Youth and Adolescence, 21,* 357-373.

Deming, J. (1989). Affective disorders in children and adolescence: A review of recent literature. *Psychotherapy in Private Practice, 7*, 43-56.

Dolan, B.M., Evans, C., and Norton, K. (1992). The Separation-Individuation Inventory. *The Journal of Nervous and Mental Disease, 180*, 529-533.

Egger H.L., Costello E.J., Erkanli, A., and Angold, A. (1999). Somatic complaints and psychopathology in children and adolescents; stomach aches, musculoskeletal pains and headaches. *Journal of the American Academy of Child and Adolescent Psychiatry,38*, 852–860.

Ehrenberg, M.F., Cox, D.N., and Koopman, R.F. (1990). The prevalence of depression in high school students. *Adolescence, 25*, 905-912.

Erikson, E. H. (1963). *Childhood and society*. New York: W. W. Norton.

Esman, A. H. (1980). Adolescent psychopathology and the rapprochement phenomenon. *Adolescent Psychiatry, 8*, 320-331.

Fenichel, O. (1945). *The Psychoanalytic Theory of Neurosis.* New York: Norton.

Fichman, L., Koestner, R., and Zuroff, D.C. (1994). Depressive styles in adolescence: Assessment, relation to social functioning, and developmental trends. *Journal of Youth and Adolescence, 23*, 315-330.

Fleming, J.E., and Offord, D.R. (1990). Epidemiology of childhood depressive disorders: A critical review. *Journal of the American Academy of Child and Adolescent Psychiatry, 29*, 571-580.

Fowler, C., Hilsenroth, M.J., and Handler, L.H. (1994). Early memories: An exploration of theoretically derived queries and their clinical utility. *Bulletin of the Menninger Clinic, 59*, 79-98.

Freud, A. (1958). Adolescence. *Psychoanalytic Study of the Child, 13*, 255-278.

Freud, S. (1914). On narcissism. *Standard Edition, 14*, 67-102. London: Hogarth Press, 1957.

Freud, S. (1917). Mourning and melancholia. *Standard Edition, 14,* 243-258. . London: Hogarth Press, 1957.

Friedman, M.H., and Laufer, M. (1997). Problems in working with adolescents. In M. Laufer (Ed.) *Adolescent breakdown and beyond.* (pp. 39-56). London: Karnac Books.

Garrison, C.Z., Addy, C.L., Jackson, K.L., McKeown, R.E., and Waller, J.L. (1992). Major depressive disorder and dysthymia in young adolescents. *American Journal of Epidemiology, 135,* 792-802.

Ge, X., Conger, R.D., and Elder, G.H. (1996). Coming of age too early. Pubertal influences on girls vulnerability to psychological distress. *Child Development, 67,* 3386-3400.

Gilligan, C. (1982). In a different voice: Psychological theory and women's development. Cambridge, MA: Harvard University Press.

Goldney, R.D. (1985). Parental representations in young women who attempt suicide. *Acta Psychiatrica Scandinavica,* 72, 230-232.

Goodman, L.A. (1960). On the exact variance of products. *Journal of the American Statistical association, 55,* 708-713.

Gore, S., Aseltine, R., and Colton, M.E. (1992). Social structure, life stress and depressive symptoms in a high-school aged population. *Journal of Health and Social Behavior, 33,* 97-113.

Grotevant, H., and Cooper, C. (1985). Patterns of interaction in family relationships and the development of identity exploration in adolescence. *Child Development, 56,* 425-438.

Gunderson, J. (1983). Characteristics of borderlines. In P. Hartcollis (Ed). *Borderline personality disorders: The concept, the syndrome, the patient.* New York: International Universities Press.

Hankin, B.L., and Abramson, L.Y. (2001). Development of gender differences in depression: An elaborated cognitive vulnerability-transactional stress theory. *Psychological Bulletin, 127,* 773-796.

Harrington, R. (1994). Affective disorders. In M. Rutter, E. Taylor, L. and L. Hersov (Eds.), *Child and adolescent psychiatry, modern approaches* (pp. 330-350). Oxford.: Blackwell Science Ltd.

Heaven, P.C.L. (2001). *The social psychology of adolescence.* Basingstoke: Palgrave.

Horner, T. M. (1985). The psychic life of the young infant: Review and critique of the psychoanalytic concepts of the symbiosis and infantile omnipotence. *American Journal of Orthopsychiatry, 55,* 324-344.

Irwin, C.E., Millstein, S.G. (1986). Biopsychosoical correlates of risk-taking behaviours during adolescence: Can the physician intervene? *Journal of Adolescent Health Care, 7,* 82-96.

Jacobson, E. (1971). *Depression.* New York: International Universities Press.

Josselson, R. (1980). Ego development in adolescence. In J. Adelson (Ed.). *Handbook of adolescent psychiatry.* New York: Wiley, pp. 188-208.

Josselson, R. (1988). The embedded self: I and thou revisited. In D.K. Lapsley and F.C. Power (Eds.), *Self, ego, and identity: Integrative approaches.* (pp. 91-106). New York: Springer-Verlag.

Kaltiala-Heino, R., Rimpelä, M., Rantanen, P., and Laippala, P. (2001). Adolescent depression: The role of discontinuities in life course and social support. *Journal of Affective Disorders, 64,* 155-166.

Kaplan, L. (1978). Oneness and separateness: From infant to individual. Jonathan Cape Ltd: London.

Karen, R. (1994). *Becoming attached: First relationships and how they shape our capacity to love*. Oxford ford University Press: Oxford.

Kirkcaldy, B., Siefen, G., and Furnham, A. (2003). Gender, anxiety-depressivity and self-image among adolescents. *European Psychiatry, 18*, 50–58.

Klein, M. (1934). A contribution to the psychogenesis of manic-depressive states. *Contributions to Psycho-Analysis.* London: Hogarth Press, 1948.

Kobak, R.R., and Sceery, A. (1988). Attachment in late adolescence: Working models, affect regulation, and working representations of self and others. *Child Development, 59*, 135-146.

Kroger, J. (1996). *Identity in adolescence: The balance between self and other* (2nd ed.). London: Routledge.

Lamont, J., Fischoff, S., and Gottlieb, H. (1976). Recall of parental behaviours in female neurotic depressives. *Journal of Clinical Psychology, 32*, 762-765.

Lapsley, D.K., Rice, K.G., and Fitzgerald, D.P. (1990). Adolescent Attachment, identity, and adjustment of college: Implications for the continuity of adaptation hypotheses. *Journal of Counseling and Development, 68*, 561-565.

Laufer, M. (1997). Problems in working with adolescents. In M. Laufer (Ed.) *Adolescent breakdown and beyond.* (pp. 3-15). London: Karnac Books.

Laursen, B. (1996). Closeness and conflict in adolescent peer relationships: Interdependence with friends and romantic partners. In W.M. Bukowski, A.F. Newcomb, and W.W. Hartup (Eds.), *The company they keep: Friendship in childhood and adolescence. Cambridge studies in social and emotional development* (pp. 186-210) New York: Cambridge University Press.

Leinonen, J.A., Solantaus, T.S., and Punamaki, R.L. (2003). Social support and the quality of parenting under economic pressure and workload in Finland: The role of family structure and parental gender. *Journal of Family Psychology, 17*, 409-418.

Levine, L. V., Tuber, S. B., Slade, A., and Ward, M. J. (1991). Mothers' mental representations and their relationship to mother-infant attachment. *Bulletin of the Menninger Clinic, 55*, 454-469.

Lichtenberg, J.D. (1983). *Psychoanalysis and Infant Research.* Hillsdale, N.J.: The Analytic Press.

Lyons-Ruth, K. (1991). Rapprochement or approchement: Mahler's theory reconsidered from the vantage point of recent research on early attachment relationship. *Psychoanalytic Psychology, 8*, 1-23.

Mahler, M.S. (1963). Thoughts about Development and Individuation., *Psychoanalytic Study of the Child, 8*, 307-324.

Mahler, M.S. (1968). *On Human Symbiosis and the Vicissitudes of Individuation.* New York: International Universities Press, Inc.

Mahler, M. S., and Gosliner, B. J. (1955). On symbiotic child psychosis: Genetic, dynamic and restitutive aspects. *Psychoanalytic Study of the Child, 10*, 195-214.

Mahler, M. S., and La Perriere, K. (1965). Mother-child interaction during Separation-Individuation. *Psychoanalytic Quarterly, 24*, 483-498.

Mahler, M. S., Pine, F., and Bergman, A. (1975). *The psychological birth of the human infant: Symbiosis and individuation*. New York: Basic Books.

Main, M., and Hesse, E. (1990). Parents' unresolved traumatic experiences are related to infant disorganized attachment status: Is frightened and/or frightening parental behavior the linking mechanism?. In M. Greenberg, D. Cicchetti, and E. M. Cummings (Eds.), *Attachment in the preschool years:_Theory, research and intervention.* (pp. 161-184). Chicago: University of Chicago Press.

Main, M., and Solomon, J. (1990). Procedures for identifying infants as disorganized disoriented during the Ainsworth Strange Situation. In M. Greenberg, D. Cicchetti, and E. M. Cummings (Eds.), *Attachment in the preschool years: Theory, research and intervention.* (pp. 121-160). Chicago: University of Chicago Press.

Main, M., and Weston, D. (1982). Avoidance of the attachment figure in infancy: Description and interpretation. In C. M. Parkes and J. Stevenson-Hinde (Eds.), *The place of attachment in human behaviour*. (pp. 203-217). London: Tavistock..

Milne, L.C., and Greenway, P. (2001) *Characteristics of the parent-adolescent relationship that predict peer attachment in adolescents.* Unpublished manuscript, Monash University, Melbourne.

Mayman, M. (1968). Early memories and character structure. *Journal of Projective Techniques and Personality Assessment*, *32*, 303-316.

National Institute of Mental Health. (1981). *Special report on depression research* (Publication No. ADM 81-1085). Washington, DC: U.S. Government Printing Office.

Newsom (2002). *Testing mediation with regression analysis.* Retrieved 26 January 2004 from {http://www.upa.pdx.edu/IOA/newsom/da2/ho_mediation.doc}.

Nolen-Hoeksema, S. (1994). An interactive model for the emergence of gender differences in depression in adolescence. *Journal of Research on Adolescence*, *4*, 519-534.

Nolen-Hoeksema, S., Morrow, J., and Fredrickson, B.L. (1993). Response styles and the duration of episodes of depressed mood. *Journal of Abnormal Psychology*, *102*, 20-28.

Nottelmann, E.D., Susman, E.J., Inoff-Germain, G., Cutler, G.B., Loriaux, D.L., and Chrousos, G.P. (1987). Developmental processes in early adolescence: Relationships between adolescent adjustment problems and chronological age, pubertal status, and puberty-related serum hormone levels. *Journal of Pediatrics*, *110,* 473-480.

Ohannessian, C.M., Lerner, R.M., von Eye, A., and Lerner, J.V. (1996). Direct and indirect relations between perceived parental acceptance, perceptions of the self, and emotional adjustment during early adolescence. *Family and Consumer Sciences Journal*, *25*, 159-183.

Parker, G. (1979). A parental bonding instrument. *British Journal of Medical Psychology*, 52, 1-10.

Parker, G., Tupling, H., and Brown, L.B. (1979). A parental bonding instrument. *British Journal of Medical Psychology*, *52*, 1-10.

Parker, G., Kiloh, L., and Hayward, L. (1987). Parental representations of neurotic and endogenous depressives. *Journal of Affective Disorders*, *13*, 75-82.

Pedersen, W. (1994). Parental relations, mental health, and delinquency in adolescents. *Adolescence*, *29*, 975-990.

Pietromonaco, P.R., and Barrett, L.F. (2000). The internal working models concept: What do we really know about the self in relation to others? *Review of General Psychiatry*, *4*, 155-175.

Preacher, K.J., and Leonardelli, G.J. (2003, 21 October). *Calculation for the Sobel test: An interactive calculation tool for mediation tests*. Retrieved 6 January 2004 from {http://www.unc.edu/~preacher/Sobel/Sobel.htm}.

Quintana, S.M., and Kerr, J. (1993). Relational needs in late Adolescent separation-individuation. *Journal of Counseling and Development, 71*, 349-354.

Quintana, S.M., and Lapsley, D.K. (1987). Adolescent attachment and identity development: A continuity of adaptation. *Journal of Adolescent Research, 2*, 393-409.

Quintana, S.M., and Lapsley, D.K. (1990). Rapprochement in late adolescent separation-individuation: A structural equations approach. *Journal of Adolescence, 13*, 371-385.

Raphael-Leff, J. (1991). *The psychological process of child bearing*. Chapman and Hall: London.

Reis, S., and Grenyer, B.F.S. (2002). Pathways to anaclitic and introjective depression. *Psychology and Psychotherapy: Theory Research and Practice, 75*, 445-459.

Rey, J.M. (1995). Perceptions of poor maternal care are associated with adolescent depression. *Journal of affective Disorders, 34*, 95-100.

Riddle, M.A., and Cho, S.C. (1989). Biological aspects of adolescent depression, In G.R. Adams, and R. Montemayor (Eds.), *Biology of adolescent behavior and development. Advances in development*: An annual book series, (Vol. 1), (pp 223-246).

Ross, M.W., Clayer, J.R., and Campbell, R.L. (1983). Parental rearing patterns and suicidal thoughts. *Acta Psychiatrica Scandinavica, 67*, 429-433.

Rubenfine, D.L. (1968). Notes on a theory of depression. *Psychoanalytic Quarterly, 37*, 400-417.

Rubin, C., Rubenstein, J., Stechler, G., Heeren, T., Halton, A., Housman, D., and Kasten, L., (1992). Depressive affect in "normal" adolescents: Relationships to life stress , family and friends. *American Journal of Orthopsychiatry, 63*, 430-441.

Rudolph, K.D., and Hammen, C. (1999). Age and gender as determinants of stress exposure, generation, and reactions in youngsters: A transactional perspective. *Child development, 70*, 660-677.

Sarnoff, C.A. (1987). *Psychotherapeutic Strategies in Late Latency Through Early Adolescence.* New Jersey: Jason, Aronson Inc.

Schafer. R. (1973). Concepts of self and identity and the experience of separation-individuation. *Psychoanalytic Quarterly, 42* 42-59.

Scheibe, S., Preuschhof, C., Cristi, C., and Bagby, R.M. (2003). Are there gender differences in major depression and its response to antidepressants. *Journal of Affective Disorders, 75*, 223-235.

Schraedley, P.K., Gotlib, I.H., and Hayward, C. (1999). Gender differences in correlates of depressive symptoms in adolescents. *Journal of Adolescent Health, 25*, 98-108.

Schwartz, D., Dodge, K.A, Pettit, G.S., and Bates, J.E. (2000). Friendship as a moderating factor in the pathway between early harsh home environment and later victimization in the peer group. *Developmental Psychology, 36*, 646-662.

Shahar, G., Blatt, S.J., and Ford, R.Q. (2003). Mixed anaclitic-introjective psychopathology in treatment-resistant inpatients undergoing psychoanalytic psychotherapy. *Psychoanalytic Psychology, 20, 84-102.*

Silberg, J., Pickles, A., Rutter, M., Hewitt, J., Simonoff, E., Maes, H., Carbonneau, R., Murrelle, L., Foley, D., and Eaves, L. (1999). The influence of genetic factors and life stress on depression among adolescent girls. *Archives of General Psychiatry, 56*, 225-232.

Silverstein, B., and Lynch, A. (1998). Gender differences in depression: The role played by parental attitudes of male superiority and maternal modeling of gender-related limitations. *Sex Roles, 38,* 539–555.

Simmons, R., and Blyth, D. (1987). *Moving into adolescence*. New York: de Gruyter.

Sobel, M.E. (1982). Asymptotic intervals for indirect effects in structural equation models. In S. Leinhart (Ed.), *Sociological methodology 1982* (pp. 290-312). San Francisco: Jossey-Bass.

Spitz, R.A. and Wolf, K.M. (1946). Anaclitic depression. *Psychoanalytic Study of the Child, 2*, 313-342.

Stein, H., Koontz, A.D., Fonagy, P., Allen, J.G., Fultz, J., Brethour, J.R., Allen, D., and Evans, R.B. (2002). Adult attachment: What are the underlying dimensions? *Psychology and psychotherapy: Theory Research and Practice*, 75, *77-91.*

Steinwand, G.M. (1984). Adolescent individuation: The culmination of a developmental line. *Journal of the American Academy of Psychoanalysis, 12*, 43-57.

Stern, D. N. (1985). *The interpersonal world of the infant*. New York: Basic Books.

Surrey, J.L. (1993). Self-in-relations: A theory of women's development. *Advanced Development 5, 1-11.*

Swanson, J.W., Linskey, A.O., Quintero-Salinas, R., Pumariega, A.J., and Holzer III, C.E. (1992). A binational school survey of depressive symptoms, drug use and suicidal ideation. *Journal of the American Academy of Child and Adolescent Psychiatry, 31*, 669-678.

Thomas A., and Forehand R. (1996). The role of paternal variables in divorced and married families: Predictability of adolescent adjustment. *American Journal of Orthopsychiatry, 63*, 126–135.

Toolan, J. (1981). Depression and suicide in children : An overview. *American Journal of Psychotherapy, 35*, 311-322.

Way, N., and Robinson, M.G. (2003). A longitudinal study of the effects of family friends and school experiences on the psychological adjustment of ethnic minority, low-SES adolescents. *Journal of Adolescent Research*, 18, 324-346.

Whitaker, A., Johnson, J., Shaffer, D., Rapoport, J.L., Kalikow, K., Walsh, B.T., Davies, M., Braiman, S., and Dolinsky, A. (1990). Uncommon troubles in young people: Prevalence estimates of selected psychiatric disorders in a nonreferred adolescent population. *Archives of General Psychiatry, 47*, 487-496.

Winnicott, D.W. (1954). The depressive position in normal emotional development. *British Journal of Medical Psychology, 28*, 89-100.

Zetzel, E.R. (1960). Introduction to the symposium on 'Depressive Illness'. *International Journal of Psycho-Analysis, 41*, 476-480.

Zung, W.W. (1965). A self-rating depression scale. *Archives of General Psychiatry, 12*, 63-70.

Zung, W.W. (1973). From art to science: The diagnosis and treatment of depression. *Archives of General Psychiatry, 29*, 328-337.

In: Abnormal Psychology: New Research
Editor: Helen D. Friedman and Paulina K. Revera
ISBN: 978-1-60692-636-9

Chapter 9

A HERMENEUTIC APPROACH TO CULTURE AND PSYCHOTHERAPY

***John Chambers Christopher*[1]*, Gary Foster*[2] *and Susan James*[3]**

[1] Health and Human Development
Montana State University; Bozeman, Montana 59717, USA
[2] Department of Philosophy; Wilfrid Laurier University;
Waterloo, Ontario, Canada N2L 3C5
[3] Educational and Counselling Psychology and Special Education;
University of British Columbia;
Vancouver, BC V6T 1Z4

ABSTRACT

Despite the growing awareness of culture within psychology, critics contend that understandings of culture remain largely superficial. Hermeneutics is a way of thinking interpretively about cultural meanings and discerning their specific manifestations that helps to remedy this situation. Hermeneutics offers a comprehensive theory of culture that (a) details how the self is embedded in culture, (b) highlights culture's inherently moral nature, and (c) provides conceptual tools for approaching culture in specific encounters. It can be utilized by psychotherapists not only to help understand clients from different cultural backgrounds but also to better recognize how the dominant Western cultural outlook, individualism, influences psychotherapy theory, research, and practice. These concepts are applied to cross-cultural cases.

Psychology and the practice of psychotherapy and counseling, according to many critics, have failed to fully address the challenges of working with minority group members, immigrants, and those dwelling in non-Western societies. Sue and Sue (1990) unequivocally maintain that when counseling theories are uncritically applied to ethnic minorities and non-Western peoples they contribute to portraying them as pathological. Mental health services and interventions are "frequently antagonistic or inappropriate to the life experiences of the culturally different client" (Sue and Sue, 1990, p. 7). Concepts, interventions, and measures developed in Western cultures are regularly extended to persons in and from non-Western cultures and research findings are interpreted at face value often resulting in an *imposed etic* and a perpetuation of the socio-political status quo (Pedersen, 1991; Prilleltensky, 1994; Sue and Sue, 1990). Not surprisingly, research indicates that groups such as African Americans have a considerable amount of distrust of the fields of counseling and psychotherapy and of Anglo psychologists (Nickerson, 1994). Research on underutilization and premature termination of mental health services by ethnic minorities lend strong support to these claims (Brinson and Kottler, 1995; Vandervert, 1995; Vernon and Roberts, 1982; Whaley, 2001).

Given this state of affairs, Sue and Sue (1990) offer a challenge to counselors and psychologists. They write:

> As mental health professionals, we have a personal and professional responsibility to (a) confront, become aware of, and take actions in dealing with our biases, stereotypes, values, and assumptions about human behavior, (b) become aware of the culturally different client's world view, values, biases, and assumptions about human behavior, and (c) develop appropriate help-giving practices, intervention strategies, and structures that take into account the historical, cultural, and environmental experiences/influences of the culturally different client. (p. 10)

Pursuing such an agenda, however, is enormously difficult when conducted within the reigning dualistic presuppositions of Western culture. Western thought tends to dichotomize life into opposing pairs such as mind/body, fact/value, good/bad, subject/object, self/other, and individual/society. These dichotomies pervade psychology as well as popular thought. For instance, academic and professional psychology have long seen themselves as objective, neutral, and culture-free enterprises dedicated to the discovery of universal and ahistorical facts and laws (Bernstein, 1978; Braginsky, 1992; Giorgi, 1970; Richardson and Christopher, 1993; Richardson, Fowers, and Guignon, 1999; Taylor, 1985a, 1985b). Western social science, shaped by positivism and more generally, empiricism, has held fast to a sharp metaphysical separation of facts and values with values seen as undesirable subjective emotional intrusions into the scientific process (Bernstein, 1978). From this mainstream view of social science, theory and practice should not be informed by cultural values.

This dualistic outlook has been largely overturned by a variety of post-positivist theorists who have considered how the pursuit of objectivity and neutrality have impeded the social sciences from understanding their own ethical and cultural roots (Christopher, 1996; Gergen, 1995; Hoshmand, 2006; Martin and Thompson, 1997; Prilleltensky, 1989; Richardson and Christopher, 1993; Richardson, Fowers, and Guignon, 1999; Slife, Reber, and Richardson, 2005; Slife, Williams, and Barlow, 2001). There is a history of seminal theorists such as Ellis (1973), May (1967), and Wachtel (1977) declaring that values and assumptions strongly shape the theory and practice of counseling and psychotherapy. In Wachtel's (1977) words, the counseling theories "that guide contemporary psychotherapeutic efforts both reflect and shape the culture's view of human potential and the good life" (p. 3). In her APA presidential address, Spence (1985) concludes that, "...whatever their intentions, scientists are the products of their society and time, and their construction of social reality is shaped by the world view and values of the culture in which they were reared" (p. 1285). Yet despite these observations, Sue and Sue (1990) are accurate when they note, "For too long we have deceived ourselves into believing that the practice of counseling and the data base that underlie the profession are morally, ethically, and politically neutral" (p. 24). It is little wonder that we have been left conceptually impoverished to identify cultural influences and deal with the moral dimension that many theorists are now saying is necessarily present in any scientific endeavor, especially those in the human sciences (Bellah, 1983; Bellah, Madsen, Sullivan, Swidler, and Tipton, 1985; Bernstein, 1978; Christopher, 1996, 2004; Cushman, 1990; Doherty, 1995; Richardson and Christopher, 1993; Sugarman and Martin, 1995; Taylor, 1989; Tjeltveit, 1989; Walsh, 1995). Consequently the role of individualism has remained disguised within the social sciences because "cultural influences may be quite pervasive, widespread, and powerful in forming the basis of "being" for ordinary people and, yet, remain elusive for those researchers who have sought to understand them" (Kitayama and Markus, 2000, p. 122).

To adequately respond to the challenge of Sue and Sue, we are faced with finding some point of leverage to understand the cultural values and assumptions of not only others but ourselves while we are situated within a cultural outlook that doesn't see itself as being a cultural outlook. Americans frequently assume that either we don't have a culture or that culture refers to superficial variations in clothing, food, and holiday customs. In a somewhat similar way, psychologists and counselors have assumed they were doing value-free and culture-free therapy. Part of the difficulty is that the definitions of culture provided in much of the cross-cultural and multicultural literature are often brief and tend to lack substantive value (Adams and Markus, 2001; Cole, 1996; Jahoda, 2002; Ratner, 2000). Another, as Maruyama (1992) makes clear, is that psychology has not generated the cognitive structures that would allow us to think contextually when we encounter diversity (see also Shweder, 1991). Instead, Sampson (1993) trenchantly argues that psychology has hastily responded to diversity with what he calls add-on eclectic strategies. So we are faced with two challenges: the first, to define culture in some way that doesn't trivialize it and assists us in discerning how we are culturally embedded and second, to learn to think culturally.

Our aim in this chapter is sketch out a hermeneutic account of culture. Philosophical hermeneutics provides a non-dualistic model of culture and the self. It is also a means of thinking interpretively about cultural meanings and discerning their specific manifestations. As a metatheory for psychology, hermeneutics can deepen our understanding of how we are shaped by culture and how much of psychological theory, research, and practice is influenced by individualism, our dominant cultural outlook. Hermeneutics is a framework for thinking about the world of our clients and the ways culture permeates every dimension of this world. This framework goes beyond just making global generalizations about what culture is. In addition to needing a comprehensive understanding of the nature of culture and its relationship to the self, psychotherapists must be able to think culturally. As Seeley (2000), following Devereaux (1958) argues, "Rather than learning about the stereotypical characteristics of particular cultures, psychotherapists need to become familiar with the general characteristics, categories, and functions of culture per se" (p. 72).

The term hermeneutics derives from the Greek word for interpretation and is related to Hermes, god of communication who ferried messages between the gods and humans. More recently, during the Protestant Reformation, hermeneutics was the theory and method of interpretation that emerged as a means of interpreting the Bible. Friederich Schleiermacher, at the turn of the eighteenth century, ushered in the contemporary understanding of hermeneutics, when he established a general interpretive methodology for uncovering the original intent of all forms of human communication, not just written texts like the Bible or legal statures. This version of hermeneutics, sometimes called *romantic hermeneutics* (Palmer, 1969; Richardson, et al., 1999) currently influences qualitative research methods (Benner, 1994; Fischer, 1980; Michrina and Richards, 1996; Packer and Addison, 1989; Ratner, 1997; Rennie, 1999; Tappan, 1997; Van Manen, 1990), theories of epistemology and clinical interpretation in psychodynamic therapies (Barclay, 1992; Bouchard and Guerette, 1991; Chessick, 1990; Eagle, 1986; Gentile, 1998; Schaefer, 1976; Spence, 1982, 1993), and narrative approaches to psychotherapy (Frank, 1987; Gergen, 1994; McNamee, 1996; Neimeyer and Mahoney, 1995; Schaefer, 1993). Following Schleiermacher in the tradition of romantic hermeneutics, Wilhelm Dilthey (1989) developed a critique of the natural science approach to the human sciences. Dilthey argued that the distinct subject-matter of the human sciences required a distinct methodology, one that acknowledged the role of interpretation in understanding the history, society and the individual. Less well known within psychology, Martin Heidegger's work in the 1920's instigated the most recent turn in hermeneutic thought, *philosophical* or *ontological hermeneutics*. Philosophical hermeneutics goes beyond methodology to consider the broader ontological questions about human nature that arise when we acknowledge that interpretation is central to human existence. This iteration of hermeneutic thought is highly influential in contemporary philosophy and social theory but is largely unknown within psychology except for a few notable exceptions (e.g., Messer, Sass, and Woolfolk, 1988; Richardson, et al., 1999; Woolfolk, 1998).

We believe that philosophical hermeneutics has numerous important contributions to make to psychology. In this chapter we outline a hermeneutic model of the self and its relationship to culture. Integrating the writings of philosophers Martin Heidegger, Hans-Georg Gadamer, Charles Taylor, and Paul Ricoeur, and the cultural anthropologist Clifford Geertz throughout the chapter, we begin by considering how the reigning Western understanding of the person, ontological individualism, makes it especially difficult to grasp how thoroughly we are shaped by culture. We then outline a hermeneutic theory of culture. Heidegger's notion of *being-in-the-world* is then reviewed as offering an alternative non-Cartesian ontology of the human agent that complements an interpretive view of culture. We also introduce Taylor's claim that culture is a moral framework that orients us to the good. We then explore how the hermeneutic notion of dialogue can provide a framework for engaging with those from different cultural backgrounds. Finally, we apply these concepts to a cross-cultural case study.

Ontological Individualism and the Challenge of Recognizing Culture

The dominant cultural outlook in the West is Individualism. In individualism, the self is the primary social reality, the basic building block of society. Individuals are seen as independent, and self-contained. They should be authentic, unique, responsible, expressive, rational. Anthropologists such as Geertz (1973), Lutz (1988), and Shweder, (1991; Shweder and Bourne, 1984) have explored how individualism may be a "peculiar idea" within human history and cross-cultural psychologists Harry Triandis (1989) estimates that individualism is the cultural outlook for only 30% of the world's population.

In the United States individualism is taken for granted as being "the way things are." The individualistic interpretation of the self is regarded as a scientific, rational, or as 'common sense' self-understanding instead of as one self-interpretation among a myriad of others. Ontological individualism casts the individual and culture as distinct and separable from each other, making it particularly difficult for us to grasp how we are shaped by culture. In ontological individualism the person is regarded in atomistic terms that render the person metaphysically separate from others, society, and nature (Bellah, Madsen, Sullivan, Swidler, and Tipton, 1985; Dumont, 1986; Lukes, 1973). Richardson, Fowers and Guignon (1999) describe this further, "We tacitly view human beings atomistically as discrete centers of experience and action concatenated in various ways into social groups, struggling to reduce inevitable conflicts with others through negotiations and temporary alliances" (p. 71). Such a self should ideally be "self-defining" (Taylor, 1975), refusing to rely upon the beliefs, values, and outlooks of others but seizing responsibility for coming to one's own identity.

Taylor (1975) contends that the emergence of this "self-defining subject" was accompanied by a new view of the universe as a brute physical domain of objects open to free and objective scientific investigation. Such a universe was best understood in mechanistic and materialistic terms as a neutral arena for the course of human history. While such an outlook makes good sense to most of us today it was a radical break with the history of ideas. Prior to the European Enlightenment beginning in the 17th century and still today in most non-Western parts of the world humans being were seen as situated in an ordered and inherently meaningful cosmos in which the individual had a defined place and role. Since the Enlightenment, this meaningful cosmos gave way to what Max Weber evocatively called the "disenchanted" world of modernity. This disenchanted perspective relies upon a sharp split between external objects and subjective experience. After this split, meanings and values are thought to reside in the realm of subjective experience. At the time this subject-object division was the kind of dramatic intellectual and cultural breakthrough that Isaiah Berlin (Berlin, Hardy, and Hausheer, 1998) would refer to as a "great liberating idea." The new view of the self as discrete and the world as disenchanted were ideological tools to liberate both scientific inquiry and the individual from the authoritarian and dogmatic excesses and oppressiveness of church, state, and society.

Taylor (1995) suggests, that the modern, disengaged, "punctual" self is as much a moral as a scientific ideal. In his writings (1975, 1989) he thoroughly documents how this individualism with its emphasis on autonomy and self-responsibility gradually evolved through many centuries of Western history (cf., Baumeister, 1986, 1987; Cushman, 1995). The modern self confronting a natural and social world to which it has no essential or defining ties "connects with ...central moral and spiritual ideas of the modern age," such as the modern ideal of "freedom as self-autonomy...to be self-responsible, to rely on one's own judgment, to find one's purpose in oneself" (1995, p. 7). This self is well-positioned to freely and rationally treat both itself and the outside world instrumentally, to alter them in desired ways, or, in later permutations of the modern self, to resist social pressure to conform and pursue self-actualization or personal authenticity as it sees fit. Culture, then, can come to be seen as a potential external threat that can somehow diminish the individual's autonomy. Critics suggest that our contemporary individualistic outlook has purchased valuable freedoms at the price of much alienation, stressing mastery and control over nature and ourselves to the detriment of other kinds of social, moral, or spiritual values in living.

Individualism functions, as Bernstein (1978) trenchantly argues, as the "disguised ideology" of the social sciences in the United States and much of Western Europe. Within psychology recent years have witnessed an increasing number of critiques of how individualism influences in unrecognized ways various fields of psychology (Christopher, 1999; Christopher, Nelson, and Nelson, 2004; Cirillo and Wapner, 1986; Cushman, 1990, 1991; Fowers and Richardson, 1993; Frank, 1978; Hogan, 1975; Kanfer, 1979; Kirschner, 1996; Perloff, 1987; Sampson, 1981, 1985, 1988, 1989; Smith, 1978; Spence, 1985; Waterman, 1981; Wolszon, 1998).

A powerful example of this underlying individualistic influence comes from what Geertz (1973) identified as the "stratigraphic" concept of the human being that dominates the social sciences. Like Bronfenbrenner's (1977) ecological model of the person, stratigraphic approaches portray the human being as a set of onion-like concentric circles, each layer of which is complete and irreducible in itself (Geertz, 1973). The innermost circle is biological, which is encircled successively by the psychological, social, and cultural domains. As Geertz puts it:

> Strip off the motley forms of culture and one finds the structural and functional regularities of social organization. Peel these off in turn and one finds the underlying psychological factors—"basic needs" or what-have-you—that support and make them possible. Peel off psychological factors and one is left with biological foundations—anatomical, physiological, neurological—of the whole edifice of human life. (p. 37)

The implication is that the psychologist can focus exclusively on the psychological "circle," leaving the levels of social and cultural organization to sociologists and anthropologists.

While these stratigraphic approaches do provide accounts in which culture is addressed, the downside is that culture can become mere extraneous context. Models and theories that take this approach adopt and reinforce the supposition that the individual is ontologically prior to the social; that it somehow makes sense to think of the individual as a biological entity existing independently of society and culture. Geertz (1973) challenges the notion that it is possible to understand the human being stripped of "the trappings of culture." In his view, which we shall turn to next, culture permeates human existence so thoroughly that the attempt to separate individuals and culture is incoherent and distorts our understanding of human nature.

A Hermeneutic View of Culture: Webs of Significance

Jackson and Meadows (1991) alert us to the fact that culture is a vague concept that most individuals never think about in any precise manner. Nevertheless, they think it essential that counselors engaged in multicultural counseling have a clear understanding of what this notion means. There is no shortage of definitions of culture in the cross-cultural and multicultural literature but these definitions are often not substantive and rarely help to bridge the gap between theory and practice (Christopher, 2001; Cole, 1996; Jahoda, 2002; Ratner, 2000).

Viewed from a hermeneutic perspective, culture is constituted by the shared meanings that make human interactions possible. These meanings form a common framework for helping people to make sense of the social (and physical) world. They form a background set of assumptions and values that not only shapes our understanding of the world but guides us practically through that world. Geertz (1973) claims that culture is a universal requirement of life, it is that which puts a particular order or structure on the lives of a people in a particular place.

Geertz (1973, 1983) makes a distinction between the notions of world view and ethos – two interdependent aspects of culture. The idea of a world view or *weltanschauung* denotes the more cognitive aspect of culture, that which describes or defines one's conception of reality. To hold a particular worldview is to have a framework for understanding the way that the world or reality works – its causal relations, various dimensions, the nature of its objects and so on. An *Ethos*, on the other hand, characterizes the more normative aspect of human existence. *Ethos* is concerned with the moral, aesthetic and affective dimensions of human life. As Geertz puts it, "A people's *ethos* is the tone, character and quality of their life, its moral and aesthetic style and mood; it is the underlying attitude towards themselves and their world that life reflects" (Geertz, 1973, p. 127).

Geertz (1973) characterizes culture, and in particular the notions of world view and *ethos* in terms of "webs of significance". These are what give meaning and coherence to our life activities. By "significance" Geertz implies something similar to what Heidegger (1962) means by the term *signification*. Heidegger characterizes the most fundamental aspects of our being-in-the world in terms of signification, care and concern. Our thoughts, feelings and actions reflect deep-seated presuppositions about what is real, important or valuable. The notion of care used by Heidegger is not simply that of a sympathetic emotional response, but refers to what we value, what consumes our energy and focus in life. These presuppositions reveal themselves to us and others through our actions, through how we actually spend our time and energy. The things through which a culture expresses itself in terms of the collective use of time and energy reveal the webs of significance or the webs of care of that culture. The actions of people from a particular culture reflect this 'caring.' Actions are embodiments of values and tell us something about what is significant in a culture (Christopher and Bickhard, in press).

These structures permeate and express themselves through the institutions and social practices of a particular culture. If we do an ethnography of everyday life, it becomes clear that this is so. For instance we ask our counseling students to write down everything they do for the first fifteen minutes after they get up in the morning. What we find is that American students often report hitting the snooze button on their alarm clocks, taking hot showers, and attending to pets. Each of these mundane behaviors may reveal to us certain aspects of our world view and *ethos*. Hot showers, for instance, require a rich background of understanding. The possibility of hot showers relies on knowledge of physics, hydrology, electricity, sanitation, and so on. This knowledge must also be applied or translated to technology including pipes, valves, boilers, etc… When we turn on the shower in the morning anticipating a stream of hot water we are relying on a vast body of knowledge – both theoretical and applied – accumulated and understood in terms of our culture's worldview which, can generally be characterized as mechanistic and materialistic. Hot showers tells us something about core cultural values. When we ask "why do we shower?" and "why do many shower one or more times daily?" these values begin to be revealed. Students tell us that evidence of odor, dirt and sweat evokes negative feedback from others. Evidence of eliminative body functions in our society is expected to be neutralized or eliminated. There is a social cost to not doing so. We still believe, along with Francis Bacon and John Wesley that "Cleanliness is next to Godliness." We associate cleanliness with responsibility, health, and wellness. It is an assumption or presupposition implicit in our cultural ethos. We take a negative view of those below a certain level of cleanliness. One characteristic of schizophrenia is a dysfunction in self-care, which many understand as a dysfunction in hygiene. Our assumptions about cleanliness then influence our understanding of what is meant by wellness, maturity and mental health. This gets expressed in the American way of life as a form of self-care, a form which sees millions of dollars spent each year on bath products. This type of self-care through cleanliness suggests the influence our Romantic heritage and its characteristic form of expressive individualism (Bellah, Madsen, Sullivan, Swidler, and Tipton, 1985; Taylor, 1985b).

This kind of ethnographic "fieldwork in familiar places" (Moody-Adams, 1997) helps us recognize the extent to which culture pervades our lives. Simple, everyday actions display an abundance of cultural presuppositions and values. Social practices like hot showers reveal to us how connected facts and values, world view and *ethos* are in our collective experience. Most of the time we do not consciously recognize these implicit values and assumptions when we engage in our everyday practices (practices such as bathing). Identifying these implicit cultural themes via an interpretive approach is illustrative of hermeneutics as a method. The implications of the interpretive approach lead to some of the core tenets of philosophical hermeneutics—for instance, that the individual is largely constituted by cultural assumptions and practices (see critiques by Cole, 1996; Shweder, 1990; Kashima, 2000, and Poortinga, 1997). And this in turn may help provide an important corrective to the dominant tendency within psychology to view culture as external to the individual.

Being-in-the-World: A Hermeneutic View of the Person

Heidegger characterizes the dominant western view of the person as based on a fundamental error. Western individualism characterizes persons as autonomous, atomistic, and independent of the world of objects and social structures. This individualistic view of humans, according to Heidegger, is itself a creation of culture, one that is derivative of a more primordial way of being that he terms *being-in-the-world* (Heidegger, 1962; cf., Campbell, Christopher and Bickhard, 2002; Christopher, 2004). Being-in-the-world refers to the way human beings are always fundamentally engaged in life or the world and do not experience the self as a separate *cogito* or thinking subject in the manner made famous by Descartes (Heidegger, 1962).

In his characterization of being-in-the-world, Heidegger wants to show the derivative nature of our experience of a subject-object duality or what Taylor (1991) calls the "reification of the disengaged first-person-singular self" (p. 306). Heidegger illustrates this by having us consider the simple task of hammering. When using tools such as a hammer, we do not normally experience this as a discrete object. Our phenomenological experience of 'hammering' is one in which the hammer is treated as part of our self. The actual experience is more unified than the abstract characterization we may give of it upon reflection (where we separate our self from the object). Normally we only come to notice the hammer as an object when something goes wrong (we hit our finger or the hammer breaks, etc…). When engaged in the task of hammering we also lose our awareness of 'I' or of our subjectivity. Such engagement eliminates the subject-object or mind-body distinction that we often posit by way of abstraction when we characterize our experience in the world intellectually. Heidegger sees our engagement in life as a more fundamental experience than this aforementioned understanding which highlights our separation from the world..

Heidegger characterizes our being-in-the-world in terms of what he calls "throwness." That is, we are thrown into this world, we do not choose to be born, that choice was made for us. Due to the nature of our throwness, we already experience the world in a certain unified way before we come to distinguish our self from objects. Even after we have recognized this separation we still experience most of our everyday activities in a more unified manner. We live our everyday life outside of the awareness of this distinction. We live as expressions of our culture and world. As Heidegger (1962) puts it:

> Ontically, of course, Dasein is not only close to us—even that which is closest: we *are* it, each of us, we ourselves. In spite of this, or rather for just this reason, it is ontologically that which is farthest. p. 36

The view that has been attributed to Descartes characterizes the "I' as the reflective or conscious part of our being, a part that is somewhat independent of our various beliefs, presuppositions and ideas. The hermeneutic view of the person suggests that these ideas and beliefs have already become part of what we mean by self or "I" by the time we become conscious of self. This learning of culture is illustrated by simple things such as a trip to McDonald's. In our culture we learn from a young age what is expected from the various participants of the McDonald's experience. When we awaken to consciousness, we find that we have already developed habits and understandings of the world that are part of how we experience the world. We find our self to be a participant in a drama that we have not constructed (Camus, 1983) or as Heidegger puts it, when we become aware of our 'self' and the world, we find that it is a world that is publicly constituted and interpreted. It is the world of the 'they' (Heidegger, 1962, p.296). We participate in this publicly interpreted world of the 'they' when eating a meal at McDonald's and reinforce cultural themes such as "time is money." We become part of the process of perpetuating and reinterpreting these cultural themes.

We can become partially aware of the effect of our cultural embeddedness, characteristic of our being-in-the-world through reflective abstraction (Bickhard and Christopher, 1994; Campbell and Bickhard, 1986; Campbell and Christopher, 1996). This may mean, however, that we will best come to understand our self, "not by inward-turning and introspection" (the Cartesian way) "but by catching sight of ourselves as we are engaged and preoccupied in everyday contexts" (Guignon, 1984, p. 232). Cognitive researchers who are recognizing the enormous role played by implicit cognitive functioning or the "adaptive unconscious" are similarly concluding we may need to "look outward to know ourselves" (Wilson, 2002). As Wilson writes, "No amount of introspection, however, can illuminate the contents of the adaptive unconscious, no matter how hard I try" (p. 163).

Our attempt to develop perspectives for reflecting on culture will always be partial and provisional. The perspectives that we develop will always be constituted through what Gadamer (1975) calls our 'prejudices' or pre-judgments. These are the beliefs and ideas that we inherit by virtue of growing up in a particular culture. Any distance that we get from culture through abstraction or critical reflection is always temporary and provisional (Gadamer, 1975). We can never fully follow the Cartesian model of detaching our self from culture. They provide a framework or horizon that enables us to make sense of the world. While we can develop partial, provisional perspectives that allow us to reflect on our culture, we unavoidably take on the meanings implicit in these practices prior to awareness. We are partly constituted by our cultures, which means that it is not possible to fully detach ourselves. Any distance that we get from our culture is always temporary and provisional (Gadamer, 1975). This does not mean, however, that we are all the same by virtue of our cultural constitution. Our individual life history or story is unique, but it develops through the shared background beliefs and meanings of our culture. As Charles Taylor puts it, this individual uniqueness consists largely of variations or various combinations of cultural themes and aspirations as expressed in an individual life. (Taylor, 1989; cf., Sugarman and Martin, 1995). The desire to separate this individual life from culture is a fairly modern phenomenon, one that we have characterized simply as individualism.

Moral Visions

Given the dualistic predilection in Western thought to bifurcate facts and values, we use the term *moral visions* to recapture the centrality of the moral, ethical, value-related dimension of our existence. Values and morals from the hermeneutic perspective are not subjective "things" that human beings tack onto their representations and perceptions. Instead values are intersubjective, unavoidable, and inextricably intertwined with facts. "Care" is presupposed in our most basic ways of being-in-the-world (Heidegger, 1962). What we do, how we allocate our time and energy, what we focus on, all reveal a structure of care. Thoughts, emotions, and behavior presuppose deeper distinctions of what is important and valuable.

This point becomes clearer if we consider the notion of folk psychologies. Every culture possesses certain presuppositions concerning human nature. The *folk* or *indigenous psychology* of a culture embodies these presuppositions and attempts to give an account of the human subject accordingly. Bruner (1990, p. 35) defines a folk psychology as:

> a set of more or less connected, more or less normative descriptions about how human beings 'tick,' what our own and other minds are like, what one can expect situated actions to be like, what are possible modes of life, how one commits oneself to them, and so on. (p. 35)

These folk psychologies tell us about the nature of emotions, motivation, psychopathology and self as understood by the culture in question. These understandings are sometimes well developed as with the various Buddhist or Hindu theories of the self. These exist and inform our conceptions of self and other at a pre-conscious level and guide our interactions regardless of whether they have been explicitly articulated. They make our understandings and interactions with others possible, drawing as they do upon both the culture's world view and its *ethos*.

A world view tells us what a person *is* according to the culture in question. It explains a culture's conception of what capabilities, characteristics, faculties and resources a person is said to possess. It also tells us about the boundaries of personhood – whether persons are conceived of as atomistic or social beings. *Ethos* characterizes the ethical dimension of a culture. *Ethos* tells us what norms or standards are appropriate to live by or what is desirable for human life. It tells us what is right and wrong and how we should behave, think, interact or feel. *Ethos* tells us what constitutes the good life as well as the mature, healthy or successful life. The world view tells what human nature is like according to a particular culture while ethos tells us how a person 'should' develop – 'what' one should become.

Folk psychologies draw on elements of a culture's world view and *ethos* not only to provide an account of what a person *is* but also what a person *should be*. Just as world view and *ethos* are always intertwined within the webs of meaning and significance that make up culture, so do they intertwine in our understandings of human nature and of our own identity. A folk psychology accordingly "summarizes not simply how things are but (often implicitly) how they should be" (Brunner, 1990, pp. 39-40). One implication is that the 'moral' or 'ethical' is entailed by our understanding of the self. Taylor (1989) even argues that "Selfhood and the good, or in another way selfhood and morality, turn out to be inextricably intertwined themes" (p. 3). Paul Ricoeur (1992) developed a hermeneutical account of selfhood which employs the notion of narrative identity, a notion which not only illustrates the social nature of selfhood but also shows how the descriptive aspects of selfhood are inseparable from the evaluative dimensions. He sees the fact value distinction as problematic when we try to examine or characterize the human subject. Ricoeur's work provides a useful complement to the sociological-historical account of selfhood that we find in Taylor (1989).

Moral visions refer to the constellations of cultural values and assumptions that constitute our understanding of the nature of the person and of the good life. Moral visions establish our sense of what the self *is* and what the self *should be*. Moral visions operate both implicitly and explicitly to orient us to what is deemed higher, deeper or more worthy; those things that give us strength, integration, wholeness, vitality, dignity, and goodness (Taylor, 1989). At the same time, moral visions delineate what we should avoid, resist, or oppose, both internally and externally. As used here, moral does not mean simply what is seen as right or wrong, but our deepest understanding of what is good, worthy, and desirable (Brinton, 1987). And these matters can vary dramatically across cultures. In traditional Chinese society, for instance, the defining moral virtue is *filial piety*, being a dutiful to one's parents. The good person is one who follows the relationships established and codified by Confucius and in this way demonstrates proper respect and maintains harmony. In Anglo-American society the good or ideal person is defined in more circumscribed and individualistic terms; rationality, autonomy, and authenticity are cardinal virtues.

Taylor (1989) describes these moral visions held by cultural groups as *inescapable moral frameworks* that orient us to what is worthy and provide direction in approaching those ideals. Like Heidegger's notion of care, moral visions are always present, even if, and perhaps especially when, they are unrecognized. As Taylor (1985a) writes, "these deepest evaluations are the ones which are least clear, least articulated, most easily subject to illusion and distortion. It is those which are closest to what I am as a subject, in the sense that shorn of them I would break down as a person, which are among the hardest for me to be clear about" (p. 40). These evaluative frameworks form a *moral topography* or moral space within which our identities take shape and our aims and ideals are intelligible (Taylor, 1987; see also McLeod and Lynch, 2000; Sugarman and Martin, 1995). A sense of the "good" person and the "good" life is implicit in all our day-to-day events. Even such apparently amoral or antisocial individuals as gang members can be shown to be animated by moral visions (Christopher, 1996; Schmitz and Christopher, 1997).

Taylor (1987) utilizes a *via negativa*—using an example of what something *is not* to help make clear what it *is*—to help us experience the moral space or topography in which we are embedded. He alleges we all have a sense of what it means to feel "out-of-joint:"

> This is conceptually expressed in a host of ways: as being lost, or condemned, or exiled, or unintegrated, or without meaning, or insubstantial, or empty, to name some categories. Corresponding to each of these descriptions of breakdown is some notion of what it would be to overcome it, to have integration, or full being, to be justified, or found, or whatever. But more, there is a notion of 'where' this integration, fullness, etc., might come from, what might bring it about. . . . In other words, these different, often indefinite and tentative senses of what integration consists of incorporate notions of where it might be found, in the sense of where the strength lies, where the sources or resources are situated, which could bring integration, or fullness about. (pp. 300-301)

In his own work Taylor is primarily interested in explicating the moral sources of Western culture. However, his framework is a powerful tool for thinking about cultural differences. It reminds us that different cultures have not only different understandings of what the person or self is but also different understandings of the good or ideal person. The coordinates of the moral topographies in which the self is situated are marked out by a diversity of goods.

Taylor believes the spatial metaphor that lies at the heart of his notion of moral topography illuminates the manner in which these inescapable moral frameworks provide a sense of identity and orientation. Our identity, in his view, is based on one's sense of location in one or more moral visions. "To define my identity," he observes, "is to define what I must be in contact with in order to function fully as a human agent, and specifically to be able to judge and discriminate and recognize what is really of worth or importance, both in general and for me" (1985b, p. 258). Orientation in and to life comes from our relative position in this moral space that allows us to situate ourselves to the goods established by our culture's *ethos*. We can sense the direction we must pursue in order to more closely approach the good life and we can discern how far we are from it.

Cultures as Moral Visions

A fundamental ontological assumption of western culture is expressed in the way that we view the relation between facts and values. Facts, representative of empirical states of affairs, are afforded more certainty or reality than values. Values are seen as subjective possessions which people choose to adopt, but are generally not seen as constitutive of who or what we are. We assume that the self is something autonomous from values and culture. Heidegger challenges this notion by claiming that "we do not, so to speak, throw a 'signification' over some naked thing which is present-at-hand, we do not stick a value on it" (1962, p. 190). According to Heidegger values are already a part of the world of facts in which we participate. The separation of facts from values is an abstraction from the everyday world in which we live. This abstraction presupposes a self that is autonomous in relation to values, but again according to Heidegger our selfhood is shaped by the meanings and social practices that precede us and which we participate in during our self-formation (Heidegger, 1962). Shweder, Mahapatra, and Miller (1987) express the way that our cultural values and assumptions are communicated implicitly through our social interactions in the following:

> [M]orally relevant interpretations of events by local guardians of the moral order (e.g. parents) are typically presented and conveyed to young children in the context of routine family life and social practices. Those moral premises are carried by the messages and meanings implicit in the emotional reactions of others (anger or disappointment or "hurt feelings" over a transgression). They are carried by the verbal exchanges--commands, threats, sanction statements, accusations, explanations, justifications, excuses--necessary to maintain routine social practices." (p. 73).

As humans we are beings whose selves are formed by the values and assumptions of our culture. It is not just that culture influences who we are, it is rather that who or what we are is reflected in our cultural answers to questions such as "what does it mean to be a person?" or "what kind of person should one become?" Heidegger expresses this condition by telling us a human being (*Dasein*) is a being who "in its very Being, that Being is an *issue* for it" (p. 32) These questions are fundamentally ethical questions, they have to do with what we value most dearly in a particular culture. Our lives exist in the space of these moral questions (Taylor, 1989). Society or culture presents us with possible answers to these questions, but our identity itself is formed by the cultural dialogue that generates both these answers as well as the questions themselves.

As we discussed on pages 5-7, American culture is defined by a predominantly individualistic moral vision. Individualism, like any cultural vision, presents answers to the aforementioned questions of what the self is and what is should be. A number of authors have tried to show how this moral vision has shaped and permeated psychology (Christopher, 1992, 1999; Christopher, Christopher, and Dunnagan, 2000; Cirillo and Wapner, 1986; Cleary, 1999; Cushman, 1991, 1995; Fowers and Richardson, 1993, 1996; Frank, 1978; Greenberg, 1994; Kirschner, 1996; Lambeth, 1994; Richardson, 1989; Richardson and Guignon, 1988; Roland, 1996; Rubin, 1997; Sampson, 1977, 1988, 2000; Spence, 1985; Sue and Sue, 1990; Sullivan, 1986; Taylor, 1985a; Waterman, 1981, 1984; Wolszon, 1998; Woolfolk and Richardson, 1984).

Most non-western cultures embrace a very different form of self-understanding based on a collectivist rather than an individualist worldview and *ethos* (Hui and Triandis, 1986; Kim, Triandis, Kagitçibasi, Choi, and Yoon, 1994; Triandis, 1989, 1995). Such cultures tend to have a more interdependent or social view of the self (Geertz, 1973, 1983; Moore, 1968; Munro, 1969). Individualistic moral visions, characteristic of western views of selfhood tend to focus on independence, separation, personal discovery, etc., whereas collectivist views stress social harmony and family relations as well as one's role within these institutions (Hui, 1984, 1988; Hui and Triandis, 1986; Kim et al., 1994; Markus and Kitayama, 1991; Triandis, 1995). It should be noted that terms such as individualism and collectivism are meant as general characterizations. They do not capture the degrees of difference between various cultures that may fall under one or the other of these characterizations.

This is an important point to remember. Moral visions are such that they do not form a single coherent perspective on life in the way that a moral, religious or political theory might.

Moral visions, embodied as they are in societies, take different forms. Individualism for instance, varies in form and expression in modern pluralistic societies. Two predominant forms of individualism, as labeled by Bellah and his colleagues are utilitarian and expressive individualism (Bellah et al., 1985). Utilitarian individualism personifies the confidence in science and technology characteristic of the sixteenth century Enlightenment and the emergence of the Utilitarian moral and political doctrine of Jeremy Bentham and John Stuart Mill. This view emphasizes rationality, rational self-interest, efficiency and individual initiative. Utilitarian individualism "takes as given certain basic human appetites and fears and sees human life as an effort by individuals to maximize their self-interest relative to their given ends" (Bellah et al., 1985, p. 336). In contrast to the scientific orientation of utilitarian individualism is the humanistic emphasis of expressive individualism. Following the Romantic reaction to the scientific dominance of the Enlightenment spirit, expressive individualism emphasizes the creative and artistic potential of the individual. This form of individualism views the good life as a life "rich in experience, open to all kinds of people, luxuriating in the sensual as well as the intellectual, above all a life of strong feeling" (Bellah et al., 1985, p. 34). Each individual "has a unique core of feeling and intuition that should unfold or be expressed if individuality is to be realized" (Bellah et al., 1985, p. 333). Bellah et al. note that contemporary American society brings together both forms of individualism in a precarious union. Utilitarian individualism tend to be the predominant way of understanding the world of industry and business, but for many people, expressive individualism characterizes the goals and desires of their personal or family life (Taylor, 1985b). Neither of these approaches takes the form of dogma, but both operate implicitly in this culture and strongly influence identity formation.

Hermeneutic Conceptual Tools for Approaching Cross-Cultural Interactions and Conflict

At this point we would like to introduce four ideas that we see as helpful in working with culture in psychotherapy. These four ideas, the hermeneutic circle, effective historical consciousness, hermeneutic dialogue, and *phronesis* are presented as optimal ways of grappling with the differences in moral visions that occur when working across cultures.

The Hermeneutic Circle and the Reconciliation of Culture-General and Culture-Specific Approaches to Multicultural Counseling

Hermeneutics helps resolve a dichotomy in the theories of multicultural counseling literature (Bezanson and James, 2005). Over the last few decades multicultural counseling theories have evolved into two categories: cultural general (etic) theories and cultural specific (emic) theories. Culture general theories of multicultural counseling provide a universal or etic approach to conceptualizing mental health issues with people of a culture other than the dominate one by examining the key issues that cut across humanity. Examples of this framework are Vontress' (1979) existential approach to cross-cultural counseling, Patterson's (1996) universal system of counseling and Fisher and colleagues' (Fischer, Jome, and

Atkinson, 1998) 'common factors' perspective. Critics of these approaches suggest that they rely on a strong therapeutic relationship but this could be sabotaged if the therapist is not aware of the complexities of the group with whom he or she is working. These universal approaches can also be seen as simply facilitating acceptance of the ways of the dominate culture (Bezanson and James, 2005).

Culture specific approaches to multicultural therapy, on the other hand, emphasize the necessity of being knowledgeable about an ethnic group in order to provide suitable counseling services. Racial and ethnic differences become the basis for theories and models, and as such a counselor must gain an in-depth understanding of the particular group that he or she is working with (Sue, 1981, Pedersen, 1997; Tatman, 2004, Trimble, 2003). Critics of this approach suggest that making culture the focus of the practice may propagate that which Shweder (2004) calls "the ethnography of difference" or "disparagement" (p. 4). Thus, defining differences between groups can result in misleading generalizations that might not be useful when working with actual clients whose backgrounds are more complex than the theories acknowledge (Bezanson and James, 2005).

The debate over the usefulness of either approach has caused theorists and practitioners to focus their energy on defending their position, possibly at the expense of developing an integrated approach that would benefit the profession. We suggest that the dichotomy implied by the 'universal' versus 'specific' debate is not an either/or situation but may become the building blocks for a multidimensional framework (Bezanson and James, 2005) when understood from a hermeneutic perspective. Necessary to the hermeneutic process of interpretation is knowledge of the relationship between *the part* and *the whole,* or what is called the hermeneutic circle. As an interpretive process, hermeneutics provides a way of understanding the cultural influences that help create the self and thus is a useful framework for developing culturally sensitive practices. When applied to psychotherapy, this approach requires the delicate task of understanding the individual in the context of their culture and understanding the culture from the perspective of the client. This view does not privilege *the part* (the individual) over *the whole* (the culture) or visa versa but rather attempts to provide a true convergence of culture specific and culture general approaches. Christopher (1996, 2001), Foster and James (2004), James and Foster (in press) and Bezanson and James (2005) provide detailed accounts of a hermeneutic approach and its applicability to psychotherapy and cultural psychology.

The most obvious critique of culture-specific approaches focuses on the numerous possibilities for stereotyping when practitioners rigidly adhere to some abstract notion of a culturally influenced concept of the individual (Bezanson and James, 2005). For instance, the therapist may expect that client behave in a certain way because they are from a particular group, rather than seeing how the sessions unfold. Consideration of *the part* (the client) and *the whole* (the culture) promotes an understanding of the interaction between the two and discourages the idea that culture can be considered separate from individuals that collectively manifest the behaviors, beliefs and values of that culture. As such, racial and ethnic differences inform practice rather than becoming the sole basis for theories and models. The individual is situated within his or her local world but an understanding of culture-specific knowledge is still valued and utilized if appropriate.

Rather then the map becoming the territory, therapy requires striking a balance by moving back and forth in order to refine the notion of the part and the whole. The process is not about having information, the specifics or the universals, but more of creating a dynamic process where neither culture-specific nor general cultural theories alone hold the means for the therapist to understand the client's world (Bezanson and James, 2005). To the degree that broad generalizations like individualism and collectivism are important it is as a starting point in the hermeneutic circle that helps to delineate a range of possibilities of human functioning. Such a preliminary view of the whole can then be critically assessed to determine the degree to which it helps to illuminate a specific client's life and experience, which in turn refines our notion of what such broad concepts as collectivism actually entail.

Counseling psychology developed out of a temporally specific *zeitgeist* of Western thought, thus it provides a specific form of culture with its own value system and beliefs that we impose on clients of different ethnicities. Culture-general theories attempt to transcend any specific culture in order to access a body of knowledge that privileges individualism and choice. Consideration of this 'counseling' culture is imperative for understanding our beliefs concerning well-being and mental health. Hermeneutics offers a framework for considering this paradigm in which therapists work. In this case, the part (the practitioner) and the whole (the helping culture) are considered and the influence of these cultural institutions as well as the values and assumptions they imply are addressed simultaneously as we work with people of different ethnicities (Bezanson and James, 2005).

The Idea of Effective Historical Consciousness

The phrase "effective historical consciousness" was coined by Hans-Georg Gadamer (1975), a major figure in the modern hermeneutics movement. This notion implies an awareness by individuals of the role that "effective history" plays in human life. Effective history is the notion that the past shapes our understanding and outlook in the present and the present provides the framework for understanding the past. Our modern notions of virtue as well as our ideas of dignity, honor and respect are shaped by their history in the context of western religious, philosophical and political dialogue. Other cultures with a different religious, philosophical and political history will understand the virtues differently. Effective historical consciousness denotes an awareness of these historical influences on our thinking, understanding and beliefs, an awareness that Gadamer sees as crucial to our own self-understandings.

Due to the fact that our identity and self-understandings are shaped by history in this way, we believe that the awareness implied in the notion of "effective historical consciousness" should help inform counseling practices. We need to find a way to communicate or teach such awareness to our clients. Such teaching would aim at making both clients and therapists aware of the influence and limitations of these historical traditions on our thinking. These traditions provide us with our moral sources and shape our sense of self. We need to preserve these traditions, but we must preserve them in a critical manner. That is, we must not see these traditions as static with an intractable authority, but rather as living, growing and in need of scrutiny. What emerges from this is a kind of critical dialogue between the client or therapist and the cultural, historical tradition that they are part of. The individual comes to understand their self, not as an isolated or atomistic being, but as part of the historical struggle of preserving what is valuable in a tradition and challenging or opposing that which is at odds with human well-being.

Hermeneutic Dialogue

Two defining aspects of culture are reflected in a particular culture's answer to the questions: "What does it mean to be human?" and "What is the good life of human beings?" The answers to these questions divide cultures by presenting what seem to be irreconcilable and fundamental differences. What makes matters worse is the apparent lack of an objective standard through which to judge the validity or soundness of a culture's answers to these questions. This would seem to suggest that these answers will be culture-bound, lacking validity outside of the framework of the particular culture in which they are created. The conclusion that we are forced to draw from this situation is that these answers will be culturally-relative (Bernstein, 1983).

Our day to day lives, however, are not normally experienced as relative in this way. Typically, our experience of life confirms the contention of Heidegger, Geertz and Taylor that the form of life we share is of fundamental importance to us and we are shaped and motivated by our social practices and cultural meanings. As North Americans, we tend to experience ideals such as individual autonomy and rights, authenticity and tolerance, not merely as possible ways of living, but as valid, legitimate or true ways of being. We often forget that people from other cultures view their own ideas about the relation between the individual and culture for instance as obvious and true as well. We often fail to recognize or we mis-recognize the nature of the moral vision of another culture when we view that culture's practices, forms of life, or cultural meanings as inferior. This does not imply that we should never disagree with the views or moral values of another culture, but before we can authentically do so we should, following Gadamer (1975), engage in a form of dialogue that recognizes (provisionally) the legitimacy of these views as claims to truth.

Dialogue, for Gadamer, allows us to genuinely attempt to understand the horizon of understanding of another cultural group. Understanding the horizon of another group (or individual) allows for the possibility of a *fusion of horizons*. Gadamer uses the metaphor of a horizon in order to illustrate the limitations inherent in human understanding. Our attempts at understanding another culture, according to Gadamer, will always be determined or shaped by our pre-judgments or prejudices. These pre-judgements consist of the various assumptions or presuppositions that we develop throughout our life by way of our participation in a particular culture or form of life. This implies that human knowledge and understanding is always partial, perspectival and fallible as we always come to understand the world within a particular horizon or from a particular vantage point (Gadamer, 1975). We ought not to view this horizon as fixed or static but as something that evolves through the ongoing dialogue in which we participate both within our culture and while engaging with other cultures. The dynamic nature of cultural horizons implies that they are never closed. We may only have one particular vantage point for making judgments at a particular time in our history, but that vantage point changes with the change and growth of our horizon. Gadamer sees this limitation not merely as a comment on the incomplete nature of our understanding but as a defining feature of the human condition.

To attain a fusion of horizons in the manner that Gadamer advocates requires an openness to the horizon or perspective of others, even granting their values a kind of provisional authority through which to judge our own values. This means that we must bracket or suspend the authority of our own views or values creating a kind of Hegelian dialectic where ideas or concepts are only fully understood when they have been challenged by opposing theses. This approach attempts to avoid the pitfall of trying to understand the perspective of others superficially by making foreign ideas fit into our own conceptual framework. This process, when successfully carried out will inevitably change our own horizon and alter our perspective on our own deeply held beliefs and values. This dialogical approach and the openness it involves creates an authentic way of relating to others according to Gadamer. It moves us from an I-It way of relating to an I-Thou relationship (Buber, 1970).

None of this implies, however, that we adopt a position of unqualified relativism. We may still hold standards and ideals but this sort of dialogical exploration moves us towards a transforming of our standards (Taylor, 1992). Our standards are altered or transformed as we come to realize the ways in which elements of other cultures may enhance or renew aspects of our own tradition or way of life. We come to realize that our own worldview and *ethos* are incomplete. They represent one possibility among many. This does not diminish the value of our own way of life, but allows us to be open to having our perspective enriched by the perspective of others. Incorporating elements of another culture may lead to qualitative growth in our own. We see this already to some degree in modern multi-cultural nations, but in such contexts, we also see the struggle involved in overcoming the tendency to reduce dialogue to monologue. The dominant culture of any society often tends to resist change from the outside as part of its own struggle for survival.

This approach does not imply that we indiscriminately accept and adopt the views or practices of others into our way of life. Gadamer introduces the process of *application* as a way of tempering the work of dialogue. The knowledge that we gain through dialogue with another culture is tested by way of critical reflection in order to see if it really does help us clarify or improve our understanding of our own situation. What we gain from the other will be tested, applied and modified according to our own concrete situation and in our own historical context. Even in this application, however, it is important to maintain an openness so that we do not apply this newfound understanding too narrowly.

Hermeneutics and Aristotle's "Phronesis"

Hermeneutic philosophers have noted the manner in which Aristotle's concept of *phronesis* resembles a hermeneutic approach to philosophy and understanding (Gadamer, 2001; Ricoeur, 1992). *Phronesis* has been generally translated into English as 'practical wisdom'. This form of practical wisdom involves the correct application of general or universal rules (theoretical) to particular, concrete circumstances. What is distinct about phronesis is the manner in which Aristotle viewed this relationship between the universal and the particular. It is not simply a matter of applying the general to the concrete in terms of a 'top-down' approach, but it involves a two-way reflection similar to that implied by the hermeneutic relationship between the part and the whole. The person who possesses the virtue of practical wisdom does not mechanically apply universal rules to concrete situations, but through experience and the gaining of wisdom learns how to apply the right rule in the correct way in a particular situation. This means that the rule itself, the universal or theoretical principle is not fully understood or does not gain its full measure of truth until one has understood it through the application. The 'part' here, as in a hermeneutic approach, helps inform the 'whole' (or the general rule) and the whole guides us in dealing with the part. For instance, to be benevolent or to possess the virtue of benevolence does not mean that we simply are generous with our money or time. The true virtue of benevolence is expressed by the person who knows who to give what in a concrete situation of need.

What this implies for psychotherapists, particularly in a pluralistic or multicultural context, is that counseling and making good decisions regarding clients who hold different values or perspectives will involve more than applying general or universal principles. Aristotle's form of practical wisdom suggests that we need to work to understand the context or concrete circumstances of a client, including their cultural, social or religious background in order to understand not only which principles should be applied but also 'how' these principles should be applied. This approach once again takes a more dialogical (as opposed to monological) view of the relation between the therapist and the client whose culture may be foreign.

Multiculturalism and Intercultural Contact

The moral visions framework outlined in the chapter provides a powerful vantage point for discerning what is at stake in cross-cultural interactions. Moral visions influence counseling theory, but they also influence practice by shaping case conceptualization, diagnoses and diagnostic systems, the direction of cure, treatment goals, and the choice of interventions. According to Szasz (1961) the "socio-ethical orientations" of the psychiatrist will "influence his [or her] ideas on what is wrong with the patients, what deserves comment or interpretation, in what possible directions change might be desirable, and so forth" (p. 116). The underlying moral visions of therapy differ to some degree across theoretical orientations. Generally, however they all draw on some variant of individualism (Christopher, 1996; Richardson, 1989). For instance, behaviorism, cognitive-behaviorism, reality therapy and psychoanalytic ego therapy all are consonant with the version of individualism that Bellah et al., refer to as *utilitarian individualism,* that encourages using reason to control the emotions and thereby achieve self-defined goals. Other approaches to therapy including humanistic and transpersonal theories, self-psychology, and certain schools of object-relations theory like that of Winnicott, as well as many feminist orientations have their roots in Romanticism and what Bellah et al. term *expressive individualism.* Expressive individualism emphasizes authenticity, spontaneity, the importance of turning inward and making contact with one's inner life, and of identifying and expressing feelings in order to attain intimacy and reconnect with humanity and nature (see Richardson, 1989.

Cross-cultural interactions entail the intersection of multiple cultures. The culture of therapy is influenced by Western culture but is not synonymous with it. Psychology as a profession and an academic field reinterprets the moral sources of Western culture and these reinterpretations in turn influence Western folk psychology. A good example of this is the psychoanalytic notion of defense which is now part of the North American folk psychologies. Furthermore, the values and assumptions underlying professional theory and practice are situated within and exist along side the cultural values and assumptions manifested in different parts of society. This results in a kind of dialectical relation between professional psychology and folk psychology. Moreover there is a dynamic tension for the psychotherapist between their professional theoretical commitments and their cultural orientation as shaped by their own family and socio-economic group. This complex intertwining and tension between different strands of Western culture results in a heterogeneous complexity of moral sources that underlie the therapist. Consequently, all counseling even when the counselor and client are of the same ethnicity is cross-cultural. Inviting in a client from a widely different culture adds exponentially to this complexity. It is this overwhelming complexity that we face, consciously or not, when engaging in multicultural counseling and intercultural contact.

Some examples of the complexity of these issues are provided by research conducted with Portuguese immigrants in Canada and the United States (James, 2002, Morrison and James, 2006). These examples raise questions about the applicability of Murray Bowen's notion of differentiation across cultures. In Bowen's work, differentiation plays a significant role in marriage and family therapy. Differentiation relies on a highly individualistic understanding of identity. Bowen defines *differentiation of self* as "the difference between people in the proportion of life energy prone to be invested and bound in relationships" (Kerr and Bowen, 1988, p. 68). According to this view, individual identity is not well developed where more energy is invested in preserving or maintaining relationships. Individuality is better developed in the more highly differentiated individual who focuses on his or her own functioning. A lack of differentiation leads to higher levels of emotion and anxiety resulting from concern for others.

> Trying to achieve a higher level of differentiation or more solid (basic) self means increasing one's capacity for emotional detachment or neutrality. More detachment or neutrality depends on changes in thinking. Such changes are reflected in the ability to be in emotional contact with a difficult, emotionally charged problem and not feel compelled to preach about what others "should" do, not rush in to "fix" the problem, and not pretend to be detached by emotionally insulating oneself. Improving one's ability to contain these emotionally driven urges is contingent on developing a way of thinking that can counterbalance them. (p.108)

The notion of differentiation, as attractive as it may be in our culture, relies on a particular, culture-bound moral vision. This reliance limits the applicability of this notion when it comes to cross-cultural psychology. For instance, our research with Portuguese immigrants indicates that they handle differentiation differently (Morrison and James, 2006). A father from the community stated,

> It's my way or no way. (Laughing) It is my way or the highway. It's one table, one plate on the table . . .. That's the way it goes (laughing). And no complaints, my older son is 27 years old. . . . And he is still here.

This communal moral vision had a number of important implications for the Portuguese community. This vision of a "good" family can be misunderstood by therapists. A number of therapists who work with Portuguese immigrants were interviewed and said that the Portuguese families were enmeshed. The interdependence can be misunderstood and rashly pathologized if it is not understood from the moral visions of the family.

Looking at the concept of the person from the perspective of the Portuguese community highlights a very different way of thinking. The dominant Western way of dividing reality into subjects and objects or self and other does not accord with the folk psychology of Portuguese immigrants. This community relies on a different conception of selfhood, one that is not primarily dualistic. Markus and Kitayama (1991) have called this the *interdependent* sense of self in which "the self is viewed as *inter*dependent with the surrounding context, and it is the "other" or the "self-in-relation-to-other" that is focal in individual experience" (p. 225). This interdependent sense of self is illustrated by an example taken from the fieldwork of Fajans (1985) among the Baining in New Guinea. She writes, "the social actor is not a rigidly defined and delimited entity" for "the boundaries of the individual and the definition of the person are neither permanent nor immutable, but alter and adapt in specific contexts" (p. 381). A Portuguese woman's description of suffering highlights this notion as well (James, 2002). "You need to suffer to redeem yourself and others. In a Catholic Church suffering is not only for yourself but also for others and for the world." Another woman concurred, "Someone, after all, has to carry the cross like Jesus Christ carried the cross for everyone. Some of us, are chosen by God to care for others and pay for their sins."

Here we see a very different sense of self, one where the sharp distinctions characteristic of the independent sense of self do not exist. Suffering, helping and meeting needs is understood in more communal terms and less in voluntary, individualistic terms. The suffering of others and the duty to help relieve suffering is part of the conception of self by virtue of being part of the community. Suffering is not divided into "my" suffering or "their" suffering. Without realizing this characteristic of a Portuguese sense of identity, a North American counselor could easily pathologize the experience of a Portuguese immigrant.

A different sense of self also affects our understanding and experience of emotions. For example, Portuguese children mentioned struggling with guilt around their desire to be more independent. Typically North American psychotherapists would attempt to make sense of guilt within the dualistic framework consistent with an independent self-construal (Christopher and Smith, 2006). In this sense, emotion terms have been understood as having a two-dimensional scaling solution (Russell, 1980); along the first dimension they can be mapped as pleasant/good versus unpleasant/bad or along the second dimension as active/high energy versus inactive/low energy. This same two dimensional pattern of results can be found in Non-Western cultures. In collectivist cultures however, a third dimension has been identified which is not found in the United States. (Markus and Kitayama, 1991). In these cultures we see other-centered emotions which stand in contrast with ego-centered ones. In Portugal other-centered emotions include suffering as we mentioned already. In addition, *saudade* refers to a mixture of sadness, love, compassion, and longing that has a real similarity to a term, *fago*, used in Micronesia for the same qualities (Lutz, 1988). Another other centered emotion used In Palau, *ta rengrir* denotes the other-centered emotion of getting along or being of one mind (Smith and Smith, 1995). *Awumbuk*, a term used by the Baining of Papua New Guinea to indicate a kind of social hangover, is an especially vivid example of interpersonal emotion.

> ...a lassitude that people feel after the departure of visitors, friends, or relatives who have resided with them....When the social group disbands, these connections are severed. The extended persona is destroyed and individuals must reconstitute their boundaries.... The departure induces a loss of social vitality and leaves the home party feeling relatively weakened and diminished, experienced as an additional weight or burden.... (Fagans, 1985, p. 380)

These other-centered or social emotions, we should add, are often neither exclusively positive nor negative. They may often include both connotations much like our idea of sweet sorrow.

The concept of other-centered emotions poses a difficult challenge to western approaches to counseling and psychotherapy. We tend to view emotions as personal and private, something that comes from our interior being (Taylor, 1989; Dreyfus and Rabinow, 1983). We see emotions as something one 'has' or 'possesses' (cf. Macpherson, 1962). By contrast, collectivist cultures often interpret emotional experiences externally, by looking to the environment or to relations with other people. These other centered emotions do not play such an important role in individualist cultures. We do often not even have a name in English for such emotions. Western society operates as if such emotions are unimportant or perhaps not even real. Mesquita (2001) tells us: "Emotions in collectivist cultures are expected to stress and reproduce the self in relation to others or the self in relation to the world, whereas emotions in individualist cultures are assumed to underline and amplify a bounded, subjective self" (p. 68). This raises an important question for counselors, namely, "how should we deal with other centered emotions?" The presence of other centered emotions may even suggest a pathological condition when viewed from an individualistic perspective. A self experiencing such emotions may appear to be divided or co-dependent.

We have noticed that the Portuguese immigrant children struggle when they try to differentiate from their parents. Portuguese parents may characterize their 'differentiated' children as "*falta de orgulho*" which roughly translates as "having no pride in one's family or culture". Parents may also feel an intense emotion with that differentiation. It is sometimes described as *agonias,* literally translated as "the agonies" (James, 2002). For instance, the community Priest said,

> Children can give people *agonias* because they are not living with faith or they are doing things that are forbidden like divorcing. And for the people it's certainly a weight on them and it gives them a tightening feeling, like claustrophobia.... *Agonias* is really anxiety about sins, the sins of your children.

In this example *agonias* seems to carry a different connotation than guilt—it has more of an interpersonal quality. We seem to have no way of representing this interpersonal dimension within the folk psychology of North American culture therefore we view it as something negative such as "co-dependency" or as being "enmeshed." From a Portuguese perspective, however, the guilt of the children and the agonies of the parents are appropriate. They are a testament to the fact that the Portuguese sense of self is interdependent, that is, it is understood as involving the hopes, aspirations and desires of one's family members. Pathology in this case would involve being detached and disconnected and not experiencing *agonias.* If a therapist working with Portuguese clients were to attempt to reduce the guilt they would demonstrate a lack of understanding for the Portuguese sense of self.

An understanding of emotion as well as its expression is also shaped by cultural norms as a number of researchers have observed (Lebra, 1976; Markus and Kitayama, 1994; Menon and Shweder, 1994; Mesquita, Frijda, and Scherer, 1997). Noting these differences, multicultural counselors have warned against drawing premature conclusions. An example of the cultural influence on emotions is expressed in interviews (James, 2002) that we conducted with therapists who treat Portuguese clients,

> A lot of them … don't exactly say what they want so it takes forever to get information from them and they go about it in a round about way and they don't directly ask what they're looking for.

Thus, the way that Portuguese negotiate seeking help can be misunderstood if therapists have different ideals and expectations of how a client should act.

Resolving these cultural differences and addressing the personal conflicts they engender will not be an easy or straightforward task. Rather than applying such hermeneutic notions as effective historical consciousness, hermeneutic dialogue, phronesis, and the hermeneutic circle, it would be much easier to try to make the problems fit into a counseling framework that we are familiar with. To do so, we believe, would fail to adequately address the problems that immigrants face. Clients who are struggling with the stress of culture shock or enculturation may be helped by our recognition of the complexity of their situation. The recognition of these cultural differences and divergent moral visions (including different assumptions about the nature of the self, the good person and the good life) can help the client to understand and deal with the social stresses better, in part by helping them recognize the enormity of what's at stake. For instance, Christopher and Smith (2006) explored how educating clients about the moral visions involved can help clients develop self-acceptance and compassion. Thus, a sensitivity to "what's at stake" may allow counselors to better help clients through a potentially traumatizing transition to a new culture. Such sensitivity may be nurtured by recognizing the significance and influence of historical factors that make up the tradition of the client. The consciousness or self of the client is shaped by this history as well as the meanings and symbols of a particular tradition. In light of this, deciding an appropriate way to help a client will involve a kind of practical wisdom that resembles Aristotle's *phronēsis*. It will not be a simple matter of applying principles of counseling theory algorithmically to the client's situation, but of making a judgement about which principles are appropriate given the concrete circumstances and historical factors involved. This is something that mature and sensitive counselors may often do intuitively as a response to problems that they encounter in cross-cultural counseling. We see this sensitivity as an important dimension of counseling that should be nurtured among therapists.

For Portuguese immigrants, negotiating the divide between family obligations and individuation is conceivably a lifelong process. In order to find a balance between the sometimes conflicting cultural influences we may need to recognize this as a process and attribute moral meaning to it. This avoids the simple and insensitive solution of assuming that the family has problems and recognizes the fact that we live in a time where moral visions are confronting each other more and more. We must recognize the implications of a more global world and of more inter-cultural societies. We must seek to help those who attempt to live bi-culturally (or even multi-culturally) understand the role of the moral visions that make up their world.

Portuguese immigrants who seek therapy are faced with a challenge. To some degree American culture and the therapies that uncritically build upon it may lack the resources to help the Portuguese immigrants cope with a situation that does not have readily apparent solutions. The emancipatory thrust of the American *ethos* emphasizes the elimination of suffering and even freedom from unhappiness, as is promised in much of the popular psychology literature. Some critics have suggested that this cultural outlook can result in a kind of tyranny of happiness (Held, 2002). A one-sided emphasis on emotional satisfaction and happiness tends to neglect, according to Frank (1973), other, more traditional, but often worthwhile values or virtues such as "the redemptive power of suffering, acceptance of one's lot in life, adherence to tradition, self-restraint and moderation" (p. 7). We see this emphasis on redemptive suffering in the Portuguese immigrant community. Instead of emphasizing liberation from pain and suffering, Portuguese culture regards this ability to suffer for others as the mark of a virtuous person.

The moral visions framework we've described was put to the test in some of our work cross-culturally in Micronesia, although the examples that follow need not be strictly cross-cultural. Our work with gang members and inmates who had been diagnosed with conduct disorder, oppositional defiant disorder, and antisocial personality disorder raised questions about what could possibly be moral in the lives of those widely regarded as immoral and antisocial. In exploring the lives of this population we found that their lives, like ours,' are clearly informed by a conception of the good (Christopher, 1996; Schmitz and Christopher, 1997.

For instance gang members indicated a commitment to such virtues as honor, respect, and dignity. Recognizing this raised our awareness of the critical distinction between certain moral sources and the interpretation and application of these moral sources in particular situations. Even if we reject the moral visions of these gang members, it is important to identify and understand the values that inform it, values that are worthwhile. Honor, dignity and a general sense of virtue are implicit in most value systems. Identifying such values may serve as an ally to the counselor in dealing with the more problematic aspects of a client's life. We do not have to discredit the whole person, but we can start with affirming the positive values contained in that person's moral vision.

Discovering and acknowledging the client's orientation towards the 'good' can have a number of therapeutic benefits. Rather than feeling that they are simply bad people, outcasts of society, or pathological, clients can feel that something very important to their sense of self has been recognized. This may open the door for a bond of communication and understanding between counselor and client. Helping the client to understand their own moral vision and the way that it influences their sense of identity (as well as their actions) may help them to think through with the counselor, alternative strategies for attaining their idea of the good life. Proceeding in this way allows the client to see change in terms of an alteration of their own moral vision rather than in terms of having a foreign moral vision imposed on them from the outside. Given the intimate connection between moral visions and one's sense of self, this would seem to be an important step in overcoming the barriers between counselor and client, especially in a cross-cultural context.

The encounter between the moral vision of the counselor and that of the client parallel's, to a large extent, the encounter between horizon's advocated by Gadamer and discussed earlier in this chapter. Just as a fusion of horizon's required an openness to the horizon of the other and a provisional granting of the truth or legitimacy of that horizon, so the encounter between counselor and client requires an initial working within the client's moral vision and a refusal to impose one's ethnocentric view of the good on the client. This in itself does not solve the problem when it comes to counseling. We have admitted that the counselor possesses his or her own moral vision or horizon and can only make sense of the world and the client (initially) through this. Not only does this vision allow us to make sense of the client, but it also helps us to prescribe a solution to the problem. If we did not think that we could help find such a solution, or if the client did not think that we could, then the therapeutic encounter would be useless. A totally neutral stance towards the client's moral vision (which in itself reveals a particular moral vision – one based on a particular view of scientific or philosophical reason) would give us nothing to prescribe. It would seem therefore, that we need to allow our moral visions to play some role in our judgments concerning a client's condition and our proposals for treating this condition without negating or disrespecting her or his moral vision.

Gadamer's (1975) "fusion of horizons" would once again seem to offer a possible solution. In order to respect the moral vision of our client, while at the same time making discriminations or judgments about what is good or healthy behavior, requires a dialogical situation not unlike the one Gadamer proposes. As we discussed earlier in the paper, hermeneutic dialogue requires a dialectic between openness and application. As counselors we need to be open to the horizon of the client and allow that horizon provisional authority in terms of our understanding of their situation. Until we openly attempt to understand the client's situation as they understand it, we are not in an authentic position to work towards a solution. Even when we have made a sincere, reflective and critical attempt at understanding this horizon, we must remember the fallible nature of our undertaking. Once we have gained insight into our client's situation or horizon, it is important to remember the second part of Gadamer's dialectic which involves a critical application of the insights attained. Applying these insights in order to make sense of the client's concrete situation helps us to avoid an uncritical or superficial understanding or adoption of the perspective of the client. Such an adoption may allow for an understanding of the client that is deeply empathetic, but not terribly useful in helping the client work through an understanding of their moral vision in a way that aids them in overcoming the confused or negative aspects. This is why the interaction between counselor and client is best understood in terms of dialogue. A true fusion of horizons will indeed be a dialogue between the two parties that leads to greater understanding on both parts. The counselor may not (and probably will not) know how he or she can help the client in their particular concrete situation until he or she has engaged in the process of dialogue involving the dialectic between openness and application.

IMPLICATIONS: BEYOND OBJECTIVISM AND RELATIVISM

> Bellah et al. (1985) have made us aware of the fact that social science makes assumptions about the nature of persons, the nature of society, and the relation between persons and society. It also, whether it admits it or not, makes assumptions about good persons and a good society and considers how far these conceptions are embodied in our actual society. (p. 301)

Should we be troubled by this condition? Should the aim of the social sciences be to eradicate such biases in order to attain a more neutral or objective understanding of the subject-matter of counseling, psychology or the social sciences in general as has been recommended by Spence (1985)?

Proponents of philosophical hermeneutics (Gadamer, 1975; Richardson and Christopher, 1993; Richardson and Woolfolk, 1994; Taylor, 1985a, 1985b; Ricoeur, 1981), social constructionism (Cushman, 1990; Gergen, 1985), and interactivism (Bickhard, 1980; Campbell and Bickhard, 1986), among others, contend that attempts to gain objective, value-free, ahistorical knowledge are both futile and misguided. These attempts presuppose the questionable subject-object and fact-value dichotomies that have been conceptual hallmarks of Western culture. Bickhard (1980) has argued that "the concept of knowledge as objective, to which we then attach values, purposes, goals, and so forth is mistaken. Objective knowledge is a myth. All knowledge is motivationally structured" (p. 33). Knowledge is a product of interpretations. These interpretations can never be purely objective due to our inescapable historicity (see Hiley, Bohman, and Shusterman, 1991; Rabinow and Sullivan, 1987). This implies that we are always situated within a particular historical horizon of understanding, one which contains its own moral vision, and we always try to make sense of the world through the cultural and personal presuppositions that this horizon gives rise to.

Gadamer (1975) called these presuppositions prejudices. He speaks of the Enlightenment spirit as one which displays a prejudice against prejudice. This prejudice against prejudice (or presuppositions) has given rise to what Bernstein (in discussing the social sciences) (1978) called the ideal of the disinterested observer "who explains, understands, interprets, or simply describes, what is" (p. xix). Hermeneutic thinkers such as Gadamer (1975) and Taylor (1989) oppose the notion of the disinterested observer telling us that it is not possible to fully remove ourselves from the prejudices of our traditions. The very ideas of objectivity and value-neutrality according to Taylor are "connected with some of the most important moral and spiritual ideals of our civilization" such as individualism (Taylor, 1987, p. 472; also see Bernstein, 1986; Cirillo and Wapner, 1986). A hermeneutic view tells us that ironically this objective or neutral approach is itself the product of a particular moral vision.

The counselor can never take the stance of a detached observer neutrally evaluating different interpretations. We are always speaking from within a set of presuppositions; thus, our understandings and interpretations can only be criticized from the base of other prejudices not in question at the moment. Of course, this does not mean that we should not attempt to be more careful and rigorous in our thinking. But, if we assume we are being neutral, unbiased, or value-free, then we are simply failing to recognize the prejudices from which we operate.

Bellah and his colleagues, recognizing the impossibility gaining objectivity and value neutrality in the social sciences, have proposed that we think in terms of *social science as moral inquiry* or *social science as public philosophy* (Bellah et al, 1985; Haan, Bellah, Rabinow, and Sullivan, 1983). Applied to counseling, this approach recognizes the fact that we are always working within the space of moral visions or cultural horizons. This means that we would have to recognize that counseling is "a tradition, or set of traditions, deeply rooted in the philosophical and humanistic (and, to more than a small extent, the religious) history of the West" (Bellah et al., 1985, p. 301). Acknowledging this fact about counseling may remind us that our beliefs about what it means to be a person and our normative assumptions about what a person should be are "contestable and that the choice of assumptions involve controversies that lie deep in the history of Western thought" (p. 301). As a form of public philosophy, counseling "would make the philosophical conversation concerning these matters its own" (p. 301).

A consequence of viewing counseling as a largely moral activity or enquiry is that we must acknowledge with Prilleltensky (1989) that our current conception of the role of ethics in counseling is too narrow. If counseling involves the encounter of moral visions between counselor and client that we have claimed, then ethics cannot merely play the role of providing ethical procedures or guidelines as outlined in our professional ethics manuals. The role of morality in the counseling is more substantive. Bickhard (1989), for instance, maintains that:

> Therapy is not just an activity to which ethical considerations can be applied, nor just an activity which makes use of moral considerations in selecting its instrumental goals. Psychotherapy is a very special kind of intrinsically ethical relating to another person. (p. 163)

This more substantive understanding of the role of ethics will also extend beyond counseling. Moral visions not only affect counseling practice, but counseling theory and research as well. This suggests that counselors should: (a) acknowledge our cultural embeddedness, (b) seek to continually clarify and question the moral visions that motivate us, (c) relentlessly attempt to discern how moral visions affect our work as counselors, and (d) regularly engage in public discourse on the nature and appropriateness of our moral visions.

This article has tried to outline a meta-theoretical account of culture by focusing on the way that moral visions permeate culture. The aim of such an account is to help counselors to acknowledge and explore their moral visions in order to have a better grasp of the role that they play in their own understanding as well as the self-understanding of their clients

The meta-theoretical account provided here aims at furthering the effort to find an account of understanding the human subject that is "beyond objectivism and relativism" (Bernstein, 1985). Such an account will acknowledge that there are no ahistorical, neutral or truly objective criteria to adopt as counselors. On the other hand, this does not lead us to adopt a fruitless relativism that suggests that all moral visions are equally good or useful. There are grounds for criticizing moral visions that exist within cultural and historical traditions. Their culture-bound nature does not render them illegitimate. Historically we have developed judgments that condemn racism, sexism, and oppression from within the context of cultural communities (MacIntyre, 1988; Ricoeur, 1981). Many of these critiques have gained currency beyond their original cultural setting and have been recognized on a more universal level. This move from a specific cultural starting point to a widening and more universal perspective suggests one possibility for defining a middle way between objectivism and relativism, a path which the authors of this article seek.

The previous example illustrates the more general attempt to move beyond objectivism and relativism implied in philosophical hermeneutics. This approach aims at truth but recognizes that the finite nature of human understanding limits us to truths that will never have complete certainty. The middle ground is found in the recognition that our moral visions are neither fully objective nor arbitrarily relative. We must acknowledge and take responsibility for our actions and their consequences, especially the effect that our judgments or prescriptions will have upon our clients. We must make choices about the source of the problem and the direction of the cure and intervene accordingly, but we must not allow ourselves or our clients to believe that these judgments are not influenced by our moral visions. Maturity in counseling, much like the maturity implied in Aristotle's practical wisdom *(phronesis)* is expressed in our capacity for making good judgments regarding the implications of our moral visions and the application of well-reasoned and critically evaluated counseling prescriptions.

Part of this maturity consists in the recognition that our judgment is fallible, our theories, conceptualizations, diagnoses and interventions are uncertain. We must make the best judgments that we can based on our experience and the best reasons and arguments we have available (Taylor, 1989). These judgments mature through thoughtful dialogue with clients, colleagues and through life experience.

Our judgments and prescriptions themselves will reflect a stance that we are taking, a moral vision by which we live. Such a vision presupposes a conception of the good which we aim to live by and which will inevitably influence our interaction with clients, even if we do not explicitly urge them to adopt our view. Counseling ultimately engages us in a discussion of the good life with the client, one which ideally leads to a dialogical conclusion or solution.

CONCLUSION

Moral visions are essential to human life as we have emphasized throughout this paper. The idea of culture itself is that of a web which is imbued with one or more moral visions. Contrary to certain modern conceptions of individualism, the individual and culture are not radically separate entities. Individuals live a certain culture by defining personhood and the concept of the good life in culture-specific terms. The intersubjective nature of cultural ideals is expressed in social practices that are often unique to particular cultures and which help create the identity of its inhabitants. We gain this identity through growing up in or participating in the practices of a particular culture. The identity that we gain through our culture is often involuntary and largely unacknowledged, at least until we begin to reflect upon who we are or contrast our identity with a different cultural group. Our encounter with other cultures allows us to understand more clearly the presuppositions inherent in our own. These presuppositions include our conception of what it means to be a person and what it means to live a good life.

We sometimes make the mistake of categorizing the behavior of others, especially those from a different culture as pathological, distorted, crazy or even evil. We often do this because we do not acknowledge the fact that our perspective is limited by our cultural horizon and the presuppositions that compose it. Understanding a particular behavior through a different set of presuppositions and background assumptions – namely those inherent in the horizon of a different culture, may change our assessment and the way that we interpret a particular behavior. As Pederson (1991) tells us, we can only avoid being "culturally encapsulated" if we allow our cultural "givens" to be questioned through dialogue so that our differences might be bridged.

This type of intercultural dialogue may not radically transform either culture's horizon. It is difficult to change something that has been deeply ingrained in us well before we were even conscious of it. What such dialogue does offer, however, is the chance to reflect on the assumptions and beliefs that we take for granted by virtue of growing up in a particular culture and adhering to a particular view of the good. This kind of dialogue may deepen, enhance and even modify our own conception of the good and the good life. This kind of transformation paralleling what Gadamer has called a fusion of horizons, may lead to cultural and personal advancement and enrichment.

REFERENCES

Adams, G., and Markus, H. R. (2001). Culture as patterns: An alternative approach to the problem of reification. *Culture and Psychology, 7*(3), 283-296.

Barclay, M. W. (1992). The utility of hermeneutic interpretation in psychotherapy. *Theoretical and Philosophical Psychology, 12*, 103-118

Baumeister, R. F. (1986). *Identity: Cultural change and the struggle for the self.* New York: Oxford University Press.

Baumeister, R. F. (1987). How the self became a problem: A psychological review of historical research. *Journal of Personality and Social Psychology, 52*, 163-176.

Bellah, R. N. (1983). The ethical aims of social inquiry. In N. Haan, R. N. Bellah, P. Rabinow and W. M. Sullivan (Eds.), (pp. 360-381). New York: Columbia University Press.

Bellah, R. N., Madsen, R., Sullivan, W. M., Swidler, A., and Tipton, S. M. (1985). *Habits of the heart: Individualism and commitment in American life.* New York: Harper and Row.

Benner, P. (1994). *Interpretive phenomenology: Embodiment, caring, and ethics in health and illness*. Thousand Oaks, CA: Sage Publications.

Berlin, I., Hardy, H., and Hausheer, R. (1998). *The proper study of mankind : An anthology of essays*. London: Pimlico.

Bernstein, R. J. (1978). *The reconstructing of social and political theory*. Philadelphia: University of Pennsylvania Press.

Bernstein, R. J. (1983). *Beyond objectivism and relativism: science, hermeneutics, and praxis*. Philadelphia: University of Pennsylvania Press.

Bickhard, M. H. (1980). *Cognition, convention, and communication*. New York: Praeger.

Bickhard, M. H. (1989). Ethical psychotherapy and psychotherapy as ethics: A response to Perrez. *New Ideas in Psychology, 7*(2), 159-164.

Bickhard, M. H., and Christopher, J. C. (1994). The influence of early experience on personality development. *New Ideas in Psychology, 12,* 229-252.

Bouchard, M. and Guerette, L. (1991). Psychotherapy as a hermeneutical experience. *Psychotherapy: Theory, Research, Practice, Training, 28*, 385-394.

Braginsky, D. D. (1992). Psychology: Handmaiden to society. In S. Koch and D. E. Leary (Eds.), *A century of psychology as science* (pp. 880-891). Washington, DC: American Psychological Association.

Brinson, J. A., and Kottler, J. A. (1995). Minorities' underutilization of counseling centers' mental health services: A case for outreach and consultation. *Journal of Mental Health Counseling, 17*, 371-385.

Brinton, C. (1987). *A history of Western morals.* New York: Paragon House. (Original work published 1959).

Bronfenbrenner, U. (1977). Toward an experimental ecology of human development. *American Psychologist, 32*, 513-531.

Bruner, J. (1990). *Acts of meaning.* Cambridge, MA: Harvard University Press.

Buber, M. (1970). *I and Thou.* New York: Charles Scribner's Sons.

Campbell, R. L., and Bickhard, M. H. (1986). *Knowing levels and developmental stages.* Basel: Karger.

Campbell, R. L., Christopher, J. C., and Bickhard, M. H. (2002). Values and the self: An interactivist foundation for moral development. *Theory and Psychology*, *12*, 795-823.

Camus, Albert. (1983). *The Myth of Sisyphus*. Markham, ON: Penguin Books, Ltd.

Chessick, R. D. (1990). Hermeneutics for psychotherapists. *American Journal of Psychotherapy, 44*, 256-273.

Christopher, J. C. (1996). Counseling's inescapable moral visions. *Journal of Counseling and Development*, *75,* 17-25.

Christopher, J. C. (1999). Situating psychological well-being: Exploring cultural values and assumptions underlying theory and research on psychological well-being. *Journal of Counseling and Development*, *77*, 141-152.

Christopher, J. C. (2001). Culture and psychotherapy: Towards a hermeneutic approach. *Psychotherapy, 38*, 115-128.

Christopher, J. C. (2004). Moral visions of developmental psychology. In B. Slife, J. S. Reber, and F. C. Richardson (Eds.), *Critical thinking about psychology: Hidden assumptions and plausible alternatives* (pp. 207-231). Washington, D. C.: APA Press.

Christopher, J. C., and Bickhard, M. H. (in press). Culture, self, and identity: Interactivist contributions to a metatheory for cultural psychology. *Culture and Psychology*.

Christopher, S., Christopher, J. C., and Dunnagan, T. (2000). Culture's impact on health risk appraisal psychological well-being questions. *American Journal of Health Behavior, 24*, 338-348.

Christopher, J. C., Nelson, T., and Nelson, M. D. (2004). Culture and character education: Problems of interpretation in a multicultural society. *Journal of Theoretical and Philosophical Psychology*, *23*, 81-101.

Christopher, J. C., and Smith, A. (2006). A Hermeneutic Approach to Culture and Psychotherapy. In R. Moody, and S. Palmer (Eds.), *Race, culture and psychotherapy: Critical perspective in multicultural practice* (pp. 265-280). New York: Brunner/Routledge.

Cirillo, L., and Wapner, S. (1986). *Value presuppositions in theories of human development*. Hillsdale, NJ: Lawrence Erlbaum.

Cleary, R. J. (1999). Bowlby's theory of attachment and loss: A feminist reconsideration. *Feminism and Psychology, 9*, 32-42.

Cole, M. (1996). *Cultural psychology: A once and future discipline*. Cambridge, MA: Harvard University Press.

Cushman, P. (1990). Why the self is empty: Toward a historically situated psychology. *American Psychologist, 45*(5), 599-611.

Cushman, P. (1991). Ideology obscured: Political uses of the self in Daniel Stern's infant. *American Psychologist, 46,* 206-219.

Cushman, P. (1995). *Constructing the self, constructing America: A cultural history of psychotherapy*: Addison-Wesley.

Devereaux, G. (1958). Cultural factors in psychoanalytic therapy. *Journal of the American Psychoanalytic Association*, *1*, 629-655.

Dilthey, W. (1989). *Introduction to the Human Sciences* (R.A. Makkreel, and F. Rodi, Trans. and Ed.), Princeton, NJ: Princeton University Press.

Doherty, W. J. (1995). *Soul searching: Why psychotherapy must promote moral responsibility*. New York: Basic Books.

Dreyfus, H. L., and Rabinow, P. (1983). *Michael Foucault: Beyond structuralism and hermeneutics*. Chicago: The University of Chicago Press.

Dumont, L. (1986). *Essays on individualism*. Chicago: University of Chicago Press.

Eagle, M. N. (1986). Psychoanalysis a hermeneutics. *Behavioral and Brain Sciences, 9*, 231-232.

Ellis, A. (1973). Humanistic psychotherapy. New York: McGraw-Hill.

Fajans, J. (1985). The person in social context: The social character in Baining "psychology." In G. M. White, J. Kirkpatrick and et al. (Eds.), *Person, self, and experience: Exploring Pacific ethnopsychologies.* (pp. 367-397). Berkeley, CA, USA: University of California Press.

Fischer, A. R., Jome, L. M., and Atkinson, D. R. (1998). Back to the future of multicultural psychotherapy with a common factors approach. *Counseling Psychologist, 26*, 602-606.

Fischer, C. T. (1980). Phenomenology and psychological assessment: Re-presentational description. *Journal of Phenomenological Psychology, 11*, 79-105.

Foster, G. and James, S. (2004). Narratives of hope and reconciliation: A hermeneutic approach to cultural therapy. *Constructivism and the Human Sciences, 9*, 67-76.

Fowers, B. J. and Richardson, F. C. (1993). Individualism and aggression: A hermeneutic analysis of Huesmann and Eron's cognitive theory of aggression. *Theory and Psychology, 3,* 353-377.

Fowers, B. J. and Richardson, F. C. (1996). Individualism, family ideology, and family therapy. *Theory and Psychology, 6,* 121-151.

Fowers, B. J., and Richardson, F. C. (1994). Why is multiculturalism good? *American Psychologist, 51*, 609-621.

Frank, J. (1978). *Psychotherapy and the human predicament.* New York: Schocken.

Frank, J. D. (1973). *Persuasion and healing: A comparative study of psychotherapy.* New York: Schocken Books.

Frank, J. D. (1987). Psychotherapy, rhetoric, and hermeneutics: Implications for practice and research. *Psychotherapy: Theory, Research, Practice, Training, 24*, 293-302.

Gadamer, H.-G. (1975). *Truth and method.* New York: Crossroad.

Gadamer, H.-G. (2001). *Reason in the Age of Science*. Cambridge, MA: The MIT Press.

Geertz, C. (1973). *The interpretation of cultures.* New York: Basic Books.

Geertz, C. (1983). *Local knowledge: Further essays in interpretive anthropology*. New York: Basic Books.

Gentile, J. (1998). Listening for deep structure: Between the a priori and the intersubjective. *Contemporary Psychoanalysis, 34*, 67-89.

Gergen, K. J. (1985). The social constuctionist movement in modern psychology. *American Psychologist, 40*, 266-275.

Gergen, K. J. (1994). *Realities and relationships: Soundings in social construction.* Cambridge, MA: Harvard University Press.

Gergen, K. J. (1995). Postmodern psychology: Resonance and reflection. *American Psychologist, 50*, 394.

Giorgi, A. (1970). *Psychology as a human science: A phenomenologically based approach.* New York: Harper and Row.

Greenberg, G. (1994). *The self on the shelf: Recovery books and the good life*. Albany: State University of New York Press.

Guignon, C. B. (1984). *Heidegger and the problem of knowledge.* Indianapolis: Hackett.

Haan, N., Bellah, R. N., Rabinow, P., and Sullivan, W. M. (1983). *Social science as moral inquiry*. New York: Columbia University Press.

Held, B. S. (2002). The tyranny of the positive attitude in America: Observation and speculation. *Journal of Clinical Psychology, 58*, 965-992.

Hegel, G.W.F. (1977). *Phenomenology of Spirit*. New York: Oxford University Press.

Heidegger, M. (1962). *Being and time* (J. Macquarrie and E. Robinson, Trans.). New York:

Hiley, D. R., Bohman, J. F., and Shusterman, R. (Eds.). (1991). *The interpretive turn: Philosophy, science, culture*. Ithaca, NY: Cornell University Press.

Hogan, R. (1975). Theoretical egocentrism and the problem of compliance. *American Psychologist, 30*, 533-540.

Hoshmand, L. T. (Ed.). (2006). *Culture, psychotherapy, and counseling.* Thousand Oaks, CA: Sage.

Hui, C. H. (1988). Measurement of individualism-collectivism. *Journal of Research in Personality, 22,* 17-36.

Hui, C. H., and Triandis, H. C. (1986). Individualism-collectivism: A study of cross-cultural researchers. *Journal of Cross-Cultural Psychology, 17,* 225-248.

Jackson, A. P., and Meadows, F. B., Jr. (1991). Getting to the bottom to understand the top. *Journal of Counseling and Development, 70*, 72-76.

Jahoda, G. (2002). The sifting sands of culture. In F. J. R. v. Vijver and A. M. Chodynicka (Eds.), *New directions in cross-cultural psychology* (pp. 91-106). Warsaw, Poland: Polish Psychological Association.

James, S. and Foster, G (in press). *Reconciling Rules with Context: A Hermeneutic Approach to Cultural Psychotherapy.*

James, S. (2002). *Agonias*: The social and sacred suffering of Azorean immigrants. *Culture, Medicine and Psychiatry, 26*, 87-110.

Kanfer, F. H. (1979). Personal control, social control, and altruism: Can society survive the age of individualism? *American Psychologist, 34*, 231-239.

Kashima, Y. (2000). Conceptions of culture and person for psychology. *Journal of Cross-Cultural Psychology, 31*, 14-32.

Kerr, M. E., and Bowen, M. (1988). *Family evaluation: An approach based on Bowen theory.* New York, NY: W. W. Norton.

Kim, U., Triandis, H. C., Kagitçibasi, C., Choi, S.-C., and Yoon, G. (Eds.). (1994). *Individualism and collectivism.* Thousand Oaks, CA: Sage.

Kirschner, S. R. (1996). *The religious and romantic origins of psychoanalysis.* New York: Cambridge University Press.

Kitayama, S., Markus, H. R., and Lieberman, C. (1995). The collective construction of self esteem: Implications for culture, self, and emotion. In J. A. Russell and J.-M. Fernâandez-Dols (Eds.), *Everyday conceptions of emotion: An introduction to the psychology, anthropology and linguistics of emotion.* (pp. 523-550). Dordrecht, Netherlands: Kluwer Academic Publishers.

Lambeth, G. S. (1995).Psychoanalytic theories of narcissism: An historical and critical analysis. Unpublished doctoral dissertation, The University of Texas at Austin.

Lebra, T. S. (1976). *Japanese patterns of behavior*. Honolulu: University of Hawaii Press.

Lukes, S. (1973). Individualism. Oxford: Basil Blackwell.

Lutz, C. A. (1988). *Unnatural emotions: Everyday sentiments on a Micronesian atoll and their challenge to Western theory*. Chicago: University of Chicago Press.

MacIntyre, A. (1988). *Whose Justice? Which Rationality?* Notre Dame, IN: University of Notre Dame Press.

Markus, H. R., and Kitayama, S. (1991). Culture and the self: Implications for cognition, emotion, and motivation. *Psychological Review,98,* 224-253.

Markus, H. R., and Kitayama, S. (1994). The cultural construction of self and emotion: Implications for social behavior. In *Emotion and culture: Empirical studies of mutual influence* (pp. 89-130). Washington, DC: American Psychological Association.

Martin, J., and Thompson, J. (1997). Between scientism and relativism: Phenomenology, hermeneutics and the new realism in psychology. *Theory and Psychology, 7*, 629-652.

Maruyama, M. (1992). *Context and complexity: Cultivating contextual understanding*. New York: Springer-Verlag.

May, R. (1967). *Psychology and the human dilemma*. Princeton, NJ: D. Van Nostrand.

McLeod, J., and Lynch, G. (2000). 'This is our life': Strong evaluation in psychotherapy narrative. *European Journal of Psychotherapy, Counselling and Health, 3*, 389-406.

McNamee, S. (1996). Psychotherapy as a social construction, *Constructing realities: Meaning-making perspectives for psychotherapists* (pp. 115-137). San Francisco, CA: Jossey-Bass.

Menon, U., and Shweder, R. A. (1994). Kali's tongue: Cultural psychology and the power of shame in Orissa, India. In S. Kitayama and H. Markus (Eds.), *Emotion and culture* (pp. 241-284). Washington, DC: American Psychological Association.

Mesquita, B. (2001). Emotions in collectivist and individualist contexts. *Journal of Personality and Social Psychology, 80*, 68-74.

Mesquita, B., Frijda, N. H., and Scherer, K. R. (1997). Culture and emotion. In J. W. Berry, P. R. Dasen and et al. (Eds.), *Basic processes and human development (2nd ed* (Vol. 2, pp. 255-297). Needham Heights, MA: Allyn and Bacon.

Messer, S. B., Sass, L. A., and Woolfolk, R. L. (1988). *Hermeneutics and psychological theory: Interpretive perspectives on personality, psychotherapy, and psychopathology.* New Brunswick, NJ: Rutgers University Press.

Michrina, B. P., and Richards, C. (1996). *Person to person: Fieldwork, dialogue, and the hermeneutic method.* Albany, NY: State University of New York Press.

Moody-Adams, M. M. (1997). *Fieldwork in familiar places: Morality, culture, and philosophy*. Cambridge, MA: Harvard University Press.

Moore, C. A. (1968). *The status of the individual in East and West.* Honolulu: University of Hawaii Press

Morrison, M. and James, S. (2006). Portuguese Immigrant Families: The Impact of Acculturation. (Manuscript submitted for publication).

Munro, D. J. (1969). *The concept of man in early China.* Stanford, CA: Stanford University Press.

Neimeyer, R. A., and Mahoney, M. J. (Eds.). (1995). *Constructivism in psychotherapy.* Washington, DC, USA: American Psychological Association.

Packer, M. J., and Addison, R. B. (Eds.). (1989). *Entering the circle: Hermeneutic investigation in psychology*. Albany, NY: State University of New York Press.

Palmer, R. E. (1969). *Hermeneutics*. Evanston, Illinois: Northwestern University Press.

Patterson, C. H. (1996). Multicultural counseling: From diversity to universality. *Journal of Counseling and Development, 74*, 227-231.

Pedersen, P. B. (1991). Multiculturalism as a generic approach to counseling. *Journal of Counseling and Development, 70*(1), 6-12.

Pederson, P. B. (1997). The cultural context of the American Counseling Associations code of ethics. *Journal of Counseling and Development*, *76*, 23-28.

Perloff, R. (1987). Self-interest and personal responsibility redux. *American Psychologist, 42*, 3-11.

Poortinga, Y. H. (1997). Towards convergence. In J. W. Berry, Y. H. Poortinga and J. Pandey (Eds.), *Handbook of cross-cultural psychology (2nd): Volume One, Theory and method* (pp. 347-387). Needham Heights, MA: Allyn and Bacon.

Prilleltensky, I. (1989). Psychology and the status quo. *American Psychologist, 44*(5), 795-802.

Prilleltensky, I. (1994). *The morals and politics of psychology: Psychological discourse and the status quo*. Albany, NY: State University of New York Press.

Rabinow, P., and Sullivan, W. M. (1987). *Interpretive social science: A second look.* Berkeley, CA: The University of California Press.

Ratner, C. (1997). *Cultural psychology and qualitative methodology: Theoretical and empirical considerations*. New York, NY: Plenum Press.

Ratner, C. (2000). Outline of a coherent, comprehensive concept of culture: The problem of fragmentary notions of culture. *Cross-Cultural Psychology Bulletin, 34*, 5-11.

Rennie, D. L. (1999). Qualitative research: A matter of hermeneutics and the sociology of knowledge, *Using qualitative methods in psychology* (pp. 3-13). Thousand Oaks, CA: Sage Publications.

Richardson, F. C. (1989). Freedom and commitment in modern psychotherapy. *Journal of Integrative and Eclectic Psychotherapy, 8,* 303-319.

Richardson, F. C., and Christopher, J. C. (1993). Social theory as practice: Metatheoretical options for social inquiry. *Theoretical and Philosophical Psychology, 13*, 137-153.

Richardson, F. C., and Guignon, C. (1988). Individualism and social interest. *Journal of Individual Psychology, 44,* 13-29.

Richardson, F. C., Fowers, B. J., and Guignon, C. B. (1999). *Re-envisioning psychology: Moral dimensions of theory and practice*. San Francisco, CA: Jossey-Bass.

Ricoeur, P. (1981). *Hermeneutics and the Human Sciences.* Cambridge, UK: Cambridge University Press.

Ricoeur, P. (1992). *Oneself as Another*. Chicago: The University of Chicago Press.

Ritzer, G. (1996). *The McDonaldization of society.* Thousand Oaks, CA: Pine Forge Press.

Roland, A. (1996). The influence of culture on the self and selfobject relationships: An Asian-North American comparison. *Psychoanalytic Dialogues, 6*, 461-475.

Rubin, J. B. (1997). Psychoanalysis is self-centered, *Soul on the couch: Spirituality, religion, and morality in contemporary psychoanalysis* (pp. 79-108). Hillsdale, NJ: The Analytic Press.

Sampson, E. E. (1977). Psychology and the American ideal. *Journal of Personality and Social Psychology, 35,* 767-782.

Sampson, E. E. (1981). Cognitive psychology as ideology. *American Psychologist, 36*(7), 730-743.

Sampson, E. E. (1985). The decentralization of identity: Toward a revised concept of personal and social order. *American Psychologist, 40*, 1203-1211.

Sampson, E. E. (1988). The debate on individualism: Indigenous psychologies of the individual and their role in personal and societal functioning. *American Psychologist, 43,* 15-22.

Sampson, E. E. (1989). The challenge of social change for psychology: Globalization and psychology's theory of the person. *American Psychologist, 44*, 914-921.

Sampson, E. E. (1993). Identity politics: Challenges to psychology's understanding. *American Psychologist, 43*, 1219-1230.

Sampson, E. E. (2000). Reinterpreting individualism and collectivism: Their religious roots and monologic versus dialogic person-other relationship. *American Psychologist, 55*, 1425-1432.

Schafer, R. (1976). *A new language for psychoanalysis*. New Haven: Yale University Press.

Schafer, R. (1993). Narration in the psychoanalytic dialogue. In E. Berman and et al. (Eds.), *Essential papers on literature and psychoanalysis.* (pp. 341-368). New York, NY: New York University Press.

Schmitz, S. E., and Christopher, J. C. (1997). Trouble in Smurftown: The moral visions of youth gangs on Guam. *Child Welfare, 76,* 411-428.

Seeley, K. M. (2000). *Cultural psychotherapy*. Northvale, NJ: Jason Aronson.

Shweder, R. A. (1990). Cultural psychology: What is it? In J. W. Stigler, R. A. Shweder and G. Herdt (Eds.), *Cultural psychology: Essays on comparative human development* (pp. 1-43). New York: Cambridge University Press.

Shweder, R. A. (1991). *Thinking through cultures: Expeditions in cultural psychology.* Cambridge, MA, US: Harvard University Press.

Shweder, R. A. (2003). Why do men barbecue? *Recipes for cultural psychology*. Cambridge, MA: Harvard University.

Shweder, R. A., and Bourne, E. J. (1984). Does the concept of the person vary cross-culturally? In R. A. Shweder and R. A. LeVine (Eds.), *Culture theory: Essays on mind, self, and emotion* (pp. 158-199). New York: Cambridge University Press.

Shweder, R.,□^{2}ahapatra, M., and Miller, J. G. (1987). Culture and moral development. In J. Kagan and S. Lamb (Eds.), *The emergence of morality in young children* (pp. 1-83). Chicago: University of Chicago Press.

Slife, B. D., Reber, J. S., and Richardson, F. C. (Eds.). (2005). *Critical thinking about psychology: Hidden assumptions and plausible alternatives*. Washington, DC: American Psychological Association.

Slife, B. D., Williams, R. N., and Barlow, S. H. (Eds.). (2001). *Critical issues in psychotherapy: Translating new ideas into practice*. Thousand Oaks, CA,: Sage Publications.

Smith, B. M. (1978). What it means to be human. In R. Fitzgerald (Ed.), (pp. 3-24). Australia: Pergamon Press.

Smith, S. T., and Smith, K. D. (1995). Turkish emotion concepts: A prototype approach. In J. A. Russell, J.-M. Fernandez-Dols and et al. (Eds.), *Everyday conceptions of emotion: An introduction to the psychology, anthropology and linguistics of emotion.* (pp. 103-119). Dordrecht, Netherlands: Kluwer Academic Publishers.

Spence, D. P. (1982). *Narrative truth and historical truth: meaning and interpretation in psychoanalysis*. New York: W. W. Norton.

Spence, D. P. (1993). The hermeneutic turn: Soft science or loyal opposition? *Psychoanalytic Dialogues, 3*, 1-10.

Spence, J. T. (1985). Achievement American style: The rewards and costs of individualism. *American Psychologist, 40,* 1285-1295.

Sue, D. W. (1981). *Counseling the culturally different.* New York: John Wiley.

Sue, D. W., and Sue, D. (1990). *Counseling the culturally different.* New York: Wiley.

Sugarman, J., and Martin, J. (1995). The moral dimension: A conceptualization and empirical demonstration of the moral nature of psychotherapeutic conversations. *Counseling Psychologist, 23*, 324-347.

Sullivan, W. M. (1986). *Reconstructing public philosophy.* Berkeley: University of California Press.

Szasz, T. S. (1961). *The myth of mental illness.* New York: Hoeber-Harper.

Tappan, M. B. (1997). Interpretive psychology: Stories, circles, and understanding lived experience. *Journal of Social Issues, 53*, 645-656.

Tatman, A. (2004). Hmong history, culture and acculturation: Implications for counseling the Hmong. *Journal of Multicultural Counseling and Development, 32*, 222-234.

Taylor, C. (1975). *Hegel.* New York: Cambridge University Press.

Taylor, C. (1985a). *Human agency and language: Philosophical papers 1.* New York: Cambridge University Press.

Taylor, C. (1985b). *Philosophy and the human sciences: Philosophical papers, 2.* New York: Cambridge University Press.

Taylor, C. (1985c). Justice After Virtue. In M. Benedikt and R. Berger (Eds.), (pp. 23-48). Vienna.

Taylor, C. (1987). The moral topography of the self. In S. B. Messer, L. A. Saas, and R. L. Woolfolk, (Eds.). *Hermeneutics and psychological theory: Interpretive perspectives on personality, psychotherapy, and psychopathology* (pp. 288-320). New Brunswick, NJ: Rutgers University Press.

Taylor, C. (1989). *Sources of the self: The making of the modern identity.* Cambridge, MA: Harvard University Press.

Taylor, C. (1991). The dialogical self. In D. R. Hiley, J. F. Bohman and R. Shusterman (Eds.), *The Interpretive Turn* (pp. 304-314). Cornell, NY: Cornell University Press.

Taylor, C. (1992). *Multiculturalism and "the politics of recognition."* Princeton, NJ: Princeton University Press.

Taylor, C. (1995). *Philosophical arguments.* Cambridge, MA: Harvard University Press.

Tjeltveit, A. C. (1989). The ubiquity of models of human beings in psychotherapy: The need for rigorous reflection. *Psychotherapy, 26*, 1-10.

Triandis, H. C. (1989). The self and social behavior in differing cultural contexts. *Psychological Review, 96,* 506-520.

Triandis, H. C. (1995). *Individualism and collectivism.* Boulder, CO: Westview.

Trimble, J. E. (2003). Forward. In D. B. Pope-Davis, H. L. K. Coleman, W. M. Liu, and R. L. Toporek (Eds.), *Handbook of multicultural competencies in counseling and psychology* (pp. x-xiii). Thousand Oaks, CA: Sage.

Van Manen, M. (1990). *Researching lived experience: Human science for an action sensitive pedagogy.* New York: State University of New York Press.

Vandervert, L. R. (1995). Chaos theory and neurological positivism--clarifications: A reply to Newman, Bickhard, Alexander and Globus. *New Ideas in Psychology, 13*, 143-148.

Vernon, S. W., and Roberts, R. E. (1982). Prevalence of treated and untreated psychiatric disorders in three ethnic groups. *Social Science and Medicine, 16*, 1575-1582.

Vontress, C. E. (1979). Cross-cultural counseling: An existential approach. *The Personnel and Guidance Journal, 58*, 117-122.

Wachtel, P. L. (1977). *Psychoanalysis and behavior therapy.* New York: Basic Books.

Walsh, R. A. (1995). The study of values in psychotherapy: A critique and call for an alternative method. *Psychotherapy Research, 5*(4), 313-326.

Waterman, A. S. (1981). Individualism and interdependence. *American Psychologist, 36,* 762-773.

Waterman, A. S. (1984). *The psychology of individualism*. New York: Praeger.

West, W. (2000). *Psychotherapy and spirituality: Crossing the line between therapy and religion.* London: Sage.

Whaley, A. L. (2001). Cultural mistrust and mental health services for African Americans: A review and meta-analysis. *Counseling Psychologist, 29*, 513-531.

Wilson, T. D. (2002). *Strangers to ourselves: Discovering the adaptive unconscious.* Cambridge, MA: Belknap Press/Harvard University Press.

Wolszon, L. R. (1998). Women's Body Image Theory and Research: A Hermeneutic Critique. *American Behavioral Scientist, 41*, 542-557.

Woolfolk, R. L. (1998). *The cure of souls: Science, values, and psychotherapy*. San Francisco, CA: Jossey-Bass.

Woolfolk, R. L., and Richardson, F. C. (1984). Behavior therapy and the ideology of modernity. *American Psychologist, 7,* 777-786.

INDEX

A

D

M

N

Q

R

S

V

W

Y

Z